World War I and the Jews

World War I and the Jews

*Conflict and Transformation in Europe,
the Middle East, and America*

Edited by
Marsha L. Rozenblit and Jonathan Karp

berghahn
NEW YORK · OXFORD
www.berghahnbooks.com

Published in 2017 by
Berghahn Books
www.berghahnbooks.com

© 2017, 2019 Marsha L. Rozenblit and Jonathan Karp
First paperback edition published in 2019

All rights reserved. Except for the quotation of short passages for the purposes of criticism and review, no part of this book may be reproduced in any form or by any means, electronic or mechanical, including photocopying, recording, or any information storage and retrieval system now known or to be invented, without written permission of the publisher.

Library of Congress Cataloging-in-Publication Data

Names: Rozenblit, Marsha L., 1950– editor. | Karp, Jonathan, 1960– editor.
Title: World War I and the Jews : conflict and transformations in Europe, the Middle East, and America / edited by Marsha L. Rozenblit and Jonathan Karp.
Description: New York : Berghahn Books, [2017] | Includes bibliographical references and index.
Identifiers: LCCN 2017014887 (print) | LCCN 2017015411 (ebook) | ISBN 9781785335938 (ebook) | ISBN 9781785335921 (hbk) | ISBN 9781789200850 (pbk)
Subjects: LCSH: World War, 1914–1918—Jews. | World War, 1914–1918—Influence. | World War, 1914–1918—Social aspects—Europe. | World War, 1914–1918—Social aspects—Middle East. | World War, 1914–1918—Social aspects—America.
Classification: LCC D639.J4 (ebook) | LCC D639.J4 W77 2017 (print) | DDC 940.3089/924—dc23
LC record available at https://lccn.loc.gov/2017014887

British Library Cataloguing in Publication Data

A catalogue record for this book is available from the British Library

ISBN 978-1-78533-592-1 (hardback)
ISBN 978-1-78920-085-0 (paperback)
ISBN 978-1-78533-593-8 (ebook)

To Judith Siegel

Our friend and a true friend of scholars

Table of Contents

Figures ix

Tables x

Maps xi

Acknowledgments xii

Introduction: On the Significance of World War I and
the Jews 1
Jonathan Karp and Marsha L. Rozenblit

Part I. Overviews

1. World War I and Its Impact on the Problem of Security
   in Jewish History 17
   David Engel

2. The European Jewish World 1914–1919: What Changed? 32
   Marsha L. Rozenblit

3. Jewish Diplomacy and the Politics of War and Peace 56
   Carole Fink

Part II. Local Studies

4. Bravery in the Borderlands, Martyrs on the Margins:
   Jewish War Heroes and World War I Narratives in France,
   1914–1940 85
   Erin Corber

5. The Budapest Jewish Community's Galician October 112
   Rebekah Klein-Pejšová

6. Confronting the Bacterial Enemy: Public Health, Philanthropy, and Jewish Responses to Typhus in Poland, 1914–1921   131
Daniel Rosenthal

7. The Union of Jewish Soldiers under Soviet Rule   151
Mihály Kálmán

8. Global Conflict, Local Politics: The Jews of Salonica and World War I   175
Paris Papamichos Chronakis

9. Recounting the Past, Shaping the Future: Ladino Literary Representations of World War I   201
Devi Mays

10. Women and the War: The Social and Economic Impact of World War I on Jewish Women in the Traditional Holy Cities of Palestine   222
Michal Ben Ya'akov

11. Baghdadi Jews in the Ottoman Military during World War I   242
Reeva Spector Simon

12. Unintentional Pluralists: Military Policy, Jewish Servicemen, and the Development of Tri-Faith America during World War I   263
Jessica Cooperman

13. American Yiddish Socialists at the Wartime Crossroads: Patriotism and Nationalism versus Proletarian Internationalism   279
Gennady Estraikh

14. Louis Marshall during World War I: Change and Continuity in Jewish Culture and Politics   303
M. M. Silver

Index   326

Figures

4.1. French postcard depicting the death of Rabbi Abraham Bloch, who, upon offering a crucifix to a wounded Catholic, fell under shellfire in 1914.   89

4.2. Monument to David Bloch in Guebwiller. Postcard from interwar period. Personal collection of Michel Rothe, reprinted with his permission.   97

6.1. Workers under the auspices of the League of Nations Epidemic Commission operate a disinfection chamber in Eastern Poland, c. 1921, using hydrogen cyanide gas. *Report of the Epidemic Commission of the League of Nations* (Geneva, 1921).   138

9.1. Cover page of Nissim Shem-Tov 'Eli's *Haggadah dela Gerra por Dia de Pesach* (Constantinople: Sosieta Anonima de Papeteria i de Impremeria, 1919).   205

10.1. Food Distribution at the Central Soup Kitchen, Jerusalem, World War I. Courtesy of the Central Zionist Archives, Jerusalem, Zadok Basan Collection, photo GNZB 401450.   229

13.1. Abraham Cahan. Courtesy of the *Forverts* Archive.   280

14.1. Meeting of the Joint Distribution Committee Executive Committee, 1918. Louis Marshall is seated front, far left. Painting by Geza Fischer, 1929. Courtesy of the American Jewish Joint Distribution Committee.   306

Tables

7.1. Veitsman's Calculations concerning Jewish POWs   155

10.1. Number of Deaths in Jerusalem among the Sephardic and Mizrachi Communities   227

Maps

1	Europe on the Eve of World War I	xiv
2	Europe after World War I	xv
3	Austria-Hungary, 1910	xvi
4	The Eastern Front during World War I	xvii
5	Ottoman Empire, 1914	xviii

Acknowledgments

Many scholars have sought to make sense of World War I, and the centennial of the outbreak of that war in 1914 has provided the opportunity for much rethinking of the impact of that long and bloody conflict on the peoples who experienced it. This volume represents one such effort. It first began to take shape around the centennial of the beginning of the Great War when Judith Siegel, the director of Academic and Public Programs at the Center for Jewish History in New York, asked a group of historians to collaborate in exploring the impact of the war on Jews in Europe, the Middle East, and America. The organizers—David Engel, Jonathan Karp, Marsha L. Rozenblit, Rebecca Kobrin, Gennady Estraikh, Marion Kaplan, and Hasia Diner—sought to combine overviews by senior scholars of the war's significance for the Jews with specific local studies based on the latest research. Participating scholars came together to share their research at the Center for Jewish History in November 2014, with co-sponsorship from the American Jewish Historical Society, the American Sephardi Federation, the Leo Baeck Institute, and the Goldstein-Goren Center for American Jewish History. This gathering provided an important opportunity for historians to engage with the serious ways that World War I transformed Jewish life.

We would like to thank all the people who made this volume possible. First, of course, we would like to thank all the scholars who joined us in 2014, including those who for various reasons did not contribute a chapter. Second, we acknowledge the generosity of the Center for Jewish History, including Michael Glickman and especially Judith Siegel, who provided extraordinary logistical support and encouraged our efforts to publish this volume. We would also like to thank Siegel's able colleague Christopher Barthel. Needless to say, none of this would have taken place without the financial support of the Center for Jewish History and its constituent organizations. We wish to express our special gratitude to the center's current director, Joel Levy, for his ongoing support of this project and for his financial support, including funds to help pay for the maps and some of the images. Co-organizers David Engel, Gennady Estraikh, Hasia Diner, Marion Kaplan, and Rebecca Kobrin proved invaluable for their ideas, their suggestions, and their insights.

Finally, we express our appreciation to all the people who helped produce this book, in particular Marion Berghahn and Chris Chappell at Berghahn Books, who supported the publication of the volume very warmly, as well as the anonymous outside evaluators; the production editor, Rebecca Rom-Frank; copyeditor Debra Hirsch Corman; and typesetter Connie Richardson. A book like this needed historical maps, and we thank Nathan Burtch, a PhD student in the Department of Geographical Sciences at the University of Maryland, for preparing the elegant maps, and the Department of History at the University of Maryland for helping to defray the costs of the maps. It has been a pleasure for the two of us to work with each other, with the authors, and with everyone else who helped produce this volume of essays.

Jonathan Karp
Marsha L. Rozenblit
November 2016

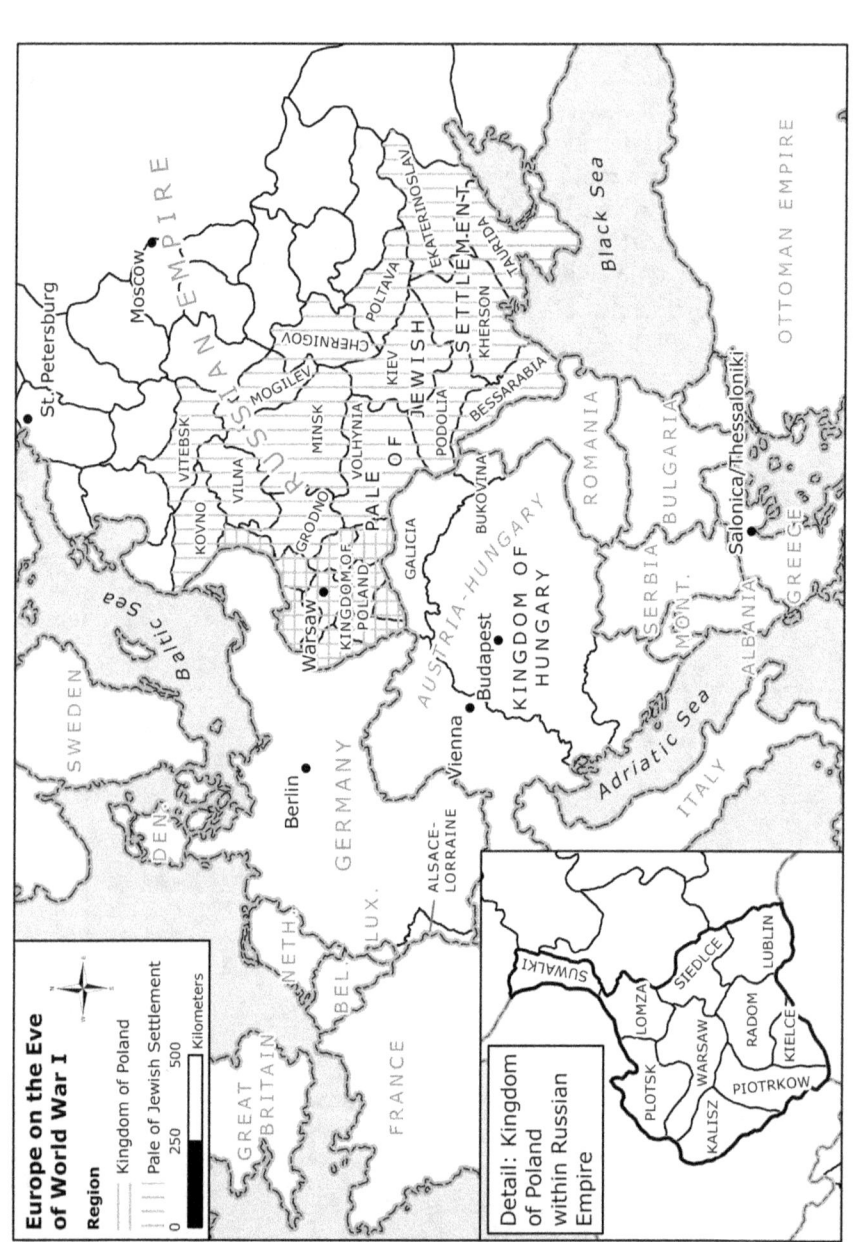

Map 1. *Europe on the Eve of World War I*

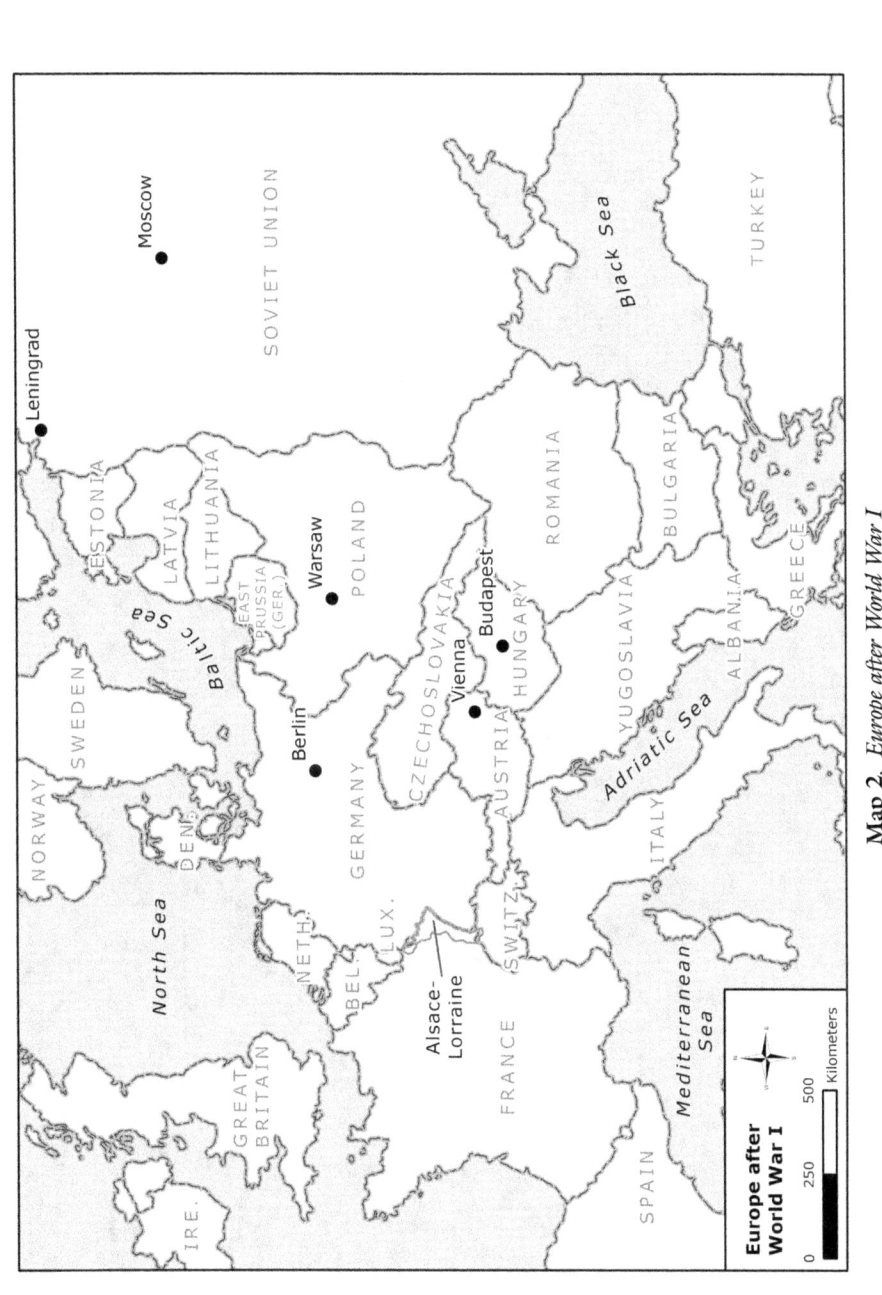

Map 2. *Europe after World War I*

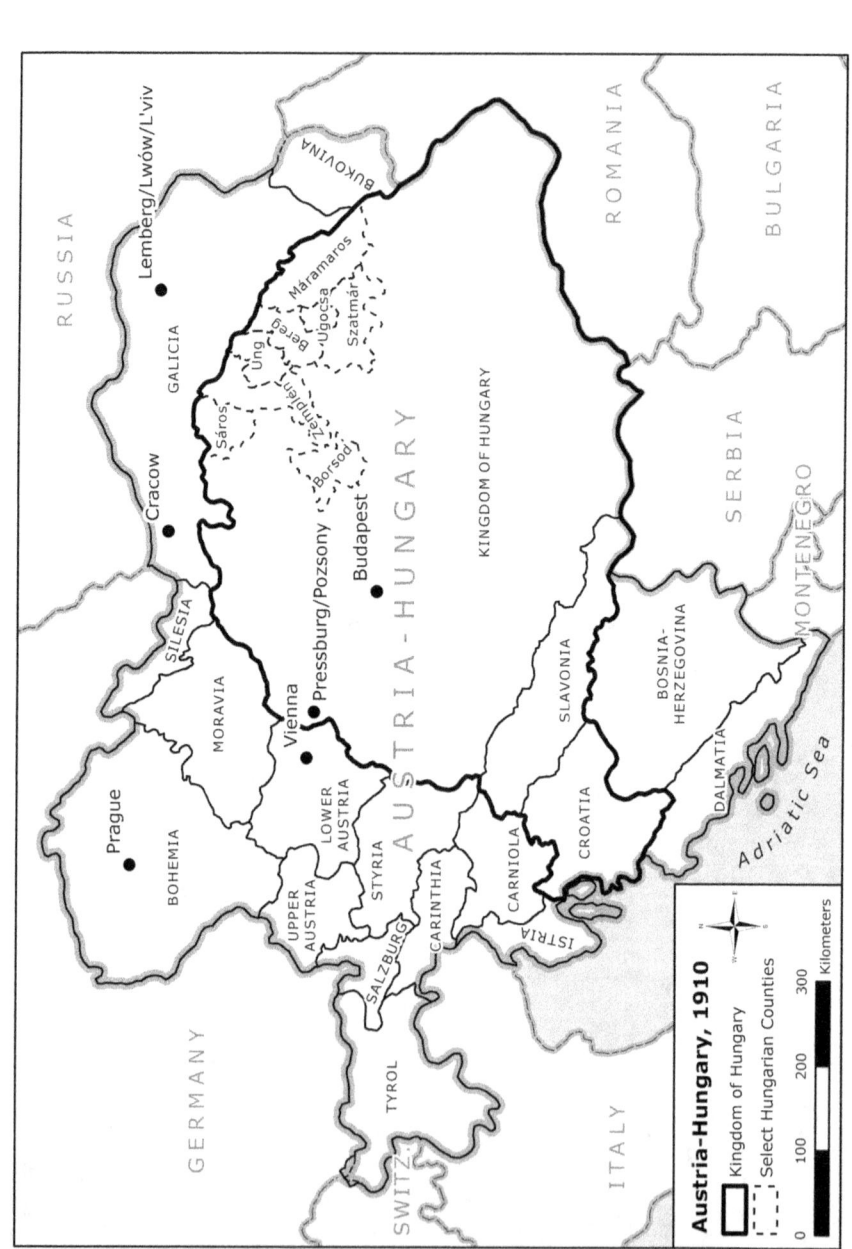

Map 3. *Austria-Hungary 1910*

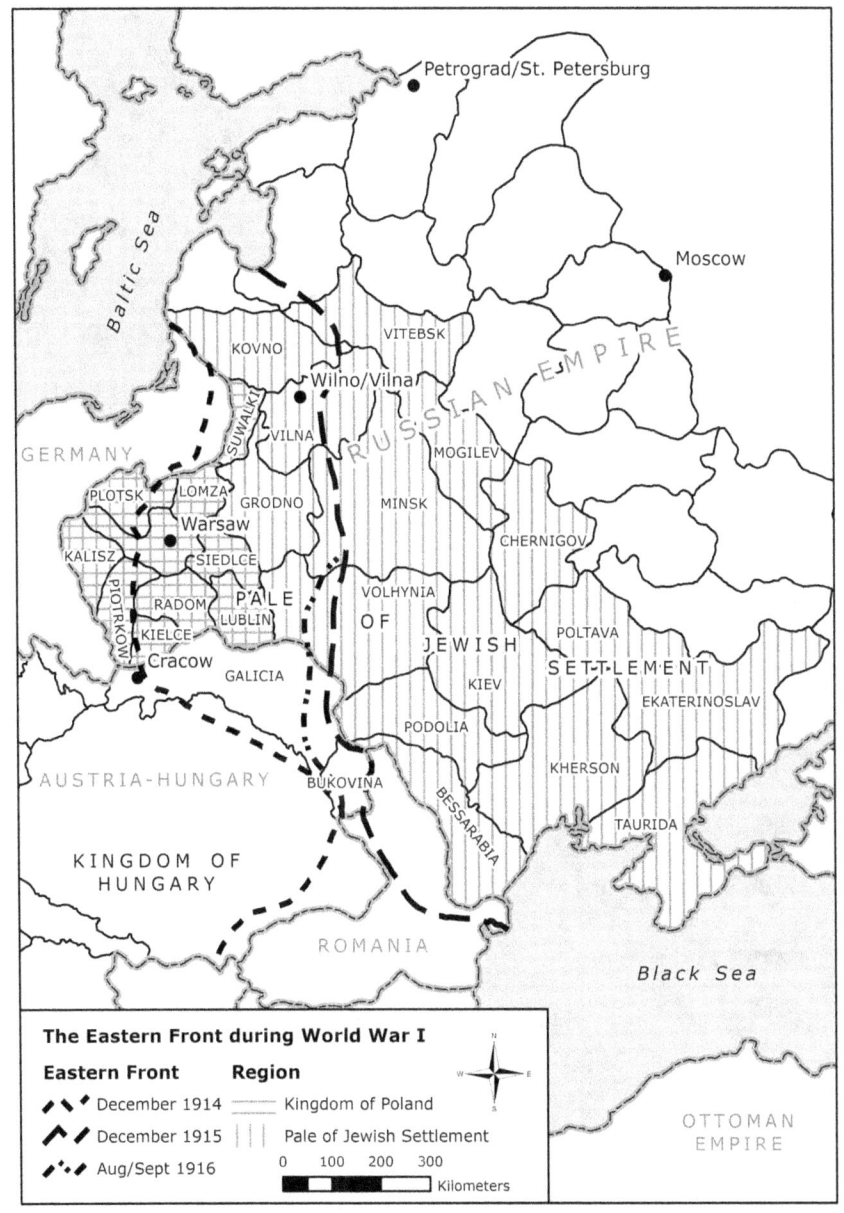

Map 4. *The Eastern Front during World War I*

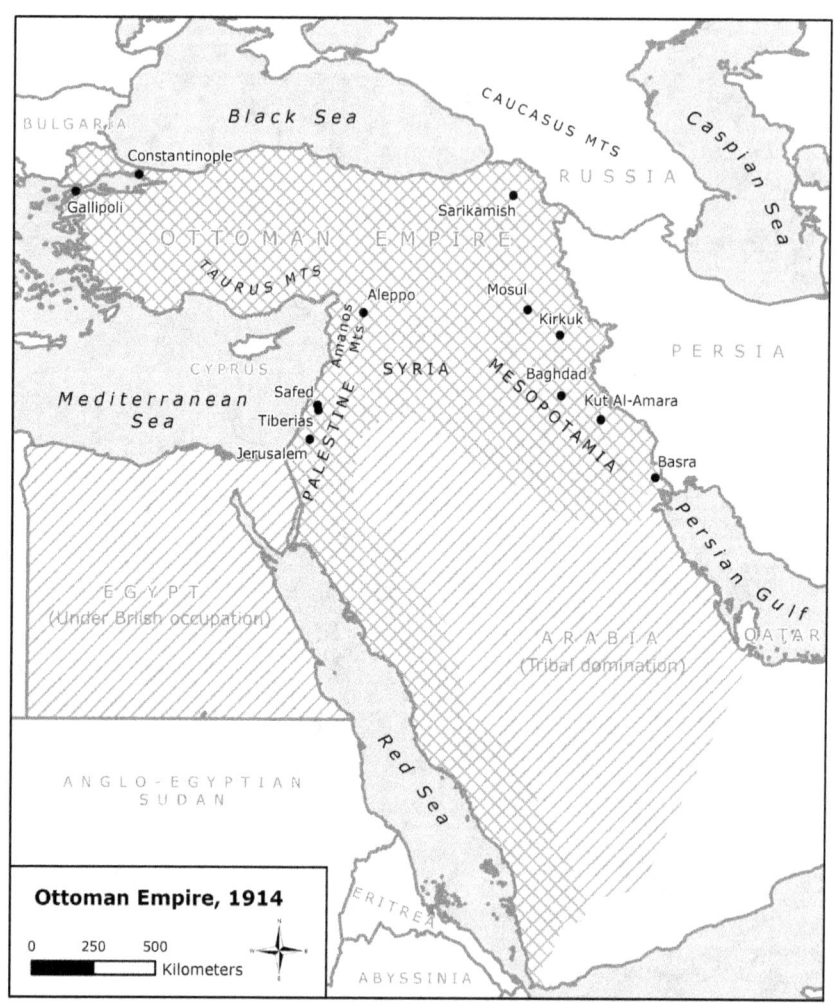

Map 5. *Ottoman Empire, 1914*

Introduction
On the Significance of World War I and the Jews
Jonathan Karp and Marsha L. Rozenblit

In *The Historian's Craft* the eminent French historian Marc Bloch offered practitioners a piece of excellent if challenging advice. Historians, wrote Bloch, must try to write about the past from two contrasting—or even contradictory—perspectives: the first with a full awareness of what later events would ensue, the second with a kind of feigned ignorance of those very same eventualities. The former, observed Bloch, would make it possible to trace a chain of historical causality, the latter to entertain awareness of historical contingency, of roads not taken.[1]

Bloch's paradox applies to the topic of this book. Some eighty years after his death (he had fought in both World Wars and was executed by the Nazis in 1944),[2] it is surprising that the present volume is one of the first academic works devoted expressly to the subject of World War I and the Jews. As the contributors make clear in the chapters that follow, this is not because World War I was without significant impact on Jewish history. On the contrary, the war profoundly affected nearly every major Jewish population around the globe.

Among the major developments occasioned by the war and its immediate aftermath, four stand out as being of paramount historical importance. First, the war offered Jewish populations in many of the combatant lands unprecedented opportunities to demonstrate their loyalty through military service and patriotic display and was thus the culmination of more than a century of debate throughout Europe and beyond over whether Jews possessed the physical and spiritual qualities required of modern citizens. Second, the conflict ultimately destroyed the imperial umbrellas under which approximately 80 percent of the world's Jews lived prior to

1914. The Russian, Habsburg, German, and Ottoman Empires were all replaced—sometimes gradually if not immediately—by a multiplicity of nation-states (or would-be nation-states) whose existence not only vastly complicated Jewish status but whose definition on the basis of ethnic and national principles typically made that existence more problematic and precarious. Third, through the issuance of the Balfour Declaration in November of 1917 and subsequently—*mutatis mutandis*—through the negotiation of the national minority clauses in the treaties emerging from the Paris Peace Conference of 1919–23, Jews won the right, hitherto denied them, to constitute a national element in international law and diplomacy, a right entitling them, in theory, to a measure of self-determination. And fourth, the war brought about a profound sense that many of the certainties that formerly governed Jewish lives were now, more than ever, open to question. This occurred in a variety of different ways: through the effective destruction of the Russian Pale of Settlement (even before the two Russian Revolutions of 1917), which despite its many hardships had also provided a protective shell around the traditional Eastern European Jewish community; through the disappointment and disillusionment many Jews came to experience as the war's seeming promise of equality often fell short in execution; or even through the appearance (or illusion) of Jewish diplomatic power that had been occasioned by the Balfour Declaration and other seeming Jewish "national" triumphs. The processes of uprooting and the dramatic shifts in Jews' sense of belonging, membership, and separate identity were a part of that larger political and psychological destabilization that was a distinct legacy of World War I for all Europeans.

These and other such major changes have been individually chronicled and explored before, of course. But the war itself as connective tissue and central organizing framework for them has generally failed to attract the attention of historians. Why is this so?

Bloch's prescription, that the historian must simultaneously know and not know what will later happen, provides part of the answer. In contrast to World War I, the impact of World War II on the Jews has been studied and written about more than any other topic in Jewish history. Each year dozens of academic monographs are published on the Holocaust, not to mention a large (if now dwindling) number of memoirs, alongside many more popular histories and historical novels. Because the Holocaust is regarded by many as the signal event of the modern Jewish experience (or by some, of *all* of Jewish experience), and because World War I has come implicitly to be seen as a prelude to its still more destructive and horrific sequel, Jewish historians may have found it difficult to conceptualize World War I and the Jews as a distinctive and discrete topic in its own right.

Surveying some of the recent one-volume histories of the Jews reinforces this impression. Paul Johnson's popular *A History of the Jews* subsumes World War I into a chapter covering the interwar and World War II periods and simply titled "Holocaust."[3] Howard N. Lupovitch's 2010 survey *Jews and Judaism in World History* encapsulates the period 1914–45 in a single chapter called "From Renewal to Destruction."[4] Other general histories and textbooks simply skip over World War I entirely (though invariably addressing individual episodes like the Balfour Declaration). Raymond P. Scheindlin's *A Short History of the Jewish People* offers no discussion of World War I per se but shifts from successive chapters on "Ottoman," "Western" and "Eastern" Jewries before 1945 to a chapter on "The Holocaust."[5] The widely used documentary history *The Jew in the Modern World* includes a chapter on the Shoah containing a wide selection of materials, but no such section on World War I and only a single document dealing specifically with the war itself.[6]

By no means is this phenomenon confined to Jewish history. The temptation has existed—almost from the period of World War II itself—to view World War I as the opening bloody salvo in a single continuous conflagration, marked by a long interregnum.[7] At the same time, what some historians have called the "Second Thirty Years War" or the "Thirty Years War of the Twentieth Century" is really but a variation on the notion that World War I marks a great turning point in world history and bears a not-distant relationship to the concept of the "short twentieth century," measured roughly from the outbreak of World War I in 1914 to the fall of communism in 1989.[8] It sometimes seems that World War I is weighted with such immense significance, and its effects are so far-reaching and long-lasting, that it cannot *also* easily be seen as a relatively self-contained episode in its own right. "Verdun and the Somme opened the way to Auschwitz and Hiroshima," asserted the historian Jack J. Roth in the 1969 volume *World War I: A Turning Point in World History*.[9] Recent studies of the Armenian genocide, which took place in the midst and in the context of World War I, underscore the same linkage. It is not that such links are false or misplaced, but only that they can have the effect of displacing the war itself and relegating it to the role of catalyst, prototype, and precursor.[10] In thinking about World War I, the *longue durée* too often seems to triumph over its antithesis, *l'histoire événementielle* (episodic history).[11]

At the same time, a countervailing tendency is also evident. Recent trends in historiography associated with the "cultural turn" have often led to a fragmentary emphasis on microhistories or on subjective representation that eschews structural and sociological accounts in favor of a focus on iconography, images, texts, and individual and collective memory. When it comes to the topic of World War I and the Jews, this narrower approach dovetails with an older emphasis, particularly pronounced in the post–World War II writing of Jewish history, that centers on the individual national territory, for example, the history of the Jews of Germany or of America. In fact it is only in recent decades that historians of the Jews have homed in on "empire" as an organizing category, though certainly an apposite one given that at the outbreak of World War I the great majority of Jews directly affected by it lived under some form of imperial rule.

At any rate, many of the important monographs that deal with some aspect of Jewish life in World War I have focused on a national territory even within the larger imperial frame. Works by Marsha L. Rozenblit on the Jews of Habsburg Austria; Egmont Zechlin, Arnold Paucker and Werner Mosse, Tim Grady, Peter C. Appelbaum, and Sarah Panter on the Jews of wartime Germany (the last including much comparative material also on Austria, England, and the United States); Abigail Jacobson's and Isaiah Friedman's studies of the Jews (and non-Jews) in wartime Palestine; Harold Shukman's examination of the conscription of Russian Jews living in Britain; Marcos Silber's recent monograph on wartime Polish Jewry; or Christopher M. Sterba's comparative study of Jewish and Italian immigrants in the American military are good examples.[12] In truth, these more national or regional studies are the very building blocks for a synthetic treatment of the sprawling topic of Jews in World War I. The archival records for a primary-source-based account of all the major Jewish communities entwined in the conflict are too vast, far-flung, and polyglot for any one historian to investigate.[13]

And yet the fact that such synthetic accounts do not exist still begs the question of why. Periodization constitutes as much of an obstacle as do linguistic divisions and territorial boundaries. This goes beyond the basic problem discussed above of subsuming the war to a long twentieth-century trajectory. In Jewish history it may seem that for the most critical events the war serves only as the occasion and immediate backdrop. In different ways this is the case with several crucial developments: the issuance of the Balfour Declaration in November of 1917; the outbreak of the Bolshevik Revolution during that same month and the ensuing civil, national liberation, and expansionist wars on Russia's western imperial border, which did not subside until 1921; and finally the series of national treaties negotiated in Paris between 1919 and 1923 that crucially affected the status of Jews in Eastern and East Central Europe during the interwar period. Like the Balfour Declaration, which was eventually incorporated into the British Mandate, these developments have histories that extend well beyond the formal periodization of World War I. The war itself forms an essential part of the framework to comprehend such events, but only a part.

There is yet one additional factor that has inhibited greater scholarly focus on the topic of Jews and World War I. In a global conflagration involving Jews from several continents and from many different countries, there really is no typical "Jewish" experience. On the contrary, the war presented individual Jewries (not to mention individual Jews) with strikingly different opportunities and experiences. British Jews (themselves stemming from all reaches of the empire), of whom about forty thousand served, certainly suffered from increased antisemitism during the war, but on the whole they experienced integration into the military and the home front that proved comparatively harmonious. One might say something similar about the much larger contingent of American Jews (about a quarter of a million serving), except that their experience was characterized in part by its sheer brevity, since the United States only became a combatant in April of 1917, while the first US expeditionary force landed in France in July of that year. German Jews proved second to none in their display of patriotism. About one hundred thousand are estimated to have served in the German armed forces, but despite the remarkably high percentage of Jewish conscripts (approximately 20 percent), their readiness for sacrifice was challenged by rising antisemitism and through a 1916 military census (*Judenzählung*) that proved humiliating and injurious to the Jewish population as a whole.

Despite this antisemitism, military service in Germany and Austria-Hungary (where three hundred thousand Jews served) resembled that of Britain and America in offering opportunities for promotion to the officer corps and for sharing in experiences of national exaltation and suffering as equal—or nearly equal—members of the national community.[14] It would be difficult to claim the same for the nearly half-million Jewish soldiers fighting in the Russian imperial army, although they did hope to gain more rights in exchange for their service, or even for the tens of thousands who served in the Ottoman armed forces. On the other hand, as several of the chapters in this volume show, World War I marked a serious setback from the relatively equal status Ottoman Jewish soldiers had enjoyed in the immediately preceding Balkan Wars of 1912–13. In World War I, despite some exceptions, Jews like other non-Muslims were typically relegated to a harsh and humiliating service in labor battalions.

These brief examples suggest just how difficult it is to venture generalizations reflecting a singular Jewish experience in World War I. And when we look at the more lasting structural effects of the war on different Jewish communities, such contrasts appear still sharper. Even compared to World War II, which of course exhibited equally divergent effects, there is an important difference. In that case the theme of the catastrophe afflicting European Jews and the efforts of various worldwide Jewries to confront it serves as a unifying core. This is not the case of World War I, and any volume that aims to cover the topic must acknowledge this problem.

Despite such challenges, we hope that the present volume will contribute to the overdue recognition of World War I as a major field in modern

Jewish history. Its central focus is indeed the war years 1914–18, but in light of the preceding discussion it is obvious that strict adherence to such a time schema would be self-defeating. A number of the chapters do focus more on the immediate postwar years, examining such phenomena as the war's subsequent memorialization, its economic legacies, Jewish diplomacy in the shaping of the postwar order, and how Jews coped with the collapse of the empires in which they lived. Nevertheless, on the whole, perspectives emphasizing the "Second Thirty Years War" and the buildup to the Holocaust are here deliberately avoided.

This volume resulted from scholarly discussions organized by the Center for Jewish History in New York City on 9–10 November 2014. Senior scholars tackled a set of overarching themes related to the Jews and World War I (diplomatic, military, political, economic, and cultural), and more junior scholars, having engaged in fresh archival research, discussed more specific issues affecting Jews in Western and Central Europe, Eastern Europe, the Ottoman Empire, and North America. We have retained much of this structure for the present volume. Part 1 includes three synthetic essays dealing with the immediate alterations in Jewish life wrought by the war, its diplomatic, financial, and philanthropic legacies, as well as its political consequences. Part 2 is structured more geographically, with chapters on different aspects of the war relating to the Jewish communities of Western, Central, and Eastern Europe, the Ottoman (or formerly Ottoman) Mediterranean and Middle East, and the United States.

In addition to underscoring the war's four major developments for modern Jewish history as outlined above, the essays collected in this volume can be organized into a handful of core motifs. The first is the thorny issue of inclusion and exclusion of the Jews. As mentioned, the war provided the first wide-ranging and global opportunity for Jews to demonstrate their patriotism through that central component of modern male citizenship: fighting for one's country. Beyond this basic point, however, World War I even offered instances of Jewish soldiery and martyrdom as exemplary of national ideals and myths. Erin Corber's fascinating and counterintuitive exploration of how French Jews and non-Jews used Jewish figures to construct images of wartime heroism reveals the significant extent to which Jews were included in narratives about French republican virtue or even epitomized such virtue (chapter 4). Not only does she describe how a Jewish chaplain who had served as a rabbi in Algeria and a Jewish soldier from Alsace—a region of France that was part of Germany from 1870 to 1918—became martyrs for France, she also explains how their very marginality, both as Jews and as individuals from outside the borders of metropolitan France, made them perfect exemplars of France's claims to embody universalist values.

In World War I, military service could function to expand conceptions and practices of equal membership for minorities like Jews. Jessica Cooperman's essay (chapter 12) on religious pluralism in the American army demonstrates how the very presence of Jewish soldiers induced reluctant military leaders to make arrangements to cater to Jewish religious needs. Blind to the evangelical mission of the YMCA (the organization tasked with catering to the spiritual needs of soldiers), military leaders initially opposed separate organizations for soldiers of different faiths, but vigorous lobbying by both Jewish and Catholic groups led the military to accept the notion that America was not just a Protestant country. M. M. Silver's study (chapter 14) of American Jewish leader Louis Marshall reinforces this theme of Jewish integration. Silver convincingly shows how in his activism on behalf of Jewish rights abroad, Marshall pursued policies that closely resembled those of Irish leaders, who, like the Jews, concerned themselves with their compatriots in the old country even while they sought integration in America. Despite Irish anti-British views and a Jewish immigrant pro-German (or rather anti-Russian) stance, leaders of both groups made loyalty to America the overarching position of their respective clienteles. And as Gennady Estraikh demonstrates in chapter 13, on American Yiddish socialists during wartime, even those who had struggled before 1917 between a commitment to internationalism and neutrality on the one hand and anti-Russian (and therefore pro-German) views on the other ended up putting their loyalty to America above prior concerns once the United States entered the war.

While France and the United States included Jews in the nation at arms, the Ottoman Empire for a variety of domestic reasons did not, choosing instead to create combat units consisting only of Muslim soldiers and relegating Jews and Christians to army labor battalions (while designating Armenians potential and actual traitors). In the eyes of many Ottoman non-Muslims, this added insult to injury, for immediately prior to World War I, during the Balkan Wars of 1912–13, they had been admitted to military service on an equal basis. Many Jews, who had been loyal Ottoman subjects, felt alienated by this evident demotion and exclusion. Devi Mays's essay (chapter 9) on Jewish responses in Constantinople to World War I shows how this dismay and disillusionment found expression in a number of Hebrew and Ladino literary works, including special Passover Haggadot that were produced during and after the war and contained stinging if thinly veiled criticisms of imperial wartime policy. Similarly, Reeva Spector Simon's contribution (chapter 11) on the Jews in wartime Baghdad concretizes this experience of alienation by detailing the harrowing experiences of Baghdad Jews pressed into a degrading and particularly coercive form of military service. Not only did they suffer terribly both in the labor battalions and on the home front, but the fact that they were no longer equal citizens undermined their loyalty to the empire.

A second theme that emerges from the essays in this volume is the tension between the local versus the imperial loyalties of Jews. Ottoman and Russian Jews may have already questioned their imperial loyalties during the war, but Jews in the Habsburg Monarchy did not. Indeed, as Marsha L. Rozenblit shows in chapter 2, "The European Jewish World 1914–1919: What Changed?," they fervently hoped that the Habsburg Monarchy would continue to exist, regarding it as their best defense against nationalist antisemitism. These former imperial subjects were devastated by the collapse of the monarchy in November 1918 and feared that the new nation-states that succeeded it would exclude them from full citizenship. On the other hand, in chapter 8, "Global Conflict, Local Politics," Paris Papamichos Chronakis persuasively argues that Jews in Salonica understood the war primarily in terms of local needs and concerns yet attached these parochial agendas, sometimes rather artificially, to conflicting sides in the war. Salonica had been an Ottoman city and became part of Greece in 1912–13 and thus part of a country that had been neutral until 1916 when it entered the anti-Ottoman entente on the side of Britain and France. Although many of the city's Jews were Francophile—largely because European modernization had occurred through the vehicle of the French language—and others sided with Germany because it was fighting Russia (the empire that oppressed its Jews), often these positions had more to do with class and ideological divisions within Salonican Jewry and within Greek politics than genuinely with international allegiances.

A third and related theme examines how the war affected transnational Jewish institutions and politics, or, more simply, the degree to which the war divided global Jewish communities or brought them more closely together. Certainly initially, the war succeeded in stretching tensions between different Jewries and their institutions to the breaking point. With the war's outbreak, as Carole Fink notes in chapter 3, on Jewish wartime diplomacy, decades-old institutional, intellectual, philanthropic, and financial ties were suddenly curtailed or in many cases severed. This could have dire consequences, especially for smaller and more peripheral concentrations of Jews. As Michal Ben Ya'akov's chapter on the fate of Jewish women in wartime Palestine makes clear (chapter 10), the war devastated the local economy of Palestine, cut Jewish (particularly Sephardic Jewish) Palestine off from traditional ethnic, familial, and philanthropic transnational ties (such as the centuries-old *halukah* fund), and consequently placed the population in a situation of extreme isolation and deprivation. Small Jewish communities in Safed, Jerusalem, and elsewhere managed to create their own makeshift relief organizations, but they could not solve the problem alone. By 1915 American Jews, in part because they were citizens of a still neutral United States, succeeded in breaking through Jewish Palestine's blockade and isolation and, via the newly created Joint Distribution Committee (JDC), brought welcome relief. And as Ben Ya'akov shows, although the Joint's official leadership was composed almost exclusively of men, it was more typically female relief workers on the ground who administered the help.

As this example suggests, more often than not the traditions of Jewish transnational philanthropy managed willy-nilly to reassert themselves and at times even transcend impulses of patriotic loyalty. Both Marsha L. Rozenblit in her aforementioned chapter and Rebecca Klein-Pejšová in chapter 5, "The Budapest Jewish Community's Galician October," emphasize that the conflict in the long run appears to have strengthened international Jewish ties through the proliferation of international relief agencies as well as through the new confrontation between settled Jewish populations and masses of Jewish refugees who required their support. On the other hand, they also provided opportunities for Jewish solidarity and augmented the collective *Klal Yisrael* mentality that M. M. Silver sees as characteristic of the war years. Indeed, the growth of a Jewish national sentiment, or at least of stronger identification with their Jewish ethnicity, typified many Jews during the war, including the Jewish socialists in New York so ably described by Gennady Estraikh. At the same time, the war could result in a Jewish community's greater isolation but also expose it to corrosive wartime forces that uprooted long-established settlements and punctured traditional insularities. Daniel Rosenthal, in his essay (chapter 6) on the wartime typhus epidemic in occupied Poland, describes the war on the Eastern Front as vaporizing there the last vestiges of "a concealed Jewish communal life." In this sense, despite ongoing ideological fragmentation, World War I created—perhaps for the first time in history—a truly globalized Jewish world, one in which effective isolation and insularity were no longer possible.

The final theme is the war's fecund impact on Jews' institutional life. As a number of the contributors discuss, the war occasioned the creation of a host of new Jewish bodies, many initially intended to further Jewish claims of loyalty to their host countries paradoxically by championing the rights of fellow Jews they claimed were being persecuted by the enemy camp. Carole Fink offers the example of the German-Jewish Committee for the Liberation of Russian Jewry, whose intent was clearly propagandist. But a number of these organizations were genuinely more philanthropic than political in intent. In response to the war, American Jews constructed not only the Joint Distribution Committee in the fall of 1914 but also the American Jewish Congress in late 1918, a month after the armistice, to coordinate postwar lobbying efforts on behalf of Eastern European Jews, including for Jewish national rights in the successor states. Similar organizations that aimed to project Jewish influence abroad (such as the Association of Jewish Organizations in Germany for the Protection of the Rights of the Jews of the East or the Comité des Délégations Juives) were founded during or immediately after the war by British, French, German, and Eastern European Jews. This trend dovetails with an important if hitherto little-emphasized transformation, that is, a shift from a long-standing Jewish tendency in transnational matters to rely on the initiatives of individual intercessors (*shtadlanim*)—wealthy notables, such as Moses Montefiore or later Jacob Schiff—to more institutional actors.[15] As David Engel shows in chapter 1, on the war's impact on Jewish security, the war's unprecedented expenses effectively destroyed the capacity of even the richest Jewish banker to seriously impact governmental policies. The war's aftermath, particularly the proliferation of small successor states to former imperial regimes, reinforced this same tendency, in which Jewish diplomacy necessarily became more institutional and bureaucratized even if less successful—at least in the fraught interwar period.

Of a far more local character, in contrast, was the Russian and later Soviet Union of Jewish Soldiers (VSEV), whose remarkable history is detailed for the first time in chapter 7, by Mihály Kálmán. Established as an umbrella organization for the many small, local bodies that had sprung up toward the end of Russia's participation in the war and that sought to aid decommissioned Jewish soldiers and veterans, VSEV survived for only a couple of years, yet in that time displayed a truly extraordinary reliance and capacity for adaptation, especially under the shifting and increasingly centralized policies of the Bolshevik regime.

Overall, *World War I and the Jews* exhibits a wide range of Jewish creative responses to the challenges and the opportunities presented by the conflict. If World War I indeed marked a major turning point in Jewish history, we hope that the essays in this volume will contribute to its further exploration.

Jonathan Karp is associate professor of history and Judaic studies at Binghamton University. He is the author of *The Politics of Jewish Commerce: Economic Thought and Emancipation in Europe, 1638–1848* (2008) and editor of several academic collections, including, with Adam Sutcliffe, *Philosemitism in History* (2012) and *The Cambridge History of Judaism in the Early Modern Period* (2017). He was executive director of the American Jewish Historical Society from 2010 to 2013.

Marsha L. Rozenblit is the Harvey M. Meyerhoff Professor of Modern Jewish History at the University of Maryland. She is the author of *The*

Jews of Vienna, 1867–1914: Assimilation and Identity (1983) and *Constructing a National Identity: The Jews of Habsburg Austria during World War I* (2001) and coeditor, with Pieter M. Judson, of *Constructing Nationalities in East Central Europe* (2005).

Notes

1. Marc Bloch, *The Historian's Craft* (Manchester, UK: Manchester University Press, 1954), pp. 35–46.
2. See Marc Bloch, *Memoirs of War, 1914–15,* trans. Carole Fink (Ithaca, NY: Cornell University Press, 1980); and Bloch, *Strange Defeat: A Statement of Evidence Written in 1940,* trans. Gerard Hopkins (New York: Octagon, 1968). For a full biography of Bloch, see Carole Fink, *Marc Bloch: A Life in History* (Cambridge: Cambridge University Press, 1989).
3. Paul Johnson, *A History of the Jews* (London: Weidenfeld and Nicolson, 1987).
4. Howard N. Lupovitch, *Jews and Judaism in World History* (London: Routledge, 2010).
5. Raymond P. Scheindlin, *A Short History of the Jewish People: From Legendary Times to Modern Statehood* (New York: Macmillan, 1998).
6. Paul Mendes-Flohr and Jehuda Reinharz, *The Jew in the Modern World: A Documentary History,* 3rd ed. (Oxford: Oxford University Press, 2011), p. 452. Of such studies the volume by John Efron, Steven Weitzman, Matthias Lehmann, and Joshua Holo is exceptional in presenting a short but separate section on World War I, which is highly substantive. See *The Jews: A History* (Upper Saddle River, NJ: Prentice Hall, 2009), pp. 334–38.
7. The notion that the two world wars were really one was expressly articulated by Charles de Gaulle in a radio broadcast of 18 September 1941. See Jay Winter and Antoine Prost, *The Great War in History: Debates and Controversies, 1914 to the Present* (Cambridge: Cambridge University Press, 2005), p. 32, n. 20.
8. Ibid., p. 29.
9. Jack J. Roth, ed., *World War I: A Turning Point in Modern History* (New York: Knopf, 1969), p. 6.
10. See, most recently, Stefan Ihrig, *Justifying Genocide: Germany and the Armenians from Bismark to Hitler* (Cambridge, MA: Harvard University Press, 2016).
11. See Immanuel Wallerstein's translation of Fernand Braudel's "Commemorating the Long Durée," *Review (Fernand Braudel Center)* 32, no. 2 (2009): 171–203, esp. 174.
12. For a collection of essays covering mostly Germany but also Austria, Russia, and Britain, see Marcus G. Patka, ed., *Weltuntergang: jüdisches Leben und Sterben im Ersten Weltkrieg* (Vienna: Styria Premium, 2014). On Habsburg Jewry, see Marsha L. Rozenblit, *Reconstructing a National Identity: The Jews of Habsburg Austria during World War I* (New York: Oxford University Press, 2001); on Germany generally, see Egmont Zechlin, *Die deutsche Politik und die Juden im ersten Weltkrieg* (Göttingen: Van den Hoeck u. Ruprecht, 1969); Werner Mosse and Arnold Paucker, eds., *Deutsches Judentum in Krieg und Revolution, 1916–1923* (Tübingen: J.C.B. Mohr, 1971). Jewish service in the German military along with the *Judenzählung* are among the most studied topics of the Jewish World War I experience. In addition to older works, see Werner Angress, "The

German Army's 'Judenzählung' of 1916: Genesis—Consequences—Significance," *Leo Baeck Institute Year Book* 23 (1978): 117–37; Michael Berger, *Eisernes Kreuz und Davidstern: die Geschichte jüdischer Soldaten in deutschen Armeen* (Berlin: Trafo, 2006); Jacob Rosenthal's published PhD dissertation from Hebrew University in Jerusalem, *"Die Ehre des jüdischen Soldaten": die Judenzählung im Ersten Weltkrieg und ihre Folgen* (Frankfurt am Main: Campus, 2007); Tim Grady, *The German-Jewish Soldiers of World War I in History and Memory* (Liverpool: Liverpool University Press, 2011); David J. Fine, *Jewish Integration in the German Army in the First World War* (Berlin: De Gruyter, 2012); Sarah Panter, *Jüdische Erfahrungen und Loyalitätskonflikte im ersten Weltkrieg* (Göttingen: Vandenhoeck & Ruprecht, 2014); Peter C. Appelbaum, *Loyal Sons: Jews in the German Army in the Great War* (London: Vallentine Mitchell, 2014); Ulrike Heikaus and Julia Köhne, eds., *Krieg! Juden zwischen den Fronten, 1914–1918* (Berlin: Hentrich & Henrich Verlag, 2014). On Poland, see Marcos Silber, *Different Nationality / Equal Citizenship: Polish Jewry's Struggle for Autonomy during the First World War* [Hebrew] (Tel Aviv: Merkaz Zalman Shazar, 2014); on Russia, see Eric Lohr, *Nationalizing the Russian Empire: The Campaign against Enemy Aliens during World War I* (Cambridge, MA: Harvard University Press, 2003); and most recently, Polly Zavadivker, *1915 Diary of S. An-sky: A Russian Jewish Writer at the Eastern Front* (Bloomington: Indiana University Press, 2015). On Ottoman Jewry during the war, see Hayim Nahmias, Avner Perets, and Shelomo Nahmias, eds., *Diary 677–678: Memoirs of a Jewish Soldier in the Ottoman Army of the First World War* [Ladino and Hebrew] (Ma'aleh Adumim: Mekhon Ma'aleh Adumim, 2004); Glenda Abramson, *Soldiers' Tales: Two Palestinian Jewish Soldiers in the Ottoman Army during the First World War* (London: Vallentine Mitchell, 2013); Moshe Sharrett, *Shall We Ever Meet Again? Letters from the Ottoman Army, 1916–1918* (Tel Aviv: Ha 'Amuta le-Moreshet Moshe Sharet, 1998); Yosef Tsarni, *Oved Amitai: A Jewish Ottoman Officer and British Captive during World War I* [Hebrew] (Zikron Ya'akov: Itai Bahur, 2014); on Jews in Ottoman Palestine, see Isaiah Friedman, *The Question of Palestine, 1914–1918: British-Jewish-Arab Relations* (New Brunswick, NJ: Transaction, 1992); Ronald Florence, *Lawrence and Aaronsohn, and the Seeds of the Arab-Israeli Conflict* (New York: Viking, 2007); Abigail Jacobson, *From Empire to Empire: Jerusalem between Ottoman and British Rule* (Syracuse, NY: Syracuse University Press, 2011). On Britain, see Harold Shukman, *War or Revolution: Russian Jews and Conscription in Britain, 1917* (London: Vallentine Mitchell, 2006); on the Jewish Legion, see Michael Keren and Shlomit Keren, *We Are Coming, Unafraid: The Jewish Legions and the Promised Land in the First World War* (Lanham, MD: Rowman & Littlefield, 2010). On immigrants in America, see Christopher M. Sterba, *Good Americans: Italian and Jewish Immigrants during World War I* (New York: Oxford University Press, 2003).

13. A noteworthy exception is Mark Levene's study of the wartime diplomacy of the Anglo-Jewish notable Lucien Wolf. Through the prism of Wolf's activities, Levene is able to paint a broad but focused portrait of European Jewry in wartime conditions. Mark Levene, *War, Jews, and the New Europe: The Diplomacy of Lucien Wolf, 1914–1919* (Oxford: Oxford University Press, 1992).

14. See Derek J. Penslar, *Jews and the Military: A History* (Princeton, NJ: Princeton University Press, 2013), pp. 166–94.

15. See, for instance, Abigail Green, *Moses Montefiore: Jewish Liberator, Imperial Hero* (Cambridge, MA: Harvard University Press, 2010).

Selected Bibliography

Primary Sources

Bloch, Marc. *The Historian's Craft*. Manchester, UK: Manchester University Press, 1954.
———. *Memoirs of War, 1914–15*. Translated by Carole Fink. Ithaca, NY: Cornell University Press, 1980.
———. *Strange Defeat: A Statement of Evidence Written in 1940*. Translated by Gerard Hopkins. New York: Octogon, 1968.

Secondary Sources

Fink, Carole. *Marc Bloch: A Life in History*. Cambridge: Cambridge University Press, 1989.
Grady, Tim. *The German-Jewish Soldiers of World War I in History and Memory*. Liverpool: Liverpool University Press, 2011.
Ihrig, Stefan. *Justifying Genocide: Germany and the Armenians from Bismark to Hitler* (Cambridge, MA: Harvard University Press, 2016).
Levene, Mark. *War, Jews, and the New Europe: The Diplomacy of Lucien Wolf, 1914–1919*. Oxford: Oxford University Press, 1992.
Panter, Sarah. *Jüdische Erfahrungen und Loyalitätskonflikte im ersten Weltkrieg*. Göttingen: Vandenhoeck & Ruprecht, 2014.
Penslar, Derek J. *Jews and the Military: A History*. Princeton, NJ: Princeton University Press, 2013.
Roth, Jack J., ed. *World War I: A Turning Point in Modern History*. New York: Knopf, 1969.
Rozenblit, Marsha L. *Reconstructing a National Identity: The Jews of Habsburg Austria during World War I*. New York: Oxford University Press, 2001.
Silber, Marcos. *Le'umiyut shonah ezrahut shavah! HaMa'amats leHasagat otonomiyah liYhudei polin beMilhemet haOlam haRishonah*. Tel Aviv: Goldstein-Goren Diaspora Research Center of Tel Aviv University and Zalman Shazar Center, 2014.
Shukman, Harold. *War or Revolution: Russian Jews and Conscription in Britain, 1917*. London: Vallentine Mitchell, 2006.
Sterba, Christopher M. *Good Americans: Italian and Jewish Immigrants during World War I*. New York: Oxford University Press, 2003.
Winter, Jay, and Antoine Prost. *The Great War in History: Debates and Controversies, 1914 to the Present*. Cambridge: Cambridge University Press, 2005.
Zavadivker, Polly. *1915 Diary of S. An-sky: A Russian Jewish Writer at the Eastern Front*. Bloomington: Indiana University Press, 2015.

Part I

Overviews

CHAPTER 1

World War I and Its Impact on the Problem of Security in Jewish History

David Engel

In 1922, more than 70 percent of the world's Jews—about 8.25 million individuals—lived under regimes that had not governed their place of residence eight years earlier, before World War I and the peace treaties that followed redrew the political map of Europe and the Middle East beyond recognition. During this interval fully half of the 5.2 million Jews who had been subjects of the Russian czar were transmuted into citizens of the new Union of Soviet Socialist Republics, with the other half divided among four new national states—Poland, Lithuania, Latvia, and Estonia—along with newly enlarged Romania. That country, in turn, saw the number of Jews within its borders triple after it acquired control over lands that had formerly belonged not only to Russia but to Austria-Hungary as well. For its part, the once-great Habsburg Empire had seen its 2.1 million Jews split among the enlarged Romania; the truncated Austrian Republic and Hungarian Regency; and the new states of Poland, Czechoslovakia, and Yugoslavia. Another erstwhile power, the Ottoman Empire, lost its 400,000 Jews to five new political units—Republican Turkey, Iraq, Syria, Lebanon, and Palestine. And in Germany, several tens of thousands of Jews passed to Polish, French, or League of Nations rule, while the remaining 550,000 former Jewish subjects of the Kaiser now enjoyed the protections of the Weimar constitution.[1]

This was a transformation of staggering proportions—surely the most extensive and most rapid collective geopolitical displacement in all of Jewish history at least since late antiquity. It encompassed more than double the slightly fewer than four million Jews who changed their country of residence via migration during the half century between 1880 and 1930.² And yet this mass early twentieth-century movement of political boundaries across areas of Jewish settlement that World War I produced has been afforded far less recognition as a development of significance for Jewish history than has the early twentieth-century mass movement of Jews across political boundaries—a movement that the war, ironically, arguably impeded.³ Nevertheless, the place of this great transformation in Jewish history and the reasons for the relative lack of attention it has received to date both merit reflection.

About the latter, only speculation is possible, for no scholar appears to have noticed it, let alone ventured to justify it explicitly. Of many possible reasons, one that appears particularly telling is that no matter how extensive the war's *quantitative* impact on Jewish political demography, its *qualitative* reverberations are easily susceptible of understatement when measured against other major processes and events in modern Jewish life. In this regard the comparison with migration is instructive. Since the beginning of the twentieth century, historians and sociologists have often depicted the mass movement of Jews from one part of the world to another as a key agent of what they have variously termed, among others, the "remaking," "modernization," "transformation," "reshaping," "construction," or "reconstruction" of Jewish society and culture as a whole over the past 150 years and more. Some have portrayed its impact as invidious, others as salutary; but few have denied its magnitude. Arthur Ruppin, a pioneer of the sociological study of Jewry, noted both valences even before World War I:

> Though [its] full significance has hardly yet been appreciated, there is no doubt that this [current] migration, [which shows no signs of abating,] is of the very greatest importance for the future of Judaism. … It means an advance from poverty and misery to prosperity and security. It means the raising of politically oppressed and degraded men to the dignity of free independent citizens of a free country. It means, finally, the substitution of the most highly developed and advanced surroundings in the world for those of a civilisation still blankly unenlightened. … [Yet it also means that] the [immigrant] Jew … submits himself absolutely to the influence of [a foreign] culture, which in a few decades, or at most in one or two generations, lures him away from Judaism, or at any rate so weakens its hold that a formal profession is all that remains of it.⁴

A century later historian Gur Alroey of Haifa University termed the principal part of that same mass migration—the movement of 2.7 million Jews out of the Russian Empire—a "quiet revolution" that "changed the face of the Jewish people … beyond recognition," a "modern version of the Exodus from Egypt [undertaken by] a people seeking to free itself from the economic slavery and persecutions that were its lot in their countries of origin and to create a new life for itself" in new homes abroad.⁵

Against such wide ranging root-and-branch displacements in the social, cultural, and economic realms, the impact of World War I on Jewish life can easily appear circumscribed and transient, especially in light of the decimation of the Jewish communities most affected by it only a quarter of a century later. After all, Jews whose place of residence changed from Austrian Lemberg to Polish Lwów after the war continued to be surrounded by the same set of neighbors, to be embedded in the same social networks, to ply the same occupation, and to speak the same language as they did before, whereas Jews who moved from Austrian Lemberg to New York City or from Polish Lwów to Paris changed all of these things emphatically and abruptly. And indeed, the war's long-term effects appear to have been difficult for scholars to discern. When Ruppin, for example, returned during the 1930s to the subject of migration and its implications for Jewish life, he lamented that "the period of Jewish mass-migrations, which in the last fifty years have reshaped Jewish life, must, for the present, be regarded as closed," but he took no notice of the war's role in catalyzing that development.[6] Quite the contrary: the fact that, by his reckoning, the number of Jews entering the United States from abroad reached 119,000 in 1921—a figure nearly equal to the annual average for the five peak immigration years of 1904 through 1908[7]—persuaded him that the war and its attendant "shortage of transport" had merely temporarily depressed a movement that was curtailed only later, presumably for reasons rooted in postwar American conditions.[8]

To be sure, the importance of World War I as a factor in diminishing the scope of Jewish international movement still awaits systematic scholarly analysis; its assessment from a sound empirical vantage point remains a desideratum. Nevertheless, Ruppin's neglect of the war as an agent of any sort of long-lasting, systemic change in the Jewish world—not only in the area of migration but in all of the manifold facets of Jewish social life that he surveyed—turns out to characterize the position of many scholars, both of his own day and of subsequent generations. Some exceptions are evident with regard to Jewish culture and identity—most notably Marsha Rozenblit's exposition of how the war, or more precisely the attendant collapse of the Austro-Hungarian Empire and its replacement by a set of nationalist successor states, rendered long-standing Jewish loyalties and self-conceptions obsolete, plunging the Jews of East Central Europe into an acute identity crisis and turning them into "an easy target during World War II."[9] More recently Marcos Silber has detailed the evolution of this situation during the war years in the Polish lands, incorporating the experience of imperial Russian as well as Habsburg Jewry and exploring its political dimensions along with its self-definitional ones.[10] Yet even these works, which place World War I squarely in the center of their analyses, portray the conflict as a catalyst for changes whose impact upon Jews was felt locally or regionally. They do not suggest that the war's consequences for Jewish history as a whole were commensurable with those of migration, or with those of any of the other grand themes—emancipation, acculturation, nationalism, embourgeoisement and proletarianization, political radicalization, and social integration—that have traditionally dominated narratives of Jewish modernity.

In fact, when World War I has figured at all in overarching narratives of the modern period, it has often been presented as having reinforced—and, for some, augmented or expedited—trends in Jewish history that had been in evidence already for some time. That tendency was noticeable already in the 1920s, when the first comprehensive work to comment on the war's political significance in Jewish history, Simon Dubnow's *Weltgeschichte des jüdischen Volkes,* labeled it the beginning of a third cycle in the dialectic of emancipation and reaction that to his mind characterized the modern era in Jewish history as a whole.[11] By the 1930s, for obvious reasons, reaction appeared to have gained the upper hand—a perspective reflected in Ismar Elbogen's *A Century of Jewish Life,* which claimed that the war had made the historically "precarious" situation of Eastern European Jewry "untenable" while concomitantly boosting the credibility of the Zionist movement.[12] The perspective from a post-Holocaust vantage point was not much different: Shmuel Ettinger's account of the modern period in the Hebrew University's *History of the Jewish People* (the famous Israeli "red book"), composed during the 1960s, noted that World War I failed to resolve three fundamental world conflicts in which "Jews and Judaism seemed to be involved" since the nineteenth century: "Revolution versus conservatism, cosmopolitanism versus national sovereignty and imperialism versus the colonial peoples' struggle for freedom and independence." That failure, according to Ettinger, was reflected in "the growing opposition of the Gentile world towards the Jews as well as the increased Jewish integration into that world after the First World War."[13] In other words, the war had merely accelerated long-standing processes in Jewish history; it had not inaugurated any new ones.

The most recent, most extensive, and most emphatic statement of that view was offered by David Vital in *A People Apart,* his nine-hundred-page discourse on the political history of the Jews of Europe between the French and the Nazi Revolutions, published in 1999. In that book Vital made explicit what his predecessors had merely suggested. In his words, "the war initiated none of the essential processes of social and cultural change to which European Jewry was subject."[14] For him, the most significant of those processes were the weakening of ties binding Jewish individuals to their community, the attraction of Jews to alternative foci of loyalty, and the expectation that full acceptance for Jews into the societies and political communities of the European states was soon at hand. According to

Vital, these trends continued apace after 1918 as they had during the long nineteenth century. The war did, however—or so he claimed—expose the dangers this course held for what he called "the survival of Jewry ... as a caste or class and of the Jews as private individuals."[15] The behaviors and attitudes he enumerated had been predicated, in his view, on the belief that European society had offered Jews the bargain of emancipation in good faith, so that if Jews kept their end of the bargain—if they behaved in a fashion "'useful' to each of the several states of which they were nationals"—they would be rewarded with "fair dealing and equitable integration."[16] But in the event, even though, as Vital noted, "the Great War ... was the supreme occasion on which the Jews of Europe were called upon to be 'useful,'"[17] their utility remained unrequited. Jewish political and religious leaders of all stripes sensed this divergence between expectations and reality, he claimed, but only a small number saw clearly how to confront it. The rest, he lamented, continued much as before, albeit with far less confidence in their "essentially sanguine approach to what lay at the heart of the Jewish condition."[18]

If, then, the principal themes in modern Jewish life continued to sound after the Great War much as they had before, the fact that more than 70 percent of the world's Jews became subject to new political regimes as a result of the conflict would indeed appear to have been of little consequence in the broad sweep of Jewish history, and the lack of attention scholars have paid to it may well be justified. But the "if" is a big one, for it presumes that the themes that the scholars in question and many others have identified as principal are the only ones that merit that designation. Yet in the experience of Jews during World War I it is possible to detect an additional grand theme, one that is not only commensurable with emancipation, acculturation, migration, and the rest in its importance for modern Jewish history, but one that developed in a strikingly different direction precisely as a result of the conflict.

That theme may be labeled the search for physical security. The label refers to a fundamental problem that has faced Jews to one degree or another throughout their history—how to ensure that whatever ill will they might face because of their identification as Jews did them the least possible tangible harm. For a brief interval following the American and French Revolutions at the end of the eighteenth century, many Jews had expected the problem to disappear altogether—a reflection of their faith in the fundamental goodness, reasonableness, and corrigibility of human beings that was typical of the European Enlightenment. Over the course of the nineteenth century, however, Jews in different parts of the world experienced a succession of incidents that dashed the expectation altogether. The 1819 "Hep! Hep!" riots in Bavaria, in which mobs looted Jewish homes and shops and demanded that Jews be expelled from several towns; the Damascus blood libel of 1840, in which French officials backed a charged that Jews had murdered a Christian monk for ritual purposes and supported the arrest and torture of local Jewish leaders; the 1858 Mortara case, in which a six-year-old Jewish boy from Bologna who had been baptized as an infant by a Christian servant in his parents' household was kidnapped by papal guards and held forcibly in Rome despite worldwide protests; the crystallization of the so-called antisemitic movement in the 1880s, first in Germany, then in other Western and Central European countries, with its call for the revocation of Jewish citizenship and the reimposition of restrictions on Jewish access to state resources and positions of political, economic, social, and cultural influence; the "Southern storms" in Imperial Russia from 1881 to 1884, in which Jews in more than 250 cities, towns, and villages fell victim to a form of sometimes murderous mob violence; the Dreyfus affair of the 1890s, in which a false charge of treason brought against a Jewish officer of the French general staff touched off anti-Jewish agitation and violence throughout France and Algeria extending over a period of months—all of these episodes, and others, helped cumulatively to persuade growing numbers of Jews that the old Enlightenment confidence in human goodness and reasonableness had been misplaced. In their wake, growing numbers of Jews became convinced that an irreducible residue of prejudice, irrationality, and ill will toward them persisted within non-Jewish society, one that could never be banished entirely but at best only rendered harmless. For Jews who had come to this conclusion, the problem of security concerned how best to attain this goal.

The nineteenth century was marked by vigorous debates among Jews over this issue. During the decades that preceded World War I, however, three fundamental assumptions came to undergird virtually all approaches. The first was that Jews throughout the world were united by a common set of temporal needs and interests in addition to spiritual ones—that is, that what happened to Jews in one part of the world necessarily concerned Jews in all other parts of the world. That assumption, which was first articulated explicitly around the middle of the nineteenth century,[19] prompted Jewish leaders in countries where Jews enjoyed a relatively high level of physical security frequently to take up the cause of Jews in countries where their security appeared more precarious. Hence, beginning with the Damascus affair, we find with increasing regularity Jewish leaders—first from France, Britain, and the United States, but later also from other Western and even Eastern European countries—either negotiating directly with governments not their own on behalf of Jewish interests in far-flung communities or cajoling their own governments to take up the cause of foreign Jews to whom they owed no legal obligation.[20] That practice, and the assumption that underlay it, was in evidence most visibly at the Congress of Berlin in 1878, where an international Jewish coalition actively and vigorously lobbied the congress on behalf of Jews in far-off Serbia, Montenegro, Bulgaria, and Romania.[21]

The aim of this activity was what we might call a liberal one—to secure civic equality for Jews within the framework of a constitution that guaranteed fundamental rights for all citizens and that limited the power of governments to abridge them. Yet liberalism did not imply a principled commitment to democracy, particularly the sort of democracy for which Woodrow Wilson famously promised that World War I would make the world safe—one that vested political power not so much in "the people" of a particular region as in specific "peoples," subsets of a region's general population identified by ethno-linguistic criteria, who claimed by right of "self-determination" to constitute states "of their own" for the exclusive benefit of their members.[22] Indeed, the second assumption that underlay the Jewish search for physical security in the decades before the war was that Jews, whom most of the emerging "peoples" claiming self-determination excluded from their circle, had a fundamental interest in maintaining large states with an ethnically neutral governing authority instead of smaller ones where political power rested with a single ethnic group.[23] That assumption was buttressed by the fact that at the beginning of the twentieth century three states alone—the Russian, Habsburg, and Ottoman Empires—governed some 60 percent of the world's Jews. These—especially the first—were precisely the countries where Jews were generally assumed to be most vulnerable. Hence interventions on behalf of large numbers of Jews could be directed toward a small number of governments, maximizing the scope and the potential effectiveness of political activity in the service of Jewish physical security.

The third underlying assumption of such activity was that the large states where Jews were most vulnerable were sensitive to pressures that a handful of extremely wealthy Jewish financiers, led by the Rothschild family, were capable of exerting upon them. Before World War I this coterie of financial magnates played a significant international role in the extension of credit to governments and to developing industries—a fact that gave them relatively easy access to political decision makers across Europe and made those decision makers in all countries sensitive to their will.[24] Moreover, many of them shared the assumption of a common worldwide Jewish interest and were accordingly prepared to use both their access and their financial leverage to intervene on behalf of coreligionists whose safety they thought precarious. Their efforts had not always borne immediate fruit, but they had achieved success at a sufficient rate to convince Jewish political leaders throughout the world that the Jewish role in the international capital market was ultimately what gave them the wherewithal to carry on their fight for physical security.[25]

World War I affected all three of these assumptions profoundly. To begin with, the intense sufferings and privations of Jews living in the areas of greatest fighting along the Eastern Front and in Palestine gave unprecedented urgency to the very question of physical security, prompting Jewish leaders outside of those areas not only to restate their concern for the safety of their threatened coreligionists but to give their commitment new institutional expression. The American Jewish Joint Distribution Committee, founded in November 1914, initially to bring relief to Jews in Palestine but later also to aid Jews along the eastern war front,[26] and the American Jewish Congress, which convened for the first time in Philadelphia in December 1918 to promote the interests of Eastern European Jewry at the impending peace conference,[27] are examples of new institutions that directed the attention of Jews in one country toward conditions for Jews abroad, but parallels can be noted in other Western countries as well, as in the 1917 reorganization of the Conjoint Foreign Committee of the Board of Deputies of British Jews and the Anglo-Jewish Association,[28] the 1918 formation of the Vereinigung jüdischer Organisationen Deutschlands zur Wahrung der Rechte der Juden des Ostens (Association of Jewish Organizations in Germany for the Protection of the Rights of the Jews of the East),[29] the creation of the international Comité des Délégations Juives in 1919,[30] and the launching of a new publication devoted to the welfare of Eastern European and Middle Eastern Jewry, *Paix et Droit*, by the Alliance Israélite Universelle in 1920. All of those bodies demonstrated a renewed determination, as the Alliance Israélite Universelle explained in a public declaration, "to raise up our less fortunate brethren in countries of oppression and persecution ..., in recognition of our origins and ... of the obligations of solidarity [those origins] impose upon us before world opinion."[31]

That task, however, was complicated immeasurably by the postwar proliferation of new, small states, most of them governed by regimes that not only were far from ethnically neutral but that regarded themselves as advocates for ethnic groups with whom Jews had recently experienced tense relations. International Jewish spokesmen were compelled consequently to negotiate with and to find avenues for applying pressure upon a significantly greater number of governments than before the war, each with its own sets of local needs, interests, concerns, constraints, and weaknesses. In many cases, moreover, both the leaders and the broader political culture of these new popularly based governments were unfamiliar to Jewish exponents who had come of age in the era of empire. Viewed in this context, the mass political displacement of Jews as a result of World War I appears to take on far greater significance in the history of the Jews than most have afforded it to date: postwar Jewish political demography made intervention on behalf of Jewish interests in the parts of the world where the majority of Jews lived a far more cumbersome, laborious, and expensive task than it had been at any time during the previous century.

In fact, the expense of effective intervention now became so great as to reduce the usefulness of the Jewish financial elite to virtual insignificance. That additional expense stemmed not only from the enlarged number of states that needed to be courted and cajoled according to different local strategies but even more because the enormous cost of the war itself had forced public expenditures in all belligerent countries to levels incommensurable with any hitherto known in human history. To offer only one illustration among many possible: in the short space of six weeks in 1916 Britain alone spent some 210 million pounds on war-related activities, more than the entire infamous debt of the Ottoman Empire that had so exercised European diplomacy in the final third of the nineteenth century.[32] The war thus rewrote all procedures for government finance in a way that significantly reduced the degree to which any individual banker could influence the actions of governments. All of the major belligerents paid for their war efforts primarily through bond issues, raising their own composite public debt by more than 600 percent in the process.[33] None of the European states possessed sufficient domestic capital resources to support such needs; even before it entered the war, the United States, long indebted to Europe, was transferring funds to the Allies in amounts that eventually reached $9.6 *billion*.[34] Similarly, none of the world's major investment banking houses that had served European governments as financial agents in previous decades could marshal such sums by traditional means; now loans underwritten by central banks, by large syndicates that spread risk widely among many backers, or increasingly by patriotic bond drives involving direct mass sale of small-denomination government notes became the norm.[35] The efforts of the British government to raise a loan of $500 million in the United States in 1915 eventually required a syndicate of nearly 1,570 banks and other financial institutions, and in the end even such a mighty coalition took well over a year to generate the target amount.[36] Gone were the days when Lord Natty Rothschild could singlehandedly enable the British government to purchase its share of the Suez Canal Company or when Jacob Schiff could influence the outcome of the Russo-Japanese War by providing Japan with significant financial resources while limiting Russian access to American capital markets. Indeed, when in early 1915 the British Foreign Office asked Lord Rothschild for advice on war finance, he effectively removed himself as a factor, recommending instead to rely more on taxes and less on loans.[37] As a result, the Rothschilds, the Warburgs, Schiff, and other Jewish financiers who had given teeth to the prewar Jewish security strategy now found themselves with hardly any bite at all.

How greatly the significance of the Jewish financial elite had diminished between the beginning of World War I and its end was starkly reflected in a May 1921 exchange between Louis Marshall, president of the American Jewish Committee and a central figure in the international Jewish search for security, and L. B. Michaelson, a Jewish attorney from New York with important connections in Polish business and financial circles. At the behest of Stanisław Arct, a senior Polish diplomat in the United States, Michaelson asked Marshall to encourage American Jewish financiers to loan substantial funds to the Polish state. The burden of Marshall's response was as follows:

> You seem to have the idea that the Jews of this country are in a position to make a loan to Poland.... I do not regard that as being at the present time practical. There is no Jewish banking house that could undertake such a burden. Government loans are not made in that way at the present time. It is only by means of a syndicate, of which practically the entire banking community becomes a part, that any Government loans can now be floated.... If a syndicate has been formed for the flotation of a Polish loan ..., I have no doubt that if Jewish bankers are invited to become members of the syndicate they would be likely to participate in it on the same basis as the other members.... Financial business is not and cannot be conducted on the theory either of an existing sentiment or that, if the loan is made, conditions affecting the Jews that have been in the past intolerable ... may be improved. A banker who conducts his affairs on such lines would ... forfeit the confidence of his clientele.[38]

Marshall's blanket eschewal of finance as a lever for improving the conditions of Jews not only in Poland but anywhere constituted a remarkable reversal of position. It indicated that World War I had created a situation in which the pursuit of physical security for the bulk of the world's Jews would henceforth need to proceed according to a new set of assumptions than the ones that had guided it in the past and with the help of new mechanisms for acting upon them. The principal new mechanism upon which the postwar security strategy relied was the system of international protection for minorities established by the Paris Peace Conference. It is no accident that Jewish spokesmen were among the most visible public advocates of this system at its inception and throughout its existence—after World War I, they had nowhere else to turn. And when the system turned out to be a broken reed, European Jewry was left defenseless against the Nazi onslaught.[39]

Viewed in this light, World War I becomes something more than a mere reinforcer of trends in Jewish history that had been proceeding apace since the nineteenth century. By impairing the degree to which the majority of the world's Jews could experience those trends from a position of relative physical security, it abruptly and decisively changed what had until then been widely figured as a triumphant Jewish march toward social integration, political enfranchisement, and cultural adaptation into a rapid descent toward physical annihilation. The geopolitical displacement it created and the neutralization of Jewish financial power that it forced turned it into what can be perceived in retrospect as the beginning of a historical path that would culminate in the Holocaust.

David Engel is Greenberg Professor of Holocaust Studies, professor and chair of Hebrew and Judaic studies, and professor of history at New York University. He is the author of seven books and more than seventy articles on various aspects of modern Jewish history, the Holocaust, and interethnic relations in Eastern Europe, including, most recently, *The Assassination of Symon Petliura and the Trial of Scholem Schwarzbard*.

Notes

1. The statistic is compiled from various sources, chief among them Arthur Ruppin, *The Jews of To-day* (London: G. Bell and Sons, 1913), pp. 30–44; Jacob Lestschinsky, *Dos idishe folk in tsifern* (Berlin: Klal Farlag, 1922); Lestschinsky, "Statistics," in *Universal Jewish Encyclopedia* (New York: Universal Jewish Encyclopedia, 1943), vol. 10, pp. 23–36.
2. See the table in Arthur Ruppin, *The Jews in the Modern World* (London: Macmillan, 1934), p. 62.
3. The statistic about boundary movements was not located in any work on the demography or political history of modern Jewry; instead it was calculated from raw data.
4. Ruppin, *Jews of To-day*, pp. 93–94.
5. Gur Alroey, *HaMahapekhah haSheketah: HaHagirah haYehudit mehaImperiyah haRusit 1875–1924* (Jerusalem: Zalman Shazar Center, 2008), p. 9.
6. Ruppin, *Jews in the Modern World*, p. 67.
7. Calculated from figures in Mark Wischnitzer, "Migrations of the Jews," in *Universal Jewish Encyclopedia*, vol. 7, p. 548.
8. Ruppin, *Jews in the Modern World*, p. 49. For a different approach, which affords the war greater weight in the migratory decline, see Arieh Tartakower, *Nedudei haYehudim baOlam* (Jerusalem: Institute for Zionist Education, 1941), pp. 17–18. Even this work, however, attributes greater weight to the collapse of global free trade during the 1920s than to the war itself.
9. Marsha L. Rozenblit, *Reconstructing a National Identity: The Jews of Habsburg Austria during World War I* (New York: Oxford University Press, 2001), p. 172.
10. Marcos Silber, *Le'umiyut shonah ezrahut shavah! HaMa'amats leHasagat otonomiyah liYhudei polin beMilhemet haOlam haRishonah* (Tel Aviv: Goldstein-Goren Diaspora Research Center of Tel Aviv University and Zalman Shazar Center, 2014).
11. S. Dubnow, *Divrei ymei am olam* (Tel Aviv: Dvir, 1958), vol. 10, p. 271. In his construction, the three great signposts of the "third emancipation" were the March 1917 revolution in Russia, the Balfour Declaration of November 1917, and the conclusion of the international treaties for the protection of minorities, beginning with the treaty

with Poland, negotiated at the Paris Peace Conference and signed at Versailles in June 1919.
12. Ismar Elbogen, *A Century of Jewish Life* (Philadelphia: Jewish Publication Society of America, 1944), p. 503.
13. S. Ettinger, "The Modern Period," in *A History of the Jewish People*, ed. H. H. Ben-Sasson (Cambridge, MA: Harvard University Press, 1976), pp. 944–46.
14. David Vital, *A People Apart: The Jews in Europe 1789–1939* (New York: Oxford University Press, 1999), p. 650.
15. Ibid., p. 644.
16. Ibid., p. 650.
17. Ibid.
18. Ibid., p. 643.
19. Most notably in the foundational document of the Alliance Israélite Universelle: *Alliance israélite universelle* (Paris: A. Wittersheim, 1860), esp. pp. 6–15.
20. See, *inter alia*, Jonathan Frankel, *The Damascus Affair: "Ritual Murder," Politics, and the Jews in 1840* (New York: Cambridge University Press, 1997), esp. pp. 432–35; Abigail Green, *Moses Montefiore: Jewish Liberator, Imperial Hero* (Cambridge, MA: Belknap Press of Harvard University Press, 2010), pp. 133–98, 258–81, 300–19, 339–58; Bertram W. Korn, *The American Reaction to the Mortara Case: 1858–1859* (Cincinnati: American Jewish Archives, 1957), pp. 21–78; Lisa Moses Leff, *Sacred Bonds of Solidarity: The Rise of Jewish Internationalism in Nineteenth-Century France* (Stanford, CA: Stanford University Press, 2006), pp. 157–99.
21. N[arcisse] Leven, *Cinquante ans d'histoire: L'Alliance israélite universelle (1860–1910)* (Paris: Felix Alcan, 1911), vol. 1, pp. 213–32; N. M. Gelber, "She'elat haYehudim lifnei haKongres haBerlinai biShenat 1878," *Zion* 8 (1943): 35–50.
22. For a concise theoretical statement of this idea as it was widely understood during the half century preceding World War I, see J[ohann] K[aspar] Bluntschli, "Nation und Volk, Nationalitätsprincip," in *Deutsches Staats-Wörterbuch,* ed. Bluntschli and K[arl] Brater (Stuttgart and Leipzig: Expedition des Staats-Wörterbuchs, 1862), vol. 7, pp. 152–60.
23. The historian Salo Baron, who was active during the 1920s in organizations seeking to advance security for Jews in postwar Europe, went so far as to formulate this assumption as a "historical law": "The status of the Jews was most favorable in pure states of nationalities (*i.e.*, states in which several ethnic groups were included, none having the position of a dominant majority); least favorable in national states (*i.e.,* where state and nationality, in the ethnic sense, were more or less identical); and varying between the two extremes in states which included only part of a nationality. ... The reason is quite obvious. The state of many nationalities found the 'foreignness' of the Jews less objectionable, since its major elements were ethnically differentiated among themselves." Salo Wittmayer Baron, *A Social and Religious History of the Jews* (New York: Columbia University Press, 1937), vol. 2, p. 39.
24. For a succinct description of this position see Karl Erich Born, *International Banking in the 19th and 20th Centuries* (New York: St. Martin's Press, 1983), pp. 30–58.
25. Among the successes that impressed contemporaneous Jewish observers were the interventions by Berlin banker Gerson Bleichröder at the Congress of Berlin in favor of equal rights for Romanian and Balkan Jews, the seemingly decisive intervention of New York financier Jacob Schiff in arranging loans for the Japanese war effort against Russia in 1904, and Schiff's victorious effort to prevent renewal of a Russian-American commercial treaty in 1911, which pitted him against US president

William Howard Taft. On these episodes see, respectively, Fritz Stern, *Gold and Iron: Bismarck, Bleichröder, and the Building of the German Empire* (New York: Alfred A. Knopf, 1977), pp. 369–93; Daniel Gutwein, "Ya'akov Schiff uMimun milhemet Rusiyah-Yapan: Perek beToledot haDiplomatiyah haYehudit," *Zion* 44 (1991): 137–72; Gary Dean Best, *To Free a People: American Jewish Leaders and the Jewish Problem in Eastern Europe, 1890–1914* (Westport, CT: Greenwood Press, 1982), pp. 166–205. More generally see Derek J. Penslar, *Shylock's Children: Economics and Jewish Identity in Modern Europe* (Berkeley: University of California Press, 2001), pp. 153–58; Daniel Gutwein, *The Divided Elite: Economics, Politics, and Anglo-Jewry* (Leiden: E. J. Brill, 1992), pp. 307–96; John Cooper, "Nathaniel Mayer Rothschild (1840–1915): The Last of the *Shtadlanim*," *Jewish Historical Studies* 43 (2011): 125–39.

26. Yehuda Bauer, *My Brother's Keeper: A History of the American Jewish Joint Distribution Committee 1929–1939* (Philadelphia: Jewish Publication Society of America, 1974), pp. 3–9.
27. Stephen Wise, *Challenging Years: The Autobiography of Stephen Wise* (London: East and West Library, 1951), pp. 131–33.
28. Mark Levene, *War, Jews, and the New Europe: The Diplomacy of Lucien Wolf 1914–1919* (Oxford: Oxford University Press for the Littman Library of Jewish Civilization, 1992), pp. 156–58.
29. Jacob Toury, "Organisational Problems of German Jewry: Steps towards the Establishment of a Central Organisation," *Leo Baeck Institute Year Book* 13 (1968): 79–84.
30. *Le Comité des Délégations Juives: Dix-sept ans d'activité* (Paris: Éditions du Comité des Délégations Juives), 1936.
31. "Paix et droit," *Paix et droit*, 1 January 1921.
32. John Steele Gordon, *An Empire of Wealth: The Epic History of American Economic Power* (New York: HarperCollins, 2004), p. 290. The Ottoman public debt stood at 106 million pounds sterling in 1881.
33. Calculated from tabular data presented in Niall Ferguson, *The Pity of War: Explaining World War I* (London: Basic Books, 1998), p. 422. Cf. James MacDonald, *A Free Nation Deep in Debt: The Financial Roots of Democracy* (New York: Farrar, Straus, and Giroux, 2003), p. 402. For a detailed discussion of the comparative role of bond issues in the war finances of the major belligerents, see Hew Strachan, *Financing the First World War* (Oxford: Oxford University Press, 2004), pp. 114–223.
34. Gordon, *Empire of Wealth*, p. 291.
35. Strachan, *Financing the First World War*, pp. 147–59; MacDonald, *A Free Nation*, pp. 400–408; Manfred Pohl, "Bankensysteme und Bankenkonzentration von den 1850er Jahren bis 1918: Allgemeine Entwicklungslinien," in *Europäische Bankengeschichte*, ed. Hans Pohl (Frankfurt am Main: Knapp, 1993), pp. 231–33.
36. Kathleen Burk, "The Diplomacy of Finance: British Financial Missions to the United States 1914-1918," *Historical Journal* 22 (1979): 354.
37. Niall Ferguson, *The House of Rothschild: The World's Banker 1849–1999* (New York: Viking, 1999), pp. 435–37, 455. See also Edwin R. A. Seligman, "The Cost of the War and How It Was Met," *American Economic Review* 9 (1919): 748.
38. Marshall to Michaelson, 26 May 1921, American Jewish Archives, Cincinnati, OH, Louis Marshall Papers, box 1591.
39. For an extended discussion, see David Engel, "Manhigim yehudim, tikhnun estrategi vehaZirah haBeinle'umit le'ahar milhemet haOlam haRishonah," *Michael* 16 (2004): CLXV-CLXXVIII (Hebrew pagination).

Selected Bibliography

Primary Sources

Bluntschli, J. K., and K. Brater, eds. *Deutsches Staats-Wörterbuch*. Stuttgart and Leipzig: Expedition des Staats-Wörterbuchs, 1862.
Leven, N. *Cinquante ans d'histoire: L'Alliance israélite universelle (1860–1910)*. Paris: Felix Alcan, 1911.
Rupin, Arthur. *The Jews of To-day*. London: G. Bell and Sons, 1913.
Wise, Stephen. *Challenging Years: The Autobiography of Stephen Wise*. London: East and West Library, 1951.

Secondary Sources

Alroey, Gur. *HaMahapekhah haSheketah: HaHagirah haYehudit mehaImperiyah haRusit 1875–1924*. Jerusalem: Zalman Shazar Center, 2008.
Baron, Salo Wittmayer. *A Social and Religious History of the Jews*. New York: Columbia University Press, 1937.
Bauer, Yehuda. *My Brother's Keeper: A History of the American Jewish Joint Distribution Committee 1929–1939*. Philadelphia: Jewish Publication Society of America, 1974.
Ben-Sasson, Haim Hillel, ed. *A History of the Jewish People*. Cambridge, MA: Harvard University Press, 1976.
Best, Gary Dean. *To Free a People: American Jewish Leaders and the Jewish Problem in Eastern Europe, 1890–1914*. Westport, CT: Greenwood Press, 1982.
Born, Karl Erich. *International Banking in the 19th and 20th Centuries*. New York: St. Martin's Press, 1983.
Cooper, John. "Nathaniel Mayer Rothschild (1840–1915): The Last of the *Shtadlanim*." *Jewish Historical Studies* 43 (2011): 125–39.
Dubnow, Simon. *Divrei ymei am olam*. Tel Aviv: Dvir, 1958.
Elbogen, Ismar. *A Century of Jewish Life*. Philadelphia: Jewish Publication Society of America, 1944.
Engel, David. "Manhigim yehudim, tikhnun estrategi vehaZirah haBeinle'umit le'ahar milhemet haOlam haRishonah." *Michael* 16 (2004): CLXV–CLXXVIII (Hebrew pagination).
Ferguson, Niall. *The House of Rothschild: The World's Banker 1849–1999*. New York: Viking, 1999.
———. *The Pity of War: Explaining World War I*. London: Basic Books, 1998.
Frankel, Jonathan. *The Damascus Affair: "Ritual Murder," Politics, and the Jews in 1840*. New York: Cambridge University Press, 1997.
Gelber, N. M. "She'elat haYehudim lifnei haKongres haBerlinai biShenat 1878," *Zion* 8 (1943): 35–50.
Gordon, John Steele. *An Empire of Wealth: The Epic History of American Economic Power*. New York: HarperCollins, 2004.
Green, Abigail. *Moses Montefiore: Jewish Liberator, Imperial Hero*. Cambridge, MA: Belknap Press of Harvard University Press, 2010.
Gutwein, Daniel. *The Divided Elite: Economics, Politics, and Anglo-Jewry*. Leiden: E. J. Brill, 1992.
———. "Ya'akov Schiff uMimun milhemet Rusiyah-Yapan: Perek beToledot haDiplomatiyah haYehudit," *Zion* 44 (1991): 137–72.

Korn, Bertram W. *The American Reaction to the Mortara Case: 1858–1859*. Cincinnati: American Jewish Archives, 1957.
Leff, Lisa Moses. *Sacred Bonds of Solidarity: The Rise of Jewish Internationalism in Nineteenth-Century France*. Stanford, CA: Stanford University Press, 2006.
Lestschinsky, Jacob. *Dos idishe folk in tsifern*. Berlin: Klal Farlag, 1922.
———. "Statistics." In *Universal Jewish Encyclopedia*, vol. 10, pp. 23–36. New York: Universal Jewish Encyclopedia, 1943.
Levene, Mark. *War, Jews, and the New Europe: The Diplomacy of Lucien Wolf 1914–1919*. Oxford: Oxford University Press for the Littman Library of Jewish Civilization, 1992.
Penslar, Derek J. *Shylock's Children: Economics and Jewish Identity in Modern Europe*. Berkeley and Los Angeles: University of California Press, 2001.
Pohl, Hans, ed. *Europäische Bankengeschichte*. Frankfurt am Main: Knapp, 1993.
Rozenblit, Marsha L. *Reconstructing a National Identity: The Jews of Habsburg Austria during World War I*. New York: Oxford University Press, 2001.
Ruppin, Arthur. *The Jews in the Modern World*. London: Macmillan, 1934.
Silber, Marcos. *Le'umiyut shonah ezrahut shavah! HaMa'amats leHasagat otonomiyah liYhudei polin beMilhemet haOlam haRishonah*. Tel Aviv: Goldstein-Goren Diaspora Research Center of Tel Aviv University and Zalman Shazar Center, 2014.
Stern, Fritz. *Gold and Iron: Bismarck, Bleichröder, and the Building of the German Empire*. New York: Alfred A. Knopf, 1977.
Strachan, Hew. *Financing the First World War*. Oxford: Oxford University Press, 2004.
Tartakower, Arieh. *Nedudei haYehudim baOlam*. Jerusalem: Institute for Zionist Education, 1941.
Toury, Jacob. "Organisational Problems of German Jewry: Steps towards the Establishment of a Central Organisation." *Leo Baeck Institute Year Book* 13 (1968): 79–84.
Vital, David. *A People Apart: The Jews in Europe 1789–1939*. New York: Oxford University Press, 1999.
Wischnitzer, Mark. "Migrations of the Jews." In *Universal Jewish Encyclopedia*, vol. 7, p. 548. New York: Universal Jewish Encyclopedia, 1942.

CHAPTER 2

The European Jewish World 1914–1919
What Changed?

Marsha L. Rozenblit

Writing his memoirs as a refugee in Brazil in 1942, the Viennese Jewish writer Stefan Zweig evoked a perfect world on the eve of World War I. It was, he noted, "the Golden Age of Security," in which people truly believed that "it was merely a matter of decades until the last vestige of evil and violence would finally be conquered." After all, so much progress had been made in the nineteenth century:

> The dim street lights of former times were replaced by electric lights.... Thanks to the telephone one could talk at a distance from person to person.... Comfort made its way from the houses of the fashionable to those of the middle class.... Hygiene spread and filth disappeared.... Progress was also made in social matters; year after year new rights were accorded to the individual, justice was administered more benignly and humanely, and even the problem of problems, the poverty of the great masses, no longer seemed insurmountable.... There was little belief in the possibility of such barbaric declines as wars between the peoples of Europe as there was in witches and ghosts. Our fathers were comfortably saturated with confidence in the unfailing and binding power of tolerance and conciliation. They honestly believed that the divergencies and the boundaries between nations and sects would gradually melt away into a common humanity and that peace and security, the highest of treasurers, would be shared by all mankind.[1]

Of course, Zweig knew that such views were absurd. After all, the enormous technological, scientific, economic, and political progress in the nineteenth century benefited only the growing middle classes in Western Europe and America, much less so in Eastern Europe, let alone the rest of the world. More importantly, World War I, the horrors of which no one could have imagined in the summer of 1914, represented exactly the kind of violence and animosity between nations that Europeans thought were a relic of a dim and distant past. Europe, which had not witnessed a major, continent-wide war since the early nineteenth century, subjected itself to four years of bloody conflict that left millions of soldiers dead and millions others maimed. The enormous casualties in the industrialized warfare of World War I made people realize that war was not, to use Zweig's own words, "a rapid excursion into the romantic, a wild, manly adventure."[2] War was mud, and rats, and rot, and ceaseless noise, and fear, and almost certain death.[3] To many Europeans, soldiers and civilians alike, it was not even clear why they were fighting, although the propaganda machines of all the belligerents churned out justifications for the war. Even soldiers who could justify the war—against an aggressive enemy, or to defend their homes from invasion, or to defeat the evil Russian Empire—grew weary of the endless slaughter. Their relatives and friends on the home front also resented both the terrible food shortages and their governments, which asked them to make the ultimate sacrifice but could not even distribute food properly.[4]

Moreover, in the wake of the war, the national differences that Zweig assumed would fade away grew stronger. The Versailles Peace Treaty created new states in East Central Europe on the basis of "national self-determination." These new states were rarely nationally or ethnically homogenous, and the dominant "nations" within them—Poles in Poland or Romanians in Romania—did not extend much toleration to the so-called "national minorities"—Ukrainians, Belorussians, Lithuanians, Germans, and Jews in Poland and Hungarians or Ukrainians in Romania—despite Versailles's requirement that they do so. Nationalist resentment against the new nationalizing states grew. Democracy also did not flourish. Most of the new states turned to authoritarian rule, and the Soviet Union became an oppressive Communist dictatorship. Some countries embraced fascism, most notably (but not only) Germany and Italy. Nazis, fascists, and Communists embarked on vicious campaigns of violence against their own citizens even before World War II.

Zweig's ironic invocation of progress reminds us how profoundly World War I altered the conditions of Jewish life in Europe. It did so primarily because the war led to the collapse of the Habsburg Monarchy and the Russian Empire. The new states that emerged in the wake of the collapse of those empires had a very different relationship with the Jews than the old empires, and the very nature of Jewish identity and political loyalties shifted enormously. A Jewish national identity—that is, that the Jews formed a nation with certain national rights—took shape in many of these states, both in the new nation-states and in the Soviet Union. Yet even before the new states came into existence, a greater sense of Jewish ethnic distinctiveness grew in many of the belligerents, including Germany, largely in response to wartime antisemitic attempts to exclude the Jews from the nation at arms. The war also hastened Jewish modernization and secularization, processes long under way before the war. Finally, the war vaunted the Zionists to prominent positions in the Jewish world, which they had not enjoyed before. None of this was either foreseen or planned in 1914.

In 1914, one could easily divide the Jews of Europe into two groups: those who had emancipation and those who had not. The almost three million Jews in Western and Central Europe—England, France, Germany, Italy, and Austria-Hungary—were emancipated, including the traditional Jewish populations of Austrian Galicia and Bukovina as well as Hungary, while almost six million Jews in Eastern Europe—the Russian Empire and Romania—were not. In 1919, by contrast, all the Jews of Europe had received citizenship in the countries in which they lived, but citizenship in the new states was far more complicated than it had been in the Western European nation-states or the old Habsburg Monarchy. In France, England, Italy, or Germany, for example, Jews had adopted a French, English, Italian, or German national identity. They spoke those languages, adopted those cultures, and identified as members of the nation in whose territory they lived. They continued to do so after World War I, so despite some problems, their world did not change fundamentally.

The Habsburg Monarchy, however, had been a supranational dynastic state that counted at least eleven different "nationalities" or *Volksstämme* (nations conceived in linguistic/ethnic terms) within its borders—Germans, Hungarians, Czechs, Poles, Ukrainians, Slovaks, Slovenes, Serbs, Croats, Romanians, and Italians. In Austria-Hungary Jews could adopt the language and culture of the peoples in whose midst they lived—German, Hungarian, Polish, or Czech primarily—or they could continue to speak Yiddish and live within the world of Jewish culture, but they did not necessarily have to adopt the national identity, the sense of belonging to the *Volk,* the ethno-cultural community of descent, of those groups whose languages they spoke. In the Hungarian half of the monarchy, which regarded itself as a quasi-sovereign nation-state, many Jews did adopt a Hungarian identity that paralleled the German identity of German Jews or the French identity of French Jews. That is, they thought they had joined the Hungarian nation. In the Austrian half of the monarchy, by contrast, Jews had the flexibility to adopt an Austrian political identity, that is, a loyalty to the supranational state that did not conceive of itself in national terms, while at the same time adopting the languages and cultures of their neighbors (or not) and identifying ethnically as Jews. Habsburg Jews—who numbered around two million in 1910—rather liked the arrangement. They thus faced a grave crisis when in 1919 they found themselves in nation-states run by nations that did not accept them as members of the national community.[5]

The Russian Empire was also a multinational empire, but here one group, the Russians, controlled the state, and they could not really conceive of other groups becoming Russian. Although the regime had made some attempts to integrate its Jews in the nineteenth century, most Jews remained distant from the Russian state and Russian society.[6] After the Russian Revolutions of 1917 ended the czarist regime, Jews received full legal equality, but the new Soviet Union wanted to secularize its Jews and make them good Communists and Soviet citizens. Despite the fact that Lenin and Stalin had rejected the idea of Jews as a nation, for pragmatic reasons (in order to inculcate Communism) the USSR recognized the Jews as a nation, one of the many nations of the Soviet Union. Therefore the regime encouraged Yiddish culture (as long as it was secular and Communist), even though it also wanted to Russianize the Jews. In the interwar period Soviet Jews were happy with the end of the czarist regime and with the personal rights and opportunities offered by the new regime, which also forcefully opposed antisemitism. Yet they faced many challenges trying to craft a new Jewish, Russian, and Soviet identity, not least of which was the regime's attempt to uproot all manifestations of religion, which made it difficult (or impossible) for Jews to observe Jewish rituals or maintain traditional Jewish schools.[7] The other new states formed from the old czarist empire (Poland or Lithuania, for example) proved even more problematic. They granted Jews citizenship but did not consider Jews members of the dominant nationality that controlled the state, and they ignored the provisions of the treaties that required them to respect minority rights, including those of the Jews. Jews here also had to contend with rampant antisemitism.[8]

That the war would change Jewish life was not even remotely suspected in the first flush of patriotism when the war began in 1914. Jews in most of the belligerent countries—Great Britain, France, Germany, Austria-Hungary, Serbia (but probably not in Russia)—shared the enthusiasm for war of their compatriots—or at least their middle-class compatriots—in August 1914. They were eager to go to war, to fight "shoulder to shoulder" with their fellow citizens against the enemy, to give their *Gut und Blut* in order to show their patriotism and loyalty. French and British Jews, although not the relatively new immigrants from Russia in their midst, were eager to fight Germany in order to demonstrate their abiding French or British patriotism. French Jews also shared the French desire to regain the provinces of Alsace and Lorraine, taken by Germany in 1871.[9] Similarly Jews in Germany eagerly went to war in the summer of 1914 to show their loyalty to their German fatherland.[10] Jews in Austria-Hungary also wanted to demonstrate their patriotism in the war with Serbia and Russia. For all these Jews, the desire to demonstrate patriotic zeal was intimately connected with a desire to refute antisemitic canards about Jewish cowardice. After all, if Jews fought and died for the Fatherland, they reasoned, the antisemites would not be able to charge the Jews with shirking military responsibility, hiding behind the lines, and getting cushy desk jobs to avoid combat. Emancipated French, English, German, and Austro-Hungarian Jews regarded the war, both at the front and at home, as an opportunity to end all remaining de facto discrimination against Jews, to convince their societies that the Jews belonged.[11] For native British Jews, patriotic sacrifice could also counter charges that Jews harbored German loyalties. Such views had a long history, but they gained traction at the beginning of the war because Russian Jewish immigrants in Britain generally supported Germany, largely because it fought Russia, the oppressor of the Jews.[12] Wartime enthusiasm was probably not shared by Jews in Russia, who were not emancipated and had no reason to be loyal to the czarist regime. Nevertheless, even Russian Jews supported the war, hoping to gain political rights in Russia as a result.[13]

German and especially Austro-Hungarian Jews had another, Jewish, reason to fight in 1914. Since they were fighting Russia, the evil empire that oppressed its Jews, they could see the war as a Jewish war, a *Rachekrieg für Kischinew*, a war of revenge for the pogroms in Russia, a war to liberate the persecuted Jews of Eastern Europe. German Jews, however, like Germany in general, mostly fought on the Western Front, against England and France, so the Jewish war of liberation was not as all-consuming as it was for Austro-Hungarian Jews, although it did allow them to equate Jewish and German aims during the war.[14] For the Jews of the Habsburg Monarchy, Russia was the primary enemy through the end of 1916, and thus they could conflate Austrian patriotism—the need to fight Austria's enemy that had invaded and occupied the provinces of Galicia and Bukovina—with a Jewish cause. From the beginning of the war, the Jewish press all over the monarchy lauded the war against Russia as a "just cause," indeed a holy war against a barbaric, evil, and rapacious enemy, the enemy of freedom and culture, and the traditional enemy of the Jews, a modern Amalek who committed atrocities against the Jews both in Russia and in occupied Galicia.[15] One soldier (whose letter was published in the Jewish press) noted, "It is a very sweet feeling … to be able to go to war against an enemy like Russia. Oh, may we be able to take revenge for the mutilated bodies of Kishinev, for the most shameful atrocities of Zhitomir, for the eyes put out in Bialystok, for the defiled Torah scrolls, for the pogroms, and for the innumerable murdered innocent children."[16] Jewish spokesmen saw the war in Manichean terms as a struggle between the forces of light (Germany and Austria-Hungary) and the forces of darkness (Russia), of culture versus barbarism, of justice versus tyranny. God would surely help the Central Powers to victory. In a sermon to celebrate Emperor Franz Joseph's eighty-fourth birthday in August 1914, Rabbi Rubin Färber of Mährisch Ostrau/Moravská Ostrava, Moravia, declared that the war was a battle of "good against evil, of light against darkness, a battle of morality against immorality, of virtue against wickedness and brutality, of law against lawlessness and barbarism." Urging his congregants to remember Amalek, he declared that God would help Austria and her Jews destroy the terrible enemy.[17] Similarly, Rabbi David Herzog of Graz, Styria, noted that "it is the holy duty of every man of culture to fight this barbaric people." For Jews in particular, the destruction of this enemy was of primary importance. The "screams of pain" of Russian Jewry "compel us to participate in the annihilation of this enemy."[18]

When Germany and Austria-Hungary drove the Russians out of Galicia in 1915, the Jews cheered, vindicated in their hope. The Zionist press, for example, expressed the "overwhelming joy" of "we Austrian Jews." After all, "the liberation of Galicia from the yoke of the Cossack hordes" represented the triumph of freedom and humanity over barbarism.[19] The occupation of most of Russian Poland, Lithuania, and other parts of western Russia by the Central Powers in 1915 also provided the Jews in Germany with a new opportunity to demonstrate the identity of Jewish concerns with German war aims in the East. Seeking to influence the German authorities in the occupied zone, they insisted that Eastern European Jews spoke German and supported Germany.[20] By contrast, Jews in Britain and France, who did care about the fate of Jews in the Russian Empire, had to downplay such concern, blaming Germany for fanning antisemitism in Russia and especially in Russian Poland and hoping that the alliance with Britain and France would somehow have a positive influence on Russian policy to the Jews.[21]

When the Central Powers definitively drove back the Russians after the Brusilov Offensive of 1916, Habsburg Jews heaved a sigh of relief and joy. With Russia effectively out of the war, Jews did not turn their attention to the war with Italy, since Italy was no enemy of the Jews. Instead, they now focused on maintaining the Habsburg Empire itself, correctly fearing that its collapse would expose them to the dangers of antisemitism and nationalism. Worried that the Jews would suffer if the Habsburg "umpire" was no longer there to ensure Jewish rights, they hoped that Galicia would remain a Habsburg crown land even if an independent Poland came into existence.[22]

Fighting and dying for their countries did not have the impact that Jews had hoped in 1914. Their patriotic sacrifice did not lead to greater inclusion of the Jews in the nations in whose midst they lived and for which they died. Indeed, antisemitism flourished during the war, mostly in its last two years and especially in Germany and Austria-Hungary. Here war weariness combined with food shortages led to shrill denunciations of the Jews for evading military service, for war profiteering, even for spreading typhus or other contagious diseases. The rise of antisemitism frightened the Jews, especially since proof of their military valor and sacrifice seemed to have no impact.[23] In Germany, antisemites convinced the army to do a military census in 1916 to "prove" that Jews hid behind the lines, and Jewish soldiers felt excluded from the nation for which they fought and died, especially since the state, which never published the results that showed that Jews did serve proportionately at the front, seemed to legitimate antisemitic charges.[24] The Habsburg army, however, regarded the Jews as utterly loyal and refused to do a similar census, so Jews felt confident in the power of the empire to protect them from antisemitism.[25] Nevertheless the sheer vituperation of antisemitic slander between 1916 and 1918 frightened the Jews enormously. Such slander was exacerbated by the presence of hundreds of thousands of Galician and Bukovinian Jewish refugees in Vienna, Bohemia and Moravia, and Hungary. Many of these refugees, who had fled from the Russian occupation, were poor Hasidim, an easy target for the antisemites.[26] In Great Britain, the issue of drafting Russian Jewish immigrants became a flashpoint for antisemitism, especially since most Russian Jews did not want to serve in the military. While in France and England antisemitism did not reach the levels it did in the Central Powers, it was still a cause for concern for Jews.[27]

Although many Jews entered the war eager to show their common bonds with their compatriots, in fact the war served to enhance Jewish identity.[28] Antisemitism and the need to mobilize against it was only one reason for increased attention to Jewish needs. In addition, Jews on the home fronts felt compelled to help Jewish soldiers in the armies. Thus, in all the belligerents Jews organized committees to provide Jewish soldiers with prayer books and other religious articles, to distribute Chanukah presents to soldiers, to provide for Passover seders, both by arranging them and by distributing matzah, to organize High Holiday services, and to make sure that there were rabbis who could attend to the religious needs of Jewish soldiers.[29] Most armies now contained Jewish chaplains, rabbis who were commissioned officers and who could organize religious services, Passover seders, kosher food, and proper Jewish burial and create a community of Jewish soldiers under arms.[30] In addition to helping soldiers, Jews mobilized to help refugees, especially in Austria-Hungary. Caring for the Galician refugees was an enormous task. Since they were war victims, the government of Austria provided financial aid to refugees and also established barracks camps (*Konzentrationslagern*) in some regions. Such aid was always insufficient, and the government turned to local Jewish communities to distribute and supplement the aid. Jewish communities in the monarchy may have helped a bit grudgingly and with an air of condescension, but they did help the refugees a great deal. Indeed, help for Galician refugees became the primary war work of all Jews, especially Jewish women, who organized committees, soup kitchens, lying-in hospitals, and other institutions to help the refugees. Such assistance fortified a sense of Jewish solidarity among all Jews during the war.[31]

Contact with Eastern European Jews also augmented Jewish identity, at least among some German Jews. During the occupation of Russian Poland, many German-Jewish soldiers came into contact with Eastern European Jews for the first time. Many were horrified by the poverty, filth, lack of modernity and bourgeois values, but others were impressed with the fortitude and culture of the Jews they encountered. Such was especially true for Zionists and for the Orthodox, who had been primed to regard Eastern European Jews as somehow "authentic Jews."[32] Habsburg Jews did not "encounter" Eastern European Jews during the war, since the monarchy contained Eastern European Jews in Galicia, Bukovina, and parts of Hungary. Jews in those regions and in Vienna were already familiar with their Eastern European brethren. Yet contact was increased because the way that the Habsburg army was organized meant that modern and traditional Jews fought together in many units, especially in regiments from Galicia and Hungary. Modern Jews were impressed with the valor of Jews from the "East" even if they hoped to make them over in a modern, more Western image.[33]

Both antisemitism and the need to help fellow Jews in distress played an important role in raising Jewish consciousness during the war in Germany and Austria-Hungary. In the Russian Empire, Russian governmental policy against Jews and other ethnic groups "nationalized" many Russian minority groups, including the Jews, thus reinforcing the sense that Jews formed a separate nation with no possibility of integration into Russian society. During World War I, Russia not only deported enemy aliens— citizens of Germany, Austria-Hungary, and the Ottoman Empire residing in Russia—to the Russian interior, it also deported large numbers of its own subjects who belonged to ethnic and religious groups—primarily Germans and Jews—whom it feared harbored anti-Russian attitudes and would spy for Germany and Austria. These deportations entailed much suffering and misery, but they also led to the hardening of ethnic boundaries and the exacerbation of ethnic conflict in the Russian Empire. The Russian army in particular deeply suspected Germans and Jews, tolerated and organized violence against them, and took the lead in deporting them from territory under direct military control in western Russia, which largely corresponded to the Pale of Settlement. In the first six months of the war, the Russian army expelled Jews from the immediate front lines to the interior, and then, in 1915, as the Russians retreated in the face of the Central Powers' successful advance into Galicia, Russian-Poland, and Lithuania, military commanders energetically and brutally expelled Jews from many areas, including the city of Warsaw, Vilna and Kovno provinces, and elsewhere in the northwest, as well as from Belorussia and Volhynia. The process was never systematic, but hundreds of thousands of Jews were deported by the Russian army, and others simply fled from the war zone. Many of these Jews went to the eastern regions of the Pale, but large numbers also ended up in the Russian interior. As a result, the Pale of Settlement ceased to be an institution of Russian policy, even if all other anti-Jewish discrimination remained. In addition, the army took many Jews hostage, threatening deportation to others if there was any sign of pro-German activity. With the stabilization of the front, the army ended this policy and even allowed many deportees to return home. Besides disrupting personal life, the deportations led to greater resentment of the regime, further politicization of Russia along ethnic/national lines, and increased Jewish political mobilization.[34]

Relief work on behalf of suffering Jewish deportees and refugees in Russia facilitated this process, since it provided the opportunity for Jewish activists, both those in Jewish political parties and those not, to propagandize among ordinary Jews.[35] Jewish political activists also greatly benefited from German occupation policy in Russian-Poland. Although the Germans left Russian anti-Jewish discriminatory laws intact, they nevertheless allowed Jewish newspapers, schools, and political parties to flourish. As a result, the Zionists, the Bundists, the Orthodox, and other groups developed their organizational structures and successfully propagandized among the Jews.[36]

The Zionist movement achieved notable success during the war years. The Zionists enjoyed a major advantage. The World Zionist Organization was both international and officially neutral in the war. In fact, the WZO moved from its German office to Copenhagen for the war. From there, it had the ear both of the Central Powers and of the Entente and was thus poised to lobby with both sides to achieve its goals. The Zionists lobbied not only for a "charter" for a Jewish homeland (or state) in Palestine, but against antisemitism, for Jewish rights, and especially for Jewish "national rights" after the war. The Zionists worked with the German and Austrian foreign offices to put pressure on their Turkish ally, and they urged the British, the French, the Germans, and later the Americans for support for a Jewish homeland. In this effort they were very successful. In November 1917 Great Britain issued the Balfour Declaration, declaring British support for a Jewish national home in Palestine. This declaration, a piece of political propaganda at the time, had no basis in international law. Nevertheless, the Zionists regarded it as the magic "charter" for a Jewish homeland and future state in Palestine, and their success in gaining

British support enabled the Zionists later to play an important role in the postwar order.

The main change in the situation of the Jews between 1914 and 1919 was generated by the collapse of the German, Habsburg, Russian, and Ottoman Empires. The collapse of imperial Germany and the creation of the more democratic Weimar Republic initially had little impact on the Jews. After all, Weimar Germany like the Kaiserreich before it was a German nation-state. Its Jews had long adopted a German cultural and national identity, and they easily transferred their loyalty to the new state, which ended residual discrimination against Jews. Only in the Weimar Republic, after all, did Jews become judges and university professors in appreciable numbers. At the same time, however, nasty antisemitism in the years immediately after the war did make many Jews feel that their wartime sacrifices had been in vain, that the German nation for which they had fought and died and suffered did not accept them as members. To be sure, resentment of the Weimar Republic and the humiliating terms of the Treaty of Versailles along with the economic consequences of the Great Depression led to the Nazi seizure of power in 1933, but that event was not even remotely thinkable in 1919. At that point, Jews in Germany felt nervous about the ability of the new regime to control rising antisemitism, but hopeful about the future, confident in their German identities. Indeed, the fact that Jews not only memorialized the Jewish dead in Jewish space but also actively participated in efforts to memorialize all German soldiers who had fallen in World War I reminded them that they belonged to the German nation.[37]

The collapse of the Habsburg Monarchy in October–November 1918 created a grave crisis for its two million Jews. They no longer had the Habsburg authorities to protect them from nationalist antisemitism. Indeed, pogroms broke out in the spring, summer, and fall of 1918 in Galicia, Bohemia, and Moravia as Habsburg power disintegrated. The worst of the pogroms, the pogrom in Lemberg/Lwów/L'viv in November 1918 in which seventy-two Jews were murdered, provided Jews with a classic example of the dangers of nationalism. Here Polish and Ukrainian nationalists battled for control of eastern Galicia. Jews insisted that they were neutral in the nationality conflict between the Poles and Ukrainians, but the Ukrainians assumed the Jews were pro-Polish, and the Poles understood Jewish neutrality as a sign that the Jews did not side with the Poles. In that context, Polish Legionnaires attacked Jews. Jews were caught between competing nationalisms without the old Habsburg "umpire" to protect them, which it had done in the past, as in the case of the pogroms of 1898 in Galicia. Jews felt sympathy with Polish aspirations for national independence but worried that the new Polish authorities could not protect them from antisemitism.[38] After all, as Joachim Schoenfeld from

Śniatyn, Galicia, noted in his memoirs, "independent Poland was born in rivers of Jewish blood."[39] Anti-Jewish violence was not only a Polish problem. In Bohemia and Moravia, hungry peasants attacked Jewish storekeepers in small towns, labeling them as "Germanizers," pro-Austrian opponents of the new Czech state.[40] Similarly in Slovakia (the northern counties of Hungary that came into Czechoslovakia), anti-Jewish violence raged, with Slovak peasants attacking Jews as supporters of the hated Hungarian landowners.[41]

Destroying the monarchy had not been a war aim of the Triple Entente and its later allies, although Italy did hope to gain territory from Austria that it believed to be Italian—South Tyrol, Trieste and its vicinity, for example—as a result of entering the war in 1915 on the side of England and France. The American president Woodrow Wilson's emphasis on the "self-determination of all nations" and his concern for the re-creation of an independent Poland in his "14 Points" that accompanied American entrance into the war encouraged nationalist activists within the Habsburg Monarchy—Poles, Ukrainians, Czechs, and South Slavs—to demand more autonomy, even independence, something they had not actually advocated earlier. Britain, France, and the United States only began to actively encourage these nationalists to think in terms of independence in the summer of 1918, when it was clear that Germany and Austria-Hungary would lose the war.[42] As a result, by late October and November, nationalists created what they imagined were nation-states for their own nations. Czech nationalists, for example, announced an independent Czechoslovakia on 28 October 1918. Of course the nationalists wanted as much territory as they could get for their new states, and that territory contained other ethnically defined nations. The new Czechoslovakia contained Czechs, Slovaks, Germans, Ukrainians, Poles, Hungarians, and Jews. Czechs dominated politically, economically, and culturally, and although they created a fictive national category of Czechoslovak, the Slovaks felt aggrieved and colonized. More importantly, the new Czech state suspected its Germans and Hungarians of disloyalty and irredentism.[43] Similarly, Poland, most of whose territory came from the old Russian Empire, but which also included Austrian Galicia, contained large numbers of Ukrainians, Belorussians, Lithuanians, Germans, and Jews. The Poles saw Poland as a Polish nation-state, and they did not accord these groups the considerations guaranteed by the Polish Minority Treaty of 1920, forced on Poland because of Allied fear that the Poles might oppress the other groups.[44]

After the collapse of the Habsburg Monarchy, many new "imagined" nation-states came into existence in East Central Europe: Czechoslovakia, Poland, and Yugoslavia. Other states expanded at the expense of the old monarchy. They claimed the territory on the basis of national self-determination, but the territories were ethnically mixed. Nevertheless, these states continued to see themselves as nation-states. Such was the case for Romania, which became much larger after 1918, acquiring Austrian Bukovina (with its mixed population of Germans, Ukrainians, Romanians, and Jews) and Hungarian Transylvania (with its mixed population of Hungarians, Romanians, Germans, and Jews), along with Russian Bessarabia. Romanians dominated and inaugurated policies that benefited Romanians and hurt the other national groups and the Jews.[45] On the other hand, some states became smaller because of the Versailles settlement. The new Hungary that emerged in 1919 was ethnically homogeneous but deeply resentful because it had lost much territory (much of which had been inhabited by non-Hungarians). In the old Kingdom of Hungary within the Habsburg Monarchy, Magyars composed only 45 percent of the population, but that percentage rose to 51 percent when the authorities included the Jews and Germans, deemed worthy of assimilation as Magyars once they had learned Hungarian. Virtually all of the inhabitants of Trianon Hungary (the Hungary created by Versailles) were Magyar, but Hungarians profoundly resented the loss of territory they had experienced, with Transylvania going to Romania, Slovakia to Czechoslovakia, and a piece of western Hungary to Austria. They would translate that resentment into anti-Jewish policy, a total about-face from Hungarian policy since the 1860s.[46] The small Austria that came into existence in November 1918 was also ethnically homogeneous. Indeed, it initially called itself "German Austria." It did not want to exist, however. Its inhabitants had never sought national independence. Since the overwhelming majority of them spoke German and felt themselves to be German, according to the principle of national self-determination, they sought *Anschluss* with Germany. The Versailles peacemakers, eager to punish Germany and Austria for the war, refused such a union, and so Austria came into existence. It was a German nation-state, but one deeply confused by its own existence.[47]

With the very important exception of Czechoslovakia, all of the states formed or enlarged from the old Habsburg Monarchy came to adopt right-wing, nationalist, authoritarian regimes in the interwar period, which included the toleration or encouragement of antisemitic practices. More importantly, they did not regard the Jews as members of the national community (despite their citizenship). Such was certainly the case in Romania, Poland, Hungary, and Austria. In many ways, Hungary is the most interesting example of the crisis inaugurated by the collapse of the Habsburg Monarchy. Ever since 1867, Hungary had been a quasi-sovereign country within the monarchy under the control of liberal aristocrats who honored an unspoken social contract with the Jews: if they adopted Magyar language and culture and counted themselves Hungarian, they would gain full equality, unlimited economic opportunity, and total protection from antisemitism, as long as they did not try to socialize with the aristocrats or control Hungarian politics. At that point, the Magyar political elite needed Jews to augment Magyar numbers. In post–World War I Hungary, however, the old elite was shunted aside by a new elite drawn from the lower gentry, which had long resented the Jews, and in any case the Magyars no longer needed Jewish numbers. As a result, despite intense Jewish identification with the Magyars and the Hungarian state, the new elite did not regard the Jews as Magyars, and the state now enacted anti-Jewish legislation, beginning with the *numerus clausus* of 1920, which placed a quota on Jews in higher education. This posed a severe crisis for the Jews, but they continued to hope that somehow they would be rewarded for their loyalty. They supported the regime of Admiral Miklós Horthy (1920–44) for many reasons, not least of which was their fear that something far worse, that is, fascist and more antisemitic, would replace it.[48] Likewise the Polish and Romanian political elites did not regard Jewish citizens as Poles or Romanians. In Austria as well, the antisemitic Christian Social Party soon took over (although an authoritarian one-party state was not created until 1934), and while it did not impose any antisemitic laws, Jews worried. Nevertheless, like the Jews in Hungary, Jews supported this regime for fear of something worse (such as the Nazis).[49]

Czechoslovakia presents a different picture. In the first place, despite serious problems, it managed to maintain a workable democracy. Moreover, the regime was neither autocratic nor antisemitic. Indeed, Jews flourished in interwar Czechoslovakia. Jews came to regard Czechoslovakia as a new, improved version of the old Habsburg Monarchy. They imagined that it was a multinational state tolerant of ethnic/national diversity, and they revered the president, Tomáš Masaryk, in much the same way as Habsburg Jews had revered the emperor, Franz Joseph. They counted on Masaryk to keep antisemitism in check and nationalist conflict at bay. Indeed, just as people had joked that the Jews were the only Austrians in (the old) Austria, they now joked that Jews were the only Czechoslovakians in Czechoslovakia.[50] Of course, Czechoslovakia was not the Habsburg Monarchy; it was in fact a Czech nation-state. Its Czech political elite suspected Germans and Hungarians of disloyalty, assuming they wanted to be included in a greater Germany or greater Hungary.[51] Such thinking put the Jews in a bind. Most of the Jews in Bohemia and Moravia, where Czech speakers formed two-thirds of the population and German speakers one-third, spoke German as their primary language. To be sure, many Jews in Bohemia already had switched their allegiance to Czech in the decades before World War I, but Moravian Jews retained their German loyalties. This allegiance to German language and culture, and the former Austrian loyalty of the Jews, angered Czech nationalists. At the same time, Czech nationalists did not think the Jews could ever really be Czech.[52] In Slovakia, the former northern counties of Hungary, modern Jews had adopted

Magyar language and loyalty in the late nineteenth century. Any connection to Magyar culture or even to the Jews in Hungary angered both Slovak and Czech nationalists. Anti-Jewish violence had erupted with great force in the immediate aftermath of the war in Slovakia, and even when it subsided, Slovak nationalists deeply resented the Jews for their Magyar loyalties or, if they tried to adopt a new Czechoslovak identity, for being pro-Czech.[53]

In this context, the Jews of Czechoslovakia—who numbered about 350,000 in the interwar period—turned more strongly to a Jewish identity. Czechoslovakia provided them with the opportunity to do so when it allowed Jews to register as members of the Jewish nation on the census. While for most residents of the state, national identity was based on language, Jews alone had the ability to choose a national identity irrespective of language. Czech leaders rather liked the idea of a Jewish national identity because it would reduce the number of Germans in the Bohemian lands and the number of Magyars in Slovakia. Many Jews liked the idea because they could declare their neutrality in the nationality conflicts and proclaim their loyalty to the state while speaking whatever language they preferred. In the census of 1920, 54 percent of all Jews in Czechoslovakia declared that they belonged to the Jewish nation. While in Bohemia only 15 percent chose a Jewish national identity (the others preferring either Czech or German), in Moravia 47 percent did so; in Slovakia, 55 percent; and in Subcarpathian Ruthenia, the home of very pious, mostly Hasidic Jews, fully 83 percent did so. Most of these Jews were not Zionists. They chose the Jewish national rubric on the census because it offered them an opportunity be neither German nor Czech, Magyar or Slovak, but Jewish and loyal to the state in which they lived.[54] Many Jews also voted for the "Jewish Party," a party loosely tied to the Zionist organization, not because they were Zionists, but because the party allowed them to assert neutrality in a political world in which national loyalties dominated, that is, in which most citizens voted for parties that represented the interests of one or another nationality, and in which options for Jewish voters were limited because the old liberal parties had disappeared.[55]

In many of the new states of East Central Europe, Jews turned to a Jewish national identity whether it was officially permitted to them or not. Indeed, one of the results of Wilson's principle of "national self-determination" was the growing national identity of the Jews of East Central and Eastern Europe. Such was the case in many of the states carved out of the old Russian Empire, including Poland and Lithuania, and even in independent Western Ukraine, which lasted only a few months. In Poland, for example, Jews could not officially claim to belong to a Jewish nation, but nevertheless many behaved and voted as if they formed a Jewish nation. Most Jews voted for self-proclaimed Jewish political parties—Zionist, Bundist, Orthodox, or bourgeois. Increasing numbers of Jews knew Polish, but Yiddish remained the dominant language of Polish Jewry, and a vibrant modern culture—newspapers, film, radio—as well as traditional religious culture existed in that language.[56]

Indeed, Jews had lobbied forcefully for what they called "Jewish national rights" in 1918 and 1919, both in the new states as well as at the Paris Peace Conference. All over East Central Europe, in the territory of the collapsing Habsburg Monarchy and in the western regions of the former czarist empire, Jews formed Jewish National Committees to demand that the Jews be recognized as a nation and granted some measure of national autonomy. These committees were invariably led by Zionists and other Jewish nationalists who felt energized by the unleashing of nationalist excitement generated at the end of the war. In some places—in Poland for example—they wanted full-scale autonomy, including allowing Jews to vote for official Jewish representatives in parliament. Elsewhere demands were more modest, calling only for recognition of the Jewish nation, the right to separate Jewish national schools at state expense, and the like. In the new Czechoslovakia, the Jewish National Committee even had the ear of the government. Indeed, Masaryk preferred to work with Zionists (who did not claim to be Czech) than with "German" or "Hungarian" Jews.[57] The Zionists also lobbied forcefully at Versailles for Jewish national rights in Eastern Europe, but they were not as successful as they would have hoped.[58] Yet the anti-Jewish violence that erupted in 1919 and 1920, especially in Ukraine, made the Allies more sympathetic to Jewish national rights than they would have been otherwise.

The collapse of the Russian Empire had an even greater impact than the collapse of Austria-Hungary. In the first place, Jews had to cope with several years of continued fighting between revolutionary and antirevolutionary forces, between Poles and Ukrainians, between the Bolsheviks and Ukrainians, and between the new Soviet Union and new nation-states that sought to augment their territories, especially Poland. In a context of violence, lawlessness, and no state control, vicious pogroms erupted, especially in Ukraine, and at least a hundred thousand Jews were killed before the Bolsheviks restored order and the Soviet-Polish border stabilized in the early 1920s.[59] Secondly, the collapse of the Russian Empire led in two very different directions. On the one hand, many of the Jews of the old empire found themselves in new nation-states—Poland and Lithuania—where they had to cope with rising antisemitism. On the other hand, about three million Jews became citizens of the new, Communist Soviet Union. Despite the horrors of the Civil War years, especially in Ukraine, the emergence of the Soviet Union led to enormous hope and excitement in Jewish circles. Jews were now citizens of a new state, all anti-Jewish restrictions ended, and Jews could live any place and pursue any career. Opportunity abounded, and Jews joined in building the "perfect" new socialist society. Moreover, the regime opposed antisemitism as a vestige of the old order, and it would not abide it in public life. In addition, in the early 1920s, as noted earlier, the Soviet Union recognized the Jews as one of the nations of the Soviet Union and encouraged Yiddish-language Jewish national culture as long as it fostered Communist ideology and not Jewish religion or Zionism. Large numbers of Jewish children thus attended state-sponsored Yiddish-language schools. Some Jews may have resented the pressure to abandon Jewish religious observance, but most, especially the young, modernized quickly, embraced their new identity as Yiddish-speaking Jews in the Soviet Communist world, and looked forward to the future. They could not anticipate the changes that Stalinism would later impose.[60]

What indeed was the impact of World War I on the Jews of Europe? In East Central and Eastern Europe the war led to a growing commitment to a Jewish national identity, a sense that Jews were one of the nationalities of the region. Jews therefore benefited from Wilson's principle of national self-determination, and they tried to use it to nationalize the Jews, to make them feel that they were members of a modern Jewish nation. To be sure, not all Jews agreed, including the large masses of religious Jews, as well as those who continued to aspire to join the other nations of the region. Nevertheless, Jewish national identity did grow in popularity in the interwar period.

Moreover, the war accelerated the modernization and secularization of the Jews all over East Central and Eastern Europe. Many traditional Jews encountered modern Jews—as well as non-Jews—in the army, and they experienced a modernized Jewish religion in the services organized by Jewish chaplains. The mass displacement of the war years, both for Galician and for Russian Jews, undid many of the bonds of traditional Jewish life, including the social pressures of tight-knit shtetl communities. As refugees, especially in the Russian interior, many Jews could no longer obtain kosher food or follow other rules of traditional Judaism. Many never returned home, ending up in the cities all over Eastern Europe, where new forms of Jewish identifications replaced many older practices. Even those who never left home experienced modernization, including mandatory public school, under German or Austrian occupation in Russian Poland. The pace of secularization and modernization increased dramatically in the interwar period, especially in the Soviet Union, but also in Poland, Lithuania, Romania, and elsewhere.

The war also led to a significant change in the status of women, accelerating earlier trends. Work on the home front, organizing to help both

Jewish soldiers and refugees, prepared many women for a greater public role. Educational opportunities for women in all the new states meant that women could pursue new careers and play new roles in the Jewish community and in society at large. Many women had to cope on their own during the war, and, if their husbands or fathers were killed, they continued to cope alone after the war. Their greater public activity both during and after the war meant that many women, and especially Jewish women's organizations, demanded a greater role in Jewish communal affairs, including the right to vote in communal elections.[61]

The war—or rather wartime suffering and dislocation, compounded in many places by nationalist agitation—also led to the startling growth of antisemitism. The rise of antisemitic invective in the last two years of the war, the proliferation of antisemitic violence after the war, and the antisemitic policies of many of the new states made many Jews fearful for the future. This antisemitism was not simply the continuation and acceleration of prewar modes of antisemitic agitation, whether religious, economic, antimodern, or connected to nationalist mobilization, although it certainly drew on those earlier forms. Nor was it just the result of wartime radicalization of nationalist exclusionism. Post–World War I antisemitism, at least in East Central Europe, was intimately connected with the creation of new nation-states, imagined as homogeneous, in which one nation dominated and refused to accept the Jews as members of that nation.[62] Yet the fact that antisemitism diminished in Czechoslovakia[63] as well as in the Soviet Union could be signs that the right kind of government could be counted on to keep antisemitism in check. No one could imagine what the future held in store.

Jewish life in East Central and Eastern Europe changed dramatically as a result of World War I. The same was not true in Western Europe—France, Germany, Italy, Great Britain—where Jewish life continued in the interwar period more or less according to patterns established before the war. Yet even in Western Europe, where Jewish nationalism never enjoyed the appeal it did in Eastern Europe, Jews increasingly came to see Jewish identity in ethnic and cultural and not solely religious terms.[64] Moreover, the growth and success of the Zionist movement during and immediately after the war also played an important role in spurring greater Jewish national consciousness.

World War I led to much death and destruction. It changed the parameters of Jewish life, especially in East Central and Eastern Europe. New possibilities and new difficulties emerged, neither of which would find resolution in the difficult interwar years. The "golden age of security" that Stefan Zweig imagined to have existed before the war would never return, but neither he nor anyone else could fathom what would happen in the future.

Marsha L. Rozenblit is the Harvey M. Meyerhoff Professor of Modern Jewish History at the University of Maryland. She is the author of *The Jews of Vienna, 1867–1914: Assimilation and Identity* (1983) and *Constructing a National Identity: The Jews of Habsburg Austria during World War I* (2001) and coeditor, with Pieter M. Judson, of *Constructing Nationalities in East Central Europe* (2005).

Notes

1. Stefan Zweig, *The World of Yesterday* (New York: Viking Press, 1943), pp. 1, 3–4.
2. Ibid., p. 226.
3. Most of the work on the horrors of combat in World War I has been done on the Western Front. See the classic works of Paul Fussell, *The Great War and Modern Memory* (New York: Oxford University Press, 1975); and Eric J. Leed, *No Man's Land: Combat and Identity in World War I* (Cambridge: Cambridge University Press, 1979).
4. For an excellent analysis of this phenomenon in Habsburg Austria, see Maureen Healy, *Vienna and the Fall of the Habsburg Empire: Total War and Everyday Life in World War I* (Cambridge: Cambridge University Press, 2004).
5. On the identities of Habsburg Jews before World War I, see Marsha L. Rozenblit, *Reconstructing a National Identity: The Jews of Habsburg Austria during World War I* (New York: Oxford University Press, 2001), pp. 3–38.
6. Benjamin Nathans, *Beyond the Pale: The Jewish Encounter with Late Imperial Russia* (Berkeley: University of California Press, 2002); John Klier, *Imperial Russia's Jewish Question, 1855–1881* (Cambridge: Cambridge University Press, 1995); Michael Stanislawski, *Tsar Nicholas I and the Jews: The Transformation of Jewish Society in Russia, 1825–1855* (Philadelphia: Jewish Publication Society, 1983).
7. Zvi Gitelman, *Jewish Nationality and Soviet Politics: The Jewish Sections of the CPSU, 1917–1930* (Princeton, NJ: Princeton University Press, 1972); Gitelman, *A Century of Ambivalence: The Jews of Russia and the Soviet Union, 1881 to the Present* (Bloomington: Indiana University Press, 2001); and Elissa Bemporad, *Becoming Soviet Jews: The Bolshevik Experiment in Minsk* (Bloomington: Indiana University Press, 2013).
8. Ezra Mendelsohn, *The Jews of East Central Europe between the World Wars* (Bloomington: Indiana University Press, 1983), pp. 10–83.
9. Paula E. Hyman, *From Dreyfus to Vichy: The Remaking of French Jewry, 1906–1939* (New York: Columbia University Press, 1979), pp. 49–62; Hyman, *The Jews of Modern France* (Berkeley: University of California Press, 1998), pp. 133–35; Pierre Birnbaum, "French Rabbis and the 'Sacred Unity' during the First World War," *European Judaism* 48, no. 1 (Spring 2015): 47–58; Todd M. Endelman, *The Jews of Britain, 1656 to 2000* (Berkeley: University of California Press, 2002), pp. 183–86; and Sarah Panter, *Jüdische Erfahrungen und Loyalitätskonflikte im Ersten Weltkrieg* (Göttingen: Vandenhoeck & Ruprecht, 2014), pp. 66–77. Panter argues that British Jews were not quite as euphoric as Jews elsewhere (p. 66).
10. Egmont Zechlin, *Die deutsche Politik und die Juden im ersten Weltkrieg* (Göttingen: Vandenhoeck & Ruprecht, 1969), pp. 86–100; Eva G. Reichmann, "Der Bewusstseinswandel der deutschen Juden," in *Deutsches Judentum in Krieg und Revolution, 1916–1923*, ed. Werner E. Mosse and Arnold Paucker (Tübingen: J. C. B. Mohr, 1971), pp. 511–612, esp. pp. 511–14; Stephen Magill, "Defense and Introspection: Ger-

man Jewry, 1914," in *Jews and Germans from 1860 to 1933: The Problematic Symbiosis*, ed. David Bronsen (Heidelberg: Winter, 1979), pp. 209–33; Peter Pulzer, *Jews and the German State: The Political History of a Minority, 1848–1933* (Oxford: Blackwell, 1992), pp. 194–207; Panter, *Jüdischer Erfahrungen und Loyalitätskonflikte*, pp. 39–53; and Derek J. Penslar, *Jews and the Military: A History* (Princeton, NJ: Princeton University Press, 2013), pp. 170–78, 185–92.

11. On Austrian Jews during World War I, see Rozenblit, *Reconstructing a National Identity*. For the role of antisemitism in German Jewish patriotism, see Panter, *Jüdische Erfahrungen und Loyalitätskonflikte*, pp. 41–43; for France, see Hyman, *From Dreyfus to Vichy*, pp. 54–57.
12. Panter, *Jüdische Erfahrungen und Loyalitätskonflikte*, pp. 75–77.
13. Gitelman, *A Century of Ambivalence*, pp. 55–58.
14. Panter, *Jüdische Erfahrungen und Loyalitätskonflikte*, pp. 47–51. For moving testimonies of German Jews on the Eastern Front, see Eugen Tannenbaum, ed., *Kriegsbriefe deutscher und österreichischen Juden* (Berlin: Neuer Verlag, 1915), pp. 1, 39, 126, 128.
15. See, for example, *Österreichische Wochenschrift*, 7 August 1914, pp. 547–48; 14 August 1914, pp. 562–63; 21 August 1914, pp. 577–79; 28 August 1914, pp. 593–95; *Jung Juda*, 21 August 1914, p. 213; *Selbstwehr*, 27 August 1914, pp. 1–2, 6; 20 September 1914, p. 2; *Jüdische Volksstimme*, 19 August 1914, p. 2; 10 September 1914, p. 1.
16. *Österreichische Wochenschrift*, 28 August 1914, p. 596. All translations from the German are my own.
17. Rubin Färber, *Unser Kaiser, ein Sendbote Gottes; Predigten zum allerhöchsten Geburtstage Sr. Maj. des Kaisers Franz Joseph I. und aus anderen patiotischen Anlässen* (Mährisch Ostrau, 1915), pp. 23–30; quotation, p. 27.
18. David Herzog, "Das Gelöbnis der Treue," in *Kriegspredigten* (Frankfurt: J. Kauffmann, 1915), pp. 14–18.
19. *Selbstwehr*, 25 June 1915, p. 1; *Jüdische Volksstimme*, 6 August 1915, p. 3.
20. Panter, *Jüdische Erfahrungen und Loyalitätskonflikte*, pp. 97–115; Zechlin, *Die deutsche Politik und die Juden*, pp. 139–236.
21. Hyman, *From Dreyfus to Vichy*, pp. 50, 52, 57; Panter, *Jüdische Erfahrungen und Loyalitätskonflikte*, pp. 131–35.
22. *Jüdische Zeitung*, 23 July 1915, p. 1; 6 August 1915, p. 2; 16 November 1916, pp. 1–2; 1 December 1916, p. 1; *Selbstwehr*, 30 July 1915, p. 7; 6 August 1915, p. 2; 20 August 1915, p. 3; 10 November 1916, p. 1; 22 December 1916, p. 1; *Österreichische Wochenschrift*, 25 June 1915, p. 469; 30 July 1915, p. 575; 27 August 1915, p. 650.
23. Bruce F. Pauley, *From Prejudice to Persecution: A History of Austrian Anti-Semitism* (Chapel Hill: University of North Carolina Press, 1992), pp. 64–72; Werner Jochmann, "Die Ausbreitung des Antisemitismus," in Mosse and Paucker, *Deutsches Judentum in Krieg und Revolution*, pp. 409–510; Péter Bihari, "A Forgotten Home Front: The Middle Classes and the 'Jewish Question' in First World War Hungary" (unpublished PhD dissertation, Central European University, 2005).
24. Werner Angress, "The German Army's 'Judenzählung' of 1916: Genesis—Consequences—Significance," *Leo Baeck Institute Year Book* 23 (1978): 117–37; Jacob Rosenthal, *"Die Ehre des jüdischen Soldaten." Die Judenzählung im Ersten Weltkrieg und ihre Folgen* (Frankfurt am Main: Campus, 2006); Panter, *Jüdische Erfahrungen und Loyalitätskonflikte*, pp. 179–89, 264–65, 281–87.
25. Austrian State Archives, Kriegsarchiv, KM Präs. 1616, 34-17/3.
26. Beatrix Hoffmann-Holter, *"Abreisendmachung": Jüdische Kriegsflüchtlinge in Wien 1914 bis 1923* (Vienna: Böhlau, 1995), pp. 125–40; Robert Nemes, "Refugees and Anti-

semitism in Hungary during the First World War," in *Sites of European Antisemitism in the Age of Mass Politics, 1880–1918*, ed. Robert Nemes and Daniel Unowsky (Waltham, MA: Brandeis University Press / Hanover, NH: University Press of New England, 2014), pp. 236–54.

27. David Caesarani, "An Embattled Minority: The Jews of Britain during the First World War," in *The Politics of Marginality: Race, the Radical Right, and Minorities in Twentieth Century Britain*, ed. T. Kushner and K. Lunn (London: Frank Cass, 1990), pp. 61–81; Panter, *Jüdische Erfahrungen und Loyalitätskonflikte*, pp. 213–23, 324–27.

28. On the growth of Jewish ethnicity among German Jews, see Reichmann, "Der Bewusstseinswandel der deutschen Juden"; Panter, *Jüdische Erfahrungen und Loyalitätskonflikte*, pp. 272–74.

29. Rozenblit, *Reconstructing a National Identity*, pp. 60–65; Marion A. Kaplan, *The Making of the Jewish Middle Class: Women, Family, and Identity in Imperial Germany* (New York: Oxford University Press, 1991), pp. 219–25.

30. Rozenblit, *Reconstructing a National Identity*, pp. 98–101; Panter, *Jüdische Erfahrungen und Loyalitätskonflikte*, pp. 190–96, 205–13, 227–31.

31. Rozenblit, *Reconstructing a National Identity*, pp. 65–81; Rebekah Klein-Pejšová, "Beyond the 'Infamous Concentration Camps of the Old Monarchy': Jewish Refugee Policy from Wartime Austria-Hungary to Interwar Czechoslovakia," *Austrian History Yearbook* 45 (2014): 150–66, esp. pp. 154–59. See also Rebekah Klein-Pejšová, "The Budapest Jewish Community's Galician October" in this volume.

32. Reichmann, "Der Bewusstseinswandel der deutschen Juden," pp. 521–70, 577–84; Steven E. Aschheim, *Brothers and Strangers: The East European Jew in German and German-Jewish Consciousness, 1800–1923* (Madison: University of Wisconsin Press, 1982), pp. 143–56; Mordechai Breuer, *Jüdische Orthodoxie im Deutschen Reich, 1871–1918: Die Sozialgeschichte einer religiösen Minderheit* (Frankfurt am Main: Jüdischer Verlag bei Athenäum, 1986), pp. 346–48.

33. See, for example, *Selbstwehr*, 5 May 1917, pp. 2–3; *Österreichische Wochenschrift*, 7 May 1915, p. 353; 27 August 1915, p. 646; *Jüdische Volksstimme*, 7 September 1915, p. 3. For a description of a Hungarian regiment, see the novel by Avigdor Hameiri, *The Great Madness*, trans. from Hebrew by Yael Lotan (Haifa: Or-Ran, 1984; orig. 1929), pp. 117, 171, 217, 221–22, 275–76.

34. Eric Lohr, *Nationalizing the Russian Empire: The Campaign against Enemy Aliens during World War I* (Cambridge, MA: Harvard University Press, 2003); on deportations of Jews, pp. 137–50, 157; Peter Gatrell, *A Whole Nation Walking: Refugees in Russia during World War I* (Bloomington: Indiana University Press, 1999), pp. 13, 16–18, 21–22, 31, 141–70, 181–86, 201–5; Michael R. Marrus, *The Unwanted: European Refugees in the Twentieth Century* (New York: Oxford University Press, 1985), pp. 61–63. For new reflections on the impact of wartime violence against minorities in Eastern Europe, see Jochen Böhler, Włodzimierz Borodziej, and Joachim von Puttkamer, eds., *Legacies of Violence: Eastern Europe's First World War* (Munich: Oldenbourg Verlag, 2014).

35. Steven J. Zipperstein, "The Politics of Relief: The Transformation of Russian Jewish Communal Life during the First World War," in *The Jews and the European Crisis, 1914–1921, Studies in Contemporary Jewry* 4 (1988):22–40.

36. Zechlin, *Die deutsche Politik und die Juden*, pp. 140–43, 153, 158, 172–78; Ezra Mendelsohn, *Zionism in Poland: The Formative Years, 1915–1926* (New Haven, CT: Yale University Press, 1981).

37. Donald Niewyk, *The Jews in Weimar Germany* (Baton Rouge: Louisiana State University Press, 1980); Cornelia Hecht, *Deutsche Juden und Antisemitismus in der Weimarer*

Republik (Bonn: Dietz, 2013); Tim Grady, *The German-Jewish Soldiers of the First World War in History and Memory* (Liverpool: Liverpool University Press, 2011), esp. pp. 13–14; 55–87; Penslar, *Jews and the Military*, pp. 178, 185–92.

38. Rozenblit, *Reconstructing a National Identity*, pp. 136–38; *Österreichische Wochenschrift*, 6 December 1918, pp. 772–74; *Jüdische Korrespondent*, 28 November 1918, pp. 1–3, 5; 5 December 1918, pp. 3–4; *Jüdische Zeitung*, 8 November 1918, p. 3; 15 November 1918, p. 1; 22 November 1918, pp. 1–4; 29 November 1918, pp. 1–4; 6 December 1918, pp. 3–5; *Selbstwehr*, 29 November 1918, p. 1; 13 December 1918, p. 3; *Jüdische Volksstimme*, 22 November 1918, p. 5; 6 December 1918, pp. 1–3. For a general description of the anti-Jewish violence, see Alexander Victor Prusin, *Nationalizing a Borderland: War, Ethnicity, and Anti-Jewish Violence in East Galicia, 1914–1920* (Tuscaloosa: University of Alabama Press, 2005). On the 1898 pogroms in Galicia, see Daniel Unowsky, "Local Violence, Regional Politics, and State Crisis: The 1898 Anti-Jewish Riots in Habsburg Galicia," in Nemes and Unowsky, *Sites of European Antisemitism*, pp. 13–35.

39. Joachim Schoenfeld, *Jewish Life in Galicia under the Austro-Hungarian Empire and in the Reborn Poland, 1898–1939* (Hoboken, NJ: Ktav, 1985), p. 201.

40. *Selbstwehr*, 29 November 1918, pp. 3–4; 6 December 1918, pp. 1–2; 13 December 1918, p. 1; 20 December 1918, pp. 3–5; 17 January, 1919, p. 1; 24 January 1919, pp. 1–3; *Jüdische Volksstimme*, 6 December 1918, p. 3. See also reports in Central Zionist Archives, Z3/217.

41. Rebekah Klein-Pejšová, *Mapping Jewish Loyalties in Interwar Slovakia* (Bloomington: Indiana University Press, 2015), pp. 25–32.

42. Z. A. B. Zeman, *The Break-Up of the Habsburg Empire 1914–1918: A Case Study in National and Social Revolution* (London: Oxford University Press, 1961); Alan Sked, *The Decline and Fall of the Habsburg Empire, 1815–1918* (London: Longman, 1989); Richard Plaschka and Karlheinz Mack, eds., *Die Auflösung der Habsburgerreiches: Zusammenbruch und Neuorientierung im Donauraum* (Munich: R. Oldenbourg, 1970); and Manfried Rauchensteiner, *Der Tod des Doppeladlers: Österreich-Ungarn und der Erste Weltkrieg* (Graz: Styria, 1993). Mark Cornwall, *The Undermining of Austria-Hungary: The Battle for Hearts and Minds* (New York: St. Martin's Press, 2000), pp. 11, 16–36, does well to remind us that Habsburg policies during the war, especially suspicion about the loyalty of its Czechs, Serbs, Slovenes, Croats, Poles, Ruthenes, and Italians, also played an important role in loosening bonds of many of those peoples to the state.

43. Carol Skolnick Leff, *National Conflict in Czechoslovakia: The Making and Remaking of a State, 1918–1987* (Princeton, NJ: Princeton University Press, 1988); Derek Sayer, *The Coasts of Bohemia: A Czech History* (Princeton, NJ: Princeton University Press, 1998).

44. Joseph Rothschild, *East Central Europe between the Two World Wars* (Seattle: University of Washington Press, 1974), pp. 27–72; Paul Robert Magocsi, *A History of Ukraine* (Seattle: University of Washington Press, 1976).

45. Irina Livezeanu, *Cultural Politics in Greater Romania: Regionalism, Nation Building and Ethnic Struggle, 1918–1939* (Ithaca, NY: Cornell University Press, 1995).

46. Rolf Fischer, "Anti-Semitism in Hungary, 1882–1932," in *Hostages of Modernization: Studies on Modern Anti-Semitism, 1870–1933/39*, ed. Herbert A. Strauss (Berlin and New York: W. de Gruyter, 1993), pp. 863–92; Rolf Fischer, *Entwicklungsstufe des Antisemitismus in Ungarn, 1867–1939* (Munich: Oldenbourg, 1988); Paul Hanebrink, *In Defense of Christian Hungary: Religion, Nationalism, and Antisemitism, 1890–1944* (Ithaca, NY: Cornell University Press, 2006).

47. Barbara Jelavich, *Modern Austria: Empire and Republic, 1800–1986* (Cambridge: Cambridge University Press, 1987), pp. 151–73.
48. Mendelsohn, *Jews of East Central Europe*, pp. 85–128.
49. Harriet Freidenreich, *Jewish Politics in Vienna, 1918–1938* (Bloomington: Indiana University Press, 1991); Sylvia Maderregger, *Die Juden in österreichischen Ständestaat, 1934–38* (Vienna: Geyer, 1973).
50. Rozenblit, *Reconstructing a National Identity*, pp. 138–43. Hillel J. Kieval, "Negotiating Czechoslovakia: The Challenges of Jewish Citizenship in a Multiethnic Nation-State," in *Insiders and Outsiders: Dilemmas of East European Jewry*, ed. Richard I. Cohen, Jonathan Frankel, and Stefani Hoffman (Oxford: Littman Library of Jewish Civilization, 2010), pp. 103–19, convincingly argues that Jews did not imagine Czechoslovakia as a supranational state, but rather as a Czech nation-state that was nevertheless expansive enough to accommodate Jewish particularism. For examples of Jewish admiration for Masaryk, see *Selbstwehr*, 20 December 1918, p. 1; *Jüdische Volksstimme*, 28 March 1919, pp. 3–4.
51. Nancy M. Wingfield, *Flag Wars and Stone Saints: How the Bohemian Lands Became Czech* (Cambridge, MA: Harvard University Press, 2007), esp. pp. 11–12, 14, 135–98, 231–60; Klein-Pejšová, *Mapping Jewish Loyalties*.
52. Hillel J. Kieval, *The Making of Czech Jewry: National Conflict and Jewish Society in Bohemia, 1870–1918* (New York: Oxford University Press, 1988); Marsha L. Rozenblit, "Jews, German Culture, and the Dilemma of National Identity: The Case of Moravia, 1848–1938," *Jewish Social Studies*, n.s., 20, no. 1 (Fall 2013): 77–120.
53. Klein-Pejšová, *Mapping Jewish Loyalties*, esp. pp. 86–114.
54. Franz Friedmann, *Einige Zahlen über die tschechoslovakischen Juden (Ein Beitrag zur Soziologie der Judenheit)* (Prague: J. A. Verb. Barissia, 1933), pp. 23–25; Kateřina Čapková, *Czechs, Germans, Jews? National Identity and the Jews of Bohemia*, trans. Derek and Marzia Paton (New York: Berghahn Books, 2012); Klein-Pejšová, *Mapping Jewish Loyalties*, pp. 47–85; and Tatjana Lichtenstein, *Zionists in Interwar Czechoslovakia: Minority Nationalism and the Politics of Belonging* (Bloomington: Indiana University Press, 2016).
55. Marie Crhova, "Jewish Politics in Central Europe: The Case of the Jewish Party in Interwar Czechoslovakia," *Jewish Studies at the Central European University* 2 (1999–2001): 271–301; Čapková, *Czechs, Germans, Jews?*, pp. 221–25. For the 1920 elections, see *Jüdisches Volksblatt*, 13 January 1920, p. 1; 16 March 1920, p. 1; 2 April 1920, pp. 1–2; 13 April 1920, pp. 1–2; 15 April 1920, pp. 1–2; 18 April 1920, p. 2; 20 April 1920, pp. 1–2; 23 April 1920, p. 1; 24 April 1920, pp. 1–2; *Jüdische Volksstimme*, 15 July 1925, pp. 1–2.
56. Mendelsohn, *Jews of East Central Europe*, pp. 43–83; Mendelsohn, *On Modern Jewish Politics* (New York: Oxford University Press, 1993), pp. 63–78. On a similar situation in interwar Lithuania, see ibid., pp. 43–44.
57. On Jewish nationalist demands in the new Czechoslovakia, see Rozenblit, *Reconstructing a National Identity*, pp. 138–50; Kieval, *The Making of Czech Jewry*, pp. 186–92. See also correspondence of Bohemian and Moravian Zionists with each other and with the World Zionist Organization in Central Zionist Archives, L6/366, Z3/217, and the reports of the *Jüdischer Nationalrat* in Prague in Z3/180, L6/85, L6/91, L6/96, L6/371.
58. Carole Fink, *Defending the Rights of Others: The Great Powers, the Jews, and International Minority Protection, 1878–1938* (Cambridge: Cambridge University Press, 2004).
59. Magocsi, *History of Ukraine*; Rothschild, *East Central Europe*.

60. Gitelman, *Jewish Nationality and Soviet Politics*; Gitelman, *A Century of Ambivalence*; Bemporad, *Becoming Soviet Jews*; Anna Shternshis, *Soviet and Kosher: Jewish Popular Culture in the Soviet Union, 1923–1939* (Bloomington: Indiana University Press, 2006); and Jeffrey Veidlinger, *In the Shadow of the Shtetl: Small-Town Jewish Life in Soviet Ukraine* (Bloomington: Indiana University Press, 2015).
61. On new opportunities for Jewish women in higher education, see Harriet Freidenreich, *Female, Jewish, Educated: The Lives of Central European University Women* (Bloomington: Indiana University Press, 2002). On Jewish women in Germany during and after World War I, see Martina Steer, "Nation, Religion, Gender: The Triple Challenge of Middle Class German-Jewish Women in World War I," *Central European History* 48 (2015): 176–98; and Marion A. Kaplan, *The Jewish Feminist Movement in Germany: The Campaigns of the Jüdischer Frauenbund, 1904–1938* (Westport, CT: Greenwood Press, 1979), pp. 156–62.
62. Similarly, Philipp Ther, "Pre-negotiated Violence: Ethnic Cleansing in the 'Long' First World War," in *Legacies of Violence*, pp. 259–84, sees postwar ethnic cleansing as resulting not from the war but from the new nation-state order (p. 283).
63. Čapková, *Czechs, Germans, Jews?*, pp. 24–25, 246–47, argues that antisemitism diminished in interwar Czechoslovakia, at least among the Czech nationalists who ran the government, because the demands of Czech nationalism had been satisfied.
64. For Germany, see Michael Brenner, *The Renaissance of Jewish Culture in Weimar Germany* (New Haven, CT: Yale University Press, 1996).

Selected Bibliography

Primary Sources

Jüdische Korrespondent, 1916–1919
Jüdische Volksstimme, 1914–1919
Jüdische Zeitung, 1914–1919
Jüdisches Volksblatt, 1920
Österreichische Wochenschrift, 1914–1919
Selbstwehr, 1914–1919
Hameiri, Avigdor. *The Great Madness*. Translated from Hebrew by Yael Lotan. Haifa: Or-Ran, 1984; orig. 1929.
Tannenbaum, Eugen, ed. *Kriegsbriefe deutscher und österreichischen Juden*. Berlin: Neuer Verlag, 1915.

Secondary Sources

Angress, Werner. "The German Army's 'Judenzählung' of 1916: Genesis—Consequences—Significance," *Leo Baeck Institute Year Book* 23 (1978): 117–37.
Bemporad, Elissa. *Becoming Soviet Jews: The Bolshevik Experiment in Minsk*. Bloomington: Indiana University Press, 2013.
Bihari, Péter. "A Forgotten Home Front: The Middle Classes and the 'Jewish Question' in First World War Hungary." Unpublished PhD dissertation, Central European University, 2005.
Birnbaum, Pierre. "French Rabbis and the 'Sacred Unity' during the First World War." *European Judaism* 48, no. 1 (Spring 2015): 47–58.

Caesarani, David. "An Embattled Minority: The Jews of Britain during the First World War." In *The Politics of Marginality: Race, the Radical Right, and Minorities in Twentieth Century Britain*, edited by T. Kushner and K. Lunn, pp. 61–81. London: Frank Cass, 1990.

Čapková, Kateřina. *Czechs, Germans, Jews? National Identity and the Jews of Bohemia*, translated by Derek and Marzia Paton. New York: Berghahn Books, 2012.

Fischer, Rolf. "Anti-Semitism in Hungary, 1882–1932." In *Hostages of Modernization: Studies on Modern Anti-Semitism, 1870–1933/39*, edited by Herbert A. Strauss, pp. 863–92. Berlin and New York: W. de Gruyter, 1993.

Freidenreich, Harriet. *Jewish Politics in Vienna, 1918–1938*. Bloomington: Indiana University Press, 1991.

Gitelman, Zvi. *Jewish Nationality and Soviet Politics: The Jewish Sections of the CPSU, 1917–1930* (Princeton, NJ: Princeton University Press, 1972).

Hoffmann-Holter, Beatrix. *"Abreisendmachung": Jüdische Kriegsflüchtlinge in Wien 1914 bis 1923*. Vienna: Böhlau, 1995.

Hyman, Paula E. *From Dreyfus to Vichy: The Remaking of French Jewry, 1906–1939*. New York: Columbia University Press, 1979.

Klein-Pejšová, Rebekah. "Beyond the 'Infamous Concentration Camps of the Old Monarchy': Jewish Refugee Policy from Wartime Austria-Hungary to Interwar Czechoslovakia." *Austrian History Yearbook* 45 (2014): 150–66.

———. *Mapping Jewish Loyalties in Interwar Slovakia*. Bloomington: Indiana University Press, 2015.

Lichtenstein, Tatjana. *Zionists in Interwar Czechoslovakia: Minority Nationalism and the Politics of Belonging*. Bloomington: Indiana University Press, 2016.

Livezeanu, Irina. *Cultural Politics in Greater Romania: Regionalism, Nation Building and Ethnic Struggle, 1918–1939*. Ithaca, NY: Cornell University Press, 1995.

Lohr, Eric. *Nationalizing the Russian Empire: The Campaign against Enemy Aliens during World War I*. Cambridge, MA: Harvard University Press, 2003.

Mendelsohn, Ezra. *The Jews of East Central Europe between the Wars*. Bloomington: Indiana University Press, 1983.

Mosse, Werner E., and Arnold Paucker, eds. *Deutsches Judentum in Krieg und Revolution, 1916–1923*. Tübingen: J. C. B. Mohr, 1971.

Panter, Sarah. *Jüdische Erfahrungen und Loyalitätskonflikte im Ersten Weltkrieg*. Göttingen: Vandenhoeck & Ruprecht, 2014.

Pauley, Bruce F. *From Prejudice to Persecution: A History of Austrian Anti-Semitism*. Chapel Hill: University of North Carolina Press, 1992.

Penslar, Derek J. *Jews and the Military: A History*. Princeton, NJ: Princeton University Press, 2013.

Prusin, Alexander Victor. *Nationalizing a Borderland: War, Ethnicity, and Anti-Jewish Violence in East Galicia, 1914–1920*. Tuscaloosa: University of Alabama Press, 2005.

Rozenblit, Marsha L. *Reconstructing a National Identity: The Jews of Habsburg Austria during World War I*. New York: Oxford University Press, 2001.

Zechlin, Egmont. *Die deutsche Politik und die Juden im ersten Weltkrieg*. Göttingen: Vandenhoeck & Ruprecht, 1969.

Zipperstein, Steven J. "The Politics of Relief: The Transformation of Russian Jewish Communal Life during the First World War," *Studies in Contemporary Jewry* 4, *The Jews and the European Crisis, 1914–1921*, edited by Jonathan Frankel, (1988): 22–40.

CHAPTER 3

Jewish Diplomacy and the Politics of War and Peace

Carole Fink

We Jews all leave for war of our own wish
Joyful to throng around our country's flag
To gain for ourselves—even if fate wills
That we pay with our blood—our
Fatherland.
— Emmanuel Saul, "To My Children"

O Sava, Sava River!
I'm a Jew on this side
Carry for me my true secret in your stream
To the sons of Serbia.
—Uri Zevi Greenberg, "Hazkarat Neshamot" [The Commemoration of Souls]

By any measure the war that erupted a century ago was a calamity for humankind and, especially, for the world's twelve million Jews. True, the outbreak of the Great War gave the Jewish people a potent opportunity to demonstrate their loyalty and gratitude to their various homelands and havens, and as Israel Zangwill proudly (and perhaps ruefully) wrote in 1915, "They are spending themselves passionately in the service of all."[1] Some 1.5 million Jewish men—approximately 2 percent of the mobilized manpower and double their proportion in the overall population—flocked to their countries' battleships and to the battlefields in Europe, Africa, the Near East, and Asia, thousands of Jewish women ministered to the wounded and to refugees, and scores of Jewish dignitaries played a leading role in their country's war effort.

As the war dragged on—from an initially conventional military conflict into a global struggle and a "total war" that mobilized the minds and lives of almost every segment of society—World War I brought more dangers than opportunity. On the Eastern and Southeastern Fronts and in the Near East, Jewish civilians suffered persecution, displacement, and death. In Central and Western Europe, antisemitism was reignited, and when the Bolsheviks seized power in Russia in November 1917, Jews were also tarred as communists.[2]

Yet at the end of these horrific four years, the Jewish people at the Paris Peace Conference achieved two major diplomatic accomplishments: a confirmation of the pledge by the world's largest empire of a Jewish homeland in Palestine, and a treaty with the new state of Poland establishing the international protection of minority rights, which became the model for similar agreements with the new and enlarged states of Eastern Europe.

Jewish diplomacy in war and peace involved a series of complex, transnational undertakings by a small, diverse, and resolute group of people without a sovereign state of their own, lacking accredited emissaries, often following competing goals, utilizing nonconventional methods, and evolving within chaotic and often violent circumstances.[3]

The prospects for a specifically Jewish diplomacy were not particularly bright in 1914. To be sure, various forms of Jewish representation had existed for centuries and had greatly expanded after 1815. Throughout the nineteenth century Jewish notables in Western Europe, as spokesmen for a historic people, had either enlisted their governments or entered into direct negotiations with foreign powers on behalf of their endangered coreligionists in Eastern Europe and the Near East. Indeed, they had achieved some success, particularly in the religious-protection clauses written into the 1878 Treaty of Berlin.[4]

Nonetheless, this modern stage of Jewish diplomacy was always a two-headed program, both assertive and defensive. On several occasions, a handful of Jewish dignitaries had wielded their financial, political, and media influence and formed effective local, national, and transnational alliances; but these initiatives were often curtailed by their governments' reluctance to serve as watchdog over the internal affairs of the Ottoman and Russian Empires or over new Balkan states such as Romania where discriminatory policies and outbursts of violence continued to produce waves of Jewish emigration westward and a mounting backlash in the receiving countries.[5]

At the beginning of the twentieth century Jewish diplomacy had been revitalized by the entry of American Jews into the international arena and also by the advent of Zionism. Nonetheless, some six million Jews remained in Eastern Europe, and their survival was threatened not only by prejudice and pogroms but also by new threats to curb immigration to

Western Europe and the United States. Moreover, in a world separated by rival alliances, the Jewish world had become splintered into competing national groups, within which there were also significant political, religious, and ideological differences. In addition, the unity of the Jewish people had been challenged by prominent Jewish socialists who rejected the entire concept of nationality.[6]

The outbreak of the Great War in 1914, although not unexpected, was dreaded by most Europeans and particularly by the Jews. Given the outsize increase of armaments and men in arms, the dramatic technological advances, and the almost equally balanced combatants, a short decisive conflict was highly improbable. Indeed, more likely—as in the US Civil War and the Balkan Wars—it would engulf masses of civilians and endanger the vulnerable Jewish communities in Eastern Europe and the still tiny settlements in Palestine. As Lucien Wolf, the Anglo-Jewish publicist and historian and secretary of the Conjoint Foreign Committee of the Board of Deputies of British Jews and the Anglo-Jewish Association gloomily predicted, "The whole thing is so stupendous that it fairly staggers me. It is not only the carnage that will be frightful but the economic exhaustion and the starvation which will be infinitely worse, and then when peace comes, the desolation and certain revolution everywhere."[7] In Berlin, the industrialist Walther Rathenau and the editor of the liberal *Berliner Tageblatt* Theodor Wolff viewed the impending crisis in similarly apocalyptic terms.[8]

The prospects of Jewish international activism were sorely limited. Indeed, British and French Jewish leaders would be immobilized by their governments' dependence on their indispensable Russian ally, a country where Jews were still denied citizenship, largely restricted to the Pale of Settlement, and curtailed in their economic rights.[9] The *Jewish Chronicle* on 31 July announced, "We protest with all our might against the mere thought of spilling blood or the squandering of resources in order that the Slavs may maintain their position against the Teutons.... We have no interest in the upholding of Russia and far less the debasing of Germany ... with whom [Britain] has no quarrel whatsoever."[10] The philosopher Victor Basch, one of the founders of the pacifist Ligue des Droits de l'Homme, publicly supported France's right to defend itself against the Reich's invasion but deemed Russia more culpable than Austria-Hungary and deplored France's tie with the "monstrous, immoral," and antisemitic government in Saint Petersburg.[11]

The Jews' international contacts, developed over many decades in scientific, scholarly, and cultural communities, humanitarian organizations, and working-class associations, were suddenly ruptured in August 1914. The global connections forged by Jewish bankers, traders, and industrialists were also shattered. The German shipping magnate Albert Ballin, whom the Kaiser at the last minute had dispatched to conduct the abortive semiofficial negotiations with British leaders, was shocked and angered by the enormous ineptitude with which his government had blundered into the war.[12] Moreover, the already frayed cross-border bonds of purely Jewish diplomacy between enemy, allied, and neutral countries were disrupted—especially with the United States; and the still small Zionist movement suffered a dramatic setback when its institutional center in Berlin was severed from its largest and most important branch in Russia.[13]

Phase One: Jews as Spokesmen for the Nation

After war was declared and their governments announced a *union sacrée* and a *Burgfrieden,* Europeans of all regions, parties, classes, and religions rallied to defend their homelands against the enemy. Thus, many Jewish dignitaries—although excluded from the sites of political and military decision-making—swallowed their forebodings, ended their political disengagement, and became spokesmen for the national cause. In a stunning volte-face the *Jewish Chronicle* in the beginning of August announced, "England has been all she could for the Jews, now the Jews will be all they can for England."[14] The famed 58-year-old psychoanalyst Sigmund Freud, upon hearing of Austria's war declaration against Serbia declared, "For the first time in thirty years, I feel myself to be an Austrian, and feel like giving this not very hopeful empire another chance.... All my libido is given to Austria-Hungary."[15] The writer Stefan Zweig proclaimed a "community of blood" between Germans and Austrians and bade adieu to his pacifist friends abroad.[16]

The most striking patriotic expression, the 23 October "Manifesto of the Ninety-Three German Intellectuals," was organized by the Jewish playwright Ludwig Fulda. Some of the world's leading scientists and artists—the self-proclaimed heirs of Goethe, Beethoven, and Kant—refuted the Reich's enemies' attacks on Prussian militarism and denied their country's responsibility for the outbreak of the war and its violations of international law in Belgium. Among its signatories were eight other prominent Jews, the painter Max Liebermann, the Austrian-born actor and director Max Reinhardt, the poet/playwright Herbert Eulenberg, the jurist Paul Laband, and the chemists Adolf von Baeyer, Fritz Haber, and Richard Willstaetter.[17]

The obligation to use their scholarly and artistic credentials to bolster their country in wartime was also strong among French Jews. The philosopher Henri Bergson, who pronounced the war a struggle between civilization and barbarism, published articles in the foreign press reciting the republic's virtues, lauding Belgian king Albert, upholding the Allies' war aims, and denouncing German imperialism. Equally fervent was the engagement of the sociologist Émile Durkheim, who in 1915 published two major propagandistic works: *Qui a voulu la guerre?* and *L'Allemagne au-dessus de tout*; along with the historian Ernst Lavisse (and with support from the French army and foreign ministry) he also published the *Lettres à tous les Français,* a series of mass-circulation pamphlets extolling the nation's genius and vitality for the purpose of raising morale but especially to impress allies and foreign neutrals. The famous Dreyfusard historian Joseph Reinach set out to write a book on the origins of the war. And under the aegis of the Quai d'Orsay, French-Jewish scholars undertook several missions to the United States to enlist their coreligionists in the Allied cause.[18]

German Jews also placed their pens at the service of their government, fighting for its existence. In his short story "Die Bestie" (The Beast), published in November 1914, Arnold Zweig depicted the murder of three upright and heroic German soldiers—innocently asleep in a barn—by a Belgian peasant, who had then proceeded to dissect their bodies.[19] In 1915 the 32-year-old poet-patriot Ernst Lissauer published the widely popular "Hymn of Hate" against perfidious England, which the government promptly circulated among the troops and promptly became the Reich's most famous marching song.[20]

Other German Jews were equally zealous. In his pamphlet *Deutschtum und Judentum,* the liberal philosopher Hermann Cohen, equating German and Jewish values, denounced Germany's "wicked" enemies. Cohen, who published pro-German propaganda in the American Jewish press, offered his services to the government as an emissary to the United States. And Martin Buber, in his lectures and articles, exalted the war spirit and exhorted his fellow Jews to serve the fatherland—even at the cost of fighting their coreligionists.[21]

German Zionists, stirred by Jewish nationalism and Russophobia and ignoring the World Zionist Movement's announcement of neutrality, offered their services to the Reich, whose aims in Eastern Europe and the Near East seemed to parallel theirs. The creation of the semiofficial Committee for the Liberation of Russian Jewry (later renamed the Committee for the East) provided a major outlet for these patriots, who drafted the proclamations and propaganda leaflets distributed by the German and Austro-Hungarian armies to the civilian population in Poland and Lithuania and produced a Yiddish magazine for the conquered territories (adding a pretext for Russia's removal of some one-half million Jewish civilians from the front lines as potential traitors). German Jews also provided agents to neutral countries, the most prominent of whom was Dr. Isaac Straus, who spent the entire war in the United States attempting to enlist American-Jewish support for the Reich but ultimately ended up in prison.[22]

There were also European Jews who from the very start refused to endorse their governments' war aims or to revile their enemies, who risked surveillance, censorship, and imprisonment, and who braved wartime travel limitations to disseminate their antiwar views and liaise with foreign colleagues.[23] In the German-speaking world they included the physicist Albert Einstein (one of the three signatories of the counter-document to the "Manifesto of the Ninety-Three"—the "Manifesto to Europeans Opposed to the War") and the Austrian journalist Alfred Hermann Fried (who fled to Switzerland to lead the international antiwar movement) along with the German philosophers Isaac Breuer and Franz Rosenzweig, the German rabbi Joseph Carlebach, and the young Zionist Gershom Scholem, as well as two Austrian-Jewish feminists, Yella Hertzka and Olga Misař, who took part in the first International Congress for Peace and Freedom convened at The Hague between 28 April and 1 May 1915 and organized by the renowned Dutch-Jewish pacifist Aletta Jacobs.[24] Jewish antiwar socialists included Rosa Luxemburg and Gustav Landauer in Germany, Léon Rosenthal in France, and Giuseppe Modigliani (the artist's brother, who opposed Sidney Sonnino and Luigi Luzzato's calls for Italy's entry into the war and was one of the signers of the Zimmerwald Manifesto in September 1915), and the Jewish Labor Bund, which refused to support czarist Russia. These figures, despite their small numbers and the almost complete absence of a Jewish content in their antiwar stance, challenged the war fever of August 1914, and as the war dragged on, they would be augmented by disillusioned coreligionists.

Phase Two: A Dedicated Jewish Diplomacy

By the end of 1915 Jewish public diplomacy had shifted from national advocacy to a defense of Jewish sufferers in Eastern Europe and in Palestine. Struck by the reports in the neutral press and eyewitness depictions of expulsions and atrocities, Jewish spokesmen directed their efforts to protective measures, which included relief for Jewish civilians. Clothed in patriotic rhetoric, these humanitarian programs—sometimes competing across the battle lines—necessitated extremely delicate forms of transnational Jewish diplomacy.

For loyalist German and Austro-Hungarian Jews, the East remained an important area of operation, still fueled by the aspiration that its Jewish inhabitants would become valuable allies and the vanguard of a new political order. After the Central Powers had conquered and divided Russian Poland in 1915, Jewish organizations in both countries lobbied for the removal of discriminatory czarist laws and edicts and for the creation of a multinational buffer state between Germany and Russia, with equal rights to Jewish communities. But their governments were unresponsive, unwilling to grant favors to their new Jewish subjects and risk Polish, Lithuanian, and Ukrainian opposition. Moreover the German government, smarting from the dire effects of the Allied blockade, singled out Polish Jews for harsh treatment, which included restrictions on their movement and confiscation of their property as well as forced loans, requisitions, heavy taxes, and deportations of forced laborers. Much to the chagrin of Jewish loyalists, Berlin and Vienna refused protection to the Jewish minority against its non-Jewish neighbors, and both governments imposed harsh measures on Jewish refugees.[25]

On the Near Eastern front, Jewish interests appeared to mesh more closely with those of the Central Powers and their Ottoman ally. Indeed, there was a notorious project launched by the flamboyant orientalist Max von Oppenheim, who, although denied a diplomatic post because of his Jewish ancestry, was ensconced for two years at the German embassy in Constantinople, where he conducted an abortive propaganda campaign among the Arabs.[26] The intervention of German and Austrian Jews on behalf of the Jewish settlers in Palestine was only slightly more successful. To win American support, Berlin and Vienna allowed their diplomats to work closely with Zionist representatives, and on at least one occasion, in March 1915, Germany convinced its Ottoman ally to halt the expulsion of foreign Russian Jews. However, the Reich leadership was unwilling to meet the Jews' key demands: to pressure Constantinople to grant citizenship to the Russian settlers and to alienate the Arabs by endorsing a Jewish homeland in Palestine.[27]

Jewish diplomacy within the Entente was even more intricate. Despite Russia's widely reported atrocities, French and British Jewish leaders—fearing accusations of betraying the war effort (compounded by mounting domestic protests over the refusal of significant numbers of Russian-Jewish immigrants to enlist in the nation's forces)—maintained almost a year of discreet silence over their coreligionists' plight in the East. Indeed, Jewish spokesmen publicly insisted that German antisemitism exceeded Russia's.[28] The first initiative came from the United States, where in 1915 the Russophobe banker Jacob Schiff wielded his financial power to demand reforms from St. Petersburg. Thereupon in August the czarist government—which had already sent large numbers of border Jewish communities into exile in the interior—announced reforms that substantially ended the Pale of Settlement.[29]

Lucien Wolf, who in August 1914 had loyally canceled the publication of his weekly propaganda bulletin *Darkest Russia* but had also chaffed at his immobility, sought to revitalize the Anglo-Jewish voice. While the French-Jewish establishment, which was tied closely to the Quai d'Orsay, remained silent, Wolf—stirred by the display of American-Jewish forcefulness—appealed for Whitehall's intervention on behalf of Russian Jews. And when, as expected, this effort was rebuffed, Wolf suddenly, in March

1916, made his daring proposal: to win US support for the Entente by endorsing Jewish settlement and colonization in Palestine. Wolf's Palestine scheme—despite its cautious, non-Zionist formulation—was shelved by the Asquith government; but the Conjoint leader had planted a seed for a new form of Anglo-Jewish collaboration, which only a year later would be taken up by his Zionist rivals.[30]

Phase Three: Jews in a Revolutionary Moment

World War I took a major turn in 1917 with a cascade of three significant events: the March Revolution in Russia, which overthrew the czarist autocracy; the entry of the United States into the war a month later, contributing America's abundant human and material resources to the Allied side; and the Bolshevik Revolution in November, which was followed by Russia's withdrawal from the war. For Jewish diplomacy it was also an epochal year, bringing freedom for Russia's minorities, the debut of American Jews into global politics, and Britain's promise of a Jewish homeland, followed by its conquest of Palestine.

However, these momentous developments had yet to take shape. In the meantime, the war's outcome was uncertain, and 1917 was a bleak year for both sides, due to the immense battle casualties and the privations suffered by the home front. Many early enthusiasts had become disillusioned; Sigmund Freud, Arnold Zweig, Victor Basch, and Stefan Zweig had all braved the censors to denounce the war; and in Zurich three Romanian-Jewish émigrés, Marcel and Georges Janco and Tristan Tzara, had founded World War I's unique art form, Dada, aimed at undermining the bourgeois societies that had forced the world into barbarism.[31]

The Jewish leadership, however, remained paralyzed. In Western and Central Europe—and particularly in Germany—the Jews had once more become scapegoats, blamed for the unending war and targeted in the press and public forums for shirking, war profiteering, defeatism, and even espionage.[32] Moreover developments in Eastern Europe were disquieting. The Central Powers' establishment of a quasi-independent Poland at the end of 1916 had eliminated the Reich Jews' special position in that country. British Jews were alarmed by the new government in Warsaw, which refused to grant any form of linguistic or cultural rights to its minorities. Moreover, the entries of Greece and Romania into the Allied camp had foreclosed any further appeals by British Jewish leaders to Whitehall to reverse or mitigate these countries' anti-Jewish practices.[33]

An alternative to passivity was a bold assertion of Jewish interests. Not unexpectedly, American Jewry had provided a striking example with the creation of the Joint Distribution Committee in 1914. Overriding the US

Jewish community's deep domestic divisions and overcoming immense bureaucratic, diplomatic, and logistic logjams, over the next three years the JDC raised and distributed some $15 million of aid to suffering communities in Poland, Russia, and Palestine.[34] Another mode was direct action. Thousands of Eastern European Jews in England, rebelling against the traditional leadership's restraint, had flocked to all-Jewish combat units, fought at Gallipoli, and would take part in the 1917 British conquest of Palestine.[35] There was also NILI, the youthful and daring Palestinian spy network whose attempt to provide intelligence to the British would be brutally crushed in 1917 by the Ottoman authorities.[36]

By far the Jews' most spectacular diplomatic breakthrough in 1917 was achieved as a rogue action by the Russian-Jewish scientist Chaim Weizmann. Weizmann defied not only the Anglo-Jewish establishment but also the officially neutral Zionist official bodies (and even risked Turkish retaliation against the Jewish settlers in Palestine), and with his supporters he negotiated directly with high British and French officials (and even at one point worked with the British to derail the US initiative to conduct peace talks with Turkey), ran a masterful press campaign, and deftly wielded his rivals' arguments about the necessity of winning over US and Russian Jews to the Allies' faltering cause and blocking German initiatives in Palestine—even making use of the new threat of Bolshevism—to convince his interlocutors of the necessity of the Zionist program. To be sure, Weizmann also had the good fortune of facing a sympathetic new British government in 1917, whose historic decision in the late spring to proceed with the attack on Palestine coincided with his plans.[37]

Nonetheless, the British pledge in November 1917 of a Jewish homeland in Palestine was not only a controversial project that split the Jewish and the non-Jewish world; it also highlighted the dilemma over the future of millions of Jews in Poland, Greece, Romania, and other parts of Eastern Europe unwilling or unable to emigrate to a tiny, impoverished, disease-ridden, and already inhabited province in the Near East under the aegis of an enemy power, the British Empire.[38]

Moreover, the Bolshevik seizure of power on 7 November 1917 cast a dark shadow over the fate of Eastern European Jewry. Trotsky's publication of all the secret treaties and informal agreements deeply embarrassed the Entente, and Lenin's exit from the war endangered the Allies' strategic situation. Almost reflexively, Western statesmen and journalists castigated Bolshevism as a German-Jewish plot, undermining popular and diplomatic support for the creation of a protective regime for the minorities of Eastern Europe.[39]

The Jews' predicament was further complicated by the treaties imposed by the victorious Central Powers in 1918 on Ukraine, Russia, and Romania and by the redrawing of boundaries between Poland and Lithuania.

Within this German New Order, extending from the Baltic to the Black Sea, some seven million Jews—including all the inhabitants of the former Pale of Settlement—would now dwell. And despite the pleas of Reich and Austrian Jews, the Jews in Poland and Romania would be dominated by rulers who were hostile to their religion, language, and culture.[40]

For Western Jewish leaders, the dismemberment of Russia was an alarming development, not only quashing their hopes for a liberalized empire, but also presaging a larger menace: the prospect of new and enlarged states in Eastern Europe whose Jewish inhabitants would be excluded from the body politic and placed under pressure to emigrate.[41] And on the other side, there was scant evidence of Allied recognition of the Jews' plight. In January 1918 British prime minister David Lloyd George and US president Woodrow Wilson signaled their support for the Poles' national aspirations, and in June the Allies, increasingly confident in victory, had extended their endorsement for self-determination to the Czechs, Serbs, Romanians, and Greeks. But they issued no statement on the need to protect minorities.[42]

Entente Jewish leaders were divided over these historic decisions. In Paris, the Alliance Israélite Universelle bowed to the French government's support of the Polish national cause; but Lucien Wolf, leading the newly established Joint Foreign Committee, went on the offensive, planting articles in the press and warning the foreign office of the threat to Jewish survival in Eastern Europe. Wolf also negotiated directly with Eastern European politicians, but Polish, Czech, and Romanian spokesmen, confident that victory was near, rejected his proposals for special rights and protection for their minority populations. American Jewish leaders entered the discussions, and Louis Marshall, head of the American Jewish Committee, also came away disappointed from his meetings with Polish leaders Ignacy Paderewski and Roman Dmowski. On Armistice Day, Marshall celebrated the Allies' victory over German militarism but appealed to President Woodrow Wilson to help prevent a reprise of the Jews' unhappy experience in Romania before World War I.[43]

The Jews and the Peace Conference

The Paris Peace Conference, one of the largest diplomatic gatherings in modern history, has long been the subject of controversy. Generations of scholars, journalists, and politicians have denounced the victors for their unwise and vindictive treatment of the Central Powers and for expanding European imperialism in the Middle East or only faintly praised them for their short-lived accomplishments.[44] Similarly, the Jewish role at the peace conference has either been criticized for the many setbacks or praised for its singular accomplishments.[45]

Highly pertinent to these debates are the realities of January 1919: Germany's unexpected collapse two months earlier that had left Britain, France, and the United States unprepared to reshape Europe and the world, the looming Bolshevik menace, and the fierce border struggles that had erupted between the new states of Eastern Europe, especially Poland and Czechoslovakia, and Hungary and Romania. Not only were the victors' war aims often contradictory and their peace programs uncoordinated, but their leaders were also subject to intense political and public pressure, while their smaller allies, ambitious and vulnerable, were at odds with each other. Similarly, the Jewish emissaries—now subject entirely to the victors' will—were deeply divided over their goals, methods, and loyalties, lacked an acknowledged leadership, and were both over- and under-confident of their place in the public realm.[46]

The Jews approached the peace conference in January 1919 with both assets and liabilities. The Zionists, widely recognized for their wartime patriotism, had already secured the backing of the world's largest empire and its allies, and in the last days of the war, the cause of minority rights had been bolstered by the graphic reports of violence in Eastern Europe and by the endorsements of neutrals, socialists, and humanitarian organizations. On the other hand, the Jewish representatives in Paris operated under several handicaps. The Jewish world still divided not only over a Jewish future in Palestine but also over minority rights. Moreover, the "Palestine priority," demanded by the Zionists and seconded by the Eastern European delegates, had placed minority rights in the background; and in this shadow existence, prior clashing agendas for minority rights—ranging from the traditional clauses providing equal citizenship and religious and personal freedom to claims of national autonomy—developed and festered.[47]

Moreover, the victors' wartime pledges of self-determination—to be sure, vague and selective—appeared to threaten more than to shield the affected minorities. However great their revulsion against the anti-Jewish violence at the end of the war, the Big Three—France's prime minister Georges Clemenceau, Lloyd George, and Wilson—neither had created the new map of Eastern Europe nor could do much to control the behavior of their truculent clients who, overnight, had gained control over millions of formerly dominant Germans and Hungarians as well as over formerly subordinate peoples. In order to create a solid barrier between the defeated Reich and Russia, they would be forced to deal with weak and stubborn politicians, such as Roman Dmowski, Eduard Beneš, Ian Brătianu, and Eleftherios Venizelos, who arrived in Paris insisting on their anti-German, anti-Bolshevik credentials and demanding full and unimpaired sovereignty over the expansive borders they were claiming. And Wilson was undoubtedly aware of Poland's three million supporters in the United States.[48]

Finally, the Jewish case at the Paris Peace Conference was vulnerable to stiff ideological as well as political resistance. The Zionists' demands—linked fatefully to Britain's military conquest of Palestine—not only contravened the idea of self-determination and raised opposition among the local Arabs, but they also drew hostility from British diplomats and soldiers in the Near East, French diplomats, and US traders and missionaries, who complained of the danger and injustice of privileging Jewish rights over those of the majority.[49]

Similarly, the demands for any form of group rights by the Eastern European Jews—however grounded in legitimate fears and political realities—not only contradicted Western ideas of democracy but also raised the victors' hackles against the prospect of endorsing separatism, weakening the new states, and giving comfort to German irredentism and inciting Bolshevik chicanery. In the words of Eugène Sée, president of the Alliance Israélite Universelle, "the business of the conference is to create a sovereign state for Poland, not for the Jews."[50] Although acting as defenders of a tiny, vulnerable people in need of special protection, the Jewish emissaries in Paris could also be portrayed by their opponents as elite, aggressive, and immoderate, especially because they made scant efforts to forge alliances with the other "suitors and suppliants" in the French capital.[51]

Palestine

The Palestine issue came up less than two weeks after the opening of the peace conference. While preparing to establish the League of Nations and dispose of the imperial realms of its ex-enemies, the Supreme Council on 30 January 1919 announced that "because of the historical mis-government by the Turks of subject peoples," Palestine, along with Armenia, Syria, Mesopotamia, and Arabia, were to be "completely severed" from the Turkish Empire and placed under a mandatory regime.[52]

Looming in the background were Great Britain's three contradictory wartime pledges: the October 1915 agreement between the British high commissioner in Egypt, Sir Henry McMahon, and the sherif of Mecca, Hussein bin Ali, in which Britain—in payment for the Arab revolt against the Ottoman Empire—had offered an independent Arab Kingdom, albeit within imprecisely defined boundaries; the May 1916 Sykes-Picot Agreement, dividing the Turkish province of Syria (including parts of Palestine) with France; and the 2 November 1917 Balfour Declaration, endorsed by the Dominions and Britain's major allies—France, Italy, Japan, and the United States.[53]

Now promised in whole or in part to no less than four parties—Great Britain, France, the Zionists, and the Arabs—Palestine was an unwelcome distraction to the peacemakers, who were focused on creating the League of Nations, writing a peace with Germany, and staving off the Bolshevik threat to Eastern Europe. The facts on the ground were significant. Not only was Great Britain in control of all of Palestine, which it ruled through a military government until an internationally recognized civilian regime could be established, but in December 1918 London had also given legitimacy to the Zionists by permitting a commission, led by Chaim Weizmann, to journey to Palestine and negotiate with British officials and with the Arab nationalist leader Emir Faisal on the future of a Jewish homeland. On the other hand, the local Arab population in Palestine, through words and deeds, had already registered its strong opposition to both British rule and Jewish immigration.[54]

The situation in Paris appeared propitious. The US president, who commanded vast economic and military resources as well as public prestige, had ostensibly signed on to the Zionist program. There seemed to be a strong commitment by Lloyd George and Balfour, and there was the extraordinary mobilization of the Jewish world, ranging from citizens of the United States, Central America, and South America to the populations of Western, Central, and Eastern Europe and to those as far away as South Africa and Australia, all endorsing the Jews' right to a national home in Palestine.[55]

But many elements clouded the picture. The Quai d'Orsay was firmly opposed to British-Jewish control over Palestine; key members of the US peace delegation were skeptical, as were some British cabinet members and influential British-, French-, and American-Jewish leaders. The support of the new German government did little to help the Zionists' cause. The Vatican under Pope Benedict XV was reportedly outraged at the prospect of Anglo-Jewish control over the holy places. And by far the strongest obstacle was the mobilization of the Muslim world, which, from India to the shores of the Arabian Sea, opposed the replacement of Muslim control over Jerusalem by Christian British governors and Jewish settlers.[56]

As early as 13 February 1919 Wilson had signaled his solution for the Palestine question: the dispatch of an inter-Allied commission to ascertain the population's choice of rulers.[57] Nonetheless, two weeks later—after the president had left Paris to win congressional support for the League of Nations—the Palestine issue came before the Supreme Council, although no major leader was present. Before a gathering of Allied foreign ministers, four Zionist spokesmen on 27 February 1919 defended the Jewish claims to Palestine, and a French anti-Zionist closely tied to the Quai d'Orsay rebutted them, whereupon Weizmann, in his retort, revealed his movement's ultimate goal: "To build up gradually a nationality which would be as Jewish as the French nation was French and the British nation British. Later on, when the Jews formed the large majority, they would be ripe to establish such a government as would answer to the state of the development of the country and to their ideals."[58]

The response was sharp and immediate. Although the Zionists exulted over Weizmann's audacious statement, Whitehall and the Quai d'Orsay were appalled, non-Zionists were horrified by his "undemocratic" project, and the Arabs of Palestine rioted. More important, Wilson, after his return on 20 March, continued to insist on the dispatch of a nonpartisan commission to Palestine. Following two months of foot-dragging by the bickering British and French, the president on 21 May announced the dispatch of two Americans to the Middle East.[59]

Why had this happened? To be sure, the president had pronounced sympathies for Zionism. Four of his Democratic supporters—Justices Louis Brandeis and Julian Mack, Harvard law professor Felix Frankfurter, and Rabbi Stephen Wise—were ardent Zionists as well as champions of the League of Nations. Moreover, prompted by his close advisor Colonel Edward House and by Secretary of State Robert Lansing, Wilson understood the need to settle the Palestine issue as soon as possible, because any delay would diminish the victors' power and prestige before the Arab *and* Jewish world.[60]

On the other side were even stronger considerations. Within the context of Wilson's ideological rivalry with Lenin, the president risked much by bowing automatically to Britain's claims to the spoils of war in the Middle East.[61] Although the president had declined Britain's half-hearted offer to assume a mandate over Palestine, America's economic and religious interests were at stake in the region. Furthermore, the president's pro-Zionist stance was tempered by the strong *anti-*Zionist sentiments of some of his supporters in the American Jewish community.[62]

We shall probably never know whether the postponement of the Palestine question was also due to Wilson's fragile health, his brittle temperament, his huge workload in Paris, or his private personal views. What is significant is that the US president in Paris on 21 May 1919 thwarted the Zionists' goal of a Great Power commitment to a Jewish homeland in Palestine that would be signed in Paris. The King-Crane Commission, led by two inexperienced individuals, briefly toured the Middle East and produced a report championing US religious, political, and economic interests and criticizing the Zionists' project, which caused a temporary propagandistic flurry but was ultimately buried in the files.[63]

Still, the delay had consequences, not only forcing the Zionists into even greater dependence on Britain but also intensifying their difficulties in Palestine. And because London needed Paris's agreement on a host of local and international issues, Britain's mandate over Palestine and its official commitment to a Jewish homeland was deferred for three years, prolonging British military rule, postponing the establishment of local institutions, and kindling volatile local conditions between Arabs and Jews.[64]

Britain's setback had other consequences. Lloyd George, although vexed by the US president, had come to recognize the risks in the Balfour Declaration. Whitehall officials complained over a thankless, dangerous commitment that would weaken the entire empire and were appalled by the Zionists' demands to control immigration, land, public works, water rights, and educational institutions in Palestine, and the British Military Administration was alarmed by the Zionists' political goals. Even Balfour had second thoughts. Thus, when Britain deferred to Wilson in May 1919, it marked the beginning of its step-by-step withdrawal from the Balfour Declaration.[65]

The Minority Treaties

Although the French had expected the Great Powers to appoint a special commission on Jewish questions, this never occurred. Instead, the conference's organization, dictated by Wilson—and particularly its monthlong focus on creating the League of Nations—diverted the statesmen's and public attention from the anti-Jewish violence at the end of the war. Moreover, after Clemenceau on 29 January 1919, using his prerogative as peace conference chair, invited a succession of Eastern European leaders—all potential French allies—to state their territorial claims, the Allies made the fateful decision to appoint separate expert committees to draw up the new borders. Lost in this process was the idea of a special Jewish committee.[66]

While the Zionists had at least had the opportunity to press their claims before the peacemakers, the Jewish advocates of minority rights were almost silent and were also sparsely represented. Not only were few German, Austrian, and Russian Jewish leaders, constrained by border restrictions, able to reach Paris, but on Wilson's instructions, the delegation representing the American Jewish Congress remained back in the United States.[67]

Thus the burden fell largely on Lucien Wolf and on Jacques Bigart, secretary of the Alliance Israélite Universelle, who submitted separate proposals for minority protection without consulting the Eastern Europeans; both, however, were excluded from peacemakers' secret deliberations.[68] Only in late February did Wolf learn what had happened in the League Commission, where Wilson had withdrawn his proposal to insert a religious-freedom clause in the League Covenant in order to block Japan's demand for a statement on racial equality. Now not only was Palestine in suspense, but a key issue of minority protection had also been dropped from the status of a recognized international obligation. If the Jews would receive any protection at all, it would have to be incorporated—as in the past—into the separate territorial treaties.[69]

A new act of violence underlined the dangers to the Jews in Eastern Europe when, on 5 April 1919, Polish soldiers shot thirty-four unarmed Jewish civilians in Pinsk. The news, transmitted over Jewish and German newswires, sped across Europe and the Atlantic and was reinforced by reports of more anti-Jewish violence during the Poles' military campaigns further east. The Warsaw government sought to calm public outrage by denying the atrocity reports and accusing the Jews of Bolshevik sympathies and sabotage. The Allies, disconcerted by an unwelcome distraction from the German treaty, unenthusiastically ordered an investigation.[70]

By that time Jewish representation had swelled in Paris with the arrival of the Americans and a large delegation of Eastern Europeans. In an attempt to unite their kindred from such disparate places as New York, London, Paris, Warsaw, Ukraine, and Palestine and create a permanent organization, the Easterners had created the Comité des Délégations Juives under an American chair, first Mack and then Marshall, and tasked it with preparing proposals on minority rights.[71]

The Comité added to the factionalism among the Jewish emissaries in Paris when Wolf and the Alliance Israélite Universelle decided to stay aloof from its expansive program, which included national autonomy and Jewish representation in the League of Nations. Marshall was given the difficult task of mediating between Westerners and Easterners: the British and French sought a moderate amount of minority protection acceptable to the Big Three and to the new states, and the latter (openly supported by Germany) demanded maximum national rights for the Jews and *all* minorities in Eastern Europe as well as Jewish representation in the League of Nations. The news of continued atrocities along the route of Polish conquests in Eastern Europe—some containing exaggerated casualty figures—made Marshall's work more difficult because it underlined the Eastern Jews' vulnerability, the obduracy of their new masters, and the Jews' dependency on the peacemakers.[72]

The impatient and pragmatic Marshall struck out independently. Without consulting Wolf, he delivered a draft to Wilson's close advisor Colonel House that called for national rights for the Jews and a substantial measure of minority protection by the League of Nations. This document, although considerably diluted by House's aide David Hunter Miller, reached the president at the end of April, where it found a receptive audience. On the eve of the arrival of the German delegation—which was expected to demand protection for the Reich's lost citizens—Wilson on 1 May proposed the creation of a special committee to draft minority clauses for the peace treaty.[73]

Thus the Committee on New States—and *not* a Minority Committee or a Jewish Rights Committee—was born. In one of the conference's curious turns, this committee (consisting of US, British, French, and occasional Italian and Japanese representation) took on a life of its own. Pleading the enormity of its task, it promptly informed the Big Three of the impossibility of covering all aspects of the minority problem in a few sentences and proposed to link the German treaty with a separate and detailed arrangement with Poland—one that would then be the model for pacts with the other new and enlarged states in Eastern Europe. Meeting in secret and dominated by Britain's able and energetic foreign office representative Sir James Headlam-Morley (who had rather close ties to Wolf), the committee in only two weeks produced a draft of history's first minority treaty.[74]

Wolf and Marshall were shocked by the results—by the elimination of any recognition of Jewish cultural and political rights and by the committee's refusal to provide a direct route for minorities to appeal to the new League of Nations. Breaking from their cautious practices, the two now worked together to "raise a row" against the new wave of anti-Jewish violence in Poland, planting articles in the press and stirring mass protests in Europe and America. However, both the British and Jewish emissary understood the limits of these demonstrations (which were warmly supported by Berlin). Indeed there was a backlash in Paris, where British, French, and US diplomats became impatient with the exaggerated pogrom reports and accused the Jews of bullying a weak and inexperienced Eastern European government instead of sympathizing with its starving and threatened population.[75] During Marshall's brief interview with Wilson on 26 May, the president refused to single out the Jews for special privileges that would undoubtedly encourage German demands. Moreover, the Polish government threatened to withhold its signature. On 31 May, in one of the peace conference's rare public meetings, the leaders of Romania, Czechoslovakia, Yugoslavia, and Greece roundly protested an infringement on their dignity and sovereignty.[76]

The Big Three, stunned by their clients' recalcitrance and racing to complete their work, backed off. The peacemakers not only watered down the Polish treaty but also, to sweeten the pill, reversed their objections and gave Warsaw a green light to capture all of eastern Galicia, adding some seven hundred thousand Jews and four million Ukrainians to the new state without—despite Marshall's pleas—any special guarantees for the large non-Polish population. Moreover Wilson, over Marshall's protests, took up Warsaw's suggestion and dispatched a US commission, led by the anti-Zionist ambassador Henry Morgenthau, to investigate all the reports of violence in Poland since the end of World War I.[77]

The Polish Minority Treaty, signed at Versailles on 28 June 1919, was a pale version of the Jewish claims. Not only were the citizenship and religious protection clauses extremely vague and weak, but also every shred of a Jewish *national* identity had been omitted from the final text. The treaty specified that *all* Polish nationals could establish, manage, and control charitable, religious, educational, and social institutions, use their own language, and practice their own religion, but the state was not obliged to fund any of these enterprises. In regions of considerable non-Polish-speaking population, the state would establish and fund only primary schools in the minority language. Minorities could set up their own local organizations but were barred from creating a national representative body or obtaining a specified number of seats in the parliament or government. The Jews were singled out in two of the treaty's articles: for the disbursement of public funds for their religious schools and for the protection of the Sabbath, except in state emergencies and in the performance of military duties; but as Wolf ruefully noted, there was no safeguard for Sunday trading, a crucial aspect of the Jews' economic survival. Finally, Article 12, the guarantee clause, placed enforcement under the responsibility of the as yet unborn Council of the League of Nations, but minorities were denied access to the League or to the Permanent Court of International Justice, where disputes were to be adjudicated.[78]

Jewish diplomacy at the peace conference had at least three serious handicaps. The Jews in the victor states recognized that their political value to their governments had plummeted, particularly in light of the peacemakers' more pressing considerations—their anti-Germanism and anti-Bolshevism, their concern for the stability of the new states of Eastern Europe and for their interests in the Arab/Muslim world, as well as their domestic political requirements. Jewish diplomats were also handicapped by their personal and political divisions, by their tactical inexperience, and by their rival agendas in Paris. Finally, the Palestine program, a specific, if contested goal, was backed by a Great Power; but the cause of Jewish minority rights—whose purpose and scope divided the Jewish world—had no Great Power endorsement and also raised powerful objections from all the new and enlarged states of Eastern Europe.

To be sure, the first step toward a Jewish homeland began in Paris. Despite Wilson's delaying tactic, within three years Britain and France had reconciled their differences, the League of Nations confirmed the Balfour Declaration, and a mandate that included the essentials of Jewish self-government in Palestine was established in 1922. Nonetheless, over the next twenty-five years the three essential questions growing out of World War I were to remain unresolved: the clash between Britain's imperial interests and the idea of self-determination, between the Zionists' claim of

Jewish sovereignty and the local Arabs' opposition, and between Zionist and non-Zionist Jews.

The Polish Minority Treaty was a more equivocal achievement. Behind the scenes Marshall and Wolf had undoubtedly helped craft a historic document, although the final text provided far less than they had hoped. On the other hand, the exaggerated sense of Jewish accomplishment also contributed to a backlash, not only in Poland's and its neighbors' noncompliance with the treaty's clauses, but also in the postwar swell of antisemitism in Europe and the United States. Moreover, with an even more divided Jewish world after 1919 and without a universal commitment to minority rights or a robust system of regional protection under the League of Nations, postwar Jewish defenders of their Eastern European brethren would find their task even more arduous than in the past.

Carole Fink, Humanities Distinguished Professor Emerita at the Ohio State University, is the author of *West Germany and Israel: Foreign Relations, Domestic Politics, and the Cold War, 1965–1974* (2019), *Writing 20th Century International History: Explorations and Examples* (2017), and *Cold War: An International History* (2nd ed. 2017). Two of her books, *Defending the Rights of Others: The Great Powers, the Jews, and International Minority Protection 1878–1938* (2004), and *The Genoa Conference, 1921–1922* (1984) were awarded the American Historical Association's George Louis Beer prize; and her *Marc Bloch: A Life in History* (1989) has been translated into six languages. She has taught European international history for more than four decades at universities in the United States, Europe, and Israel.

Notes

1. Israel Zangwill, "The War and the Jews," *New York Times Current History,* 1 September 1915, pp. 1155–59, quotation p. 1156.
2. Useful general works include Abraham Duker, *Jews in the World War: A Brief Historical Sketch* (New York: American Jewish Committee, 1939); Zosa Szajkowski, *Jews, Wars, and Communism* (New York: Ktav, 1972); Jonathan Frankel, "The Paradoxical Politics of Marginality: Thoughts on the Jewish Situation during the Years 1914–21," in *The Jews and the European Crisis* (New York and Oxford: Oxford University Press, 1988), pp. 3–21; Jacob Katz, "World War I: A Crossroads in the History of European Jewry," *Yad Vashem Studies* 27 (1999): 11–21; David Vital, *A People Apart: The Jews in Europe, 1789–1939* (New York: Oxford University Press, 1999).
3. Oscar Janowsky, *The Jews and Minority Rights (1898–1919)* (New York: Columbia University Press, 1933); Mark Levene, *War, Jews, and the New Europe: The Diplomacy of Lucien Wolf, 1914–1919* (Oxford and New York: Oxford University Press, 1992); Isaiah Friedman, *The Question of Palestine, 1914–1918: British-Jewish-Arab Relations* (New Brunswick, NJ: Transaction, 1992); Carole Fink, *Defending the Rights of Others: The Great Powers, the Jews, and International Minority Protection, 1878–1938* (Cambridge: Cambridge University Press, 2004).

4. See esp. Abigail Green, "The Limits of Intervention: Coercive Diplomacy and the Jewish Question in the Nineteenth Century," *International History Review* 36, no. 3 (June 2014): 473–92; also Immanuel Geiss, "Die jüdische Frage auf dem Berliner Kongress 1878," *Jahrbuch des Instituts für Deutsche Geschichte 10* (1981): 413–22.
5. Fink, *Defending the Rights of Others*, pp. 34–45.
6. Ibid., pp. 45–57.
7. Wolf to Sir Henry Primrose, August 7, 1914, CJH [Center for Jewish History], YIVO Archive [YIVO], Mowschowitch Collection, 3440.
8. Walther Rathenau, "Zur Lage," *Berliner Tageblatt*, 31 July 1914; Theodor Wolff, Diary Entry 25–26 July 1914, in *Tagebücher, 1914–1919* (Boppard am Rhein: Harald Boldt Verlag, 1984), p. 51; Adolf Gasser, "Theodor Wolff zum Kriegsausbruch 1914," *Schweizerische Zeitschrift für Geschichte* 35, no. 1 (1985): 47–53.
9. Heinz-Dietrich Löwe, "Government Policies and the Tradition of Russian Antisemitism, 1772–1917," *Patterns of Prejudice* 27, no. 1 (March 1993): 58–63.
10. "Neutrality and the War," *Jewish Chronicle*, 31 July 1914.
11. Victor Basch, *La Guerre et 1914 et le droit* (Paris: Marcel Rivière, 1915); also Bernard Ludwig, "Victor Basch et l'Allemagne," *Revue d'Allemagne et des Pays de Langue Allemande* 36, no. 3–4 (2004): 343–46.
12. Susan Viborg, "Erster Weltkrieg: Albert Ballin," *Die Zeit*, 29 July 2014, http://www.zeit.de/2014/08/erster-weltkrieg-albert-ballin-warburg (accessed 9 September 2015); also Alfred Vagts, "The Golden Chains: The Jew and Wilhelminic Imperialism," *Maryland Historian* 4, no. 1 (June 1973): 47–58.
13. David Aberbach, "Zionist Patriotism in Europe, 1897–1942: Ambiguities in Jewish Nationalism," *International History Review* 31, no. 2 (June 2009): 286–93; Jay Ticker, "Max Bodenheimer, Advocate of Pro-German Zionism at the Beginning of World War I," *Jewish Social Studies* 43, no. 1 (Winter 1981): 11–30; David Vital, *Zionism: The Crucial Phase* (Oxford: Clarendon Press, 1987).
14. "Jews and the War," *Jewish Chronicle*, 7 August 1914.
15. Ernest Jones, *Sigmund Freud: Life and Work* (New York: Basic Books, 1953–57), vol. 2, p. 172; also Peter Gay, "Freud et la guerre," *Vingtième Siècle* 41 (January–March 1994): 86–92.
16. Stefan Zweig, "Ein Wort von Deutschland," *Neue Freie Presse*, 6 August 1914; Zweig, "Die Schlaflose Welt," *Neue Freie Presse*, 18 August 1914; Zweig, "An die Freunde im Fremdländer," *Berliner Tageblatt*, 19 September 1914.
17. Jürgen Ungern-Sternberg and Wolfgang Ungern-Sternberg, *Der Aufruf an die Kulturwelt: das Manifest der 93 und die Anfänge der Kriegspropaganda im Ersten Weltkrieg* (Stuttgart: F. Steiner, 1996); Marie-Eve Chagnon, "Le Manifeste des 93: La mobilisation des académies françaises et allemandes au déclenchement de la Première Guerre mondiale (1914–1915)," *French Historical Studies* 35, no. 1 (Winter 2012): 123–47.
18. Philippe Landau, *Les Juifs de France et la Grande Guerre* (Paris: CNRS, 1999).
19. Jost Hermand, *Engagement als Lebensform: über Arnold Zweig* (Berlin: Sigma, 1992), pp. 25–36; also *Arnold Zweig: 1867: Werk und Leben in Dokumenten und Bildern*, ed. Georg Wenzel (Berlin: Aufbau-Verlag, 1978), pp. 62–63.
20. C. C. Aronsfeld, "Ernst Lissauer and the Hymn of Hate," *History Today* 37, no. 2 (December 1987): 48–51; Elisabeth Albanis, "Ostracised for Loyalty: Ernst Lissauer's Propaganda Writing and Its Reception," *Leo Baeck Institute Year Book* 43 (1998): 195–224. The translation of Lissauer's fiery message backfired, drawing pointed criticism from the neutral press and creating a propaganda field day for British bands and cartoonists.

21. Julius Schoeps, "Kriegsbegeisterung und Ernüchterung: Über das Selbstverständnis und die Befindlichkeiten deutscher Juden im Ersten Weltkrieg und danach," *Zeitschrift für Religionsgeschichte* 66, no. 1 (2014): 76–89; Ulrich Sieg, *Jüdische Intellektuelle im Ersten Weltkrieg* (Berlin: Akademie Verlag, 2001); Philippe-Efraïm Landau, "Juifs Français et Allemands dans la Grande Guerre," *Vingtième Siècle* 47 (July–September 1995): 70–76.
22. Stefan Vogt, "The First World War, German Nationalism, and the Transformation of German Zionism," *Leo Baeck Institute Year Book* 57, no. 1 (January 2012): 267–91; Vogt, "Zionismus und Weltpolitik: Die Auseinandersetzung der deutschen Zionisten mit dem deutschen Imperialismus und Kolonialismus 1890–1918," *Zeitschrift für Geschichtswissenschaft* 60, no. 7/8 (2012): 596–617.
23. Rivka Horwitz, "Voices of Opposition to the First World War among Jewish Thinkers," *Leo Baeck Institute Year Book* 33, no. 1 (1988): 233–59; also Evelyn Wilcock, *Pacifism and the Jews* (Stroud, Gloustershire: Hawthorn Press, 1994), pp. 1–57; "Pazifismus im Weltkrieg," in Marcus Patka, *Weltuntergang: Jüdisches Leben und Sterben im Ersten Weltkrieg* (Vienna: Jüdisches Museums, 2014), pp. 194–97.
24. Afterward Jacobs carried her peace message to the capitals of Europe and even traveled to the United States in an unsuccessful effort to secure Woodrow Wilson's support for her peace efforts. On Jewish antiwar figures: Hubert Goenner and Giuseppe Castagnetti, "Albert Einstein as Pacifist and Democrat in World War I," *Science in Context* 9, no. 4 (December 1996): 325–86; Daniel Laqua, "Pacifism in Fin-de-Siècle Austria," *Historical Journal* 57, no. 1 (March 2014): 199–224; Jay Howard Geller, "The Scholem Brothers and the Path of German Jewry, 1914–1939," *Shofar* 30, no. 2 (Winter 2012): 52–73; Sandi Cooper, "Women and the World Order," *Women's Studies Quarterly* 27, nos. 1–2 (Spring–Summer 1999): 99–105; Eckhard Müller, "Zum Kampf der revolutionären Antikriegsbewegung in Deutschland während des Ersten Weltkrieges," *Militärgeschichte* 24, no. 4 (1985): 303–14; Paul Breines, "The Jew as Revolutionary: The Case of Gustav Landauer," *Leo Baeck Institute Year Book* 12 (1967): 75–84.
25. Egmont Zechlin, *Die deutsche Politik und die Juden im Ersten Weltkrieg* (Göttingen: Vandenhoeck und Ruprecht 1969); Steven Aschheim, "Eastern Jews, German Jews and Germany's Ostpolitik in the First World War," *Leo Baeck Institute Year Book* 28 (1983): 351–66; Pam Maclean, "Control and Cleanliness: German-Jewish Relations in Occupied Eastern Europe during the First World War," *War and Society* 6, no. 2 (October 1988): 47–69; Jürgen Matthäus, "German 'Judenpolitik' in Lithuania during the First World War," *Leo Baeck Institute Year Book* 43 (1998): 155–74; Rebekah Klein-Pejšová, "Beyond the 'Infamous Concentration Camps of the Old Monarchy': Jewish Refugee Policy from Wartime Austria-Hungary to Interwar Czechoslovakia," *Austrian History Yearbook* 45 (2014): 150–66.
26. Mehmet Yerçil, "The Passion of Max von Oppenheim: Archaeology and Intrigue in the Middle East from Wilhelm II to Hitler," *German History* 32, no. 1 (March 2014): 149–52; Wolfgang Schwanitz, "Max von Oppenheim und der Heilige Krieg: Zwei Denkschriften zur Revolutionierung islamischer Gebiete 1914 und 1940," *Sozial.Geschichte: Zeitschrift für Historische Analyse des 20. und 21. Jahrhunderts* 19, no. 3 (October 2004): 28–59.
27. Robert Tarek Fischer, "Ballhausplatz und Davidstern: Die k. u. k. Diplomatie und die Österreichisch-Ungarischen Juden Palästinas in der Krisenzeit des Ersten Weltkrieges, 1914–1918," *Mitteilungen des Österreichischen Staatsarchivs* 50 (2003): 301–36; Hans-

jörg Eiff, "Die jüdische Heimstätte in Palästina und der deutschen Aussenpolitik, 1914–1918," *Zeitschrift für Geschichtswissenschaft* 60, no. 3 (2012): 205—7.
28. Sam Johnson, "Breaking or Making the Silence? British Jews and East European Jewish Relief, 1914-1917," *Modern Judaism* 30, no. 1 (February 2010): 95–100; also Elkan Levy, "Antisemitism in England at War, 1914–16," *Patterns of Prejudice* 4, no. 5 (September 1970): 27–30; David Ceserani, "An Embattled Minority: The Jews in Britain during the First World War," *Immigrants & Minorities* 8, no. 1–2 (March 1989): 61–82.
29. *American Jewish Year Book* 17 (1915–16): 244–49; *New York Times*, 17 September 1915; also C. C. Aronsfeld, "Jewish Bankers and the Tsar," *Jewish Social Studies* 35, no. 2 (April 1973): 103–4; Eric Lohr, "The Russian Army and the Jews: Mass Deportation, Hostages, and Violence during World War I," *Russian Review* 60, no. 3 (July 2001): 404–19.
30. Chimen Abramsky, "Lucien Wolf's Efforts for the Jewish Communities in Central and Eastern Europe," *Jewish Historical Studies* 29 (1982): 281–86; cf. Mark Levene, "Lucien Wolf: Crypto-Zionist, Anti-Zionist or Opportunist 'Par-Excellence'?," *Studies in Zionism* 12, no. 2 (1991): 133–48.
31. Arthur Marwick, "War and the Arts," *War and Society* 2, no. 1 (January 1995): 65–86. Repudiation of initial war enthusiasm: Anthony Sampson, "Freud on the State, Violence, and War," *Diacritics* 35, no. 3 (Fall 2005): 78–91; Adi Gordon, "Against *Vox Populi*—Arnold Zweig's Struggle with Political Passions," *Tel Aviver Jahrbuch für Deutsche Geschichte* 38 (2010): 131–45; Emmanuel Naquet [on Basch], "Entre justice et patrie: la Ligue des droits de l'homme et la Grande Guerre," *Le Mouvement Social* 183 (April–June 1998): 93–109; Rüdiger Görner, "The Drama of Prophesy: On Stefan Zweig and 'Jeremiah,'" *Jewish Quarterly* 58, no. 1 (2011): 44–46.
32. Examples of wartime antisemitism: Elkan Levy, "Antisemitism in England at War, 1914–16," *Patterns of Prejudice* 4, no. 5 (September 1970): 27–30; Julia Bush, "East London Jews and the First World War," *London Journal* 6, no. 2 (December 1980): 147–61; Laurent Joly, "D'une guerre à l'autre: L'Action française et les Juifs, de l'Union sacrée à la Revolution nationale (1914–1944)," *Revue d'Histoire Moderne & Contemporaine* 59, no. 4 (October–December 2012): 97–124; Stéphane Letouré, "Le compositeur Camille Saint-Saëns face à l'accusation d'être juif: Itinéraire d'une rumeur," *Revue des Etudes Juives* 172, nos. 3–4 (July–December 2013): 371–82; Wolfram Wette, "Reichstag und 'Kriegsgewinnlerei' (1916–18)," *Militärgeschichtliche Zeitschrift* 2 (1984): 31–56; Patrick Dassen, "De joden als de interne vijand: De groei van het antisemitisme in Duitsland tijdens de Eerste Wereldoorlog" [The Jews as the Internal Enemy: The Growth of Antisemitism in Germany during the First World War] *Leidschrift Historisch Tijdschrift* 29, no. 1 (2014): 23–41. On the Reich's notorious Jewish Census: Werner Angress, "The German Army's 'Judenzählung' of 1916: Genesis—Consequences—Significance," *Leo Baeck Institute Year Book* 23 (1978): 117–37.
33. Fink, *Defending the Rights of Others*, pp. 78–79.
34. Chiara Tessaris, "The War Relief Work of the American Jewish Joint Distribution Committee in Poland and Lithuania, 1915–18," *East European Jewish Affairs* 40, no. 2 (August 2010): 127–44; Jaclyn Granick, "Waging Relief: The Politics and Logistics of American Jewish War Relief in Europe and the Near East 1914–1918," *First World War Studies* 5, no. 1 (January 2014): 55–68.
35. Cecil Bloom, "Colonel Patterson: Soldier and Zionist," *Jewish Historical Studies* 31 (1988): 231–48.

36. Eliezer Tauber, "The Capture of the NILI Spies," *Intelligence and National Security* 6, no. 4 (1991): 701–10.
37. Jehuda Reinharz, "Chaim Weizmann: Statesman Without a State," *Modern Judaism* 12, no. 3 (October 1992): 225–42; Devorah Barzilay-Yegar, "Crisis as Turning Point: Chaim Weizmann in World War I," *Studies in Zionism* 6 (1982): 241–54; James Edward Renton, "The Historiography of the Balfour Declaration: Toward a Multi-Causal Framework," *Journal of Israeli History* 19, no. 2 (September 1998): 109–28; William M. Mathew, "The Balfour Declaration and the Palestine Mandate, 1917–1923: British Imperialist Imperatives," *British Journal of Middle Eastern Studies* 40, no. 3 (July 2013): 231–50.
38. Fink, *Defending the Rights of Others*, pp. 88–89.
39. Chimen Abramsky, *War, Revolution, and the Jewish Dilemma* (London: H. K. Lewis, 1975), pp. 24–26.
40. Fink, *Defending the Rights of Others*, pp. 90–96.
41. Borislav Chernev, "The Brest-Litovsk Moment: Self Determination Discourse in Eastern Europe before Wilsonianism," *Diplomacy and Statecraft* 22, no. 3 (September 2011): 369–87.
42. Fink, *Defending the Rights of Others*, pp. 96–98.
43. Ibid., pp. 98–100.
44. Alan Sharp, *The Versailles Settlement: Peacemaking in Paris 1919* (Basingstoke: Macmillan, 1991); Sharp, *Consequences of Peace: The Versailles Settlement Aftermath and Legacy, 1919–2010* (London: Haus, 2010); Erik Goldstein, *The First World War Peace Settlements, 1919–1925* (New York: Longman, 2002); Margaret Macmillan, *Paris 1919: Six Months That Changed the World* (New York: Random House, 2002).
45. Older works: Janowsky, *The Jews and Minority Rights*; Erwin Viefhaus, *Die Minderheitenfrage und die Entstehung der Minderheitenschutzverträge 1919* (Würzburg: Holzner, 1960). More recent studies: Mark Levene, "Nationalism and Its Alternatives in the International Arena: The Jewish Question at Paris, 1919," *Journal of Contemporary History* 28, no. 3 (July 1993): 511–32; Tatjana Lichtenstein, "Jewish Power and Powerlessness: Prague Zionists and the Paris Peace Conference," *East European Jewish Affairs* 44, no. 1 (April 2014): 2–20.
46. Fink, *Defending the Rights of Others*, pp. 133–51.
47. Wolf Diary, 18, 21, 28 February, 1, 3 March 1919, Mocatta Library, University of London.
48. Derek Heater, "Woodrow Wilson and National Self Determination," *Modern History Review* 7, no. 3 (February 1996): 6–8; M. B. Biskupski, "Re-creating Central Europe: The United States 'Inquiry' into the Future of Poland in 1918," *International History Review* 12, no. 2 (June 1990): 249–79; Liliana Riga and James Kennedy, "Mitteleuropa as Middle America? 'The Inquiry' and the Mapping of East Central Europe in 1919," *Ab Imperio* 4 (2006): 271–300.
49. Tomis Kapitan, "Self Determination and International Order," *Monist* 89, no. 2 (April 2006): 356–70.
50. Minutes of the meeting of the Comité des Delegations Juives auprès de la Conférence de la Paix, 31 March 1919, Central Zionist Archives, Jerusalem, A405/77/IB.
51. Stephen Bonsal, *Suitors and Suppliants: The Little Nations at Versailles* (New York: Prentice Hall, 1946).
52. *Foreign Relations of the United States: The Paris Peace Conference* [hereafter FRUS PPC] 3: 795–96.

53. Carole Fink, "The Palestine Question at the Paris Peace Conference," in *Peacemaking, Peacemakers, and Diplomacy, 1880–1939: Essays in Honour of Professor Alan Sharp*, ed. Gaynor Johnson (Newcastle upon Tyne: Cambridge Scholars, 2010), p. 122.
54. Ibid., pp. 122–23.
55. Ibid., p. 123.
56. Ibid. Also Evyatar Friesel, "Baron Edmond de Rothschild and the Zionists, 1918–1919," *Zion* 38, no. 1/4 (1973): 116–36.
57. FRUS PPC 3: 1015–18.
58. FRUS PPC 4: 169–70; Vital, *Zionism*, pp. 350–57.
59. FRUS PPC 5: 1–14.
60. A. Walworth, *Wilson and His Peacemakers: American Diplomacy at the Paris Peace Conference, 1919* (New York: Norton, 1978), pp. 481–83.
61. Dietrich Geyer, "Wilson und Lenin: Ideologie und Friedenssicherung in Ost-Europa, 1917–1919," *Jahrbücher für Geschichte Osteuropas* 3, no. 4 (1955): 430–41.
62. A. Lilienthal, *The Zionist Connection: What Price Peace?* (New York: Dodd Mead, 1978).
63. "The King Crane Commission of 1919: The Articulation of Political Anti-Zionism," *American Jewish Archives* 29, no. 1 (January 1977): 22–52; cf. Harry N. Howard, *The King Crane Commission: An American Inquiry in the Middle East* (Beirut: Khayats, 1963); James Gelvin, "The Ironic Legacy of the King-Crane Commission," in *The Middle East and the United States: An Historical Assessment*, ed. David W. Lesch (Boulder, CO: Westview Press, 1996), pp. 13–29.
64. Fink, "Palestine Question," pp. 127–30.
65. Ibid.; Vital, *Zionism*, pp. 366–76.
66. FRUS PPC 3: 852. Critique: F. S. Marston, *The Peace Conference of 1919: Organisation and Procedure* (Oxford: Oxford University Press, 1944), pp. 54–68.
67. Fink, *Defending the Rights of Others*, pp. 148–49, 150–51.
68. Ibid., pp. 149–50.
69. On the damaging failure in the League Commission, ibid., pp. 152–60; Wolf Diary, 26 February, 18 April 1919.
70. Jerzy Tomaszewski, "Pińsk, 5 April 1919," *Polin* 1 (1986): 227--51; Fink, *Defending the Rights of Others*, pp. 173–86.
71. Fink, *Defending the Rights of Others*, pp. 196–97; Wolf [the Comité's foremost opponent], Diary, 24 March 1919.
72. Janowsky, *Jews and Minority Rights*, p. 319.
73. Marshall to House, Paris, 15 April 1919, American Jewish Archives, Louis Marshall Papers 52 (written on Comité letterhead); David Hunter Miller, *My Diary at the Conference of Paris* (New York: Appeal, 1924), 1: Entries 19, 20, 30 April 1919, Memorandum, 25 April 1919; Miller to House, 29 April 1919, House to Wilson, 29 April 1919, House Papers Yale University 81/2721, 121a/4298; Marshall to his children, 28 April 1919, American Jewish Archives, Louis Marshall Papers 82 ("We are staking all on one card—a rather risky proceeding; but then what is one to do when there are no others?").
74. Fink, *Defending the Rights of Others*, pp. 211–17.
75. Ibid., pp. 217–24.
76. Meeting with Wilson, 26 May 1919, Louis Marshall Papers 131, American Jewish Archives; Secret 31 May plenary, FRUS PPC 3: 397–410.
77. Fink, *Defending the Rights of Others*, pp. 243–57.
78. Full text in FRUS PPC 13: 791–808.

Selected Bibliography

Primary Sources

Abramson, Glenda, ed. *Hebrew Writing of the First World War.* London and Portland, OR: Valentine Mitchell, 2008.

Appelbaum, Peter, trans. *German Jewish Poetry of the First World War.* http://www.firstworldwar.warpoetry.co.uk/germanjewishpoetsbios.html.

Foreign Relations of the United States: The Paris Peace Conference. Washington, DC: Government Printing Office, 1942–47.

Louis Marshall Papers, American Jewish Archives, Cincinnati, OH.

Lucien Wolf / David Mowschowitz Papers, YIVO Institute for Jewish Research, Center for Jewish History, New York, NY.

Lucien Wolf Diary, Mocatta Library, University of London.

Miller, David Hunter. *My Diary at the Conference of Paris.* New York: Appeal, 1924.

Wolff, Theodor. *Tagebücher, 1914–1919.* Boppard am Rhein: Harald Boldt Verlag, 1984.

Secondary Sources

Abramsky, Chimen. *War, Revolution, and the Jewish Dilemma.* London: H. K. Lewis, 1975.

Angress, Werner. "The German Army's 'Judenzählung' of 1916: Genesis—Consequences—Significance," *Leo Baeck Institute Year Book* 23 (1978): 117–37.

Cesarani, David. "An Embattled Minority: The Jews in Britain during the First World War." *Immigrants & Minorities* 8, nos. 1–2 (March 1989): 61–82.

Duker, Abraham. *Jews in the World War: A Brief Historical Sketch.* New York: American Jewish Committee, 1939.

Eiff, Hansjörg. "Die jüdische Heimstätte in Palästina und der deutschen Aussenpolitik, 1914–1918." *Zeitschrift für Geschichtswissenschaft* 60, no. 3 (2012): 205–27.

Fink, Carole. *Defending the Rights of Others: The Great Powers, the Jews, and International Minority Protection, 1878–1938.* Cambridge: Cambridge University Press, 2004.

Frankel, Jonathan. "The Paradoxical Politics of Marginality: Thoughts on the Jewish Situation during the Years 1914–21." *Studies in Contemporary Jewry* 4 (1988): 3–21.

Friedman, Isaiah. *The Question of Palestine, 1914–1918: British-Jewish-Arab Relations.* New Brunswick, NJ: Transaction, 1992.

Granick, Jaclyn. "Waging Relief: The Politics and Logistics of American Jewish War Relief in Europe and the Near East 1914–1918." *First World War Studies* 5, no. 1 (January 2014): 55–68.

Janowsky, Oscar. *The Jews and Minority Rights (1898–1919).* New York: Columbia University Press, 1933.

Katz, Jacob. "World War I: A Crossroads in the History of European Jewry." *Yad Vashem Studies* 27 (1999): 11–21.

Landau, Philippe. *Les Juifs de France et la Grande Guerre.* Paris: CNRS, 1999.

Levene, Mark. *War, Jews, and the New Europe: The Diplomacy of Lucien Wolf, 1914–1919.* Oxford and New York: Oxford University Press, 1992.

Lohr, Eric. "The Russian Army and the Jews: Mass Deportation, Hostages, and Violence during World War I." *Russian Review* 60, no. 3 (July 2001): 404–19.

Mathew, William M. "The Balfour Declaration and the Palestine Mandate, 1917–1923: British Imperialist Imperatives." *British Journal of Middle Eastern Studies* 40, no. 3 (July 2013): 231–50.

Patka, Marcus G. *Weltuntergang: Jüdisches Leben und Sterben im Ersten Weltkrieg.* Vienna: Jüdisches Museums, 2014.
Sharp, Alan. *Consequences of Peace: The Versailles Settlement Aftermath and Legacy, 1919–2010.* London: Haus, 2010.
Sieg, Ulrich. *Jüdische Intellektuelle im Ersten Weltkrieg.* Berlin: Akademie Verlag, 2001.
Szajkowski, Zosa. *Jews, Wars, and Communism.* New York: Ktav, 1972.
Vital, David. *A People Apart: The Jews in Europe, 1789–1939.* New York: Oxford University Press, 1999.
———. *Zionism: The Crucial Phase.* Oxford: Clarendon Press, 1987.
Wilcock, Evelyn. *Pacifism and the Jews.* Stroud, Gloustershire: Hawthorn Press, 1994.
Zechlin, Egmont. *Die deutsche Politik und die Juden im Ersten Weltkrieg.* Göttingen: Vandenhoeck und Ruprecht, 1969.

Part II

Local Studies

CHAPTER 4

Bravery in the Borderlands, Martyrs on the Margins

Jewish War Heroes and World War I Narratives in France, 1914–1940

Erin Corber

The most striking image of World War I, the battlefield cemetery, is a ubiquitous feature of the northeastern French landscape. Endless rows of uniform white crosses dot the former battlefields of the Western Front, leaving deep impressions of the human and environmental ravages of a brutal war. Replicated in military sites and commemorative spaces around the world, these spectacular and somber vistas are synonymous with World War I, a conflict that caused unprecedented casualties, and for France, on home soil. On the former bloody battlefields of Verdun, the Douaumont Ossuary (1932) was designed to create order out of chaos, a place of worship and contemplation, a "reliquary of the nation, an august temple to the war dead."[1] Others, like the Thiepval Memorial (1928–32), employed abstract modernist forms to commemorate the deaths of thousands of French and Commonwealth soldiers at the Battle of the Somme. Beyond the battlefields, and in a flurry of postwar construction, villages, towns, and communes raised funds, held design contests, and built thousands of local memorials to their own men who had bravely sacrificed their lives for the French Republic.[2] In spite of their "variety of sameness," commemorative and monumental art told different stories about France's experience and memory of the war.[3]

The French combat soldier, the scruffy blue-clad *poilu,* reigned supreme over all symbols. During the interwar period, the generic *poilu* was used to tell different kinds of war stories on battlefields, on public squares, and in cemeteries across the nation: victory, sacrifice, brotherhood, patriotism, defeat, and courage. The collective unity of French sacrifice was also expressed in the body of the unknown soldier, buried in 1920 underneath the Arc de Triomphe in Paris, a gesture that enabled the state "to overcome party lines and ... cultural divides to give discontented, traumatized populations an outlet for grief."[4] However, the *poilu* stands apart from other symbols because it not only operated as a static framing device for mourning and remembrance after the war, but was also a living embodiment of the nation during the war, through four years of carnage on home and battle fronts, in state propaganda, and in popular culture.

Shifting the discussion from postwar commemoration to a broader one about the concept of a "war hero" allows us to rethink the periodization from two distinct periods of war and postwar to a more nuanced transwar era, encompassing World War I and its aftermath (1914–40). Indeed, commemoration and mourning did not simply begin after the armistice. More than stand as a martyr in its aftermath, the life and death of the combat soldier personified patriotism during the uncertain and seemingly unending years of war. He sacrificed his life to protect France's mothers, wives, and children, to vanquish the *Boche* enemy, and to return Alsace-Lorraine to *la patrie*. A 1918 collection of tales of war heroism reveal a simple formula for this universal war hero: a hero was a young man who put on a uniform and served bravely alongside others in uniform, stood fast under fire, was wounded while defending the nation, and died tragically on the battlefield. The hero was everyman, every *poilu,* and every son of the republic.[5]

Pliable and relatable, the image of the combat soldier was used by right-wing anti-parliamentary nationalists, Republicans and Radicals, Catholic Ultramontanists, and even Socialist pacifists for a variety of purposes. He transcended political, religious, and social divides, representing the nation at large. Soldiers and civilians wrote and sang songs and poets wrote verse about these ragged heroes.[6] *Poilus* populated postcards, consumer advertising, state and community propaganda, and other media and material culture throughout the war, as well as in its aftermath.

Yet within this cultural lexicon of universalism—what Antoine Prost calls the "civil religion of France" or the "republican cult of the war dead"— there were some exceptions.[7] For instance, while the image of the colonial soldier was often employed in wartime propaganda to "affirm ... French imperial rule," racial ideas still informed military, political, and public understandings of nonwhite war experiences as fundamentally different from those of white metropolitan troops.[8] This phenomenon is only one part of a much longer history and larger critique of the Republican Empire.

This chapter addresses two striking exceptions that challenge the image of a universalist French commemorative culture during this trans-war period. These curious monuments built in the interwar period reified these two marginal individuals as vital examples of the soul of France in various ways, and by diverse groups of people, for interesting reasons. The first is a granite stele on the battlefield of Taintrux, inaugurated in 1934, and the second, a statue erected in 1922 in a quiet wood in the small Alsatian town of Guebwiller.[9] These monuments recall war heroes, neither of them *poilus*. Nevertheless their unique stories were told and retold in diverse settings during and after the war and captured the imagination of Frenchmen nationwide. These men occupied geographic and imaginary borderlands: the colonial imaginary space of French Algeria, and the Franco-German borderlands of Alsace-Lorraine. Finally, and significantly, these two monuments are dedicated to war heroes who were also Jews.

This essay interrogates a curious disconnect between two observations I will make about these cases. On the one hand, the trans-war commemorative culture of collective sacrifice and universal heroism was largely built around the figure of the martyred French combat soldier. The *poilu* reinforced solidarity and patriotism on the home front during the war, and he embodied a collective national culture of mourning and reconstruction in the tumult of its aftermath.[10] On the other hand, the case studies of David Bloch of Guebwiller and Grand Rabbi of Lyon and former Grand Rabbi of Algiers Abraham Bloch (no relation) suggest that Jewish war heroes performed a variety of important cultural and political functions for Jews and other Frenchmen during the war and in its aftermath. That their stories became heroic tales demonstrates how these two men—liminal as Jews, noncombatants, and representatives of geographic and imaginary borderlands—were particularly useful "tools" with which both Jews and other Frenchmen could attempt to reconcile universalist republican war memory with diverse particular experiences and meanings of sacrifice, trauma, and national identity.

Jews were both outsiders and insiders in French society.[11] The first to be emancipated in Europe, France's Jews were also consistent targets of right-wing nationalist and conservative movements throughout the nineteenth century who understood the "Jewish Question," in its many forms, to encompass the problems of modern society.[12] In spite of the outbreak of virulent and often violent antisemitism around the turn of the century, during the war, Jews were declared a fundamental part of the Sacred Union of French peoples and a member of the "diverse spiritual families of France."[13] While the image of brave colonial servicemen might have encouraged national independence movements and threatened the stability of state and empire, a French Jewish war hero could safely represent the two contradictory values of unity and diversity, of universalism and peculiarity. These Jewish war heroes' noncombatant status highlighted the diversity of contributions made on the battlefield and on the home front. Finally, David Bloch and Rabbi Abraham Bloch were geographically liminal. They embodied complex French borderlands: Alsace-Lorraine, the Franco-German lands at the heart of territorial conflict between France and Germany, and the overseas territory of Algeria, administratively a French department, but in practice part of a large network of colonial spaces deeply invested in the work of war.

Remarkably, these Jewish war heroes were celebrated not only by their coreligionists. They also incarnated alternate archetypes of heroism for non-Jewish Frenchmen and challenged a singular republican model of universal martyrdom.[14] It was not only in the quality and content of their military service, but also in the kind of commemorative culture that was created by Jews, and that employed Jews, that European Jewry's World War I stories merit further investigation. In the case of France, celebrating Jewish war heroes was not only a way for Jews to protect themselves from antisemitic accusations of cosmopolitanism and cowardice. The phenomenon of a public civic commemoration of Jewish war heroes also suggests peculiar functions the image of the Jew could perform for non-Jewish Frenchmen. In the trans-war years, French Jews were, to borrow Ronald Schechter's observation about the Jews in the eighteenth century, "good to think" with about France's war experience beyond the universalist republican categories offered by the generic heroic narrative of the *poilu*.[15]

Man of Spirit and Man of Action: A Rabbi on the Battlefield

In summer 1914, fifty-year-old Grand Rabbi of Lyon Abraham Bloch voluntarily enlisted in the French armed forces as a chaplain. Many years of living in North Africa serving as Grand Rabbi of Algiers had taken a toll on his physical health, but in letters home from basic training, he reassured his wife that outdoor living invigorated him. In late August, he put on his military chaplain uniform—long black robes identical to those of the army's Catholic and Protestant chaplains—and set off eastward with the Fourteenth Army Corps for what would later be known as the Battle of the Marne.[16]

On Saturday, 29 August 1914, the chaplain was killed and a hero was born. In the village of Taintrux near Saint Dié, hundreds of French soldiers were killed in a German ambush. A single witness to the event, the

Catholic chaplain Father Jamin, wrote a letter to Bloch's family on 11 September:

> The Germans were leveling a farm, where 150 wounded men were being treated, with shells ... the makeshift military hospital had to be evacuated under a storm of gunfire ... a wounded man mistook the rabbi for a Catholic priest ... without hesitation and with no concern for personal danger, the rabbi went to find a crucifix to bring to the soldier ... symbol of his faith. After completing this act of charity, the rabbi left the farm house with another wounded man, helping him to the closest ambulance, and was hit by a shell only a few metres away.[17]

The French Jewish press immediately painted Rabbi Bloch as the Jewish community's first war hero. Two weeks later, the liberal *Archives Israélites* published the sermon from the memorial service at the Synagogue de la Victoire in Paris.[18] While the sermon quoted parts of Jamin's letter verbatim, it left out Bloch's final act—his blessing of the Catholic soldier. The Grand Rabbi of Paris declared Rabbi Bloch a hero *for* Jews because he was a patriot who voluntarily gave his life to the French nation.

In the early weeks of war, the first death of a Jewish cleric was a powerful symbol for Jewish investment in the war effort and of the harmony between Judaism and patriotism. "Most of the French rabbinate is nobly serving under French flags," the Grand Rabbi of Paris reminded his audience during Bloch's memorial, "and we must not cry, because our dear

Figure 4.1. *French postcard depicting the death of Rabbi Abraham Bloch, who, upon offering a crucifix to a wounded Catholic, fell under shellfire in 1914.*

Bloch's death is one of the most glorious deaths that one can dream for."[19] In the omission of this gesture of interfaith camaraderie and humanity, it was Bloch's death *as a Jew*—rather than any specific act or comportment—that was emphasized. In this light, every man of Jewish faith could and should be a hero. "This victim's name will never die, he will stand as a saintly halo of his family, of the rabbinate, and of French Jews and Judaism. He will serve to future generations as an example of a French Jew, who, pushed by his conscience and duty, put patriotism above all other virtues, confirming the beautiful motto of the synagogue, 'Homeland and Religion.'"[20]

The reification of Rabbi Bloch's death in these early weeks can be contextualized within a moment of uncertainty within the French Jewish religious establishment. Clergymen had great practical importance, particularly in the first hours of mobilization. In autumn 1914, editorials in the Jewish press declared the need for greater clerical presence in the armed forces to protect Jews against the proselytizing zeal of their Christian counterparts.[21] While this purported danger was likely exaggerated, before the war France's Jews had theoretically been protected by the stability of the established communities within the republican consistorial system, a hallmark of French Judaism. Upon general mobilization, the Central Consistory panicked at the immediate integration of France's Jewish minority into units largely populated by Christian soldiers and clergy—an anxiety that highlights Pierre Birnbaum's argument that the substructures of French national identity were more Christian than the republican mold had made evident.[22]

This initial panic reminds us of both the perceived and real significance of the established religious community and the rabbinate during the war. Most notable was the Central Consistory's mindfulness of the diversity of its field of work and, in particular, of the peculiar needs of diverse Jews in the armed forces. Rabbis were in particularly high demand as chaplains in military units with large numbers of Algerian Jewish servicemen, who were seen by the Jewish community as typically more religious and observant than metropolitan Jews. Chaplains were hailed as providers of spiritual and moral support for these observant troops who were far from their homes.[23] Rabbis' social duties expanded too, ranging from visiting wounded soldiers in hospitals, to facilitating communication between servicemen and faraway family members, and even arranging for exhumation of remains from the battlefront for the purposes of Jewish ritual burial, an illegal practice.[24]

There was also important work to be done on the home front. During the war, the Central Consistory endeavored tirelessly to preserve France's Jewish community while simultaneously helping to accommodate and assimilate newly arrived Jewish immigrants from Eastern Europe.[25] Not a generation from the virulent public antisemitism unleashed in the metropole and colonies by the Dreyfus affair, coinciding with a wave of immigration bringing tens of thousands of Eastern European Jews to the republic, many French Jewish activists, philanthropists, and community elite had a vested interest in both of these goals.[26] The Central Consistory undertook and supported numerous charitable initiatives to ease the pains of poverty among newly arrived foreigners in Paris during the deprivation of the war years.[27] Much of the wartime Jewish press emphasized Jewish immigrants' love of the republic and regularly applauded the patriotism and voluntarism of "the immigrant Jews ... mostly Russian and Romanian," who, "from the first day of war," have "paid a grateful tribute to the country that has greeted them with such hospitality."[28]

Not simply a figure of practical importance for those many Jews on home and battlefront, Rabbi Abraham Bloch—a man of both faith and community—conveyed the patriotism of the religious establishment in the early years of the war. His death became a trope for brave religious men, Jewish and non-Jewish, who stepped out of the pulpit and into the line of fire. Among a number of similar examples of Jewish resistance and rabbinic courage, in December 1914, *Archives Israélites* reported on the heroic acts of the octogenarian Alsatian Rabbi Shlomo Bamburger. The elderly Bamburger, donning his prayer shawls and phylacteries, reportedly offered himself to the general commanding the German armies as a hostage in return for the safety of the commune of Cernay.[29]

The drama of an individual display of a rabbi's courage on the home front could not compete with the spectacle of a rabbi in military uniform putting his life in danger among soldiers on a battlefield. Rabbi-soldiers commonly appeared in the French Jewish press. *Archives Israélites* regularly published letters from Grand Rabbi of Besançon Paul Haguenauer, military chaplain with the Seventh Army Corps, offering his observations on French-Jewish soldiers' experiences of war.[30] The French-Jewish press also devoted enormous space to reports on the brave acts of chaplains on the battlefront. On 20 May 1915, *Archives Israélites* printed a story about Haïm Stourdzé, the "rabbi-soldier" who served gallantly alongside his fellow countrymen, refusing to sign documents or carry money on Saturdays.[31] Stourdzé survived the war into the mid-1930s, yet neither he nor any other French rabbi who served in uniform as soldier or chaplain attained Bloch's legendary status.

Bloch's Algerian connection further served the Central Consistory in its attempt to unify and fortify a diverse Jewish community spread over the metropole and its overseas territories. The conservative Jewish newspaper *L'Univers Israélite* made particular note of Bloch's role in antisemitic riots in Algeria before the war, emphasizing his equilibrium under the stresses of violence, his courage to lead his community out from the upheaval, and his "knowledge of men"—all themes used to describe Rabbi Bloch in his final moments at Saint-Dié.[32] Bloch's former domain, the consistorial synagogue in Algiers, was a popular location for patriotic memorial services during which diverse military and civil authorities mixed to commemorate the war dead and "celebrate the successes of our armies."[33] At one memorial service, the Grand Rabbi of Algiers proclaimed that the war dead, who died as "good Catholics, good Protestants, good Muslims, and good Jews," all fell as "good Frenchmen ... they only have one religion: the religion of the flag. It is for this religion, for this flag that they have given their lives ... most nobly ... as the first of our duties, to love and cherish ... to live and die for our nation."[34] Bloch tied the patriots of North Africa to those of the metropole, highlighting the diversity and magnitude of this "religion of the flag."[35]

A Poster Boy for the Sacred Union

As the war raged on and the death toll rose, the established Jewish community effectively recast Rabbi Bloch as a Jewish war hero for all Frenchmen. We see this in the shift of emphasis from the sacrifice of his death to that of his final interfaith gesture of goodwill described in Jamin's testimony. By 1915, even the most religiously conservative elements of the Jewish establishment recognized Bloch's *mitzvah* (righteous deed) to a gentile soldier. During the war, Zionist poet André Spire extolled the virtue of French Jews' union with the French polity and celebrated Jewish-gentile relationships. Three rabbis, he wrote, who served as soldiers or chaplains, including Bloch, were killed, "cementing the union between Jews and Christians, which has shown itself to be largely solid until this point." Spire emphasized Bloch's last deed, patriotic in its humanity. He reproduced Jamin's letter in full, a text originally published in *L'Univers Israélite* in 1915, elevating the bond between Catholics, Protestants, and Jews under fire.[36]

Bloch's sacrifice stood apart from most soldiers' deaths because its particular circumstances fit squarely into a particular vocabulary of wartime discourse. In parliament in 1914, President Raymond Poincaré declared the birth of a "Sacred Union of Peoples," a political construct aimed to quell political and social tensions for the duration of the war.[37] The abstract rhetoric of unity employed different tools to engage the broader public, and Bloch's story helped the Sacred Union make concrete sense to the public as a set of relationships between Jews and Christians. "The hearts of all Frenchmen," the editor of *Archives Israélites* wrote in 1914, "with no distinction of religion or political affiliation, all beat in unison."[38]

This story resonated well beyond the Jewish community and embodied a national strategy to forge interfaith friendships for the war effort.

As a poster boy for the abstract concept of "Sacred Union," Rabbi Bloch's model of the heroic religious patriot captured the imagination of Frenchmen of different political and religious persuasions. Even the most virulent antimilitarists of the socialist *La Guerre Sociale* applauded Catholic priests who were helping Jews in their final moments on the battlefield.[39] After the razing of the Reims Cathedral in late September 1914, the Parisian daily *La Liberté* featured a spectacular commentary on the correspondence between the Grand Rabbi of France and the archbishop of Reims, the manifestation of a "beautiful harmony" of France's diverse faith communities and "a decisive promise to prolong this generous entente" as this "immense battle rages on."[40] Furthermore, beyond his gesture, Bloch's entire life and career were lionized as heroic by the Société Académique de l'Histoire International, who painted Rabbi Bloch as political hero from his first to last breath, including his rabbinic services in Algiers, which proved he was also patriotic in his humanitarianism—not only a man of faith, but also a patriotic liberal.[41]

The most poignant example of Bloch's appeal as a French hero was his inclusion in Maurice Barrès's 1917 bestseller *Les diverses familles spirituelles de la France*. Not a generation earlier, in his 1898 platform for his right-wing National Socialist party (not to be confused with the National Socialist German Workers' Party in Germany), the antisemitic, anti-Dreyfusard polemicist famously declared that Jews, "from formerly persecuted, have become dominators."[42] He changed his tune during the war, devoting an entire chapter to France's national and foreign Jews in his 1917 bestseller. In Barrès's version, Rabbi Bloch died in Father Jamin's arms: "No comment here would add anything to the deep human empathy that inspires an act so full of human tenderness."[43] Fraternity among French men had found its perfect model: "This image will not perish."[44] Whether he was speaking from true conviction or playing into the patriotic propaganda of total war, Barrès was certainly correct. The concord between Jews and Christians was evident in an emerging interfaith commemorative culture of mourning, within which clerical representatives of different faiths were publicly visible in local communal and national memorial events. Memorials such as these were blueprints for civic commemoration through the 1920s and 1930s.[45]

In addition to a variety of postcards and prints produced throughout the war and its aftermath, the interwar period saw the proliferation of Bloch-themed poetry. Written by French men and women and printed in a variety of publications, these works set Rabbi Bloch center stage as a poetic hero, demonstrating the degree to which the story had become assimilated into popular French culture. Henri Martin, a teacher, writer, and member of the Vosgian Legion of the Federal Union of Veterans, composed poetry about Bloch's generous act of humanity, evidence to all of the divine spirit animating the French nation.

> At the foot of a mountain covered with notched evergreen trees
> Under the glare of shells from the first battles
> In stripped fields where shellfire whistles
> One of our troops gravely injured
> Feels himself dying, bloody, holds in his entrails
> With no help, with no hope, as with no funeral
> When along comes a chaplain, only steps away
> He can't absolve him, as he is an *Israélite*
> But great is his nobility in his elite soul.[46]

Outside *ancien-combattant* circles, popular art and culture magazines featured verse on Bloch's heroic tale that shaped the story in interesting ways. In a 1934 issue of *La Revue Moderne Illustrée des Arts et de la Vie*, a poem titled "Humanity" retold the story as a Christian tale of sacrifice, reflecting what Jay Winter has described as a turn back to tradition as a way to come to terms with the losses of the war.[47] In this poem, the rabbi was a Christ figure, demonstrating the story's pervasiveness in diverse popular cultures and the degree to which Rabbi Bloch served as a matrix of meanings for a variety of peoples and interests.[48]

> Resembling a messiah, like Jesus's brother
> For the Second time, a Jew rises to martyrdom
> To save his next man, for the Second time
> A Jew offers his life! A Jew dies on the cross!
> It is in your home—sweet land—that beings such as these exist.[49]

The Rabbi and the Refugee Crisis

Rabbi Bloch's heroism remained relevant amidst the disorder of the interwar years. On the heels of France's pyrrhic victory came another international upheaval, the arrival of thousands of Jewish refugees from collapsed empires in Europe fleeing poor economic conditions, state disorder, and rising antisemitism, seeking asylum in the French Republic, land of equality, liberty, and fraternity. By the mid- to late 1930s, and within a national economy struggling to stay functional during the massive worldwide depression, flight from Nazi Germany and Austria transformed this upheaval into a crisis, casting republican universalism and French citizenship and identity into question.[50]

Amidst these national and international crises, and in the face of increasingly negative responses to immigration, Bloch's sacrifice was reinterpreted by some as evidence of French Judaism's total assimilation and compatibility with French nationalism. For right-wing lawyer Edmond Bloch (no relation to the rabbi), a French-Jewish *ancien-combattant* who established a national Jewish veterans' association in France in 1934, the Union Patriotique des Français Israélites (UPFI), Rabbi Bloch was the French Jew par excellence. In opposition to the left-wing Popular Front led by Léon Blum, Edmond Bloch represented a fringe of right-wing Jewish-French nationalists that took cues from other right-wing nationalists, seeing their desperate foreign coreligionists as a threat to their assimilated status. In an attempt to minimize the onslaught of local and national expressions of antisemitism and xenophobia in the mid-1930s, the UPFI distanced itself from its foreign coreligionists, often choosing to align itself with right-wing ideals emphasizing French nationality, and denied admission to non-naturalized and foreign Jews.[51]

Present at the turn of the century during the first large wave of Eastern European immigration, this vocabulary of Jewish difference had developed at the heart of the French Jewish community during the war years among Jewish elite as well as the more general Jewish public. During the war, *Archives Israélites* readers frequently read letters from Eastern European Jewish volunteers. For instance, Charles Gourewitch, a 23-year-old Russian Jew in the French Foreign Legion, was shot on an information reconnaissance mission near Blois in October 1914. In February, *Archives Israélites* published the last letter he posted to his aunt and uncle in Paris, underscoring his patriotism.[52] In spite of the fact that Gourewitch had arrived in France five years earlier and had sacrificed himself for the national cause, he was still referred to as "this foreign Jew," suggesting that even his death was not enough to transform him into a Frenchman.

In 1934, Edmond Bloch and the nationalist UPFI spearheaded the installation of the granite stele at Taintrux commemorating Rabbi Bloch, inviting French Jewish authorities, governmental figures, and French military dignitaries to attend a series of secular commemoration rituals concluding inside the local synagogue. Locals were invited to attend the ceremony on the battlefield, where "La Marseillaise" was sung, and Frenchmen of all faiths mounted wreaths on the monument.[53] One account described the ceremony for this "exemplary hero" as emotional and fortifying. In the face of the inhuman barbarism of German Aryanism, the article read, Bloch's heroism stands as a testimony for the spiritual strength of "our sweet France."[54] For this group, Rabbi Bloch stood for the Frenchness—cultural, historical, and ethnic—of her assimilated Jewish nationals. By 1936, the UPFI had all but dissolved, but the stele remained, a symbol of a moment of powerful French-Jewish nationalist—even exclusionary—sentiment in the mid-1930s.

Not all Jewish veterans felt the same way about Rabbi Bloch. While right-wing Jewish nationalists fashioned him into a symbol for "Jewish Frenchmen," Eastern European Jewish activists in France made their claim on the rabbi for the largesse of his act of voluntarism. In the hands of Eastern European Jewish volunteers, Rabbi Bloch's heroic tale came to stand for the more general, all-encompassing heroism of the volunteer. Maurice Vanikoff, Russian-born *engagé volontaire* and president of the association for the (largely Jewish) immigrant volunteer servicemen, commented in the organization's press organ that, as a volunteer, Rabbi Bloch was a hero for foreign Jews, a symbol for their bravery and loyalty to their adopted nation. "Our hateful enemies ... have accused us of materialism, and we gave them the Bible. They denounced our laziness, and we offered them 12,000 volunteers. They condemn our fanaticism, and we gave them Abraham Bloch."[55] Vanikoff's words reveal both confidence and despair in the face of rising antisemitism and an impending conflict he judged would likely implicate the Jewish people of French and foreign extraction alike.

David Bloch of Guebwiller

The example of the young David Bloch of Guebwiller offers a second case study of Jewish heroism during World War I. In the summer of 1940, German armies left a trail of destruction as they advanced to occupy and annex the former Reichsland (Alsace-Lorraine) to the Third Reich, paying particular attention to demolishing spaces of distinct local importance.[56] Along with Strasbourg's grand synagogue on quai Kléber, synagogues, buildings, and monuments of communal significance in Alsace and Lorraine were systematically destroyed in the summer of 1940.[57] This included a relatively unimpressive monument tucked into a wood in the small Alsatian town of Guebwiller.

This monument, erected by the local community in the 1920s, commemorated the death of a twenty-year-old Jewish man during World War I. A Michelin yearbook produced for its local factory workers told the following story: Born and raised in German Alsace, David Bloch shirked his German military obligations in 1914 and enlisted as a foreign volunteer with the French military. In 1916 he journeyed undercover into enemy territory as a spy. The plane on which he was traveling crashed, and Bloch escaped the burning wreckage, only to be captured by German authorities. While he refused to give up his identity, he was accidentally betrayed by his father, who immediately identified his son when authorities brought him to the station at Mulhouse to see him. David was exe-

Figure 4.2. *Monument to David Bloch in Guebwiller. Postcard from interwar period. Personal collection of Michel Rothe, reprinted with his permission.*

cuted for high treason on 1 April 1916, and the notice of his execution was advertised widely in Mulhouse on that very day.[58]

This young man's sacrifice became a symbol for a variety of commemorative strategies. David Bloch held extraordinary meaning for local Jewish and non-Jewish pro-French Alsatians. Thus when German forces marched into Alsace during the next war and authorities came across a monument that was built to commemorate the French patriotism of this Alsatian Jewish volunteer, they removed and destroyed what they saw as a memorial to a World War I traitor.

Not unlike the case of Rabbi Bloch, age and voluntarism played into memorial representations of David Bloch. Emphasis on Rabbi Bloch's middle age highlighted the grandeur of his gesture. However, David's heroic death was elevated and underscored by the constant reference to his young age.[59] His youthful face accompanied articles in the French press, and the local monument depicted David's likeness, rather than the abstract stele used to commemorate the older Rabbi Bloch. At the monument's inauguration in 1922, the minister of the liberated regions made special mention of the "many young men of Guebwiller who enlisted as volunteers and died under our flags, and also those who suffered the terrible destiny to fall while in enemy uniform."[60] In their specific attention to the "young," these comments attribute a sort of youthful and excusable confusion to the Alsatians who served imperial Germany rather than shirking and volunteering for France. The minister's comments make evident that David's decision to ally himself with the French cause stood in stark contrast to those who had put on German uniforms: that is to say, if only these young men had been more mature, more knowledgeable, older, they may have recognized their true duty was not to the Kaiser, but to *la patrie*, the French Republic.

Beyond age, David's voluntarism was an important part of what made him a French Jewish hero. This heroic tale overrode any accusations of Jewish treachery and untrustworthiness that had run rampant during the Dreyfus affair.[61] David stood as proof that Alsatian Jews were, and always had been, French. In the eastern provinces, Jewish religious and community authorities highlighted the unequivocally French character of Alsatian Jews in commemorations that honored their coreligionists among non-Jewish Frenchmen and other Alsatians. In Jewish ceremonies mourning "French soldiers and Alsatian soldiers of French background who had fallen on fields of glory," religious authorities noted the Bloch affair. In one such event in Colmar in May 1919, the synagogue was decorated in "resplendent" tricolor banners provided for by the municipality. Prayers were said for all the French war dead, and the names of Colmar's fallen Jews and neighboring areas were read aloud, including that of "David Bloch the aviator of Guebwiller, who, charged with a secret mission requiring him to land behind German lines, was shot because he would not share information with the enemy."[62]

A Jew as an Alsatian Son of France

In Alsace, amidst a swell of regionalism and a so-called Alsatian malaise in the 1920s, David Bloch's Jewishness stood in for a steadfast pro-French patriotism. After Alsace's return to France in 1918, Alsatians displayed significant resistance to the imposition of the 1905 concordat, opposing a violation of their local tradition of "close connection between church and state" that had flourished under German rule between 1870 and 1918.[63] Alsatian autonomist movements, seeking "self-rule or separation from France, with an implied linkage to Germany," arose in opposition to moderate regionalists, who advocated reintegration into "a France that respected local customs."[64] In this climate of uncertainty, pro-French Alsatians claimed David Bloch as a hero of Alsace-Lorraine's long history of commitment to France while under the Imperial German yoke.

Local pro-French activists and community leaders understood that amidst the upheavals of épuration, a process during which thousands of Germans were forced to return to their country of origin and institutions were placed under French control, pro-French attitudes were not a fait accompli.[65] Indication of a popular movement to build support for the region's reincorporation into the Third Republic, a slew of books and pamphlets with incendiary titles published after the war, many of which included David Bloch's story, interpreted the period of German annexation as a dark one of abusive occupation.[66]

For pro-French Alsatians, the story of a Jewish patriot marked the enduring Frenchness of the eastern provinces. After the Franco-Prussian War, those living in the new imperial territory of Alsace-Lorraine were given the choice either to remain in the Reichsland or to leave, the latter option selected by approximately 11 percent of the region's total population. Not wishing to lose the political rights and status they had possessed under the former French system, many Jews chose to retain their French citizenship. Between 1871 and 1914, twelve thousand Jews left Alsace and Lorraine, many of them settling in Paris.[67]

Jews, however, did not disappear from Alsace during this period. Industrialization and urbanization offered economic opportunities to rural Alsatian Jews, many of whom chose to move to the cities, and great numbers of German Jews settled there for the same reason.[68] Between the migration of rural Jews to the Alsatian cities, those who remained in Strasbourg and other urban centers, and the migration of German Jews to the booming Reichsland, Alsatian Jewish life did not end in 1871, but rather transformed.⁶⁹ Jews were highly represented in industrial and commercial life.⁷⁰ Moreover, it was during this period that the Strasbourg Jewish community built and inaugurated its great synagogue on the quai Kléber, in one of the most visible and central locations in the city. Still, Alsatian Jews often occupied prominent roles in "pro-French patriotic organizations and activities" in the Reichsland as a response to German cultural and national security prejudices against Alsatians and Lorrainers, and especially Jews, prejudices that were "deeply embedded in the German political system."⁷¹

From the other side, French visions of annexed Alsace were equally complex. In spite of the proliferation of pro-French attitudes in these territories, David Bloch was also part of a world that, from 1871, was subject to not only some degree of French curiosity and nostalgia, but also one of suspicion and discrimination "from many who distrusted their German-sounding names and accents and doubted their very 'Frenchness.'"⁷² In this "strange" borderland, and as the prime beneficiaries of emancipation, Jewish Alsatians could figure as icons of French republican commitment.⁷³ This position was confirmed by the participation of Alsatian and other French Jewish clergy in wartime discussions of reclaiming these borderlands, one of the core Allied war aims.⁷⁴

That it was among non-Jews that that David Bloch found his biggest and most vocal community of admirers is remarkable, not least because of the war's temporal proximity to the explosive Dreyfus affair, a scandal that had erupted only decades earlier over the national loyalty of a Jewish army captain whose Jewishness and Alsatian roots made him, his critics alleged, particularly susceptible to treason. Anti-republican conservatives made it clear that neither Jews nor Alsatians could be fully trusted.⁷⁵ While Rabbi Bloch's heroic tale fit neatly into a timeless and instantly recognizable religious typology, David's story evoked an explosive recent history of spies and military treachery, discrimination, racism, and public debates about the fate of the republic. With France under fire, and the *union sacrée* theoretically muting all political and social difference, these major fissures seemed to disappear. Ironically, Captain Dreyfus's supposedly treacherous characteristics permitted David Bloch to become an actual spy during World War I: knowledge of German language, international connections, and intimate knowledge of the Alsatian urban and natural landscape. Rather than an enemy of the state, David was branded a hero for these same competencies and qualities.

While Rabbi Bloch's stele was funded and erected by the UPFI during the refugee crisis to fashion the rabbi into a true *French*-Jewish hero, David Bloch's memorial was funded by his town and installed almost immediately after the war in 1922, signaling an urgency to set in stone Alsace's identity as pro-French. In this context, David Bloch's monument celebrated at once an Alsatian-French patriot, a French martyr, and, to Germany, a traitor. The monument, designed by Emmanuel Hannaux, a Jewish artist from Metz who had already gained some fame for designing a *poilu* monument in his hometown, included David perched atop a pedestal designed by local Jewish architect Pierre Blum, in a peaceful wood along the promenade Déroulède.[76]

Evidence suggests David Bloch was an important symbol for the local and broader Alsatian community. While local Jews were instrumental, it seems likely that it was the town, in fact, that was responsible for funding and building the monument. Jewish religious authorities did speak about David Bloch in their congregations, but there was minimal Jewish official presence and nearly no mention of his Jewish background at the community ceremony, which took place at the site rather than inside the local synagogue. The minister of the liberated territories presided over the ceremony, featuring moving speeches given by the mayor, the president of a veterans' association, a local lawyer involved in the negotiation with German authorities to release Bloch from their custody, and the abbot Émile Wetterlé, a local pro-French deputy and Catholic official.[77]

The blending of religious and secular in Rabbi Bloch's commemoration was also at play in David's. In a speech published in the 1923 pamphlet "An Alsacian Hero: David Bloch" by the Societé Alsacienne, Wetterlé used a combination of muted republican secular themes and Christian religious motifs to describe Bloch's contribution to the war effort as patriotic and his death as martyrdom. Evoking the trial and crucifixion of Christ, Wetterlé reconstructed in vivid detail David's fated trial. Only once in the pamphlet/speech is his Jewish background mentioned, a reference to a "good *israélite* family of our town," a singular phrase signposting the persistence of pro-French attitudes throughout the Reichsland period. After all, the crime for which David Bloch was executed, he argued, was "loving France too much."[78]

After recounting the tale of Bloch's voluntary enlistment, capture, questioning, and execution, Wetterlé explained that "the Great War transformed thousands of young men, who were not prepared for this glorious role, into heroes ... a great patriotic wind that passed over the land ... quickly elevated that which was best in the most ordinary of souls, and inspired countless acts of devotion and self-sacrifice that fill the pages of the most beautiful and moving pages of our national history."[79] On the outbreak of war and with no hesitation, David chose to serve under the flags of "his real homeland,"[80] along with thousands of Alsatians who volunteered for service in the French army.[81]

When Alsatian Jewish authorities linked David Bloch to the French character of the eastern provinces, it served to broadcast Alsace's Jews' special relationship with French republicanism that had fashioned them into citizens before any other nation in Europe. Non-Jewish French Alsatians employed this historic relationship to underscore their own French identity. In this newly recovered territory in postwar political flux, and for similar reasons, David Bloch figured for many non-Jewish locals as a vehicle for restating Alsatian commitment to France against a rising tide of pro-German autonomism. In his youth and in his Jewishness, David Bloch helped eastern French communities think through the complex local histories of occupation, resistance, and bloody war.

Conclusions and Beginnings

During the French Indochina War, "a hybrid war, a war of changing focus and purpose, a national war of international dimensions," the image of the French soldier was reworked from a protective, patriotic, brave representation of the generous spirit of the republican empire to a mutilated, despairing, agonized warrior-victim, relating back to "the most enduring model of this traditional paradigm," the French combat soldier of World War I.[82] In its own way, World War I was also a war of changing focus and purpose, and nowhere was this clearer than in the commemoration of heroes standing in contrast to the republican cult of the *poilu*.

Rabbi Abraham Bloch and David Bloch of Guebwiller were powerful symbols for Jews and other Frenchmen that were shaped and reshaped throughout war as well as its aftermath. In his marginality as a noncombatant, a clergyman, a volunteer of middle age, and a Jew with an Algerian connection, Rabbi Bloch and his death offered an alternative vocabulary with which to make sense of the war experience within the totalizing "civic religion" of republicanism. The rabbi embodied a pliable interpretation of the abstract *union sacrée* for all its constituents during the war and its aftermath. In his liminality as a Jew, Rabbi Bloch could appeal to the faithful while not threatening the secular nature of the republic, and his colonial connection evoked a transnational quality useful for Jews and other Frenchmen. For David Bloch's admirers, his liminality gave him the power to cross boundaries, his young age gave his voluntarism potency, and his Jewishness stood in for the enduring Frenchness of the eastern provinces in a postwar era of political flux.

In addition to offering new insight into the evolving tensions between universalism and particularism, these case studies suggest that approaching French history from its margins—in this case, its Jews—may help us challenge long-held assumptions about French political and commemorative culture in the twentieth century. These stories also serve as evidence for the vibrancy of Jewish life in trans-war France, as well as the impact of the war experience on Jewish public culture. Rather than a fragmented and isolated community in the years before Vichy and the Holocaust, France's Jews retained vital connections to the political and cultural currents of this moment. This chapter offers a glimpse into the Frenchness of Jewish history and the Jewishness of French history.

Coda: An Exemplary Hero of World War II

Rabbi Abraham Bloch was reborn as a Vosgian icon in the 1950s and folded into a local history of resistance during World War II. The eastern provincial press linked the heroism of the entire village of Taintrux under the Nazi occupation to that of Rabbi Bloch himself. In 1940, the Nazis tore down the stele, which was then hidden by three villagers. Rabbi Bloch, a local hero, "one whose legendary story we all know well," became the inspiration for this village's resistance.[83] In the late 1950s, the stele was restored, a testament to "military courage, self-sacrifice, and religious greatness."[84] This may be a final chapter to the story of this Jewish war hero, whose name and story were literally set and reset in stone alongside landscapes of identical crosses marking the sacrifices of countless men from a hundred years ago, whose names and stories are now lost to time.

Erin Corber, a historian of France and French Jewry, is a research associate of the Institute for Canadian Jewish Studies at Concordia University, Montreal. Previously, she was the Inaugural Simon and Riva Spatz Visiting Chair of Jewish Studies at Dalhousie University in Halifax, Nova Scotia, the Lydia and David Zimmern Memorial Fellow at the United States Holocaust Memorial Museum, a postdoctoral fellow at the Institute for Advanced Study at New Europe College in Bucharest, Romania, and visiting assistant professor of European history at the University of Maine at Orono. Corber's publications include "Men of Thought, Men of Action: The Great War, Masculinity, and the Modernization of the French Rabbinate," Jewish Culture and History 14, no. 1 (April 2013); and "The Kids on Oberlin Street: Place, Space, and Jewish Community in Late Interwar Strasbourg," Urban History 43, no. 4 (November 2016).

Notes

1. *L'Echo de l'Ossuaire de Douaumont et des Champs de Bataille de Verdun* (Administration du comité de l'ossuaire de Douaumont, Nancy), no. 3, November–December 1921, pp. 1–2.
2. Daniel Sherman estimates that local World War I monuments are "omnipresent in France," with numbers approaching the total number of French townships in the

1920s—thirty-six thousand. Daniel J. Sherman, "Art, Commerce, and the Production of Memory in France after World War I," in *Commemorations: The Politics of National Identity*, ed. John Gillis (Princeton, NJ: Princeton University Press, 1994), p. 187. In the definitive study of commemorative culture in interwar France, Sherman demonstrates how, at the local level, design choices often ignited fierce debate over a community's identity and its relationship to the state. Local and national symbols did not always mix. The crosses ubiquitous over a battlefield commemorative space could refer to a local Christian piety but could also stir "memories of church-state conflict" from the turn of the century. Daniel Sherman, *The Construction of Memory in Interwar France* (Chicago: University of Chicago Press, 1999), p. 217. For more on religious imagery in postwar European culture, see Jay Winter, *Sites of Memory, Sites of Mourning: The Great War in European Cultural History* (Cambridge: Cambridge University Press, 1994).

3. See Sherman, *Construction of Memory in Interwar France*, pp. 186–214.
4. Laura Wittman, *The Tomb of the Unknown Soldier, Modern Mourning, and the Reinvention of the Mystical Body* (Toronto: University of Toronto Press, 2011), p. 7.
5. See, for instance, Capitaine Delvert, *Quelques Héros* (Paris: Librairie Militaire Berger-Levy, 1918).
6. See Regina M. Sweeney, *Singing Our Way to Victory: French Cultural Politics and Music during the Great War* (Middletown: Wesleyan University Press, 2001).
7. Antoine Prost, "Les monuments aux morts," in *Les lieux de mémoire*, vol. 1, *La République*, ed. Pierre Nora (Paris: Gallimard, 1984), pp. 195–225.
8. The policy of emphasizing French colonial contributions to the war was meant to counter the German war aim of promoting independence for the colonial world. To keep the empire intact was a vital war aim for the British and the French. See Andrew Jarboe, "Indian and African Soldiers in British, French, and German Propaganda during the First World War," in *World War I and Propaganda*, ed. Troy Paddock (Leiden: Brill, 2014), pp. 181–198. For more on race, see Richard S. Fogarty, *Race and War in France: Colonial Subjects in the French Army, 1914–1918* (Baltimore: Johns Hopkins University Press, 2008); Dana S. Hale, *Races on Display: French Representations of Colonial Peoples, 1886–1940* (Bloomington: Indiana University Press, 2008).
9. The statue was torn down during the Nazi occupation of Alsace, then rebuilt in 1965.
10. Not all *poilus* were simply patriotic. There were variations, including those exuding "nationalistic exaltation," some triumphant, some aggrieved, some funerary-patriotic, and some, in their refusal to acknowledge or signal the sacrifice's legitimacy, move toward critique and/or outright pacifism. For more, see Antoine Prost, *Republican Identities in War and Peace: Representations of France in the 19th and 20th Centuries* (London: Bloomsbury, 2002), pp. 22–23.
11. Many scholars have used this binary to describe the condition of Jews in modern societies. See, for example, Richard Cohen, Jonathan Frankel, and Stefani Hoffman, eds., *Insiders and Outsiders: Dilemmas of East European Jewry* (New York: Littman Library of Jewish Civilization, 2010); Dagmar C. G. Lorenz and Gabriele Weinberger, eds., *Insiders and Outsiders: Jewish and Gentile Culture in Germany and Austria* (Detroit: Wayne State University Press, 1994); David Biale, Michael Galchinsky, and Susannah Heschel, eds., *Insider/Outsider: American Jews and Multiculturalism* (Berkeley: University of California Press, 1998); and Pierre Birnbaum, *La 'République juive'* (Paris: Arthème Fayard, 1988).
12. Coinciding with a major wave of Eastern European Jewish immigration, Jews in France suffered from very public and often violent outbursts of antisemitism during

the Dreyfus affair in the 1890s. For more, see Pierre Birnbaum, *Le moment antisémite: un tour de la France en 1898* (Paris: Fayard, 1998).
13. North African Jewish troops and Eastern European Jewish volunteers served separately in military units, but French Jews served alongside their non-Jewish brothers in arms in French units. For more on Jews in the French military during World War I, see Philippe E. Landau, *Les Juifs de France et la Grande Guerre* (Paris: CNRS Editions, 1999); for more on Jews and the military, see Derek Penslar, *Jews and the Military: A History* (Princeton, NJ: Princeton University Press, 2013). Maurice Barrès, a leading voice of the antisemitic right, president of the nationalist Ligue des Patriotes, and an outspoken enemy of Alfred Dreyfus during his trials at the turn of the century, muted his antisemitism during World War I in his bestseller *Les diverses familles spirituelles de la France* (Paris: Émile-Paul Frères, Éditeurs, 1917).
14. As Gregor, Rohmer, and Roseman argue, "Minority groups existed not only as outsiders, they also engaged the center and thereby altered its contours and character." Neil Gregor, Nils Roemer, and Mark Roseman, eds., *German History from the Margins* (Bloomington: Indiana University Press, 2006).
15. Ronald Schechter, *Obstinate Hebrews: Representations of Jews in France, 1715–1815* (Berkeley: University of California Press, 2003).
16. Some of Bloch's correspondence is stored in the Collection Bloch at the Archives du Séminaire Israélite de France, Paris (SIF) BLOCH 1. Jamin's testimony is also included in this collection. Jamin's account is also quoted and translated in Sylvain Halff, "The Participation of the Jews of France in the Great War," *American Jewish Yearbook* (New York: American Jewish Committee, Jewish Publication Society, 1920), pp. 31–97.
17. SIF BLOCH 1; and Halff, "Participation of the Jews of France," pp. 61–62. Aside from a unit medic's field notes from that day, Jamin's remains the only eyewitness account of the extraordinary story of Rabbi Bloch's sacrifice. Also see chapter 12 in Philippe E. Landau, *Les Juifs de France et la Grande Guerre*, pp. 195–203; Paul Netter, *Un Grand Rabbin dans la Grande Guerre* (Paris: Italiques, 2013).
18. "A la mémoire du grand rabbin Abraham Bloch, tué à l'ennemi," *Archives Israélites*, 17 September 1914.
19. Ibid. All translations from the French are my own.
20. Ibid.
21. *Archives Israelites*, 19 November 1914.
22. See Pierre Birnbaum, *La 'République juive,'* in which this observation contributes to Birnbaum's overall reassessment of French antisemitism during the Third Republic.
23. In a letter to the French Service de Santé, responsible for the appointment of religious chaplains in the armed forces, the Grand Rabbi of the Central Consistory in France made note of the importance of dedicated Jewish chaplains to support military units with large numbers of Jewish Algerians. Archives du consistoire central des israélites (Paris), Dossier 14-18, 6K, Letter from Grand Rabbi to Service de Santé, II. "Rabbins algériens," n.d.
24. See E. Corber, "L'esprit du corps: Bodies, Communities, and the Reconstruction of Jewish Life in France, 1914–1940" (PhD dissertation, Indiana University, Bloomington, 2013), pp. 111–12.
25. The Consistory System, designed by Napoleon I to organize and administer Jewish religious and communal life throughout the provinces, was centered in Paris.
26. See, for instance, Birnbaum, *Le moment antisémite*; Michael Marrus, *The Politics of Assimilation: A Study of the French Jewish Community at the Time of the Dreyfus Affair* (New

York: Clarenden Press, 1971). Marrus describes the perceived threat posed by the new immigrant community of "outsiders" to their assimilated French Jewish counterparts.
27. Jewish communal authorities, particularly in Paris, were uniquely prepared to shoulder philanthropic projects during the war that often doubled as communal regeneration initiatives in the long term. For more, see E. Corber, "L'esprit du corps."
28. For example, "Les israélites immigrés au service de la France," *Archives Israélites*, 27 August 1914.
29. "Une cité alsacienne sauvée par le Rabbin," in *Archives Israélites*, 24 December 1914.
30. Haguenauer, awarded the Légion d'honneur in 1932, spent most of the 1930s and 1940s in Nancy, where he was appointed Grand Rabbi after World War I. He and his wife were deported to Auschwitz in 1944.
31. "Le rabbin-soldat," *Archives Israélites*, 20 May 1915.
32. "Hommage au Grand-Rabbin Abraham Bloch, 1859–1914," *L'Univers Israélite*, 1 January 1915.
33. "Service patriotique à la synagogue d'Alger," *Archives Israélites*, 17 December 1914.
34. Ibid.
35. The Jewish press would continue to draw links between the sacrifices of metropolitan Jews and those of North Africa, even by publishing material written by former anti-semites. One editorial in *Archives Israélites* penned by Victor Daveluy, "an avowed antisemite," demonstrated a dramatic transformation in his position on Jews in citing a number of cases in which Algerian Jews displayed bravery under fire on the battlefront and in which he himself came into contact with generous and patriotic "Jewish zouaves." Victor Daveluy, "Hommage aux soldats israélites algériens," *Archives Israélites*, 24 August 1916.
36. André Spire, *Les Juifs et la Guerre* (Paris: Payot, 1917), pp. 142–52
37. Poincaré, *Au service de la France*, vol. 4, *L'Union sacrée (1914)* (Paris, 1927), pp. 547–58.
38. "Haut les coeurs," *Archives Israélites*, 15 October 1914.
39. André Spire, *Les Juifs et la Guerre*; see Annexe 3 for reference to *La Guerre Sociale*, 9 March, 1915.
40. Ibid.
41. *Le Mémorial de la guerre de 1914–15* (Paris: Société académique de l'histoire international, 1915).
42. Maurice Barrès, *Le programme de Nancy*, 1898.
43. Maurice Barrès, *Les diverses familles spirituelles de la France* (Paris: Émile-Paul Frères, 1917), p. 93.
44. Ibid.
45. This was an interesting development in the French Republic, where church and state had been divorced for over a decade. Christian iconography was only one part of religion's presence in war commemoration. Religious authorities of different faiths were frequently included in national services during and after the war in France, and Catholic authorities in particular sought to "restate the *union sacrée* in ceremony." Leonard V. Smith et al., *France and the Great War 1914–1918* (Cambridge: Cambridge University Press, 2003), esp. "Commemoration: Memory and the Struggle for Meaning," pp. 159–67. For more on the broader topic of religion and the commemoration of war deaths in France, see Annette Becker, *War and Faith: The Religious Imagination in France, 1914–1930* (Oxford: Berg, 1998); Becker, "Faith, Ideologies, and the 'Cultures of War,'" trans. John Horne, in *A Companion to World War I*, ed. John Horne (Oxford: Wiley-Blackwell, 2012), pp. 234–47. For more on the British case, see John Wolffe,

Great Deaths: Grieving, Religion, and Nationhood in Victorian and Edwardian Britain (Oxford: Oxford University Press, 2000).

46. Henri Martin, "Abraham Bloch," notes from *Légion Vosgien des mutilés, anciens combattants, veuves, orphelins, ascendants, et prisonniers de guerre* (Épinal, n.d.), in SIF Collection Bloch, Box 2.
47. Winter, *Sites of Memory, Sites of Mourning*.
48. For more examples of poetry, see Bloch ephemera in SIF Collection Bloch, Box 2.
49. Georges Gérard, "Humanité," in *La Revue Moderne Illustrée des Arts et de la Vie*, 1934 (n.d.), SIF Collection Bloch, Box 2.
50. For more on the topic of migration to France during the refugee crisis of the 1930s, see Mary Dewhurst Lewis, *The Boundaries of the Republic: Migrant Rights and the Limits of Universalism in France, 1918–1940* (Stanford, CA: Stanford University Press, 2007).
51. For more on Edmond Bloch and the UPFI, see Muriel Pichon, *Les Français juifs, 1914–1950: récit d'un désenchantement* (Toulouse: Presses Universitaires du Mirail, 2009), pp. 116–31.
52. "La Dernière Lettre d'un Volontaire Israélite," *Archives Israélites*, 11 February 1915.
53. *Bulletin UPFI*, December 1934.
54. *L'Est Republicain*, 5 September 1934.
55. *Le Volontaire Juif, Organe Mensuel du Comité d'Entente des Associations Volontaires Juifs de France*, no. 30, July–October 1934.
56. Most of the area had been evacuated in 1939, and many Jews had scattered through what would become the southern zone of France.
57. Hitler Youth squads were responsible for setting the synagogue alight, but in fact it was a local Strasbourgeois company that received the contract to tear down the rest of the building after the fire. See Jean-Marc Dreyfus, "Alsace-Lorraine," in *The Greater German Reich and the Jews: Nazi Persecution Policies in the Annexed Territories, 1935–1945*, Wolf Grüner and Joerg Osterloh, eds., (New York: Berghahn, 2015). Also see Jean Daltroff, *La Synagogue du quai Kléber à Strasbourg (1898–1941)* (Strasbourg: ID L'Édition, 2012).
58. Michelin & cie, *Colmar—Mulhouse—Schlestadt: À la mémoire des ouvriers et employés des usines Michelin morts glorieusement pour la patrie* (Clermont-Ferrand: Michelin et cie, 1920).
59. This is certainly not the first instance of a hero's age being evoked to valorize his sacrifice. For an interesting case study of the meanings and uses of the "youthful hero" in British military and political culture in the eighteenth century, see D. A. B. Ronald, *Youth, Heroism, and War Propaganda: Britain and the Young Maritime Hero, 1745–1840* (New York: Bloomsbury, 2015), in which the author argues that youth had a symbolic power in an emerging "vibrant, national and predominantly urban extra-parliamentary political culture," associated with war propaganda, especially in conflict at sea (pp. 1–18).
60. "M. Reibel en Alsace," *Le Journal (Paris)*, 28 August 1922.
61. Paula Hyman argues that while "antisemitism as an organized, independent movement may have waned" before the outbreak of war in 1914, "antisemitism as a cultural practice and as a component of anti-Republican nationalism did not." Paula Hyman, *The Jews of Modern France* (Berkeley: University of California Press, 1998), p. 113.
62. "Colmar: cérémonie religieuse et patriotique," *L'Univers Israélite*, 16 May 1919. A year later, another commemorative ceremony took place at the consistorial synagogue in Metz, where the dead from the Eleventh Aerial Regiment were honored and during

which the rabbi made a special note of "the aviator David Bloch, of Guebwiller, for whom a monument ... will be erected next September in his hometown." *Le Juif* (Strasbourg), no. 30, 17 July 1920.
63. Samuel Goodfellow, "Fascism and Regionalism in Interwar Alsace," *National Identities* 12, no. 2 (June 2010): 133–45.
64. Because this debate between regionalists and autonomists cut across traditional political and religious divides, fascism was eventually able to manipulate "collective emotions and impulses that crave identity." Goodfellow, "Fascism and Regionalism in Interwar Alsace," p. 135. For more on the topic, see Samuel Goodfellow, *Between the Swastika and the Cross of Lorraine: Fascisms in Interwar Alsace* (DeKalb: Northern Illinois University Press, 1999).
65. For more on this process, see Philipp Ther, *The Dark Side of Nation States: Ethnic Cleansing in Modern Europe* (New York: Berghahn Books, 2014), esp. pp. 68–78.
66. André Fribourg, *Le poigne allemande en Lorraine et en Alsace, 1871–1914–1918* (Paris: H. Floury, 1918); Fribourg, "Les Alsaciens-Lorrains sous la Poigne Allemande," in *Notre Alsace, Notre Lorraine,* ed. L'Abbé Wetterlé and Carlos Fischer, no. 34, 20 November 1919; Florent-Matter, *L'Alsace-Lorraine pendant la Guerre: Les Alsaciens-Lorrains contre l'Allemagne* (Nancy: Berger-Levrault, 1918).
67. Esther Benbassa, *The Jews of France: A History from Antiquity to the Present* (Princeton, NJ: Princeton University Press, 1999), p. 100.
68. Strasbourg's Jewish population had grown consistently from 68 in 1789 to 3,088 in 1871, to 4,605 in 1900. In 1921, after the war, the Jewish population of the Alsatian capital was at 5,844, and in 1931, Strasbourg's Jewish community was at an all-time high of 8,402. See E. Schnurmann, *La Population Juive en Alsace* (Paris: Librairie du Recueil Sirey, 1936). In 1806, "9% of the Jews of the Bas-Rhin department lived in Strasbourg. In 1931, 57.7%." Schnurmann noted that Jews had a "pronounced tendency to establish themselves in the capital cities ... proven by the uninterrupted migration of Alsatian Jews to Paris, and the expansion of Strasbourg's Jewish community" (p. 16).
69. Vicki Caron has argued for the diversity and variation of communal reactions to the German annexation. Vicki Caron, *Between France and Germany: The Jews of Alsace-Lorraine, 1871–1918* (Stanford, CA: Stanford University Press, 1988), p. 25
70. For more on this history, see Jean Daltroff, "1871–1918 en Alsace: l'accueil contrasté des Juifs venus d'ailleurs," in *Regards sur la culture judeo-alsacienne: Des identités en partage,* ed. Freddy Raphaël (Strasbourg: La nuée bleue, 2001), pp. 113–29.
71. Ibid., p. 117.
72. Michael Nolan, *The Inverted Mirror: Mythologizing the Enemy in France and Germany, 1898–1914* (New York: Berghahn Books, 2005), p. 72.
73. Alsatian Jews were only emancipated in 1791 after significant debate over their economic and social "regeneration." For more, see Caron, *Between France and Germany*; Paula Hyman, *The Emancipation of the Jews of Alsace: Acculturation and Tradition in the Nineteenth Century* (New Haven, CT: Yale University Press, 1991).
74. *Archives Israélites* reported that at an event in New York in the summer of 1917, an American rabbi spoke alongside Catholic and Protestant clergy, stating "Alsace-Lorraine has shown us that a people will not change their nationality against their will" and that "she had good reason to have an obstinate and unwavering faith in France." Furthermore, this rabbi argued, "The injustices that Alsace-Lorraine has suffered are today the injustices the whole world is suffering. But the hour of liberation is arriving soon. The liberated peoples of the world: England, Italy, Russia, and the United States

have declared that Alsace Lorraine will leave the bloody arms of Prussia to return to the ravaged arms of France." "Un rabbin américain plaidant la cause de l'Alsace-Lorraine," *Archives Israélites,* 12 July 1917. See more in Caron, *Between France and Germany.*
75. Maurice Barrès, champion of the *union sacrée,* had been a chief anti-Dreyfusard during the affair. For more in-depth discussions on the affair, its reverberations, and its political and cultural meanings, see Ruth Harris, *Dreyfus: Politics, Emotion, and the Scandal of the Century* (New York: Macmillan, 2010); Christopher Forth, *The Dreyfus Affair and the Crisis of French Manhood* (Baltimore: Johns Hopkins University Press, 2004).
76. "L'inauguration du monument," in *Un Héros Alsacien: David Bloch,* Préface de M. l'abbé Wetterlé (Colmar: Alsatia, 1923).
77. "Déplacements ministeriels et inaugurations de monuments," *La Croix* (Paris), 29 August 1922; also see description of the event and speakers in "M. Reibel en Alsace: Inauguration du monument David Bloch," *Le Journal* (Paris), 29 August 1922. Émile Wetterlé, a well-known Alsatian figure, was a staunch supporter of Alsatian reintegration into France after the war. See Wetterlé, *L'Alsace doit rester Française* (Paris: Delgrave, 1917).
78. "Un Héros Alsacien: David Bloch," Préface de M. L'abbé Wetterlé.
79. Ibid.
80. Ibid.
81. Christopher Fischer points out that discrimination against both Alsatians and Jews in the German army was a large factor in the decision of approximately 17,500 Alsatians to serve France instead. This included "the 3,000 soldiers who fled to France at the war's outbreak, 12,500 Alsatians already in France, and over 1,500 Alsatian prisoners of war from the German army" who chose to join the French side during the war. Christopher Fischer, *Alsace to the Alsatians? Visions and Divisions of Alsatian Regionalism, 1870–1939* (New York: Berghahn Books, 2010), p. 123.
82. Nicola Cooper, "Heroes and Martyrs: The Changing Mythical Status of the French Army during the Franco-Indochinese War," in *France at War in the Twentieth Century: Myth, Metaphor, Propaganda,* ed. D. Kelly and V. Holman (New York: Berghahn Books, 2000).
83. *L'Illustré de l'Est,* 22 November 1957.
84. Ibid.

Selected Bibliography
Primary Sources

Archives du Consistoire Central des Israélites de France (Paris), Dossier 14-18
Archives Israélites (Paris)
La Croix (Paris)
Le Journal (Paris)
Le Juif / La Tribune Juive (Strasbourg)
L'Univers Israélite (Paris)

Barrès, Maurice. *Les diverses familles spirituelles de la France.* Paris: Émile-Paul Frères, Éditeurs, 1917.
Florent-Matter. *L'Alsace-Lorraine pendant la Guerre: Les Alsaciens-Lorrains contre l'Allemagne.* Nancy: Berger-Levrault, 1918.

Fribourg, André. *Le poigne allemande en Lorraine et en Alsace, 1871–1914–1918*. Paris: H. Floury, 1918.

———. "Les Alsaciens-Lorrains sous la Poigne Allemande." In *Notre Alsace, Notre Lorraine*, edited by L'Abbé Wetterlé and Carlos Fischer, no. 34, 20 November 1919.

Halff, Sylvain. "The Participation of the Jews of France in the Great War." In *American Jewish Yearbook*, pp. 31–97. New York: American Jewish Committee, Jewish Publication Society, 1920.

Schnurmann, E. *La Population Juive en Alsace*. Paris: Librairie du Recueil Sirey, 1936.

Spire, André. *Les Juifs et la Guerre*. Paris: Payot, 1917.

Un Héros Alsacien: David Bloch. Colmar: Alsatia, 1923.

Secondary Sources

Becker, Annette. *War and Faith: The Religious Imagination in France, 1914–1930*. Oxford: Berg, 1998.

Birnbaum, Pierre. *La 'République juive.'* Paris: Arthème Fayard, 1988.

———. *Le moment antisémite: un tour de la France en 1898*. Paris: Fayard, 1998.

Caron, Vicki. *Between France and Germany: The Jews of Alsace-Lorraine, 1871–1918*. Stanford, CA: Stanford University Press, 1988.

Corber, Erin. "*L'esprit du corps*: Bodies, Communities, and the Reconstruction of Jewish Life in France, 1914–1940." Unpublished PhD dissertation, Indiana University, Bloomington, 2013.

Daltroff, Jean. "1871–1918 en Alsace: l'accueil contrasté des Juifs venus d'ailleurs." In *Regards sur la culture judeo-alsacienne: Des identités en partage*, edited by Freddy Raphaël, pp. 113–29. Strasbourg: La nuée bleue, 2001.

———. *La Synagogue du quai Kléber à Strasbourg (1898–1941)*. Strasbourg: ID L'Édition, 2012.

Fischer, Christopher. *Alsace to the Alsatians? Visions and Divisions of Alsatian Regionalism, 1870–1939*. New York: Berghahn Books, 2010.

Fogarty, Richard S. *Race and War in France: Colonial Subjects in the French Army, 1914–1918*. Baltimore: Johns Hopkins University Press, 2008.

Gillis, John, ed. *Commemorations: The Politics of National Identity*. Princeton, NJ: Princeton University Press, 1994.

Goodfellow, Samuel. *Between the Swastika and the Cross of Lorraine: Fascisms in Interwar Alsace*. DeKalb: Northern Illinois University Press, 1999.

Hale, Dana. *Races on Display: French Representations of Colonial Peoples, 1886–1940*. Bloomington: Indiana University Press, 2008.

Hyman, Paula. *The Emancipation of the Jews of Alsace: Acculturation and Tradition in the Nineteenth Century*. New Haven, CT: Yale University Press, 1991.

Landau, Philippe E. *Les Juifs de France et la Grande Guerre*. Paris: CNRS Editions, 1999.

Netter, Paul. *Un Grand Rabbin dans la Grande Guerre*. Paris: Italiques, 2013.

Nolan, Michael. *The Inverted Mirror: Mythologizing the Enemy in France and Germany, 1898–1914*. New York: Berghahn Books, 2005.

Penslar, Derek. *Jews and the Military: A History*. Princeton, NJ: Princeton University Press, 2013.

Prost, Antoine. "Les monuments aux morts." In *Les lieux de mémoire*, vol. 1, *La République*, edited by Pierre Nora., pp. 195–225. Paris: Gallimard, 1984.

Ronald, D. A. B. *Youth, Heroism, and War Propaganda: Britain and the Young Maritime Hero, 1745–1840.* New York: Bloomsbury, 2015.
Schechter, Ronald. *Obstinate Hebrews: Representations of Jews in France, 1715–1815.* Berkeley: University of California Press, 2003.
Sherman, Daniel. *The Construction of Memory in Interwar France.* Chicago: University of Chicago Press, 1999.
Ther, Philipp. *The Dark Side of Nation States: Ethnic Cleansing in Modern Europe.* New York: Berghahn Books, 2014.
Winter, Jay. *Sites of Memory, Sites of Mourning: The Great War in European Cultural History.* Cambridge: Cambridge University Press, 1994.
Wittman, Laura. *The Tomb of the Unknown Soldier: Modern Mourning and the Reinvention of the Mystical Body.* Toronto: University of Toronto Press, 2011.

CHAPTER 5

The Budapest Jewish Community's Galician October

Rebekah Klein-Pejšová

It is not difficult for us to imagine the sight of Budapest's railway stations crowded with refugees. After all, images of refugees in the stations filled the media during the expansion of the Syrian refugee crisis in the summer of 2015. "Budapest's Keleti [Eastern] train station has become a de facto refugee camp," the *New York Times* reported in September 2015, in an article featuring a photograph of refugee families, mainly from Syria, making do with blankets and tents on the broad concrete floors and underground passageways of the station, waiting to move on.[1] Throughout the twentieth century and beyond, railway stations have served as crucial sites of sojourn and contact for refugees in times of mass displacement—where people have eaten and slept, sought news about relatives and friends, experienced reunions, received assistance, and engaged with political and social organizations.[2] In the early days of World War I, Budapest's train stations served as the liminal sites from which a set of staggered, closed-train transports of at least two thousand Galician Jewish refugees, arranged and financed by the Budapest Jewish community, were sent from Budapest to Vienna or to the refugee camp in the Moravian border town Ungarisch Hradisch/Hradiště Uherské, which the Austrian government had established in October 1914 to accommodate Austrian war refugees without financial means.[3] Why did the Budapest Jewish community undertake this action? How can we evaluate its initiative? This article argues that the arrival of Hungarian Jewish refugees from the then northeastern Hungarian counties of Sáros, Zemplén, Ung, Bereg, and Mármaros into the Hungarian capital that October was the primary reason why the Budapest Jewish community decided to provide for the removal of the Galician Jewish refugees from Hungarian to Austrian territory.

Thousands of Galician Jews began arriving by train and on foot in Budapest in September 1914, shortly after the outbreak of war. They were understood as "foreigners" by Hungary, despite the fact that Hungary and Austria formed a dual state under a joint ruler. Since the constitutional compromise of 1867 created the Dual Monarchy of Austria-Hungary, the two halves functioned as quasi sovereign countries joined together by a shared head of state and three common ministries: foreign affairs, war, and finance. The Austrian emperor served as the king of Hungary. As Galicia formed a constituent territory of Austria, the inhabitants of Galicia were citizens of Austria, though not of Hungary. An estimated 200,000 to 300,000 Jews had fled Galicia in August as terrified witnesses to the fate of Jews just across the border in Russia, who had been expelled from their borderland homes and sent deep into the interior of the empire by military commanders convinced that Jews were spying for the enemy.[4] They fled the dreaded Russian army's arrival in Galicia in fear of their lives.[5] Invading Russian forces looted and burned Jewish houses and shops as they moved westward across Galicia toward Kraków from September through November that first autumn of the war.[6] Approximately 15,000 Jews fled from Przemyśl, 8,000 from Zaleszczyki, and thousands more from Buczacz and Śniatyn.[7]

The Eastern Front cut through Russia's western borderlands, in addition to Austrian Galicia and Bukovina, which together were home to three-quarters of the world's Jewish population, about five million people. Approximately three-quarters of the Jewish population in the Austrian half of the Dual Monarchy lived in Austria's northeastern provinces of Galicia and Bukovina. According to the 1910 Austrian census, 871,906 Jews lived in Galicia, or 11 percent of the total population, and in Bukovina Jews numbered 102,919, or 13 percent of the total population.[8] Jews and non-Jews from Galicia and Bukovina fled in the hundreds of thousands to Hungary, Bohemia, Moravia, and Vienna.[9] Galicia endured ten months of occupation by the Russian army. By June 1915, when the Central Powers regained control over Galicia, making repatriation possible, about 500,000 Galician Jews had been dislocated.[10] Their dislocation formed a substantial part of the unprecedented mass civilian population displacement across the European continent catalyzed by World War I and the accompanying collapse of Europe's multinational empires.[11]

The Galician Jewish refugee presence throughout Hungary during the war reminded the country's population that large-scale Galician Jewish migration southward into Hungary formed the demographic base of contemporary Hungarian Jewry. Galician Jews were predominantly pious rural village or small-town Jews, who spoke Yiddish and practiced either traditional Judaism or a Hasidic lifestyle. Galicia was also an important base of development for the Haskalah, or Jewish Enlightenment, in the Habsburg Monarchy. Jews from Galicia began to migrate southward into Hungary in the 1780s due to the economic depression in Galicia that followed its annexation by the Habsburgs during the Polish partitions of 1772 through 1795. Chiefly owing to this immigration, the Jewish population in Hungary grew from about 83,000 in 1787 to 130,000 in 1805. The Hungarian Jewish population continued to grow by approximately 40 to 50 percent every twenty years until 1880, when immigration from Galicia slowed. According to the 1880 Hungarian census, the Jewish population of the country then stood at 624,000. It increased to 910,000 by 1910.[12]

The scale of Jewish immigration into Hungary and the high degree of Jews' adaptation to the parameters of the Hungarian state attested to Hungarian Jewish success. Yet it was also a source of deep insecurity, for putting an end to immigration into Hungary and doing away with Orthodoxy were conditions the great Hungarian statesmen of the 1840s Reform Era József Eötvös and Ferenc Deák urged their Jewish friends to fulfill if they wished to achieve emancipation in Hungary.[13] When the Hungarian government indeed granted emancipation to the Jews in 1867, at the time of the creation of the Dual Monarchy of Austria-Hungary, it was again de facto conditional. The government offered Hungarian Jews protection from popular antisemitism and cleared a path for their social mobility through education and religious equality. In return, it expected the Jews' unwavering loyalty to the state. This meant political support, cultural Magyarization, and social assimilation that included the renunciation of Jewish cultural, behavioral, and religious "peculiarities," which many Hungarian Jews did diligently work to achieve. They did so in a wide variety of ways, ranging from simply declaring Hungarian as their mother tongue on the census while maintaining their traditional lifestyle on the one hand, to fully identifying themselves with the Magyars at the other extreme.[14] When the war came, Hungarian Jews, like their counterparts in Austria, believed it to be their chance to join in the common war effort, to dispel antisemitism with their intrepid rise to arms, and to gain full acceptance in the Hungarian national community.[15] Yet the conspicuous Jewish refugee presence throughout the war and the peculiarities of the wartime refugee crisis on Hungarian territory produced intense interest in the so-called Jewish Question on all levels. Hungarian Jews quickly recognized that they were in no way exempt from the spike in antisemitism with which the Galician Jewish refugees were received by the broader Hungarian society.

Refugees of all backgrounds experienced hostility across the European continent during World War I. Local populations denounced refugees as "opportunists" and "deserters" in broad strokes, "whores" whose presence sharply heightened rates of epidemic disease, crime, and prostitution. They blamed refugees for driving up food prices while driving down wages. Refugees everywhere stood accused of thievery and of otherwise unfairly procuring scarce resources.[16] In the Austro-Hungarian countryside and in the capital cities Vienna and Budapest, the arrival and lingering presence of Jewish refugees during the war exacerbated existing anti-Jewish sentiment and wartime stereotypes of Jews as profiteers, hawkers, smugglers, and shirkers. According to locals' complaints, Jewish refugees loitered in large groups on the streets and in coffeehouses, lived off government aid, engaged in profiteering and dishonest business practices, and shirked military duty.[17]

This article focuses on the wartime Jewish refugee crisis in Austria-Hungary on the territory of Hungary, rather than in major centers further west—such as the imperial capital in Vienna—during the first autumn of the war. The shift to Hungary strikingly underscores the linkage between citizenship and resource distribution, financial solvency and movement, and highlights the diversity of Hungarian Jewry before 1918. The article probes the Budapest Jewish community's cooperation with the Hungarian wartime administration in clearing Hungarian territory of Austrian—that is, Galician Jewish—refugees against a backdrop of the wider Hungarian Jewish response to the Jewish refugee crisis in Austria-Hungary. It offers a snapshot of the dynamics of mass civilian displacement during World War I. How did perceptions of loyalty and concepts of patriotic obligation figure into the often hasty and improvisational nature of refugee assistance in the initial phase of the war?

From Improvisation to Policy

The Budapest Jewish community's welfare committee waited in the Keleti railway station the first Friday afternoon of October 1914 with warm meals intended for the eight hundred Galician Jewish refugees expected to arrive before sundown, the beginning of the Jewish Sabbath. The refugees did not appear. Not only did the train not arrive at the expected time, but it did not arrive at the expected place. The welfare committee later learned that refugees had only been permitted to travel to the depot station on the outskirts of the city (Ferencváros), and only there would food distribution be allowed.[18] Angered by the troubles and hunger caused by the service disruption, the liberal Hungarian Jewish daily *Egyenlőség* printed a scathing condemnation of the Hungarian administration's handling of refugee matters under the minister of the interior, Sándor János:

> By now, it is hardly an accident that the lengthy journey [undertaken by the refugees] occurs under terrible, overcrowded conditions. The weary people, for whom,

according to the beautiful words of the minister of the interior's official memo cited here, "there shall be the increased care of society and mandatory protection of the state, and who are worthy of care for their poor health," and who, according to the just communication of the Security Council, "may reside anywhere on the territory of the country if they are able to live from their own means," are not allowed to disembark from the train despite the [numbers] of the ailing among them, weakened from exhaustion ... nor may those disembark who are forbidden Saturday travel for religious reasons. Only one child sick from diphtheria and its mother may, with a great deal of [persuasion], be lifted out of the cattle car. The rest must travel on Friday night, on Saturday, and maybe further, who knows where, who knows how far, due to the greater interest in military [needs].[19]

In contrast to the considerable government aid available to the Galician refugees in Vienna, lamented *Egyenlőség*, refugee aid in Hungary was either nonexistent or obstructed. While Galician Jews from Lemberg/Lwów/L'viv, Stanislau/Stanisławów, and other Jewish communities enjoyed Yom Kippur services led by Rabbi Ezekiel Caro of Lemberg/Lwów/L'viv, grateful for Vienna's hospitality and fraternal feeling, they complained in letters to the German-language Budapest daily *Pester Lloyd* that many hundreds among them, including people of sufficient means to support themselves, were not permitted to enter Hungarian cities. They were turned away from Mármarossziget in the northeast, for example, and sent to Hungary's border.[20]

Hungarian refugee policy shifted considerably during the first chaotic weeks of the wartime refugee influx. In early September, the lord lieutenant of Zemplén County in Sátoraljaújhely improvised refugee provisions from Hungarian treasury monies and provided for temporary accommodations for refugees without means in Szatmár County. Hungarian authorities soon arranged Jewish refugee transfer to Nikolsburg/Mikulov in western Austria (Moravia), where the Israelitische Allianz zu Wien, a Jewish charitable organization, handled refugee provisions.[21] The Allianz sent Galician Jewish refugees on as soon as possible to other locations in Moravia where they would receive Austrian state aid as Austrian citizens, and it also provided kosher meals.[22] The Allianz worked with the newly established American Jewish Joint Distribution Committee (AJDC), until the United States entered the war in 1917, to serve Jewish refugee needs all over Austria-Hungary. The Allianz and the AJDC maintained soup kitchens, tea rooms, and warm rooms. They founded orphanages, homes for the elderly, and homes for the sick, while building barracks for refugee accommodations, providing clothing, linens, and one crown daily for food.[23]

The Hungarian administration relied on support from diasporic Jewish organizations to provide relief, while maintaining that the Austrian state was responsible for taking care of displaced Austrian citizens of the Dual Monarchy with its own funds. Hungary did not feel obliged to support

Galician refugees since they were Austrian, not Hungarian, citizens. Official Hungarian policy emerged from the chaotic September improvisations, chiefly derived from considerations of refugee citizenship, wealth, and health, and with the ultimate goal of full repatriation. Thus aid policy toward the Galician Jewish refugees on the territory of Hungary depended on their Austrian citizenship. As Austrian citizens, they were entitled to receive state aid from the Austrian treasury. They could only receive this aid, however, on the territory of Austria, with the exception of limited, temporary Austrian state aid provided for refugees sojourning in Budapest before transfer to Austria.[24] The Hungarian government permitted refugees with sufficient financial means to provide for themselves to remain in Hungary, where they would be required to report regularly on their continuing financial solvency. Border police sent refugees with means on to the Dual Monarchy's urban centers in Hungary and in Austria.[25]

From October 1914, Hungary sent arriving Austrian refugees without means directly to Austria and more consequently transported those sojourning in Budapest to the western Austrian border town Ungarisch Hradisch/Hradiště Uherské in Moravia.[26] Since wartime conditions gave train transport of wounded soldiers, munitions, and other military supplies highest priority, refugees most frequently made the journey to Moravia on foot, shouldering their belongings, or in the better case, by wagon.[27] Ungarisch Hradisch/Hradiště Uherské quickly became the main Jewish refugee way station and transportation hub from where refugees went on to tens of smaller camps and improvised accommodation centers in Moravia and Bohemia. Refugees remained in these controlled sites until they could repatriate.[28] Hungarian authorities did take health into consideration in organizing refugee movement. Above all, the state wished to contain the spread of illness and disease from refugees to soldiers and to the general public. Because military personnel convalesced in Pőstyén/Piešťany, for example, the Hungarian authorities prohibited Galician Jewish refugee movement through and sojourn in the town.[29] Later the authorities did permit Galician Jewish refugees without means who suffered from documented serious illnesses to remain in Hungary during the winter of 1914–15, rather than set off on the arduous trek to Austria. The Hungarian administration expected that they move on to Ungarisch Hradisch/Hradiště Uherské as soon as possible, with confirmation that they had done so from the relevant local Jewish community.[30]

Transports to Austria

By the first week of October 1914, the board of the Budapest Jewish community was sending regular updates to minister of the interior Sándor

János concerning the transports of Galician Jewish refugees to Austria. The memos were short. A single sentence confirmed the personal identity of the Galician Jews listed on the attached passenger register. Each passenger listed had undergone a medical exam and received a free train ticket for the trip in a closed, escorted wagon, all organized by the Budapest Jewish community.[31] Several previous administrative communications emphasized the importance of confirming that the refugees had been medically examined before their departure for Austria.[32] The trains left throughout the month of October on weekdays, avoiding travel on the Jewish Sabbath, from one of the two main railway stations, East (Keleti) and West (Nyugati), with a destination of either Vienna or Ungarisch Hradisch/Hradiště Uherské, where arrangement would be made for their sojourn in western Austria until repatriation became possible in Galicia.[33]

In his study of Galician Jewish refugees in Vienna, David Rechter argues that acculturated Jews were embarrassed by the Galician Jewish refugee presence. In Budapest, he notes, the local Jewish community leadership "reportedly went so far as to request the refugees' expulsion."[34] I have not found specific evidence of a "request" on the part of the Budapest Jewish community, but archival evidence indicates that the community leadership did indeed orchestrate and fund refugee removal from Budapest to Vienna. Somewhat belatedly, more than a week after the transports commenced, a report appeared in the record apprising the state's police and railway officials of the Budapest Jewish community's arrangements with the Ministry of the Interior regarding provision for Galician Jewish refugee movement.[35]

While enough compelling evidence certainly exists pointing to the unease of acculturated well-to-do Jews with the Galician Jewish refugees and the awkwardness of their interactions, this was not the only reason why the Budapest Jewish community took the radical step of organizing their removal from the Hungarian capital. Something else had changed. The arrival of Hungarian Jewish refugees from northeastern Hungary, about whom we hear much less in the literature, and for whom the Hungarian state would be obliged to assist with funds from the Hungarian treasury, appears to be the more important contributing factor in making this decision. Their entry into the city, along with the steep rise in antisemitic incitement, led Budapest Jews to make more effective demonstrations of patriotic obligation, including the wartime patriotic obligation of the Hungarian Jewish refugees themselves. Discussion in the Jewish press of Hungarian Jewish soldiers' numbers and sacrifices went hand in hand with heightened refugee aid activities in the train stations and in Jewish communal buildings and with the Galician Jewish refugees' departure. We gain more insight into the Budapest Jewish community's unusual actions in relation to the Galician Jewish refugees through their response to Jewish refugee arrival from Hungary's northeastern counties.

As the Eastern Front cut westward through Galicia, thousands of Hungarian citizens from Hungary's northeastern counties—Sáros, Zemplén, Ung, Bereg, and Mármaros—also fled before the dreaded Russian army. "The Hungarian refugees have arrived into the tracks of the Galician refugees," wrote *Egyenlőség* on 11 October 1914. "The enemy is not particular. After acquiring a position in Galicia and Bukovina—although weakened—it has also paid a visit in Ung and Mármaros."[36] Most of the population fled from their homes in the newly occupied zone following the departure of a great number of their civil and religious leaders. Jewish refugees from northeastern Hungary came in large numbers to the capital, though even more of them escaped to urban centers in the countryside. Hungarian funds to assist the displaced from the kingdom's affected regions in the Hungarian towns where they sojourned was forthcoming, although increasingly problematic within wartime budget constraints. Displaced Jewish families from Zboró and Kurima in Sáros County found refuge in Nyiregyhaza, an important urban center in the northern plain region, just far enough away from the Russian-occupied zone. The Hungarian Ministry of the Interior even allocated some additional funds to the Nyiregyhaza administration for refugee care months later following a report from the town's chief rabbi that refugees there would not be able to return to their homes by June as previously expected. Nearly all the Jews in Zboró had fled after Russian troops burned down the synagogue and the rabbi's house. The displaced rabbi of Kurima along with nine family members also received aid and accommodation in Nyiregyhaza, including monies for provisions and a simple apartment.[37]

Hungarian citizens of all backgrounds fled before the approaching Eastern Front of the war regardless of religion, yet the Jews were the most visible refugees. "[Everyone sees] the Jews because they are of another religion, they differ so greatly from the majority of the population in their attire ... the clothing and hairstyles of a great many pious Jews from Upper Hungary are not only noticeable within the mass of the normal population, but immediately obvious," *Egyenlőség* opined.[38] Acculturated Budapest Jewry felt just as uneasy about the devout Hungarian Jews from the northeast who maintained Jewish cultural, behavioral, and religious particularities despite their loyalty to and support for Hungary as they did about the pious Jews from Galicia. They wished to take them out of the public eye and provide them with Jewish communal aid rather than state funds to avoid contributing to the wartime drain on the economy and the anticipated accompanying antisemitism. Each refugee was entitled to receive 78 *fillér* from the Hungarian state treasury, about 35 percent of the average daily wage in 1914, or enough for two kilograms of rye bread. The Budapest Jewish community paid the rest, as the prescribed amount was scarcely sufficient to cover the refugees' most basic needs.[39]

Egyenlőség sorrowfully announced the commencement of "the special kind of 'patriotism' whose existence derives from declaring others unpatriotic—jingoism."[40] The Jews, continued the paper, were under attack again for their alleged lack of patriotism; they were suspected of all sorts of treacherous acts. Antisemites suspected that Jews had betrayed the nation, and they accused the Jews from Máramaros and Ung, supposedly like the Galician Jews, of guiding the Russian troops through unfamiliar territory, leading them to the Hungarian troops.[41] To counter such increasingly frequent accusations in the antisemitic press, *Egyenlőség* enumerated the broad scope of Jewish contribution to the Hungarian war effort: 150,000 Jewish soldiers stood ready to fight on the battlefields, joined by some 15,000 Jewish reserve officers and doctors; Jews had contributed more than ten million crowns to war bonds; Jews in Budapest and in the rest of the country had established countless soup kitchens, hospitals, and aid centers; the Jews bled, the Jews died, the Jews helped. The Jews had "worked miracles."[42] Articles extolling the Hungarian Jewish community's assistance to refugees and generous financial contributions to the war effort and above all praising the profound patriotism, heroism, loyalty, and sacrifice of Jewish soldiers filled the Hungarian Jewish press. *Egyenlőség* would create a column dedicated to listing the names of fallen Jewish soldiers from the Kingdom of Hungary two months later in December 1914. But Jewish refugees were more visible than Jewish soldiers.

With the arrival of the first Hungarian Jewish refugees, it became known from a memo of the Ministry of Interior circulated more widely than perhaps intended that the Hungarian administration did not wish to allow both the Galician and the Hungarian Jewish refugees to remain on Hungarian territory at the same time. The Galician Jewish refugees would have to go. The administration counted on an influx of Hungarian Jews displaced from the northeast for whom the state bore responsibility for social welfare. Existing but limited state resources would be necessary to care for them, as Hungarian citizens. Vilmos Vázsonyi, respected Hungarian politician of Jewish origin who would be minister of justice for brief terms in 1917 and 1918, suggested that the departure of the Galician refugees from Hungary would have to be arranged.[43] By the time Vázsonyi's proposal appeared in print, the transports of Galician Jewish refugees organized by the Budapest Jewish community were of course already under way. They were directly tied to the arrival of the Hungarian Jewish refugees.

But how long would the Hungarian Jewish refugees remain internally displaced? In late October 1914, *Egyenlőség* published a front-page plea to the Hungarian refugees to return home. Whether from Galicia or northeastern Hungary, the presence of the pious Jewish refugees in Budapest embarrassed the local Jewish community and made them feel uneasy. With the Hungarian Jewish refugees, however, the newspaper could appeal to the refugees' sense of patriotism and wartime responsibility as Hungarian citizens, in the Hungarian language:

> Truly with love we received our fellow citizens who fled from Máramaros and other northern regions of the country into our communities.... We had a twofold obligation to rush to their aid: one patriotic and one humanitarian.... But lo! Our heroic brethren have driven the enemy from our country. Security, calm, and order have returned to the temporarily [*ideig-óráig*] occupied regions. We feel that by now it is the duty of the refugees to return to their homes, to continue their work, their trades, and their occupations.... Everyone fulfilled their obligations to the refugees; now it is their turn.[44]

Hungarian Jewish Responses to the October Transports

Elsewhere in Hungary, particularly in the counties north of Budapest that the refugees passed through in their movement toward the capital, provincial Jewish communities began to intervene with the government in Budapest on behalf of the Austrian (Galician) Jewish refugees. They intervened not to ensure the refugees could travel more quickly and easily to Vienna by train, but rather so that the Austrian state aid intended for their assistance on Austrian territory might be diverted to them just where they were in Hungary so that their travel would not be necessary. Was it not a dual state with shared wartime obligations?

Rabbi Koloman Wéber, chief rabbi of the Orthodox Jewish community in Pőstyén/Piešťany, fought tirelessly with administrators of the Dual Monarchy to divert aid to the Galician Jewish refugees sojourning in his community. His successes with the Austrian and Hungarian Ministries of the Interior on their behalf secured his reputation as a celebrated wartime refugee advocate.[45] The Orthodox Jewish communities of Pozsony/Pressburg (later Bratislava) and Stomfa/Štupava soon followed suit, requesting that Austrian state aid be directed to them to provide for hundreds of refugee families. "After much wandering," the petition from the Stomfa community asserted, "[the refugees] have found refuge and a place of calm in the bosom of our community."[46] Why, then, was it necessary to force them further on a treacherous winter trek? The Galician-born Dr. Joseph Samuel Bloch, editor of the Vienna-based *Österreichische Wochenschrift* and staunch defender of Jewish rights, sent a telegram to the Hungarian prime minister Count István Tisza on behalf of the Galician Jewish refugees sojourning in Galanta, reminding Tisza that the sons of the refugees were off fighting the enemy in the Carpathians.[47]

Rabbi Snyder of the Orthodox Jewish community in Győr, an admirer of Rabbi Wéber, also petitioned the Austrian and Hungarian ministers of the interior for the disbursement of Austrian funds to the refugees sojourning in his town, based on the argument that refugees in the provinces should receive the same provisional Austrian aid as that available to those in Budapest. But his entreaty was not approved.[48] Since the goal was repatriation following short-term clearance of the Austrian refugees from Hungarian territory, the administration found it undesirable to dispense funds in the countryside.[49]

Jewish communities found it to be their moral imperative and humanitarian duty to step in even though their efforts obstructed the ability of the regional administration to carry out its duties. The lord lieutenant of Borsod County triumphantly reported in February 1915 that in spite of the local Jewish community's obstructionist activity, he had managed to successfully transport the majority of Galician Jewish refugees in his region to Ungarisch Hradisch/Hradiště Uherské. He derided the "role of protector" played by Rabbi Mayer Schück of the Orthodox Jewish community in Ónod since the arrival of the refugees in the fall. Rabbi Schück "would like to settle the whole of Galician Jewry around him," noted the lord lieutenant in his report, an actuality that accounted for the large numbers of refugees who had found haven in Borsod County. The refugees remained in the care of the Ónod Jewish community for nearly eight weeks, as well as in the neighboring communities of Felsőzsolcza, Sajólád, and Ujdiósgyőr.[50] Not wanting to give the impression that he had "left humanitarian principles outside of his consideration," the lord lieutenant added that he had allowed individuals of means to organize their own provisions, and he had permitted the elderly and the ill to remain in Borsod County.[51]

The Zionist literary and intellectual monthly *Múlt és Jövő* (Past and Future) believed that the Budapest Jewish community lacked compassion and morality in its handling of the Galician Jewish refugees and that the community did not act in the best interest of Jewry as a whole. The journal regularly published articles intended to familiarize Hungarian Jewry with contemporary Galician Jewish society and culture, as well as poems, letters, and other literary work sympathetic to their plight during the war. A contribution by Rabbi Antál Kertész, an army chaplain who had served in the Ninety-Seventh Reserve Unit and had been a Russian prisoner of war in Lemberg/Lwów/L'viv for over two months, decried the treatment of the Galician Jews by their coreligionists in Hungary:

> Those who have been the most afflicted victims of the raging world war again have to reach for their walking sticks. On top of all their troubles lies the fact that not only Christians, but also—I cannot deny it—some of our coreligionists exhibit a certain animosity toward the Galician Jews.[52]

Kertész pleaded with his fellow Hungarians to bear in mind that "these *payos-* and kaftan-wearing" Galician Jewish refugees, and their kin in Lemberg/Lwów/L'viv, Stanislau/Stanisławów, Stryj, and Sambor, provided warm food, drink, and clean underwear to the sons of Hungarian Jewry who fell into Russian captivity. For this reason, he implored Hungarian Jews to show compassion toward their unfortunate coreligionists—"in spite of their faults."[53]

The Hungarian government's renewed repatriation effort for Austrian Jewish refugees sojourning in Budapest in spring 1915, and the Budapest Jewish community's efforts to facilitate it, seemed particularly egregious. The effort seems to reverse a decision recently reached by both the Austrian and Hungarian administrations that Budapest would be an exceptional site on Hungarian territory where Austrian Jewish refugees without means might receive Austrian state aid if they were not engaged in or convicted of criminal activity.[54] In the view of the Jewish press, the Refugee Aid Committee, composed of five Orthodox and five Neolog (liberal) Jews under the guidance of the vice-mayor's office of Budapest, was responsible for advising the Hungarian administration to order the immediate removal of the remaining refugees.[55] The Jewish press wondered if the Refugee Aid Committee had been aware of its great responsibility to the refugees, in addition to Jewry as a whole. It urged the committee to concentrate on the rights, honor, and dignity of the Jewish refugees, as "their honor is indeed our honor, their dignity is our dignity, and their rights are our rights."[56]

Despite the efforts of the Refugee Aid Committee, repatriation was not so easily accomplished. A great number of refugees had no homes or towns to which to return, as they had been destroyed. Of the thousands of Austrian and Hungarian Jewish refugees who entered Hungary during the first weeks of the war and sojourned throughout the country, with and without financial means, hundreds remained for the duration of the war and even beyond the armistice. Repatriation became an attainable policy goal only after the Central Powers drove the occupying Russian army out of most of Galicia and Bukovina in June 1915. The Hungarian minister of the interior set 15 August as the deadline for all Austrian Jewish refugees remaining on Hungarian territory to return to their homes. The administration did not allocate trains for the purpose of refugee repatriation. The long journey back would have to be undertaken again on foot, at least 550 kilometers for most people, northward from Budapest through the countryside to Stryj, Brody, Turka, Halicz, and Buczacz. The Hungarian administration made an exception for Hungarian Jewish refugees coming from Sáros and Zemplén Counties, in the country's northeast, where heavy fighting still continued.[57]

When large numbers of refugees remained in Hungary following the 15 August repatriation deadline, Hungarian police harshly stepped up enforcement of the measures, reported the *Jüdische Zeitung*. The police began to forcibly remove refugees from their accommodations. One refugee family in Budapest was evicted in October from an apartment in which they had lived for nearly a year and sent to a detention center (*Schubhaus*).⁵⁸ Thousands more stayed scattered throughout Hungary well into fall 1915. The Israelitische Allianz zu Wien estimated that about 30,000 Jewish refugees still remained in Nagyvárad/Grosswardein/ Oradea at the end of 1915, but the organization did not have reliable figures available for either Budapest or other Hungarian regions. At the same time, approximately 100,000 refugees without means sojourned in Vienna, 84,318 in Bohemia, and 121,099 in Moravia.⁵⁹ Vienna closed its doors to further refugee entry in early December 1914, sending arrivals without means to refugee camps in Moravian and Bohemian towns and villages. The Austrian authorities permitted refugees with means to remain in Vienna.⁶⁰

Nearly 1,500 out of a previous count of 25,000 Austrian Jewish refugees remained in Budapest well into the summer of 1916. The able-bodied refugees had gone elsewhere, leaving behind a refugee population that was predominantly elderly and infirm. The remainder of the refugee population in Budapest consisted of Galician rabbis who had received permission not to be resettled in towns in Bohemia and Moravia where there were no Jewish communities, in addition to children permitted to enroll in Budapest schools for the academic year 1917–18 along with their families.⁶¹ Whatever progress had been made in repatriating Austrian and Hungarian Jewish refugees up through the summer of 1916 was disrupted by further Entente incursions on the Eastern Front. The Brusilov Offensive and the Romanian invasion of Transylvania sent thousands more fleeing from their homes toward the end of the summer. By the end of 1916, more than 20,000 Jewish refugees sojourned in Budapest and the Hungarian provinces.⁶²

The Hungarian minister of the interior made another push for refugee repatriation in September 1917, citing dire shortages of provisions and accommodations. Alarmed Budapest Jews sent a telegram sent to the emperor-king, decrying the Hungarian authorities for "[rounding] up [the refugees] like dogs on the street" and sending them away.⁶³ In November, the administration announced that more than 9,000 of the estimated 25,000 refugees had been removed, and the other 16,000 would soon leave. The *Österreichische Wochenschrift* noted the use of the term "Galizianer" in a derogatory manner in the Hungarian House of Representatives during the discussion of this issue.⁶⁴

The final wartime attempt at total refugee repatriation came in April 1918. The few hundred Austrian Jewish refugees sojourning in the provinces and in Budapest, regardless of whether with or without means, were ordered to report to the police in the capital and depart for their original residences from assigned transport centers.⁶⁵ Several hundred Galician

Jewish refugees nevertheless remained on the territory of Hungary at the close of the war, some of them settling down in various communities on an individual basis in small numbers.[66]

"Patriotic Obligation"

Was there another course of action available to the Budapest Jewish community when it made the choice to assist in removing Galician Jewish refugees from Budapest in October 1914? How can we evaluate its initiative? Given the poor and chaotic conditions for refugee aid and accommodation in Hungary in comparison with Austria and the easily recognizable fact that the Hungarian administration intended to send this group of refugees to Austria in any case because of the arrival of the Hungarian Jewish refugees, to what extent is it appropriate to take a dim view of its decision?

Justification for the Budapest Jewish community's arrangement lies with its provision for refugee movement by train rather than on foot. Since transfer of military supplies and transport of soldiers were the highest wartime priority, it was rarely possible for refugees to travel by train. Travel on foot to destinations in Austria was a terrible hardship, especially as the temperature dropped, when we consider the many old people and children within the refugee population, as well as the hostility of the wider population toward refugees in general and toward Jewish refugees in particular. The fact that Galician Jewish refugees would have to travel on foot to Austria was the main impetus for the difficult decision made by many Hungarian Jewish communities in the provinces to simply provide for the refugees themselves, out of pocket, against the wishes of the Hungarian administration. That the Budapest Jewish community was able to secure numerous train transfers to Vienna and Ungarisch Hradisch/Hradiště Uherské, even if in sealed escorted trains, attests to the strength of its efforts vis-à-vis the state administration.

The whole October action indicates that the Budapest Jewish community may have found a way to assure itself of its compliance with rapidly evolving Hungarian state policy toward the refugees and to feel it had done right by the refugees in terms of its perception of the limitations of humanitarian assistance. In addition, removing the refugees would help clear Hungary of a more traditional, largely unacculturated Jewish population whose mass influx into Hungary in the view of Budapest Jewish leaders threatened to tear the Hungarian Jewish emancipation contract. The quartet of Hungarian Jewish patriotic obligation—ending immigration, doing away with Orthodoxy, renouncing Jewish particularities, and demonstrating unwavering loyalty to the state—was given good due diligence in the Budapest Jewish community's Galician October. Budapest

Jewish leaders proved themselves willing and able to champion a refugee policy thoroughly in tune with the desires of the Hungarian administration, yet one that rang flat on the broad stage of Hungarian Jewry.

Rebekah Klein-Pejšová is Jewish studies associate professor of history and head of the Human Rights Program at Purdue University, specializing in modern Jewish and East Central European history. She is the author of *Mapping Jewish Loyalties in Interwar Slovakia* (Indiana University Press, 2015) and contributor to *The Holocaust in Hungary Seventy Years Later* (CEU Jewish Studies Program and CEU Press, 2016) and *Europe on the Move: The Great War and Its Refugees, 1914–1918* (forthcoming, Manchester University Press).

Notes

1. Anemona Hartocollis, "Traveling in Europe's River of Migrants," *New York Times*, 2 September 2015.
2. Anna Cichopek-Gajraj, *Beyond Violence: Jewish Survivors in Poland and Slovakia, 1944–48* (Cambridge: Cambridge University Press, 2014), p. 39.
3. Magyar Országos Levéltár [Hungarian National Archives, hereinafter MOL], fond Belügyminiszterium [Ministry of the Interior] K148, Elnöki Iratok [Presidential Files] (PF) 1915, Box 37, Folder 80.
4. Michael Marrus, *The Unwanted: European Refugees from the First World War through the Cold War* (Philadelphia: Temple University Press, 2002), p. 62; and Peter Gatrell, *A Whole Empire Walking* (Bloomington: Indiana University Press, 1999), pp. 16–17. Russian troops often perceived the Yiddish vernacular of the Jews as German, heightening their suspicion that Jews were spies or could potentially spy for the enemy.
5. Marsha L. Rozenblit, *Reconstructing a National Identity: The Jews of Habsburg Austria during World War I* (New York: Oxford University Press, 2001), p. 50.
6. David Rechter, *The Jews of Vienna and the First World War* (London: Littman Library of Jewish Civilization, 2001), p. 69.
7. Ibid.
8. Rozenblit, *Reconstructing a National Identity*, p. 15.
9. Ibid., p. 66.
10. American Jewish Committee, *Jews in the Eastern War Zone* (New York, 1916), pp. 84–87.
11. Peter Gatrell, *The Making of the Modern Refugee* (Oxford: Oxford University Press, 2015), p. 2.
12. William O. McCagg, Jr., *A History of Habsburg Jews, 1670–1918* (Bloomington: Indiana University Press, 1989), p. 125.
13. Ibid., pp. 133–34.
14. Victor Karady, "Religious Divisions, Socio-economic Stratification and the Modernization of Hungarian Jewry after the Emancipation," in *Jews in the Hungarian Economy, 1760–1945*, ed. Michael Silber (Jerusalem: Magnes Press, 1992), p. 162. Victor Karady terms this the "assimilationist social contract" in his pivotal study. See Rebekah

Klein-Pejšová, *Mapping Jewish Loyalties in Interwar Slovakia* (Bloomington: Indiana University Press, 2015), pp. 3–12, for discussion of heterogeneous Hungarian Jewish accommodationist practices.
15. Rozenblit, *Reconstructing a National Identity*, pp. 39–58.
16. Gatrell, *The Making of the Modern Refugee*, p. 35.
17. Rozenblit, *Reconstructing a National Identity*, pp. 78–79, 109, and elsewhere; and Rechter, *Jews of Vienna*, pp. 78, 92, 97.
18. "A háboru menekültjei [The War Refugees]," *Egyenlőség* [Equality], 4 October 1914.
19. Ibid. All translations are my own.
20. Ibid. Rozenblit, *Reconstructing a National Identity*, p. 65, notes: "Although the Austrian government provided financial assistance to all the refugees, such aid proved inadequate to meet the overwhelming need."
21. MOL, fond K148, PF 1914, file 37, inv. no. 8488; and "A Galiciai menekültek támogatása [Galician Refugee Support]," *Egyenlőség*, 27 September 1914.
22. "A Galiciai menekültek támogatása [Galician Refugee Support]," *Egyenlőség*, 27 September 1914.
23. *Reports Received by the Joint Distribution Committee for the Distribution of Funds for Jewish War Sufferers* (New York, 1916), pp. 108–9.
24. MOL, fond K148, PF 1917, Box 600, File 37, inv. no. 22447; and Rebekah Klein-Pejšová, "Beyond the 'Infamous Concentration Camps of the Old Monarchy': Jewish Refugee Policy from Wartime Austria-Hungary to Interwar Czechoslovakia," *Austrian History Yearbook* 45 (2014): 156.
25. MOL, fond K148, PF 1914, File 37, inv. no. 8488.
26. MOL, fond K148, PF 1914, File 37, inv. nos. 8488, 8663; and MOL, fond K148, PF 1915, File 37, inv. no. 80.
27. MOL, fond K148, PF 1915, Box 493, File 37, inv. no. 55.
28. MOL, fond K148, PF 1914, Box 37, Folders 8488 and 8663; MOL, fond K148, PF 1915, Box 37, Folder 80.
29. MOL, fond K148, PF 1915, Box 37, inv. no. 80.
30. MOL, fond K148, PF 1915, Box 493, Folder 37, inv. no. 55; MOL, fond K148, PF 1916, Box 542, Folder 37, inv. no. 457.
31. MOL, fond K148, PF 1915, Box 37, Folder 80.
32. MOL, fond K148, PF 1915, Box 37, Folder 80, inv. nos. 62–65.
33. MOL, fond K148, PF 1915, Box 37, Folder 80.
34. Rechter, *Jews of Vienna*, p. 73n.
35. MOL, fond K148, PF 1915, Box 37, Folder 80, inv. nos. 41–43, 17 October 1914.
36. "A menekültek [The Refugees]," *Egyenlőség*, 11 October 1914.
37. "Report from the mayor of Nyiregyhaza to the Ministry of the Interior in Budapest June 20, 1915," MOL, fond K148, PF 1915, Box 504, Folder 37; and "Report from the mayor of Nyiregyhaza to the Ministry of the Interior in Budapest April 9, 1915," MOL fond K148, PF 1915, Box 503, Folder 37. There were 645 Jews living in Zboró in 1900. JewishGen, "Zborov, Slovakia" (accessed 31 August 2015), http://data.jewishgen.org/wconnect/wc.dll?jg~jgsys~community~-847442.
38. "A menekültek [The Refugees]," *Egyenlőség*, 11 October 1914.
39. Ibid.; and Tomas Cvrcek, "Wages, Prices, and Living Standards in the Habsburg Empire, 1827–1910," *Journal of Economic History* 73, no. 1 (March 2013): 1–37.
40. "Már kezdik [It's Begun]," *Egyenlőség*, 18 October 1914.
41. Ibid.
42. Ibid.

43. "A menekültek [The Refugees]," *Egyenlőség*, 11 October 1914.
44. "Szózat a menekültekhez [An Appeal to the Refugees]," *Egyenlőség*, 25 October 1914. The call was premature. The successful counteroffensive removing the Russian presence from Austria-Hungary took place in spring 1915. Paul Robert Magocsi, *Historical Atlas of Central Europe*, rev. ed. (Seattle: University of Washington Press, 2002), p. 123.
45. MOL, fond K148, PF 1915, Box 494, Folder 37. Rabbi Wéber's initial telegram to the Austrian Ministry of the Interior; MOL, fond K148, PF 1915, Box 494, Folder 37. Rabbi Wéber's petition for fund disbursement to the Hungarian Ministry of the Interior, 19 January 1915; MOL, fond K148, EI 1915, Box 494, Folder 37. Approval for disbursement from the Hungarian Ministry of the Interior; 'Pöstyén,' *Ungarländische Jüdische Zeitung (UJZ)*, 24 January 1915.
46. MOL, fond K148, PF 1915, Box 501, Folder 37. Petition from the Orthodox Jewish community of Stomfa to the Ministry of the Interior in Budapest, 8 February 1915; and Klein-Pejšová, "Beyond the 'Infamous Concentration Camps of the Old Monarchy,'" p. 158.
47. MOL, fond K148, PF 1915, Box 501, Folder 37, inv. no. 578; and Klein-Pejšová, "Beyond the 'Infamous Concentration Camps of the Old Monarchy,'" p. 158. For more on Joseph Samuel Bloch, see Ian Reifowitz, *Imagining an Austrian Nation: Joseph Samuel Bloch and the Search for a Multiethnic Austrian Identity, 1846–1919* (Boulder, CO: East European Monographs, 2003).
48. MOL, fond K148, PF 1915, Box 37, Folder 55, inv. no. 586; MOL, fond K148, PF 1915, Box 37, Folder 55, inv. no. 590.
49. "Die Flüchtlinge in den Provinz-Gemeinden," *Ungarländische jüdische Zeitung*, 14 March 1915.
50. MOL K148, PF 1915, Box 501, Folder 37.
51. Ibid.
52. "Azok a Galiciai Zsidók [The Galician Jews]," *Múlt és Jövő*, May 1915, p. 194.
53. Ibid.
54. "Ausweisung der galizischen Kreigsflüchtlinge aus Budapest und den ungarischen Provinzstädten," *Österreichische Wochenschrift*, 7 May 1915. The *ÖW* reprinted the dual governmental communiqué ("Vereinbarung der beiden Regierungen über die Behandlung der galizischen Flüchtlinge in Ungarn") originally published in the *Neue Freie Presse* on 27 April 1915.
55. *Allgemeine Jüdische Zeitung*, 1 May 1915, reprinted in "Ausweisung der galizischen Kreigsflüchtlinge aus Budapest und den ungarischen Provinzstädten," *Österreichische Wochenschrift*, 7 May 1915.
56. "Abscheid der Galizianer," *Ungarländische Jüdische Zeitung*, 11 April 1915.
57. MOL, K148, PF 1915, Box 504, File 37.
58. "Aus der jüdischen Welt," *Jüdische Zeitung*, 15 October 1915.
59. *Reports Received by the Joint Distribution Committee of Funds for Jewish War Sufferers* (New York, 1916), p. 117.
60. Rechter, *Jews of Vienna*, p. 78.
61. MOL, K148, PF 1916, Box 544, File 37.
62. *Bericht der Israelitischen Allianz zu Wien* 44 (1916): 10–12, in Rechter, *Jews of Vienna*, p. 81.
63. "Die Ausweisung der Fremden aus Budapest," *Österreichische Wochenschrift*, 12 October 1917, cited in *Egyenlőség*. The emperor of Austria also served as the king of Hungary.

64. "Die Frage der galizischen Flüchtlinge im ungarischen Abgeordnetenhause," *Österreichische Wochenschrift*, 16 November 1917.
65. "Budapest weist die Galizianer aus," *Österreichische Wochenschrift*, 26 April 1918; Klein-Pejšová, "Beyond the 'Infamous Concentration Camps of the Old Monarchy,'" p. 159.
66. Slovak National Archives, fond MPS, Box 392, Folder 609, report summarizing the care of war refugees, submitted to the minister for the administration of Slovakia on 11 March 1921.

Selected Bibliography
Primary Sources

Allgemeine Jüdische Zeitung, 1915.
American Jewish Committee, *Jews in the Eastern War Zone* (New York, 1916).
Egyenlőség [*Equality*], 1914.
Jüdische Zeitung, 1915.
Magyar Országos Levéltár [Hungarian National Archives], fond Belügyminiszterium [Ministry of the Interior] K148, Elnöki Iratok [Presidential Files] (PF) 1915, Box 37, Folder 80.
Múlt és Jövő, 1915.
Österreichische Wochenschrift, 1915, 1917–18.
Reports Received by the Joint Distribution Committee for the Distribution of Funds for Jewish War Sufferers (New York, 1916).
Slovak National Archives, fond Ministerstvo s plnou mocou pre správu Slovenska (MPS), Box 392, Folder 609.
Ungarländische Jüdische Zeitung, 1915.

Secondary Sources

Cichopek-Gajraj, Anna. *Beyond Violence: Jewish Survivors in Poland and Slovakia, 1944–48*. Cambridge: Cambridge University Press, 2014.
Cvrcek, Tomas. "Wages, Prices, and Living Standards in the Habsburg Empire, 1827–1910." *Journal of Economic History* 73 (March 2013): 1–37.
Gatrell, Peter. *The Making of the Modern Refugee*. Oxford: Oxford University Press, 2015.
———. *A Whole Empire Walking*. Bloomington: Indiana University Press, 1999.
Karady, Victor. "Religious Divisions, Socio-economic Stratification and the Modernization of Hungarian Jewry after the Emancipation." In *Jews in the Hungarian Economy, 1760–1945*, edited by Michael Silber, pp. 161–84. Jerusalem: Magnes Press, 1992.
Klein-Pejšová, Rebekah. "Beyond the 'Infamous Concentration Camps of the Old Monarchy': Jewish Refugee Policy from Wartime Austria-Hungary to Interwar Czechoslovakia." *Austrian History Yearbook* 45 (2014): 1–17.
———. *Mapping Jewish Loyalties in Interwar Slovakia*. Bloomington: Indiana University Press, 2015.
Magocsi, Paul Robert. *Historical Atlas of Central Europe*. Rev. ed. Seattle: University of Washington Press, 2002.
Marrus, Michael. *The Unwanted: European Refugees from the First World War through the Cold War*. Philadelphia: Temple University Press, 2002.

McCagg, William O., Jr. *A History of Habsburg Jews, 1670–1918*. Bloomington: Indiana University Press, 1989.
Rechter, David. *The Jews of Vienna and the First World War.* London: Littman Library of Jewish Civilization, 2001.
Rozenblit, Marsha L. *Reconstructing a National Identity: The Jews of Habsburg Austria during World War I.* New York: Oxford University Press, 2001.

CHAPTER 6

Confronting the Bacterial Enemy
Public Health, Philanthropy, and Jewish Responses to Typhus in Poland, 1914–1921

Daniel Rosenthal

In a public plea for action in 1917, a Warsaw journalist asserted:

> Among all the plagues that claim large numbers of victims each year in Poland, typhus ranks first. While other awful diseases like smallpox or typhoid fever have a certain course of treatment with injections to fight the disease, science has of yet not found such a remedy against epidemic typhus. We only know that transmission is through the bite of the clothing louse carrying infected blood. The medical arts must focus on eradicating the intermediary. Such efforts in [Poland] focus on the delousing of houses and the occupants of those residences with typhus.[1]

Despite this clear call for action, typhus remained among the deadliest challenges that Jews in Eastern Europe faced during World War I. As an insular population of urban dwellers, Jews were particularly susceptible to the conditions that allowed for the proliferation and transmission of the disease. Unlike the rash of pogroms that broke out in the years following World War I, epidemics caused by bacteria, chief among them typhus, found victims in every major Jewish population center.

This chapter assesses epidemic typhus among the Jewish population in the German-controlled areas of Russian Poland—one of the primary battlegrounds of the Eastern Front—during and immediately after World War I. In particular, it addresses Jewish responses to the epidemic, public health responses targeted at Jews, and Jewish acceptance of a high mortality rate as the price of maintaining social and cultural particularity. Eastern

European Jews had previously suffered through numerous epidemics, most notably cholera and tuberculosis, but they had never witnessed the deployment of such a massive and thoroughly modern public health campaign to stop the spread of an epidemic.[2] During and after the war, Jews were subjected to different hygienic regimes, first by the civil administration in German-occupied Poland and later by a mix of American troops working under the American Relief Administration, the Red Cross, the new Polish government, and the American Jewish Joint Distribution Committee.

Between 1915, when cases of typhus were first reported in large numbers, and 1921, when the spread of the disease had waned in Poland as public health initiatives finally gained acceptance and wartime conditions were alleviated, Polish Jews were forced to confront an unprecedented level of mass death and intrusion into their private lives by foreign medical regimes. The war brought home a confrontation between new perspectives on medicine—in which bacteria was a physical enemy to confront head-on—and the desire to preserve Jewish insularity. For the majority of Polish Jews, poor and religious, the war broke down the last attempt to maintain a concealed and unseen traditional life without interference from state-sponsored medical bureaucracy. The reluctance of Jews to fully accept the efforts made to improve communal health—employing drastic measures to avoid compliance with public health regulations, including trading in certificates of disinfection and burning down delousing centers—indicated a fundamental distrust of state institutions, even when supported and vouched for by local Jewish religious and medical professionals and funded by Jewish philanthropies from across the Atlantic.[3] Only after the conclusion of the Polish-Soviet War, when epidemic disease had fallen considerably and the methods of typhus prevention had been substantiated with tangible proof and backed by a diverse contingent of Jewish leaders and medical professionals, did most Jews finally accept public health measures.

Previous scholarship on Jewish public health during World War I has tended to focus on only one aspect of wartime response, either philanthropy, the treatment of disease, or the impact of war and pogroms on Jewish life in the Polish lands.[4] While this scholarship is useful in assessing the level of aid provided to Jewish communities and the violence directed at Jews, little is understood of how the vast majority of the population contended with the confluence of external aid, modern medicine, and mass death during an era of total war. Scholars have focused on the means and organizational structures used to provide aid but leave out the objects of these efforts.

This chapter's analysis of the Jewish responses to the efforts to halt the outbreak of epidemic disease supports the growing understanding of the harsh realities of the German occupation of Poland that overturn long-held assumptions of a benign civilian administration.[5] Moreover, the efforts to eradicate typhus by the Kaiser's medical officials on the ground in Poland show that Jews were extremely hesitant to cooperate with German authorities, in part due to their distrust of government bodies in general, but also because of the treatment meted out by German soldiers.[6] Eastern European Jews were inherently distrustful of the state given their experiences in the Russian Empire, but the realities of the war made most Jews resent German treatment regardless of their feelings toward the overthrow of czarist rule.

The focus on German-occupied Russian Poland also makes clear how the Polish branch of the OZE, the St. Petersburg–based Society for the Protection of the Health of the Jewish Population, founded in 1912, transformed into the Warsaw-based national TOZ (Towarzystwo Ochrony Zdrowia Ludności Żydowskiej, Society for the Protection of the Health of the Jewish Population) in 1921. Second, the health policies—not merely epidemic control—implemented during the war by the occupation forces would set the stage for a national public health policy during the existence of the Polish Republic from 1918 until 1939. Finally, the cities of German-occupied Poland attracted large numbers of Jewish refugees once the fighting had moved eastward, and the urban congestion and the poor conditions that newcomers endured bred disease. Łódź, for instance, reported a typhus epidemic as early as the beginning of March in 1915.[7] It was in the territory that would become the Second Polish Republic that German and American forces conducted the most drastic efforts to combat louse-borne typhus, creating a *cordon sanitaire* that aimed to defuse the bacterial threat.

I will first discuss the efforts during and after the Great War to implement public health policy to stem epidemic typhus and the ways these efforts were financed. This discussion will be followed by an analysis of the rates of infection and mortality among Jews in Poland during the war. Finally, I will address how Jews crafted responses to medical and philanthropic efforts aimed at disease prevention, particularly as such responses related to the management of the victims of the epidemic.

From the outset of the war in 1914, only nominal aid was provided to Jews in the western Russian Empire. Finding themselves in the line of fire as early as August 1914, the Jews in this region were among the first victims of the war and were subject to the disorderly conflagrations within the historical territory of Poland that saw much of the fighting on the Eastern Front. Historiography and contemporary accounts point to numerous sources of aid, both foreign and domestic, but generally historians and contemporary observers indicate that aid was not distributed equitably, efficiently, or on a regular basis. The ethnographer and author S. An-sky (pen name of Shloyme Zanvyl Rapoport), a representative of the Jewish Committee for the Relief of War Victims (EKOPO), detailed how as a front-line aid worker he distributed rubles to needy communities and individuals that he met along his travels.[8] When he was out of money or when he encountered a particular case in which aid would make a discernible difference, he returned to Kiev or St. Petersburg to acquire the necessary funds.

OZE—unlike EKOPO, which was established in Moscow in 1915—was in charge of developing health initiatives for the Jewish population of the western Russian Empire. An-sky's detailed narrative on the destructive effect of the war on Jews living in the path of combat shows that neither organization was able to adequately aid the population. Moreover, there was neither the requisite medical specialization nor the infrastructure in the empire to combat epidemics like typhus that spread rapidly among the affected civilian populations.

In the winter of 1914–15, when the first epidemics of war-related typhus broke out, the czarist army still controlled Congress Poland and had occupied much of Galicia, with its large Jewish population.[9] In the face of myriad issues impacting the hundreds of thousands of Eastern European Jewish refugees displaced within the first year of fighting, Jewish organizations could engage in little more than stopgap measures in aiding the victims of war.[10]

OZE, either independently or through associated relief channels, attempted to combat this deterioration by opening "ambulatoria, hospitals for infectious diseases, organized sanitary supervision, etc. The divisions were sent to such places which were mostly affected by the war, and where epidemics were raging," like Lublin, Łomża, and Warsaw. Over the course of four months in late 1914 and early 1915, OZE reported that 3,863 Jews received medical treatment for communicable disease in these areas.[11] While this data seems to indicate a great deal of aid, statistics belie the chaos that greeted the efforts by sanitary commissions, medical professionals, and aid workers struggling to maintain the health of the Jewish and non-Jewish populations.[12] An-sky wrote in detail of the absolute chaos that governed the organization's relief efforts in Russian Poland in the first months of the war. In late fall of 1914, he found himself in Warsaw, scrambling to carry out orders to put together hospital facilities for thousands of sick and wounded soldiers within a matter of days.[13] As he indicates, such hasty aid activity was the norm during the period of Russian wartime control of Congress Poland.[14]

The hasty measures were of little use by mid-1915 when hundreds of thousands of Jews sought refuge in the larger cities, particularly Warsaw and Łódź. Warsaw alone took in thirty thousand refugees by the beginning of 1915, bringing the number of out-and-out Jewish paupers in the city to one hundred thousand.[15] Urban overcrowding and a renewed German and Austrian effort to push the czar's forces eastward—again bringing the front lines through the places where millions of Jews were living—served as the final elements that set the stage for epidemic disease to take hold of the Jewish population.

After a major offensive in summer 1915 pushed the Russian army far to the east, the Central Powers established a joint system of occupation in Russian Poland, and Germany established a military regime called *Ober Ost* in the western Russian Empire. This new administration improved the situation for Jews to a degree, but these improvements were not without cost.[16] Jews generally felt that although there had been sporadic pogroms by the czarist forces (chiefly blamed on Cossack brigades), Russian leadership and its lack of organization had proved less harmful on the whole. Jewish storeowners especially found that the czar's troops paid fair prices for goods and were decent customers. Conversely, the Germans implemented a more orderly regime, but because of requisitions, the economic situation was substantially harsher for Jews.[17]

German forces were quick to establish a civil regime in the territory of Congress Poland that would be responsible for ensuring the public's health, in large measure to prevent the westward spread of disease. Fifty German officers from the medical service were mobilized to aid in sanitizing the formerly Russian-controlled districts.[18] At the head was Gottfried Frey, a pragmatic physician and bureaucrat familiar with tensions in Prussia between Germans and ethnic Poles. Frey was aided by entomologists specializing in lice and by Ludwig Haas, a liberal member of the Reichstag and head of the department for Jewish affairs of the German civil administration, who, along with two Orthodox rabbis attached to the military, was the chief liaison to the Polish Jewish population.[19] Under Frey's direction, over three hundred mobile disinfection units and another three hundred formalin disinfection chambers were employed throughout Congress Poland and the western Russian Empire. According to German estimates, over three million individuals and half a million residences were disinfected by the end of the occupation.[20] Nevertheless, even after the declaration of the client Kingdom of Poland in late 1916, which theoretically allowed for the establishment of independent Polish public health services, German medical personnel still headed up efforts to disinfect the Polish populace.

While public health officials aimed to prevent the spread of disease throughout Poland, often their efforts were focused specifically on the Jewish population. The antisemitic belief that Jews were filthy, and the actual squalid conditions in the Jewish districts of Polish cities, fueled the idea that anti-typhus efforts should be targeted toward Jews, especially the poor. German tactics for disinfecting the population were severe, often forcing the closure of institutions and businesses deemed unclean or lousy and requiring the masses in need of disinfection to endure long periods of immodesty. Those individuals, typically Jewish itinerant beggars and peddlers deemed incapable of maintaining appropriate standards of cleanliness, were forcibly disinfected on a regular basis.[21] German authorities did not initially intend to use such tactics, but in their minds, the reticence of the Jewish population to readily accept treatment that was in their own best interest required the use of the military to carry out disinfections.[22] (German authorities felt that Catholic Poles were more cooperative and willing to undergo disinfection and delousing, although it is not clear how much of the perception about Jews was based on antisemitism.) According to both German and Jewish accounts, harsher measures were introduced toward the end of World War I as the Jewish population in the Polish lands started to actively resist the German medical campaign. Polish Jews, apart from those few who were "on the level of Western and Central European culture," were accused of fleeing disinfection centers, burning such centers down, and creating a lively black market in medical certificates proving disinfection.[23]

With the German retreat following the armistice in late 1918, Poland's population was left in a precarious position. Years of war and military requisitions had left the country with little food or resources. The cold weather and the outbreak of hostilities between the new powers in the area over territory led to further migration, again straining the resources of urban centers and contributing to further outbreaks of typhus. Only in the summer of the following year, after a spike in the mortality rate in many cities of the new Polish Republic—again, hitting the Jewish population hardest—did the American Relief Administration under the leadership of Herbert Hoover dispatch a small contingent of American military medical personnel to attempt to stem the spread of typhus.[24]

Colonel Harry Gilchrist led this endeavor from a base in Warsaw. His mostly handpicked staff of medical personnel carried mobile disinfection equipment throughout Poland, always staying clear of the fighting between the Poles and the Bolsheviks. Their efforts were not necessarily more successful than German efforts, although the population, Christians and Jews alike, seemed more willing to engage with this public health campaign, perhaps in part because the Americans were not seen as occupiers and there was no historical animosity between Poles and the United States, as there was with either Germany or Russia.[25]

The Americans were able to set up targeted efforts along the eastern reaches of Poland with four disinfection and delousing railcars. Additional targeted efforts, so-called internal *cordons sanitaires,* focused on those cities like Lemberg/Lwów/L'viv (now officially Lwów) and Vilna/Wilno that had the highest rates of typhus in 1919. These efforts focused on disinfecting refugees and the itinerant. Typically, the Americans employed steam or kerosene as a disinfectant, although there was also experimentation with hydrocyanic acid for use as a pesticide.

The American forces tackling this outbreak were forced to direct much of their efforts at the former Austrian province of Galicia. Conditions in this poor region—long a part of the Habsburg Empire—deteriorated after November 1918 as Polish and Ukrainian forces fought for dominance in eastern Galicia. Jews were caught in the middle of this conflict, suffering displacement and shortages of basic necessities. As a result, Galicia's Jewish population was decimated by typhus in 1919 and 1920 before American and Polish health officials were able to bring the public health crisis under control.[26]

Between late 1919 and early 1921, American personnel disinfected hundreds of thousands of individuals within the republic and in the eastern borderlands to prevent the westward spread of epidemic disease and to help build Poland's public health infrastructure. The exact figures, despite efforts at careful record keeping, are not clear, since many individuals and residences were disinfected multiple times. However, we know, for instance, that the Vilna/Wilno section of the American expedition disinfected a total of 32,487 individuals, as well as 1,846 railcars, during the short time it was active in 1920. In Lwów, over 35,000 individuals were inspected each week during the second half of 1920 and early 1921; out of these, roughly 5 percent were disinfected due to suspicion of being symptomatic or showing signs of louse infestation.[27]

The Americans worked with League of Nations and Polish officials to help the newly independent country develop a public health system that was equipped to treat and quarantine those with communicable disease. By March 1920, twenty-nine hospitals throughout Polish territory had been equipped with 2,155 epidemic beds.[28] Generally, there was a good deal of cooperation between the Americans, the Poles, and the medical representatives of the League of Nations. The Polish Republic was thus able to quickly work toward meeting the League's new guidelines on establishing sufficient public health facilities for the population.[29]

Although Americans troops were only present in Poland at the end of World War I, American money had been flowing into the region in the form of aid from the beginning of the conflict. Financial aid for efforts to combat disease in Eastern Europe and to provide for Jewish refugees fleeing the war zone started flowing as early as fall 1914, with much of the funds originating in the United States. The American Jewish Joint Distribution Committee was established in 1914 specifically for the purpose of collecting donations for needy Jews overseas.[30] During the war itself, the JDC funneled over $3 million to the German-based Jüdisches Hilfskomite für Polen und Litauen, which took responsibility for distributing this aid to Polish Jews under German occupation.[31]

Figure 6.1. *Workers under the auspices of the League of Nations Epidemic Commission operate a disinfection chamber in Eastern Poland, c. 1921, using hydrogen cyanide gas.* Report of the Epidemic Commission of the League of Nations *(Geneva, 1921).*

Toward the end of the war, violence against Jews increased, and American Jews became incensed with pogroms directed against their coreligionists. The JDC transformed this anger into a philanthropic campaign that raised $5 million for Polish Jews in 1920 alone.[32] However, it became substantially more difficult for the JDC to distribute these funds to those in greatest need. The organization used its chief envoys—among them Felix Warburg and Boris Bogen—to deliver cash in person after 1918, but they were considerably hindered by the number of currencies of widely different valuations that circulated in Central and Eastern Europe. Often, the coordinators of this overseas aid were forced to carry around large amounts of American dollars, which, according to their official reports, they distributed haphazardly to those Jewish organizations or individuals who seemed in greatest need. Some thought was given to arranging more systematic aid, such as importing winter clothing for children, but those endeavors usually proved more difficult than useful. With the fear of typhus in particular, philanthropists were less inclined to provide clothing. In the case of other goods, envoys realized that locals, even in destitute areas, were better able to procure necessities.[33] Regardless of the means of distribution used by JDC personnel, it was often impossible to ensure how the funds were used by the most needy and whether money even arrived where it was needed to bolster Jewish public health.

Jewish philanthropic organizations, despite tales of success detailed in propaganda literature, arguably had little ability to stem the spread of epidemic typhus. Advanced knowledge of epidemiology and the pathology of typhus was still relegated to specialized medical researchers and military doctors interested in stopping the spread of epidemics. As a result, philanthropic efforts were of little use in establishing the facilities needed to prevent louse-borne typhus. Moreover, there was often no working relationship between JDC envoys and the leadership of those American medical officers tasked by the Hoover-led American Relief Administration to stop the spread of disease in Europe.[34]

Typhus had both a quantifiable and qualitative impact on Polish Jewry. Historian Ignacy Schiper provided the most dramatic statistics. In his estimation, Warsaw lost 9,000 Jews in 1916, 14,410 in 1917, and 13,000 in 1918, compared to a pre- and postwar average of 4,500 to 5,000 dead per year.[35] As the disease with the highest mortality rate in the absence of comprehensive treatment, typhus was primarily responsible for this dramatic increase in mortality.

While the importance of statistics for understanding and addressing the needs of a society was already realized in Eastern Europe by the mid-nineteenth century, World War I highlighted the difficulty of accurate data collection as well as the unreliability of mortality figures and the rate of infection. Such problems were especially acute in Jewish urban slums, where there were large numbers of epidemic victims and where the population generally held a degree of contempt for or suspicion of public health officials—whether Jewish or not. The data for the city of Warsaw highlights the unreliability of any claims about the number of those ill with typhus. Jewish observers in the city in early 1918 contended that 70 percent of those ill with the disease were Jews.[36] Official statistics from the municipality from late 1917, however, show that of the 407 people who died from typhus during the course of one week in mid-November, Christians made up approximately 60 percent of the total number of victims.[37] Even if the mortality rate among Jews was much lower than among the Christian population—which was not typically the case—this would not explain such a major discrepancy in the figures.

Such inaccuracies in data are not surprising given that, apart from a few specialists, the medical understanding of disease transmission and pathology was rudimentary. More tellingly, many, Jews included, referred to typhus as "hunger typhus" (*hunger-tifus*) based on the fundamental misunderstanding that malnourishment could cause bacterial infection.[38] Moreover, even German physicians attached to the imperial army often misdiagnosed cases of typhus as influenza.[39]

Jewish responses to epidemic-proportion typhus, as well as to the ill and to the casualties of the disease, indicate a population struggling to maintain religious and social insularity against new forms of official intrusion. By their own accounts, Polish Jews, including doctors among them, were reticent to change their sanitary habits, even in the face of epidemic illness and evidence of the benefits of proper sanitation and hygiene. After the German occupation, the population was confronted with numerous forms of health propaganda in Yiddish, Polish, and German warning of the dangers of lice and of living in filth.[40] One proclamation indicated that such efforts "will not cause a disruption to the lives of the population and will provide the basis for cleaning [all living accommodations] in all the houses on some streets, also the occupants must thoroughly sterilize all clothing. ... The population must understand that all actions are for the good of your very existence and ... the well-being and health of Warsaw."[41]

Regardless of their personal feelings, many leaders of Hasidic dynasties in Poland and their non-Hasidic counterparts engaged in public education programs beginning in 1916 to help inform the Jewish population of the need for improved sanitation within Jewish communities. During a rabbinical conference held in the town of Włocławek in northern Poland in the fall of 1916, the heads of eleven Hasidic courts were joined by district and German medical officials in a public meeting that aimed to dispel myths surrounding typhus and provide the Jews with proper guidance on how to handle the crisis. During this meeting, Dr. Ludwig

Haas, the head of Jewish affairs in occupied Poland and a member of the Reichstag, remarked that "the Jew who does not maintain cleanliness cannot be considered a *frum* [devout] and believing Jew; the Torah also warns many times that you must maintain cleanliness!"[42] Although much of the discussion during this conference covered the prevention of disease transmission, including large-scale disinfection, the meeting aimed at rallying the Jewish religious leadership in Poland to tackle the public health crisis and to gain support from their followers who remained skeptical and suspicious of German efforts.

The eleven rabbis in attendance were all convinced of the benefit of these medical efforts, even going so far as to work to limit or prohibit the presence of itinerant beggars who relied on coreligionists for handouts. These beggars, long a fixture of Jewish communities throughout Europe, were seen as a major factor in the spread of louse-borne typhus.[43] While the majority of Jews had long considered Jewish beggars a nuisance and embarrassment, the war was the first time that they came to view these beggars as an existential threat, and rabbinical leadership crafted plans to quarantine these individuals throughout Polish territory.

Despite the good intentions of Poland's rabbis, there is little indication that these religious leaders had the ability to change public perception. Hasidic rabbis had only minimal medical or scientific knowledge, making it doubtful that they possessed the ability to effectively convey this information—and the significance of the public health campaign—to their communities.[44] Given that the rates of infection only increased after 1916, it is safe to assume that these public information campaigns were complete failures and perhaps only served to further alienate Jews from German efforts to regulate health within occupied Poland.

Enacting sanitation measures was problematic for most Jews, even if they possessed the desire to rid themselves of those causes of disease that resulted from poor hygiene. With few changes of clothes, it was difficult to completely eradicate all forms of clothing lice without enduring some form of humiliation. During both German and American efforts to forcibly disinfect and delouse Jews and their residences between 1916 and 1921, the vast majority of those treated were severely embarrassed by having to wait around disinfection stations naked and shorn of most of their body hair. (Although the comparisons to later Nazi treatment of Jews are inevitable, it is important to remember that these efforts were funded in part by North American Jews and sanctioned by most religious leaders.) In the crowded apartments common in larger cities, bathing was also not an easy task. Some Jews turned to ritual bathing in the *mikvah*, but such efforts—submersion in stagnant water with no soap—did not aid hygiene. Contrary to antisemitic allegations that these pools bred disease, however, immersion in *mikvaot* did not contribute to its transmission.[45]

Another order from the Reich Presidium, dated 22 November 1916, made it a crime to fail to report the presence of any ill individuals throughout the German zone of occupation. Even failing to report the suspicion of the presence of disease was a crime that could have amounted to substantial fines or six months in prison. This regulation also included mandatory reporting of the dead, putting additional pressure on Jewish funeral bureaus to remain in contact with German civil authorities.[46] Before the establishment of modern hospitals in Poland at the end of the nineteenth century, illness and death were private matters in Jewish life, to be handled by family and the appropriate religious functionaries. Reporting sick or dead individuals to outside authorities was perceived as a great indignity, and it was a major factor in the efforts by Jews to conceal the sick. Likewise, Jewish undertakers and cemetery employees, often religious themselves or sympathetic to religious Jews, held no qualms about disobeying German authorities if it meant sparing the deceased the indignity of a burial not performed according to halakha, Jewish religious law.[47] This obfuscation displays a desire for full autonomy regardless of the sanitary ramifications rather than a willful attempt to stymie the German sanitary regime.

The desire for complete religious freedom aside, Jewish functionaries, particularly the *hevra kadisha* (literally, holy society) that prepared corpses for burial, disregarded even the most basic tenets of disease prevention when handling the victims of typhus. There is no evidence that such practices were ever modified before the beginning of World War II, as there were no fundamental changes to any of the Jewish mortuary facilities in Poland's major cities, nor to corpse-handling practices.[48]

German medical officials were horrified by the lack of sanitation in Jewish community-owned morgues that stood within the grounds of Jewish cemeteries. When investigating conditions at the mortuary located on the grounds of the Gęsia Street cemetery in Warsaw, Gottfried Frey was appalled by the fact that bodies were routinely haphazardly scattered throughout the facility and then washed with the same unclean water used for multiple corpses (Jewish law requires all bodies to be washed and wrapped in shrouds before burial). He noted that caskets were not used in the majority of cases, forcing many Jews to directly handle infectious corpses. Even more alarming to him was that the water, which he described as "gutter water," used for hand washing by the *hevra kadisha* and mourners upon exiting the cemetery was never changed.[49] Such was the confrontation between German standards of hygiene and the routine practice of Jewish ritual in Polish urban environments in the early twentieth century.

Moreover, the Jewish cemeteries in most major cities in Poland were already at capacity before the beginning of World War I.[50] The high rate of mortality during the war only further exacerbated this issue. In some cities mortality had risen by over 50 percent over the course of the war, leading to a full-scale burial crisis. In many of these areas, local Jewish leaders attempted to negotiate with officials and landowners to sell them land for the expansion of Jewish cemeteries. These requests were often ignored, forcing the community to purchase land well outside a city's limits or to create makeshift plots within the existing cemetery grounds.[51]

Often the administrators of Jewish cemeteries in German-occupied Poland were forced to find creative solutions to bury the dead. New plots were created in between existing graves, or the requirements for the dimensions of graves were loosened. Descriptions of wartime Jewish graves describe the plots as being only just wide enough for the body without a casket and never more than one meter deep.[52] The depth may be an indication that plots were reused and that bodies were being buried one on top of the other, so-called burial in layers.[53] In 1922, following the establishment of the Polish Republic, the Jewish communities of Warsaw and Kraków determined that following the increase in wartime deaths, it was necessary for grave diggers to begin digging deeper graves in order to prepare for this practice.[54]

In perhaps the most telling Jewish response to the crisis of typhus, a gathering of approximately ten thousand Jews met in the main Jewish cemetery on Gęsia Street in Warsaw in 1917 (unfortunately, we do not know the specific date for this event) to conduct what is known as a *shvartze khasene* (literally, "black wedding" in Yiddish). This superstitious folk practice brought together two young poor Jews (both virgins and often orphans) for an arranged marriage conducted on cemetery grounds.[55] This practice aimed to confuse the angel of death (*malekh ha-maves*) and prevent additional casualties from an illness plaguing a particular Jewish community. German medical officials documented several cases of such *shvartze khasenes* that were conducted during World War I to prevent the spread of epidemic disease, but the 1917 wedding in Warsaw was the only documented case specifically targeted at halting typhus. This event, which is perhaps the largest such wedding recorded in Jewish history, indicates the continued resonance of these types of folk practices even within the modern metropolis of Warsaw. Those who participated perhaps needed to feel that Jews were taking action against the rampant spread of disease even if they doubted the efficacy of this type of religious esotericism.

Deaths from typhus subsided only with the settlement of the postwar conflicts in Eastern Europe and the establishment of modern medical facilities based on American and Western European models. Nevertheless, despite being the population hit hardest by the epidemic, Jews were still hesitant to accept the lessons of wartime epidemiology. The intrusion into private homes and the indignities of disinfection—real or perceived—

were costs that Jews were not willing to accept, even in the face of high rates of mortality. The failed propaganda campaign to spread awareness of the causes and prevention of typhus led by rabbinical leadership in Poland indicates the lack of trust or understanding the Jewish public had in modern medicine, as well as the decentralized and weak nature of Jewish leadership.

The prevalence of antisemitism among German and American medical officials was not a significant factor in the success or failure of typhus-eradication campaigns. Rather, the efforts to stamp out the epidemic in the Polish lands seems to have fostered many of the antisemitic tropes common in the interwar period, including the notion that Eastern European Jews, the so-called *Ostjuden*, were lousy and unable to maintain any semblance of hygienic standards. These impressions were also spread by representatives of the JDC and the Jewish members of the German military, who were shocked at the conditions in which their coreligionists lived.

Ultimately, the confrontation between Western medical regimens and the Jewish population in Russian Poland under German occupation and in the new Polish Republic highlights the uncertainty with which Eastern European Jews approached the new technologies and medical understandings of the early twentieth century. Many individuals died and many more were infected due to Jewish insularity and the fear of outside intrusion, a sentiment that is understandable given historical indignities leveled against the Jewish population as a result of czarist policies. This long collective memory fueled Jewish intractability even as new and variegated threats emerged during the chaos, violence, and upheaval of the Great War.

Daniel Rosenthal currently teaches history and Jewish studies at the Charles E. Smith Jewish Day School. Previously, he taught at the University of Haifa (where he held postdoctoral fellowship through the Israeli Inter-university Academic Partnership in Russian and East European Studies), the University of Toronto, and the University of Western Ontario. His research and publications focus on the confrontation between economics and Jewish religious practice in the daily existence of Jews in modern Eastern Europe.

Notes

1. "The Campaign against Spotted Typhus in Warsaw" [Yiddish], *Der Moment*, 16 August 1917, N. 192. All translations are my own.
2. I. C., "Shterblishkayt fun tifus ba odeser idn," *Bleter far idishe demografiye, statistik, un ekonomik* 1, no. 2 (15 April 1923), pp. 82–85.

3. "Rabbinical Conference in Włocławek" [Yiddish], *Der Moment*, 17 September 1916, N. 217. See also Gottfried Frey, "Das Gesundheitswesen im deutschen Verwaltungsgebiet von Polen in den Jahren 1914–1918," *Arbeiten aus dem Reichsgesundheitsamt* 51, no. 4 (December 1919), p. 724; and Frank M. Schuster, *Zwischen allen Fronten: Osteuropäische Juden während des Ersten Weltkrieges (1914–1919)* (Cologne: Böhlau, 2004), pp. 215–16.
4. On philanthropic efforts, see Chiara Tessaris, "The War Relief Work of the American Jewish Joint Distribution Committee in Poland and Lithuania, 1915–18," *East European Jewish Affairs* 40, 2 (August 2010): 127–44; and Joseph C. Hyman, *Twenty-Five Years of American Aid to Jews Overseas: A Record of the Joint Distribution Committee* (New York: AJJDC, 1939). For a good overview of Polish efforts to aid Catholics in the "Congress Kingdom" of Poland during the war, see Marek Przeniosło, "Organizacje Samopomocy Społecznej W Królestwie Polskim W Latach I Wojny Światowej," *Niepodległość I Pamięć* 33, no. 1 (2011): 57–72. On the impact of war on Jewish life in Eastern Europe before 1921, see Sh. An-sky, *Gezamalte shriftn*, vols. 4–6 (Warsaw, 1928); Piotr Wróbel, "The Jews of Galicia under Austrian-Polish Rule, 1869–1918," *Austrian History Yearbook* 25 (1994): 97–138; Pam Maclean, "Control and Cleanliness: German-Jewish Relations in Occupied Eastern Europe during the First World War," *War and Society* 6, no. 2 (September 1988): 47–69; Alexander Prusin, *Nationalizing a Borderland: War, Ethnicity, and Anti-Jewish Violence in East Galicia, 1914–1920* (Tuscaloosa: University of Alabama Press, 2005); and John Klier and Shlomo Lambroza, eds., *Pogroms: Anti-Jewish Violence in Modern Russian History* (Cambridge: Cambridge University Press, 1992). On the understanding of medical developments in Europe by Jews, see John M. Efron, *Medicine and the German Jews: A History* (New Haven, CT: Yale University Press, 2001).
5. General histories that cover the period gloss over German treatment of Jewish civilians in war zones, focusing, if at all, on the *Judenzählung* as the central instance of ill-treatment of the Jews during World War I. See, for example, Zosa Szajkowski, "The German Appeal to the Jews of Poland, August 1914," *Jewish Quarterly Review* vol. 59, no. 4 (April 1969): 311–20; and Lloyd P. Gartner, *History of the Jews in Modern Times* (Oxford: Oxford University Press, 2001), pp. 267–72.
6. Schuster, *Zwischen allen Fronten*, pp. 122–28.
7. *Der Moment*, 8 March 1915, N. 48, 3.
8. Thomas Fallows, "Politics and the War Effort in Russia: The Union of Zemstvos and the Organization of the Food Supply, 1914–1916," *Slavic Review* 37, no. 1 (1978): 70–90. See also Kalman Weiser, *Jewish People, Yiddish Nation: Noah Prylucki and the Folkists in Poland* (Toronto: University of Toronto Press, 2011), pp. 120–21.
9. *Der Moment*, 8 March 1915, N. 48, 3.
10. Hundreds of thousands of Galician Jews fled to the interior of the Habsburg Empire from the invading Russian army, straining the resources of aid organization within the western cities of the empire. See Marsha L. Rozenblit, *Reconstructing a National Identity: The Jews of Habsburg Austria during World War I* (New York: Oxford University Press, 2001), pp. 65–81.
11. "From the Report of OZE: 'The Beginning of the War … ,'" 23 February 1918, American Jewish Joint Distribution Committee Archives, NYAR1418:03363.
12. While this article discusses the conditions of the Jewish population, Polish Catholics in the Russian Empire were also forced to organize their own self-help organizations. Especially in the Russian Empire, no state-controlled medical relief was available as was the case in Britain or France. See, for instance, Elżbieta Więckowska, "Organizacja

Sekcji Sanitarnej Krakowskiego Biskupiego Komitetu Niesienia Pomocy Dotkniętym Klęską Wojny (1914–1918): Społeczne Aspekty Historii Medycyny," *Medycyna Nowożytna: Studia Nad Historią Medycyny* 2, no. 1 (1995): 92–93; Marek Mądzik, "Polskie Organizacje Niesienia Pomocy Ofiarom Wojny Na Wołyniu W Latach I Wojny Światowej," *Ucrainica Polonica* 1 (2004): 112–120; Mariusz Korzeniowski, "Rejon zachodni Centralnego Komitetu Obywatelskiego—powstanie i początki działalności," *Studiów z Dziejów Rosji i Europy Środkowo-Wschodnie* 29 (1994): 29–46; and Przeniosło, "Organizacje Samopomocy Społecznej," pp. 57–59.

13. An-sky, *Gezamelte shriftn*, vol. 4, pp. 17–26.
14. Ibid. Also see Maria Stecka, *Żydzi w Polsce* (Warsaw: Księgarnia i Skład Nut Perzyński, Niklewicz i S-ka, 1921), pp. 56–59. Stecka provides figures that illuminate general conditions for Jews during the war.
15. Weiser, *Jewish People*, pp. 120–121.
16. Semion Goldin, "Deportation of Jews by the Russian Military Command, 1914–1915," *Jews in Eastern Europe* 1, no. 41 (2000): 58; Jacob Joshua Golub, "OSE: Pioneer of Jewish Health," *Jewish Social Service Quarterly* 14, no. 4 (June 1938): 366; and Vejas Gabriel Liulevicius, "German-Occupied Eastern Europe," in *A Companion to World War I*, ed. John Horne (Chichester, UK; Malden, MA: Wiley-Blackwell, 2010), pp. 447–52.
17. Goldin, "Deportation of Jews by the Russian Military Command," p. 58; Schuster, *Zwischen allen Fronten*, pp. 129–31.
18. Paul Weindling, *Epidemics in Eastern Europe, 1890–1945* (Oxford: Oxford University Press, 2000), p. 97.
19. Alexander Carlebach, "A German Rabbi Goes East," *Leo Baeck Institute Year Book* 6, no. 1 (1961): 62.
20. Weindling, *Epidemics in Eastern Europe*, p. 97.
21. Ibid.
22. Frey, "Das Gesundheitswesen im deutschen Verwaltungsgebiet von Polen in den Jahren 1914–1918," pp. 723–24.
23. Frey in particular makes this sharp distinction. See ibid., p. 724. On the issue of the confrontation between German Jews and Eastern European Jews during the war, see Arnold Zweig, *Das Ostjüdische Antlitz* (Berlin: Welt Verlag, 1922); and Steven Aschheim, *Brothers and Strangers: The East European Jew in German and German Jewish Consciousness, 1800–1923* (Madison: University of Wisconsin Press, 1982), pp. 139–53.
24. Alfred E. Cornebise, *Typhus and Doughboys: The American Polish Typhus Relief Expedition, 1919–1921* (Newark, DE: University of Delaware Press, 1982), pp. 141–43.
25. Ibid.
26. *Wiadomości statystyczne o mieście Lwowie, 1912–1922* (Lwów: Nakładem gminy Król. Stól. m. Lwowa, 1926), esp. pp. 39 and 40. While epidemic typhus was responsible for just 0.57 out of every 100 Christians who died in the city of Lwów in 1919, the disease killed 3.4 out of every 100 Jews who died that year. Typhus took the lives of 300 percent more people than any other epidemic disease.
27. League of Nations, *Report of the Epidemic Commission of the League of Nations* (Geneva: League of Nations, 1921), p. 30.
28. Ibid., p. 40.
29. See the progress documented in Carl Prausnitz, *Report on the Work of the Conferences of Directors of Schools of Hygiene* (Geneva: League of Nations Health Organization, 1930), pp. 89–99.

30. Tessaris, "War Relief Work," p. 127; Hyman, *Twenty-Five Years of American Aid,* pp. 7–11; and Zosa Szajkowski, "Private and Organized American Jewish Overseas Relief, 1914–1938," *American Jewish Historical Quarterly* 57 (1967): 52–106.
31. Michael Beizer, "American Jewish Joint Distribution Committee," *YIVO Encyclopedia of Jews in Eastern Europe* (2010), http://www.yivoencyclopedia.org/article.aspx/American_Jewish_Joint_Distribution_Committee (accessed October 3, 2014).
32. Hyman, *Twenty-Five Years of American Aid,* pp. 7–11.
33. "Report of Boris Bogen," undated, Records of the New York Headquarters of the American Jewish Joint Distribution Committee, 1921–1932, NY AR192132, http://archives.jdc.org/.
34. Cornebise, *Typhus and Doughboys,* pp. 15–18; letter from Harriet B. Lowenstein to Albert Lucas, 3 April 1919, Records of the American Jewish Joint Distribution Committee, 1919–1921, NY AR191921, http://archives.jdc.org/; letter from Cyrus Adler to Mr. Warburg, 9 April 1919, op. cit.; Meeting of the Commissioners to Poland of the Joint Distribution Committee, 21 March 1919, op. cit.
35. Ignacy Schiper, *Cmentarze żydowskie w Warszawie* (Warsaw, 1938), pp. 224–25.
36. *Der Moment,* 27 May 1918, N. 112.
37. Ibid., 10 January 1918, N. 9.
38. Frey, "Das Gesundheitswesen im deutschen Verwaltungsgebiet von Polen in den Jahren 1914–1918," p. 728.
39. Weindling, *Epidemics in Eastern Europe,* p. 103.
40. Ibid., pp. 101–2. Also see the presentation of *Ostjuden* in Carlebach, "A German Rabbi Goes East"; and Aschheim, *Brothers and Strangers.*
41. *Der Moment,* 21 January 1916, N. 18
42. Ibid., 18 September 1916, N. 218.
43. Frey, "Das Gesundheitswesen im deutschen Verwaltungsgebiet von Polen in den Jahren 1914–1918," p. 730; *Der Moment,* 18 September 1916, N. 218.
44. Frey, "Das Gesundheitswesen im deutschen Verwaltungsgebiet von Polen in den Jahren 1914–1918," p. 725.
45. Ibid., p. 726. See also Schuster, *Zwischen allen Fronten,* pp. 314–16.
46. *Der Moment,* 6 October 1917, N. 230.
47. While such practices had occurred for decades, only during the interwar period is there concrete evidence of coordinated efforts to conceal the Jewish dead from Polish civil and medical authorities. Many Jews correctly assumed that bodies would be subjected to postmortem examination and delayed burial, both of which Jews considered signs of disrespect for the corpse. See Leon Przysuskier, *Cmentarze żydowskie w Warszawie: przewodnik ilustrowany* (Warsaw: Józef Pinkiert, 1992), pp. I–IV.
48. See, for instance, *Haynt,* 29 September 1937, N. 222. According to this article, burial practices were either the same or worse than what German officials described in their reports. There were cases in which poor Jews did not even receive full burial rites and were interred as quickly as possible.
49. Frey, "Das Gesundheitswesen im deutschen Verwaltungsgebiet von Polen in den Jahren 1914–1918," pp. 725–26.
50. On the need to buy cemetery land in Kraków during World War I, see Kraków Jewish Religious Community to the Kraków Municipal Magistrate, 19 December 1917, Kraków Jewish Religious Community, RG 715/2, Archives of the Jewish Historical Institute, Warsaw. The Kraków *kehile* (the organized Jewish community) recognized as early as 1912 that the Miodowa Street cemetery established in 1800 had already reached capacity. Different ideas were circulated about how to create more room for

burials, including the purchasing of one large piece of land in the Podgórze neighborhood or buying four different properties closer to the existing cemeteries in the Kazimierz district near the city's center. It was quickly established by the *kehile* that the new grounds could not be established in Kazimierz due to a lack of space and the difficulty of situating burial grounds near densely populated residential areas.

51. One particularly well documented example of this practice comes from Stanislau/Stanisławów in Galicia. Although outside the area of focus of this article, the situation there resembled that in Russian Poland, including in the German zone of occupation. See Cemetery Report, 8 September 1923, Stanisławów Jewish Religious Community, and Stanisławów Jewish Religious Community to the Stanisławów Municipal Magistrate, 25 May 1920, Stanisławów Jewish Religious Community, HM2/9131.1, Central Archives for the History of the Jewish People, Jerusalem. A similar case from Warsaw can be found in Schiper, *Cmentarze żydowskie w Warszawie*, pp. 224–25.
52. Frey, "Das Gesundheitswesen im deutschen Verwaltungsgebiet von Polen in den Jahren 1914–1918," pp. 725–26.
53. Rav Hai Gaon (Hai ben Sharira), the *av beyt din* (chief religious authority) of the Pumbedita academy toward the end of the tenth and beginning of the eleventh century, first enumerated the permissibility of this practice in a responsum that was included by Jacob ben Asher in the *Tur* (Yoreh De'ah 363). However, as the *Shulhan Arukh* (Yoreh De'ah 362:1, 4) states, one should leave a space of six *tefahim* (either 48 or 57.6 cm) of earth between the two graves.
54. Kraków Jewish Religious Community to the Warsaw Jewish Religious Community, 3 February 1922, Kraków Jewish Religious Community, RG 715/2, AŻIH. Some major Jewish communities, particularly that in Łóme, did not experience these issues, as their cemeteries were big enough to accommodate the increase in burials.
55. See Hanna Wągrzynek, "Black Weddings among the Jews," in *Holy Dissent: Jewish and Christian Mystics in Eastern Europe*, ed. Glenn Dynner (Detroit: Wayne State University, 2011), pp. 55–68. Apparently, many "black weddings" were held between 1939 and 1942 in the hopes of staving off the devastation of the Nazi occupation.

Selected Bibliography
Primary Sources

An-sky, Sh. *Gezamalte shriftn*. Vols. 4–6. Warsaw, 1928.
Frey, Gottfried. "Das Gesundheitswesen im deutschen Verwaltungsgebiet von Polen in den Jahren 1914–1918." *Arbeiten aus dem Reichsgesundheitsamt* 51, no. 4 (December 1919): 583–733.
I. C. "Shterblishkayt fun tifus ba odeser idn." *Bleter far idishe demografiye, statistik, un ekonomik* 1, no. 2 (15 April 1923): 82–85.
League of Nations. *Report of the Epidemic Commission of the League of Nations*. Geneva: League of Nations, 1921.
Prausnitz, Carl. *Report on the Work of the Conferences of Directors of Schools of Hygiene*. Geneva: League of Nations Health Organization, 1930.
Wiadomości statystyczne o mieście Lwowie, 1912–1922. Lwów: Nakładem gminy Król. Stół. m. Lwowa, 1926.
Zweig, Arnold. *Das Ostjüdische Antlitz*. Berlin: Welt Verlag, 1922.

Secondary Sources

Aschheim, Steven. *Brothers and Strangers: The East European Jew in German and German Jewish Consciousness, 1800–1923*. Madison: University of Wisconsin Press, 1982.
Carlebach, Alexander. "A German Rabbi Goes East." *Leo Baeck Institute Year Book* 6, no. 1 (1961): 60–121.
Cornebise, Alfred E. *Typhus and Doughboys: The American Polish Typhus Relief Expedition, 1919–1921*. Newark, DE: University of Delaware Press, 1982.
Efron, John M. *Medicine and the German Jews: A History*. New Haven, CT: Yale University Press, 2001.
Fallows, Thomas. "Politics and the War Effort in Russia: The Union of Zemstvos and the Organization of the Food Supply, 1914–1916." *Slavic Review* 37, no. 1 (1978): 70–90.
Gartner, Lloyd P. *History of the Jews in Modern Times*. Oxford: Oxford University Press, 2001.
Goldin, Semion. "Deportation of Jews by the Russian Military Command, 1914–1915." *Jews in Eastern Europe* 1, no. 41 (2000): 40–73.
Golub, Jacob Joshua. "OSE: Pioneer of Jewish Health." *Jewish Social Service Quarterly* 14, no. 4 (June 1938): 365–71.
Hyman, Joseph C. *Twenty-Five Years of American Aid to Jews Overseas: A Record of the Joint Distribution Committee*. New York: AJJDC, 1939.
Klier, John, and Shlomo Lambroza, eds. *Pogroms: Anti-Jewish Violence in Modern Russian History*. Cambridge: Cambridge University Press, 1992.
Korzeniowski, Mariusz. "Rejon zachodni Centralnego Komitetu Obywatelskiego—powstanie i początki działalności." *Studiów z Dziejów Rosji i Europy Środkowo-Wschodnie* 29 (1994): 29–46.
Koss, Andrew N. "War Within, War Without: Russian Refugee Rabbis during World War I." *AJS Review* 34, no. 2 (November 2010): 231–63.
Liulevicius, Vejas Gabriel. "German-Occupied Eastern Europe." In *A Companion to World War I*, ed. John Horne, pp. 447–52. Chichester, UK: Wiley-Blackwell, 2010.
Maclean, Pam. "Control and Cleanliness: German-Jewish Relations in Occupied Eastern Europe during the First World War." *War and Society* 6, no. 2 (September 1988): 47–69.
Mądzik, Marek. "Polskie Organizacje Niesienia Pomocy Ofiarom Wojny Na Wołyniu W Latach I Wojny Światowej." *Ucrainica Polonica* 1 (2004): 112–20.
Prusin, Alexander. *Nationalizing a Borderland: War, Ethnicity, and Anti-Jewish Violence in East Galicia, 1914–1920*. Tuscaloosa: University of Alabama Press, 2005.
Przeniosło, Marek. "Organizacje Samopomocy Społecznej W Królestwie Polskim W Latach I Wojny Światowej." *Niepodległość I Pamięć* 33:1 (2011): 57–72.
Przysuskier, Leon. *Cmentarze żydowskie w Warszawie: przewodnik ilustrowany*. Warsaw: Józef Pinkiert, 1992.
Rozenblit, Marsha L. *Reconstructing a National Identity: The Jews of Habsburg Austria during World War I*. New York: Oxford University Press, 2001.
Schiper, Ignacy. *Cmentarze żydowskie w Warszawie*. Warsaw, 1938.
Schuster, Frank M. *Zwischen allen Fronten: Osteuropäische Juden während des Ersten Weltkrieges (1914–1919)*. Cologne: Böhlau, 2004.
Stecka, Maria. *Żydzi w Polsce*. Warsaw: Księgarnia i Skład Nut Perzyński, Niklewicz i S-ka, 1921.
Szajkowski, Zosa. "The German Appeal to the Jews of Poland, August 1914." *The Jewish Quarterly Review* 59, no. 4 (April 1969): 311–20.

———. "Private and Organized American Jewish Overseas Relief, 1914–1938." *American Jewish Historical Quarterly* 57 (1967): 52–106.

Tessaris, Chiara. "The War Relief Work of the American Jewish Joint Distribution Committee in Poland and Lithuania, 1915–18." *East European Jewish Affairs* 40, no. 2 (August 2010): 127–44.

Wągrzynek, Hanna. "Black Weddings among the Jews." In *Holy Dissent: Jewish and Christian Mystics in Eastern Europe,* ed. Glenn Dynner, pp. 55–68. Detroit: Wayne State University, 2011.

Weindling, Paul. *Epidemics in Eastern Europe, 1890–1945.* Oxford: Oxford University Press, 2000.

Weiser, Kalman. *Jewish People, Yiddish Nation: Noah Prylucki and the Folkists in Poland.* Toronto: University of Toronto Press, 2011.

Więckowska, Elżbieta. "Organizacja Sekcji Sanitarnej Krakowskiego Biskupiego Komitetu Niesienia Pomocy Dotkniętym Klęską Wojny (1914–1918): Społeczne Aspekty Historii Medycyny." *Medycyna Nowożytna: Studia Nad Historią Medycyny* 2, no. 1 (1995): 91–114.

Wróbel, Piotr. "The Jews of Galicia under Austrian-Polish Rule, 1869–1918." *Austrian History Yearbook* 25 (1994): 97–138.

CHAPTER 7

The Union of Jewish Soldiers under Soviet Rule

Mihály Kálmán

Approximately half a million Jews fought in the Russian Imperial Army during the Great War, which saw mass violence and forced dislocations directed against the Jews of Russia while opening up unprecedented possibilities for transforming Jewish society.[1] Following the demise of the czarist empire after the February Revolution of 1917, Jewish political, cultural, relief, and economic organizations mushroomed and Jewish soldiers' organizations were established throughout the former Russian Empire. This chapter examines the fate of one of these organizations, the All-Russian Union of Jewish Soldiers (VSEV). Its brief and tumultuous history can serve as a barometer of the challenges faced not just by Jewish soldiers at the end of Russia's involvement in World War I but more broadly by the Russian Jewish community as a whole as it sought to adapt its own urgent concerns to the ideological and political demands of the new Soviet regime.

In mid-1917, the aspiring umbrella organization of Jewish soldiers' associations, VSEV, was established in Kiev—only to be decapitated shortly thereafter in January 1918 as Ukrainian authorities forcibly dispersed its gathering, killing the chairman of the organization.[2] Nevertheless, the phenomena that called the VSEV to life, such as the collapse of the front and demobilization, the material and cultural needs of sick, jobless, homeless Jewish POWs and soldiers, and the threat of pogroms, continued to present Russian Jews with enormous challenges. Despite the outbreak of hostilities between Russia and Ukraine, the VSEV managed to relocate to Petrograd and later Moscow and succeeded in positioning itself as a major Jewish organization, in frequent contact with the highest rungs of government.

The democratization of refugee relief under the Old Regime and its transformation into what the historian Peter Holquist called a "parastatal complex" were spurred on by the February Revolution, and the emergence of relief organizations among various nationalities created an important nexus where representatives of different political strands and social strata could cooperate in moving toward a common national goal.[3] The flood of Jewish refugees and deportees during the war spawned and consolidated Jewish relief activism, and similar to other national elites and nationality-based relief organizations, those of Russian Jewry endeavored to shape national consciousness by engaging in relief, educational, and cultural activities.[4] At the same time, Jewish relief work underwent sea changes before and during the war, its democratization resulting in the rise of professionals and intellectuals to leadership roles, challenging the authority of established Jewish notables and disseminating democratic and revolutionary ideas.[5] For Jews, relief work represented a veritable experiment in self-government,[6] and like most European governments, the czsarist regime and the Provisional Government were eager to utilize the services offered by Jewish relief organizations. After the October Revolution, the Soviet government viewed such organizations as potential conduits for the transmission of its ideology to the Jewish street.[7]

The VSEV's claim to legitimacy as the representative of Jewish soldiers and the ties it built to other Jewish organizations enabled it to operate with considerable autonomy. This was the case even though its activities were often in direct contravention of professed Soviet policies. The freedom of organization brought about by the revolutions, combined with the pressing needs facing Jewish soldiers, propelled the VSEV to frantically devise and launch a variety of relief projects aimed at alleviating the troubles of its constituents. In addition to popularizing Jewish culture, carving out a Jewish economic sphere, and relief efforts, the VSEV placed a special emphasis on using the military skills of its members for self-defense. The successes and limitations of the VSEV under Soviet rule demonstrate the extent to which autonomous Jewish organizations were able to appeal to a broad pool of potential volunteers and activists and maneuver through the corridors of power, while seeking compromises with the increasingly overbearing Soviet-Jewish authorities.

Thus, the organization's cooperation with, subordination to, and eventual dissolution by Soviet-Jewish authorities in mid-1918 shed light on the pressures faced by many a Jewish organization eager to survive in the Soviet state-in-the-making.

Cultural and Relief Work

On 28 March 1918, as the German army was advancing on the city, the Temporary Central Committee of the All-Russian Union of Jewish Soldiers (VTsEKOVSEV) convened for the first time in Moscow, where it relocated from Petrograd along with numerous Soviet institutions.[8] While liaising with the recently established Jewish Commissariat (Evkom)—the Soviet state organ in charge of Jewish affairs—the VSEV made explicit its intention to preserve organizational autonomy.[9] At the same time, it published an open letter in the first issue of the Evkom's new journal, requesting Evkom's backing for securing governmental aid to the VSEV and proposing cooperation in the spheres of economic, legal, and labor aid, as well as re-evacuation—that is, helping Jews return to their hometowns that had been occupied by the Central Powers.[10] Cooperation with the Evkom did not prevent the VSEV from pursuing cultural and relief initiatives, establishing separate spaces where Jewish soldiers could recover, socialize, or work together. It organized events for Sabbath and holidays, as well as concerts and lectures on Jewish literary topics. The Society for Spreading Enlightenment among Jews (OPE) offered access to its large Moscow library for VSEV members, and the VSEV prepared to set up its own library, opening a reading room with daily deliveries of Russian and Yiddish newspapers.[11] A club decorated with pictures of Jewish writers, political activists, and artists was set up in February.[12] The VSEV also intended to showcase Jewish literary, theatrical, and musical works, forming choirs to popularize Jewish songs instead of the more typical fare of soldiers', students', and Gypsy songs. As a substitute for popular American plays, the VSEV sought to provide "Jewish" drama training for soldiers with the help of the Peretz Drama Association and the Habima Theater.[13]

In October 1917, the Zionist leader Meir Grossman had chastised the Russian Jewish community's "strange apathy," the lack of attention to the "few hundred thousand Jewish sons [who] live without a Jewish [or Yiddish] book or letter, torn off from Jewish society." Grossman juxtaposed this attitude both to that shown by other nationalities in Russia after the February Revolution and to that of the German, Austrian, and American Jewish communities catering to Jewish soldiers' needs. Decrying in particular the disappearance of the custom of communities providing kosher meals for Jewish soldiers and inviting them for Sabbath and holidays, he urged Russian Jewry to "correct their mistakes, the heavy injustice" committed against Jewish soldiers.[14]

In its Russian period, catering kosher meals and offering cultural events to Jewish soldiers became central to the VSEV's mission of providing physical and spiritual relief. The organization's clubs were to function as schools of Yiddish literacy and as venues for lectures on literary, scientific, and political topics. Dining halls, in turn, were to serve meals and incentivize club attendance, replacing the dirty private eateries offering subpar meals for hefty prices.[15] The war also brought about the modernization of philanthropy, replacing individual hospitality with institutional resources. The VSEV was determined to provide kosher meals in order to alleviate the psychological challenges faced by Jewish recruits and fulfill their aspirations to have a semblance of a Jewish environment while trapped "in the bloody atmosphere of the barracks ..., [enduring] the foreign military drills and the hostile-tormenting attitude of comrades-in misfortune ..., languishing in the unholy stuffiness of *treyf* cauldrons."[16]

Although self-defense remained a priority for the VSEV, the relatively small number of pogroms in 1918 allowed it to concentrate on aiding and "productivizing" Jewish POWs and veterans, thereby raising the VSEV's status to that of a nationwide, established organization. At the end of February 1918, the VSEV presented a plan to all major Jewish organizations to reinvigorate the Jewish cooperative movement, gather information on POWs, and ascertain the number of those wishing to return to Russia, asking them to obtain tools for industrial and agricultural production from Austria and Germany. Credit cooperatives, legal aid, and medical-sanitary aid were also to be organized, and aside from a property tax levied on all Russian Jews, fund-raising among Jews abroad was also planned.[17] In order to coordinate the re-evacuation of refugees and advance the organization's legitimacy by further embedding it into the fabric of Jewish society, in April the VTsEKOVSEV—now located in Moscow—initiated the formation of a United Jewish Committee (UJC), with representatives from all major Jewish public organizations.[18] However, the revived project was plagued by partisanship and interorganizational bickering, and the VSEV soon perceived that it was being squeezed out from the UJC; indeed, its representatives were not included even in the fact-finding delegation gathering information on POWs.[19] After the Moscow Jewish community left the UJC, the VSEV followed suit, and the organization disintegrated.[20] Persisting in its commitment to helping POWs, the VSEV in April–May gathered information on them, made efforts to establish contacts with the main German-Jewish relief organization, the Hilfsverein, and organized courses for instructors slated to provide social, economic, and labor relief.[21]

On 8–10 May, the Second All-Russian VSEV Conference took place in Moscow, with twenty-five delegates representing sixteen cities across Russia out of twenty-two VSEV branches.[22] Presenting on the POW question, Osip Veitsman took stock of the enormous task at hand, providing estimates on the number of Jewish POWs.[23] He suggested setting up a refuge, sanatoria, and dormitories, all serviced by the POWs themselves and subsidized by state funds. Veitsman also advocated the creation of informational juridical and registration bureaus to gather data about Jewish POWs, assist their distribution to dormitories and hospitals, and help them get in touch with their families. The informational-juridical bureaus were also to provide POWs with certificates for allowances and pensions, as well as with legal help and information on their property.[24]

Given Russian Jewry's overwhelmingly non-agrarian occupational structure, and with the disruption of commerce and production plaguing the country, many Jewish POWs were unable to return to their trades. However, since many of them had been employed in technically advanced German and Austrian factories, the conference accepted Veitsman's proposal to make use of their work experience. To this end, Veitsman also proposed opposing restrictions on the return of POWs and mobilizing the help of Austrian and German Jewry.[25] The Zionist head of the Moscow self-defense, Matus Gershman, added that not only had Jewish POWs gotten used to discipline and productive labor, but they were already "revolutionized to some extent and socially-psychologically ... healthy." He thus suggested that POWs not return to the ranks of artisans characterized by "stagnation and social flabbiness" and unable to compete with the prices and quality of the factories. Instead, the resolutions included Gershman's proposal to carve out an autonomous Jewish economic sphere by establishing credit cooperatives and organizing competitive large-scale production on a cooperative basis.[26]

The resolutions also stipulated that VSEV instructors recruit soldiers to Jewish labor bureaus or organize Jewish sections under general ones and form cooperatives jointly with public organizations, especially the Society of Skilled Trades (ORT). As the directives for instructors expectantly stated, "The present anarchic situation in the country, the local conditions, and especially local authorities, create ... unexpectedly great possibilities for creative work."[27] Such an opportunity, for instance, came in the form of an offer from the Northern Oblast Production Administration, which

Table 7.1. *Veitsman's Calculations Concerning Jewish POWs*

	Healthy	Tuberculosis	Sick	Overall sick	Total
Ukraine	26,500	10,000	7,000	17,000	43,500
Lithuania and Belorussia	17,000	7,600	3,400	11,000	28,000
Poland	16,000	7,200	3,300	10,500	26,500
Baltics	1,000	300	200	500	1,500
Russia	3,500	1,200	800	2,000	5,000
Total	64,000	26,300	14,700	41,000	105,000

Source: RGASPI 273/1/4/2ob.

in June 1918 asked the VSEV to cooperate in the production of shoes, offering to provide materials if craftsmen, workshops, and tools were made available.[28]

In line with the conference resolutions on relief and following the proposal of a group of VSEV member physicians to set up a medical-sanitary department, representatives were sent to Aleksino, Elets, and Samara in May to explore the possibility of setting up sanatoria, and efforts were made to raise funds from the Commissariat for Social Welfare.[29] Authorities in the former two localities provided premises for sanatoria,[30] and by mid-June the VSEV reached an agreement with the Society for the Protection of the Health of the Jewish Population (OZE) on cooperating in POW relief. Meanwhile, the VSEV urged local branches to involve Jewish communities and explore the possibility of setting up sanatoria and refuges at state expense, with symbolic funds from the TsEKOVSEV.[31] Soon, however, it became obvious that the VSEV lacked the necessary funds; it considered transferring the sanatorium in Elets to the Society for the Protection of Health entirely and in June had recourse to the OZE to fund the Aleksino sanatorium.[32] At the same time, the VSVE set up a sanatorium near Tula for two hundred patients, formed POW, medical-sanitary, and informational-juridical departments, and established a permanent presence at the Lefortovo POW sorting point in Moscow, providing twenty rubles per day to POWs, until it ran out of funds.[33]

Overburdened, in early April the VSEV requested 15,000 rubles from the Moscow Jewish community, but despite earlier promises it never received a response. Similarly, the 640,000-ruble aid the VSEV had requested from the Evkom did not materialize.[34] The VSEV thus remained badly underfinanced: in May 1918 it received nearly 8,000 rubles from donations, the same amount from local branches, while two VTsEKOVSEV members provided an additional 2,740 rubles. However, the funds were immediately spent, mostly on per diems and reimbursements for instructors, on the publication and distribution of printed materials, and on VSEV officials' salaries.[35] In mid-May, the TsEKOVSEV decided to request 25 percent of local branches' income, but the cash-strapped organizations were often not in a position to finance the center.[36]

These relief operations provided an opportunity for the VSEV to form at least temporary alliances with other major Jewish organizations as well as to present itself as an organization catering to the needs of the "revolutionized" and potentially most productive segment of the Jewish population. This, in turn, allowed the VSEV to obtain tenuous support from Soviet authorities, thereby confirming its legitimacy as an organization assisting overstretched state institutions. Indeed, the VSEV's relief efforts were welcomed and badly needed: according to a report from May, the VSEV, an "association of the very objects of communal help," was the only organization carrying out effective work among the Jewish POWs arriving in Moscow in appalling conditions.[37]

Self-Defense and the Second Conference

Still in Petrograd, on 10 March VSEV delegates attended a meeting devoted to self-defense, convened by the Evkom. Speaking on behalf of the VSEV, Joseph Trumpeldor emphasized that it considered self-defense units necessary, particularly since the German advance and the evacuation of Soviet institutions threatened to create a power vacuum. The majority supported the formation of an Evkom-controlled self-defense in cooperation with the Red Guards and the Red Army, but a number of Evkom members asserted that the Soviet government was strong enough to defend its citizens and insisted that self-defense would only benefit the Jewish bourgeoisie or might eventually turn into a White Guard. Finally, the tension was resolved by the Evkom: Il'ia Dubkovskii, the deputy of the all-powerful Evkom commissar Simon Dimanshtein, assured the delegates that in principle the Evkom supported self-defense, and Dimanshtein—at this time still quite lenient toward Jewish organizations and intent on channeling them into the Evkom—himself expressed the opinion that self-defense might be formed as a section of the Evkom, provided that members were only admitted upon the recommendation of revolutionary organizations.[38] Thus, the resolutions provisioned a self-defense commission consisting of representatives from the meeting's delegates, the Evkom, the VSEV, and Trumpeldor's former Joint Jewish Detachment.[39]

In Moscow, the VTsEKOVSEV member Moisei Dubrovinskii represented the VSEV at a joint session of Jewish political parties devoted to self-defense on 2 March,[40] and the VSEV began organizing self-defense immediately. By the middle of the month 180 people had signed up to the unit, which was allotted some 550 rubles by the VSEV.[41] Around the same time, the Evkom invited all Jewish parties to discuss the formation of an Evkom branch for Moscow and Moscow Oblast; the VSEV obtained a place at the meeting and was put in charge of elaborating plans to help POWs and combat pogroms.[42] By the end of March, the plans were sent to the Evkom, signaling the VSEV's realization that only by cooperating with the Evkom did they have a chance to influence Soviet policies on Jewish self-defense.[43]

In early April, the Moscow VSEV officially initiated the formation of self-defense units.[44] The Moscow Jewish community opposed the idea but expressed a willingness to agree to a VSEV intelligence unit in charge of providing warnings on antisemitic agitation. The VSEV, however, considered the existence of such a unit without a self-defense component to be useless, and it set up a department to elaborate plans for organizing self-defense and petitioning authorities for weapons.[45] It also asked the Moscow Soviet to legalize and subordinate to itself the self-defense function;[46] by April, 367 of the 662 VSEV members in Moscow were included into self-defense units.[47] Although the Moscow Evkom and the Military Commissariat drew up plans for Jewish self-defense, the Moscow Soviet of People's Commissars rejected these at the end of April, only undertaking to conduct anti-pogrom agitation, to assign Red units to combat pogroms and to recruit members of parties on the Soviet platform to the Red Army.[48]

With one-third of the delegates, Zionists generally supportive of self-defense had a plurality at the Second Conference that opened a few days later, and fifteen of the twenty-five delegates had prior involvement in self-defense.[49] The self-defense theses—evoking the most heated debates—were presented by Iakov Brams (Fareynikte) and coauthored by Solomon Aleksandrovich (SR), both ranking self-defense members from Petrograd.[50] Providing a historical overview of Jewish self-defense, the theses noted that no sovereign power could tolerate independent nationality-based armed groups, as that would be "tantamount to admitting its own powerlessness to defend all its citizens."[51] Thus, self-defense remained a vexed issue, with the czsarist government's malevolence and fear of left-leaning revolutionaries replaced by the Soviet government's opposition to self-defense based on its misguided official optimism and confidence in its ability to prevent pogroms.[52] Decrying the Evkom's and Soviet authorities' opposition to and half-hearted measures toward combating pogroms, Brams also called out the volte-face of the Bund's attitude toward self-defense. The leading advocate of the use of force in 1903–6, the Bund now put the unity of the "democratic front" before Jewish self-defense. Gravitating toward the Bolsheviks, Bundists now often viewed self-defense as chauvinistic, siphoning off forces from the fight against counterrevolution and into the hands of the Jewish bourgeoisie, while also fanning the flames of antisemitism. In turn, Brams praised Zionists, who though too weak and inexperienced in clandestine work to contribute significantly to self-defense in 1903–5, had become after the February Revolution the vanguard of Jewish self-defense and the VSEV.[53]

Although Brams acknowledged that self-defense under the Evkom seemed unthinkable, he believed that cooperation with the state as well as with Jewish communities was necessary. Thus, he advised VSEV branches to negotiate with local authorities that often acted independently of central directives and to warn them that by refusing to permit self-defense they would become accomplices to pogroms. Self-defense staffs were to be subordinated to Jewish communities politically and tactically while retaining strategic autonomy. Communities and wealthy Jews were expected to provide funding as well as legitimacy, which however also necessitated a democratization of self-defense. The theses thus advised that Jewish soldiers not monopolize self-defense, and once a unit was armed and legalized, the VSEV should forfeit control over it, restricting itself to forming its military core. Rejecting party control, Brams warned that legalization was possible only by averting "the minutest pretext ... for accusing the self-defense [organization] of sympathy to this or that party grouping, and by restricting it to functions of supervising order."[54]

In a retort to the theses' historical segment, Gershman and another Zionist, the Saratov self-defense leader Khaim Fel'dberg, emphasized Zionist efforts for self-defense in 1881–82 and 1903 and denounced socialists' current opposition to it. Moreover, Gershman advocated for a nationwide self-defense organization and drafting all Jews between seventeen and forty-five years of age, while also underlining that the VSEV could contribute to the revolutionizing of Jewish organizations. The zeal of the Zionist was countered by two former Jewish Socialist Workers' Party members, the Bundist Moisei Murinson and the Smolensk self-defense instructor and future Soviet historian David Baevskii. While Baevskii found the permanent arming of a specific nationality altogether anomalous, Murinson agreed to support a permanent nationwide self-defense organization under the VSEV, though he warned that if "separatist tendencies" were observed—that is, if it were to turn into a nationalist force undermining government authority—parties and public organizations should take the task of forming self-defense into their own hands.[55]

In order to ease tensions and move toward a united stance before further disagreements broke out, a closed session was held, where the coauthor of the theses, Aleksandrovich, again underlined that illegal, clandestine self-defense organizations—while at times useful—had limited efficiency. He proposed a permanent, militarized organization under the control of the VSEV rather than of parties, legalized by local authorities.[56] By the next session, Aleksandrovich argued that while Jews should demand protection from the Soviet government as citizens, they should not entrust the government with their lives. He thus subscribed to Gershman's plan for a universal draft, declaring that a draft dodger "will not be considered a son of our people." Similarly, Solomon Borunskii from Moscow suggested that all Jews capable of handling weapons be drafted and emphatically ruled out any cooperation with non-Jews. However, the Moscow VSEV leader Aleksandr Vilenkin, perhaps the most authoritative voice on military matters, warned that it might result in demoralization and mass desertion.

In response to the proposal to have self-defense units legalized locally, a delegate from Kursk also countered that although at times local authorities did indeed permit self-defense, they often demanded that it consist of non-Jews as well as Jews.⁵⁷ For some units, local legalization was made possible by complying with the party line while Soviet symbolism could be satisfied by making units less conspicuously Jewish. For instance, Iakov Khvilevitskii from Orsha reported that while his branch could not have its self-defense unit legalized, calling it the "Detachment for Guarding the City" allowed the unit to remain at least in a quasi-legal limbo.⁵⁸

Shimelovich, the Jewish Commissariat's representative at the conference, tried to reassure the delegates that the Soviet government would not allow pogroms but was reluctant to arm Jewish soldiers due to a lack of assurance that they would not turn against it. Adhering to the party line on the counterrevolutionary nature of pogroms, he added that arming Jews would in principle mean that all other nationalities had to be armed, since all were equally threatened by the counterrevolution. Instead, he supported the arming of workers who were "on the Soviet platform" and of organized Jewish workers, regardless of party affiliation. Being the head of the department responsible for Evkom operations in the provinces and for Jewish workers' clubs, Shimelovich suggested storing weapons in the latter, where they would be distributed if a pogrom were to erupt, allowing Jews and non-Jews to jointly suppress it. His proposal, however, was supported by only one delegate.⁵⁹

The VSEV was determined to avoid party and Evkom control over self-defense, and many even questioned the advisability and possibility of cooperating with Soviet authorities. While warning against criticizing the Evkom, Vilenkin was nevertheless intent on pressuring it into allowing self-defense to remain independent, so that "the fate of the Jewish people must not be tied to a certain party."⁶⁰ Shpunt, a former commander in Trumpeldor's Joint Detachment and member of the Zionist Military Organization, lashed out both against Brams's theses full of "party bickering and belletristics" and the Evkom proposal, categorically rejecting the notion that Soviet authorities could be trusted to give out weapons.⁶¹

Baevskii, the Smolensk delegate who had opposed national military organizations, now lent cautious support to illegal self-defense led by soldiers rather than party members. However, a number of branches warned that such plans would be difficult to fulfill. Kamenchik from Tambov countered that illegal self-defense could not be organized in central gubernias where authorities had greater control. Therefore the VSEV should strive to establish a centrally legalized self-defense organization. Closer to the neutral zone between Soviet Russia and the Ukrainian Hetmanate, delegates from Orel, Kursk, and Roslavl' reported that illegal self-defense was equally impossible to organize in the militarized border zone and advocated a nationwide campaign for its legalization.⁶²

Echoing the Evkom line, the Bundist Murinson from Moscow opposed illegal self-defense on the grounds that a strong Soviet state would not allow pogroms, while a weak one would need to direct all its forces—including Jewish soldiers—against the enemy. Sensing the firm opposition of the Evkom and the Bund, Vilenkin proposed to exploit the discrepancies between centrally dictated policies and the individual initiatives and considerations of local authorities. Instead of pursuing the apparently hopeless legalization in the center, local branches were to secure permission on lower levels or organize illegally. Veitsman, also from Moscow, preferred a semi-legal self-defense to a legal one and called local branches to organize units, train people, and create intelligence units and weapon stashes. Finally, Aleksandrovich proposed forming self-defense under the mantle of house guards or gymnastics clubs under the aegis of the VSEV.[63]

The resolutions on self-defense reflected a compromise between a decentralized, locally sanctioned (potentially illegal or semi-legal) self-defense and a state-mandated nationwide force, in other words, more or less between the provinces and the capitals. While attempting to avert accusations of disloyalty on the part of its armed forces, the VSEV firmly rejected party control over it and insisted on preserving such a force's neutrality and organizational autonomy. The delegates declared it necessary immediately to form a nationwide self-defense force involving all Jewish organizations acting in cooperation with the authorities. At the same time, while the VSEV promised to do everything in its power to achieve the legalization of self-defense in the center, it left it to local branches to define their own specific course of action—as long as the self-defense units were apolitical and remained aloof from the civil war, while seeking only to defend Jewish honor, life, and property. Finally, the resolutions warned Soviet authorities to stop hindering the formation of nonpartisan Jewish self-defense organizations and the arming of Jewish soldiers, lest they become inadvertent accomplices to pogroms.[64]

Organizing Self-Defense

About a week after the Second Conference resolved to seek legal standing for self-defense, the VSEV began negotiations with the Jewish community and the Evkom to this end.[65] Although it seems that the VSEV received tenuous support, the commissar for military affairs Bonch-Bruevich, in a fiery, thirty-minute-long speech, categorically refused the request of a VSEV delegation to arm even a nonpartisan self-defense force.[66] Thus, before the end of May the TsEKOVSEV informed local branches that there was no hope of legalizing self-defense and receiving weapons and urged them to devise new ways of organizing self-defense in case legalization could not be achieved locally. At the same time, the circular noted that the Evkom was planning to set up anti-pogrom detachments led by local self-governments, admit members upon the recommendation of the labor unions and communal organizations, and base the detachments in workers' clubs. In turn, the VSEV implored the branches to lobby for the formation of such detachments and for admission based on VSEV recommendations, to ensure that most detachment members were Jewish or people who could be relied on to combat pogroms. As the circular warned, however, the branches had to prepare for the formation of independent VSEV self-defense units should the Evkom fail to fulfill its promises.[67]

Although the Evkom's plan was scrapped by central authorities, in some cases it was nevertheless actualized on the local level. In Smolensk, for instance, the VSEV members were registered through the labor unions in early May, likely in order to be able to join the self-defense.[68] However, given that the Evkom was present in only about a dozen cities in 1918, the possibility of forming self-defense units under its supervision was necessarily curtailed.[69] In Vologda, a VSEV branch was officially organized on 6 May, and almost seventy people registered on the first day. Since there was no Evkom in the city, the VSEV branch began negotiations with the city administration as well as with the Bund, the Fareynikte, and the Poale Tsion parties about the possibility of forming a self-defense unit, and at the end of June the TsEKOVSEV sanctioned the decision to cooperate with parties.[70] In Kineshma, the formation of a self-defense unit was postponed, as the local VSEV branch decided to wait until an Evkom unit was organized. Despite the directives provided in the circular, they considered it impossible to apply to the local Soviet for permission, given the small size of the VSEV.[71]

The VSEV also faced opposition from the Bund. VSEV instructors sent to Samara, Tambov, and Voronezh in April 1918 reported that the Bund considered the VSEV "not only superfluous but harmful for democracy and useful only for the bourgeoisie." Such a party line, however, did not prevent local Bund committees from organizing their own armed units. In the case of Voronezh, at the meeting convened by the VSEV instructor to organize a detachment, the Bund representative openly called participants to join the Bund detachment instead.[72] At the same time, the Jewish community of Smolensk was joined by a Bundist representative of the Soldiers' Soviet in repeatedly requesting that Soviet authorities arm a nonpartisan Jewish self-defense unit. Seeing his pleas fall on deaf ears, the Bundist soldier himself established a VSEV branch in early May. However, local authorities banned the organization, and even after a pogrom ravaged Smolensk in mid-May, Jews were refused weapons.[73]

Despite the lack of legalization, in mid-June the Moscow Evkom permitted the VSEV to hold shooting training for self-defense members at state-owned shooting ranges, and measures were elaborated for self-defense in Moscow and the provinces.[74] Local VSEV branches were sent notarized copies of the permission to use shooting ranges and were advised to use it for seeking similar authorizations from local military commissariats, allowing for large-scale training in order to select the most capable self-defense members and build group cohesion.[75] In Moscow, the VSEV Self-Defense Department planned to work with a head instructor and two to four paid instructors to select the best shots among self-defense members, whose addresses were meticulously registered in order to facilitate swift mobilization.[76] In mid-September, however, a Moscow VSEV session decided that since those undergoing the VSEV military training program were often subject to Red Army draft, training would be superfluous. The VSEV thus decided to halt training and close down its military school in Aleksino but reminded former trainees that they were obliged to appear at VSEV self-defense organizations in case of pogroms.[77]

Under the Commissar

As the Soviet state moved to "statize" public life, the Evkom, which initially relied on Jewish organizations for support while also trying to wield influence over them, increasingly began to encroach upon Jewish organizations.[78] Nor could the VSEV, by this time a visible presence, escape the urge of the Evkom to impose the dictatorship of the proletariat on the Jewish street. On June 26, the Evkom appointed one Mikhail Tsvibak as commissar to the VSEV, and his relationship with the organization was strained from the start. Upon his appointment, Tsvibak asked to be presented a list of and information on all TsEKOVSEV members, adding that thereafter outgoing documents were invalid without his signature. A few days later, he demanded to be immediately provided with all protocols of the Second Conference and that POWs no longer be registered on VSEV membership cards.[79] Within weeks, tensions between the Evkom and the VSEV erupted because of the latter's insistence on continuing Jewish relief work.

In mid-June the TsEKOVSEV complained to the Evkom that their petitions for equipping a dorm had been refused on the grounds that the VSEV was conducting relief work that catered to a single nationality. The VSEV asserted that their intentions were predicated not on "considerations of a chauvinistic-nationalist character" but on the realization that the "everyday [*bytovye*] and economic conditions" of Jewish POWs warranted a particular treatment, especially the observance of kashrut laws, which Jewish soldiers had not been able to follow during the war. In addition, the VSEV pointed out that while non-Jews returned to their villages with beneficial dietary and climate conditions, numerous Jewish POWs were unable to return to their hometowns on the territories occupied by the Central Powers, whence most of them came, and in the cities they had been driven to criminality, into the "army of bagmen and profiteers." Thus, the VSEV argued that it had to take care of a larger share of POWs in the cities than organizations catering to non-Jewish POWs.[80]

The issue of Jewish relief also surfaced when in mid-July Mark Zel'des from the TsEKOVSEV deliberated upon the fate of the VSEV's Kazan' sanatorium with Evkom representatives. Planning for the sanatorium began in late May, and by mid-June the local VSEV received funding and rented an appropriate building. The equipment was paid for by the Social Welfare Commissariat, the VSEV was responsible for maintenance expenses, and the institution was to be governed by the VSEV's Medical-Sanitary Department. While the TsEKOVSEV insisted on providing care exclusively for Jews, the commissariat refused to give even half of the available places to Jewish patients, offering a mere 5 to 6 percent. In an attempt to divide the organization, the Evkom thus tried to go over its head by contacting only Zel'des personally to work on the sanatorium issue.[81]

Such cases of overreach on the part of the Evkom did cause serious tensions within the VSEV. Shortly after the Kazan' sanatorium incident, Gershman and Aleksandrovich handed in their resignations, announcing their disagreement with the Evkom's apparent intention to exclude the VSEV from the operation of the Kazan' sanatorium and transform it into one of its auxiliary institutions under the thumb of the overbearing and interfering commissar. While Brams agreed that the commissar disrupted the collegial atmosphere in the VSEV, he insisted on preserving the VSEV's autonomy even while cooperating with the Evkom, while also seeking to repel—as it did in the case of the sanatorium—Evkom's aggressive measures.[82] Two days later, the tension mounted to the extent that the TsEKOVSEV voted on the dispersal of the VSEV and its replacement by a bureau for helping POWs as a subdepartment within the Society for the Protection of the Health of the Jewish Population. However, the majority of the members opted to continue working independently and to protest against the breach of their autonomy, thus prompting the resignation of Shpunt, who was of the opposite opinion.[83]

Economic woes did not cease to plague the VSEV either; by the end of June, the TsEKOVSEV warned the branches that due to their inertia and the lack of funds transmitted to the center, the expansion of the VSEV network to the southeast and Siberia had been halted, and the central apparatus might even cease to function.[84] Financial troubles notwithstanding, in its circular in early July the TsEKOVSEV urged local committees to set up juridical-informational bureaus, fulfilling the same functions as they did vis-à-vis the central office.[85]

Underfunded local branches, however, were often not up to the tasks that fell on them. Although on 6 September, the Evkom promised the VSEV to discuss the possibility of providing financial help for refugees; it was concerned about the VSEV's ability to manage relief operations. It asked to be informed whether the Jewish refugees in Briansk were being aided by the local Jewish community and organizations and whether the POWs were being sent to Orsha.[86] However, reports from August indicated that the VSEV operations were crumbling in Orsha as well; the registration of POWs and refugees was not being carried out by the local branch, and only the OZE had the means to provide them with a meager bread ration and financial aid.[87]

In late September, the TsEKOVSEV was still busy taking over a dining hall from Moscow OZE, dispatching representatives to Russian cities, and coordinating work with POW relief organizations.[88] A worrying sign of the impending end, however, was a general gathering of the Moscow VSEV planned for 6 October, though postponed due to the lack of interest. The VSEV warned its members that the "absenteeism of comrades threatens the VSEV with the disruption of its activities and leads to the full dissolution of the organization," pleading with them not to forfeit the results already achieved and to continue their work, particularly in the sphere of self-defense.[89]

Despite such internal crises, in the end it was external pressure that forced the VSEV out of existence. Its fate was sealed at the First Conference of the Jewish Sections of the Communist Party (Evsektsiia) and the Evkom, held 20–27 October 1918. Shimelovich, the Evkom delegate to the Second Conference, proposed a thesis announcing that the Evkom was unwilling "to give any weapons to our bourgeoisie, but we must arm our workers ... to fight pogroms and defend Soviet power," and the resolutions of the conference called for the liquidation of all Jewish bourgeois organizations.[90]

Instead of self-defense, planning thus began to draw Jews en masse into the Red Army, which saw the greatest single mobilization drive of the civil war era between October and December 1918. On 9 November, the Evkom and the Evsektsiia resolved to call upon Jewish workers to join the Vilna Regiment of the Western Division, where a special Jewish detachment was to be established,[91] and on 17 November the Evkom decided to close down the VSEV, citing its inactivity and uselessness for the laboring masses.[92] While Soviet-Jewish authorities also took control of major Jewish relief organizations, for a time they were allowed at least a shaky existence, as their disbanding would have presented the government with an insurmountable task of caring for hundreds of thousands of Jewish refugees.[93] As for the VSEV, however, despite shifting its focus to relief activities, its claim to Jewish military endeavors proved a thorn in the side of Soviet and Soviet-Jewish authorities, which thus used the first major attempt at the induction of Jews to the Red Army as an opportunity to disband the VSEV.[94]

Conclusion

The relief and self-defense projects of the VSEV provided a sphere of grassroots activism for Jewish soldiers, reintegrating them into Russian society and the Jewish community after years of warfare. Imploring Jewish soldiers to articulate their interests and needs, the VSEV aimed to cater to these, while putting into use its membership's unique capabilities—be it familiarity with German shoe production technologies or battle-worthiness—for the benefit of Russian Jewry as a whole. In addition, the VSEV aimed to advance the political awakening of newly emancipated Jewish soldiers, welding them into a community, as well as a military, economic, and humanitarian force. As a communique inviting soldiers to the Second Conference put it:

> In the moment of the downfall of society, of general apathy on the Russian as well as the Jewish street, we, Jewish soldiers, demobilized and veterans, all participants of the World War, have to take into our own hands the issue of defending our rights and interests. The time has passed when one related to Jewish soldiers in the best case with benevolence and sympathy, but in any case as to an inferior creature. The Jewish soldier grew, realized himself, understood that he cannot and does not have to be merely an onlooker upon everything that is going on around him. The Jewish soldier does not want to be a mercenary in Jewish society anymore; he wants to build his own life, his fate, regardless of the difficulties, conditions, circumstances, and political events. The Jewish soldier grew politically and at present already raises his own voice and goes out to the arena of social and economic life on his own.[95]

According a historic role to Jewish soldiers, the Moscow Zionist Il'ia Sosnovik at the Second VSEV Conference emphasized their potential to serve and transform Jewish society through the VSEV, "an organization that—at this crucial moment—would be able to take into its own hands the defense not only of soldiers themselves but of the entire Jewish people ... the civic and political rights achieved by the revolution.... Jewish society is tired, apathetic; it lacks resources and will. New forces, vitally interested in awakening Jewish society and making it do something, are needed."[96]

Just as soldiers were singled out as the vanguard of the revolution, so too did the VSEV lay claim to being the vehicle of change in Jewish society, and the promise of partaking in this enterprise proved to be attractive to numerous Jewish soldiers. Self-defense served as a cornerstone of VSEV activities on account of the military training of members. The VSEV aimed thereby to appropriate an uncharted but far-reaching territory in Jewish political life—the physical protection of all Jews. Such a challenge to the state's monopoly of violence, to the influence of Soviet-Jewish authorities, and to the unity of the front, however, hastened the VSEV's disbanding, while sharp disagreements over self-defense along party lines undermined the unity of the organization.

The VSEV's conflicts over military affairs were paralleled by those over nationality-based relief activities. Attempts to act in coordination with major Jewish public organizations also evoked the ire of the Evkom, anxious to safeguard and extend its influence. While delegates at the Second Conference seemed eager to cooperate with Jewish communities and organizations, the Evkom representative warned that these were "buried by the times" and insisted that the only possible future lay in cooperating with the Soviet government.[97] Increasingly, the internal tensions resulting from the pressure to cooperate with or subordinate itself to the government clashed with the VSEV's concomitant desire for autonomy and took a heavy toll on the organization. The uneasy cooperation alienated leaders and members alike, resulting in resignations and declining participation. At the same time, the VSEV's staunchly nonpartisan stance and insistence on independence was also increasingly untenable in the face of the party's—and Soviet-Jewish authorities'—growing sway over public life and due to the Red Army's hunger for battle-seasoned soldiers.

Mihály Kálmán is a postdoctoral fellow in Jewish studies at the Central European University in Budapest. His research follows Jewish military and paramilitary organizations during the Russian Civil War and the concomitant pogroms, as well as the transplantation of self-defense activists' narratives and the application of their experience to Mandatory Palestine. He has also published on Hungarian-Jewish Olympians.

Notes

1. See, e.g., Jonathan Frankel, "The Paradoxical Politics of Marginality: Thoughts on the Jewish Situation during the Years 1914–1921," in *Crisis, Revolution and Russian Jews,* ed. Jonathan Frankel (New York: Cambridge University Press, 2009), pp. 142–43, 145–46. On wartime violence and deportations, see, e.g., Eric Lohr, "1915 and the War Pogrom Paradigm in the Russian Empire," in *Anti-Jewish Violence: Rethinking the Pogrom in East European History,* ed. Israel Bartal et al. (Bloomington: Indiana University Press, 2011), pp. 41–51.
2. On Jewish soldiers' organizations and the VSEV (*Vserossiiskii soiuz evreev-voinov*), see Vladyslav Hrynevych and Liudmyla Hrynevych, "Deiatel'nost' soiuza evreev-voinov

Kievskogo voennogo okruga (iul' 1917–ianvar' 1918 gg.)," *Vestnik Evreiskogo universiteta v Moskve* 6, no. 24 (2001): 207–48 [The Activities of the Union of Jewish Soldiers of the Kiev Military District (July 1917–January 1918)]; Vladyslav Hrynevych and Liudmyla Hrynevych, *Natsional'ne viis'kove pytannia v diial'nosti Soiuzu ievreiv-voiniv KVO: (lypen' 1917–sichen' 1918 rr)* [National Military Questions in the Activities of the Union of Jewish Soldiers of the Kiev Military District (July 1917–January 1918)] (Kiev: Natsional'na akademiia nauk Ukrainy, Instytut istorii Ukrainy NAN Ukrainy, Instytut politychnykh i etnonatsional'nykh doslidzhen', 2001); Iaroslav Tynchenko, *Pid zirkoiu Davida: Evreis'ki natsional'ni formuvannia v Ukrainy v 1917–1920 rokakh* [Under the Star of David: Jewish National Units in Ukraine in 1917–1920] (Kiev: Tempora, 2014), pp. 16–56.
3. Peter Gatrell, *A Whole Empire Walking: Refugees in Russia during World War I* (Bloomington: Indiana University Press, 1999), pp. 171–87; Peter Holquist, *Making War, Forging Revolution: Russia's Continuum of Crisis, 1914–1921* (Cambridge, MA: Harvard University Press, 2002), p. 4.
4. Mark von Hagen, "War and the Transformation of Loyalties and Identities in the Russian Empire, 1914–1918," *Annali Fondazione Giangiacomo Feltrinelli* 34 (Russia in the Age of Wars 1914–1945) (1998): 18; Mark von Hagen, "The *Levée en masse* from Russian Empire to Soviet Union, 1874–1938," in *The People in Arms: Military Myth and Mobilization since the French Revolution,* ed. Daniel Moran and Arthur Waldron (Cambridge: Cambridge University Press, 2003), p. 170; Gatrell, *A Whole Empire Walking,* pp. 141–44, 168–70; Peter Gatrell and Nick Baron, "Population Displacement, State-Building, and Social Identity in the Lands of the Former Russian Empire, 1917–23," *Kritika* 4, no. 1 (2003): 57, 61–66; Eric Lohr, "War Nationalism," in Eric Lohr, Alexander Semyonov, and Vera Tolz, eds., *Empire and Nationalism at War: The Russian Empire in World War I* (Bloomington: Slavica, 2014): 96–97.
5. Steven Zipperstein, "The Politics of Relief: The Transformation of Jewish Communal Life During the First World War," in *The Jews and the European Crisis, 1914–1921,* ed. Jonathan Frankel, *Studies in Contemporary Jewry* 4 (1988), pp. 29, 32–36; Mikhail Beizer, *Evrei Leningrada, 1917–1939: Natsional'naia zhizn' i sovetizatsiia* [The Jews of Leningrad, 1917–1939: National Life and Sovietization] (Moscow and Jerusalem: Mosty kul'tury, 1999), p. 237. As Rabinovitch notes, however, most organizations remained dependent on the funding and support of Jewish notables; Simon Rabinovitch, *Jewish Rights, National Rites: Nationalism and Autonomy in Late Imperial and Revolutionary Russia* (Stanford, CA: Stanford University Press, 2014), pp. 192–97.
6. Rabinovitch, *Jewish Rights,* pp. 180–85.
7. Frankel, "The Paradoxical Politics of Marginality," pp. 140–42.
8. VTsEKOVSEV (*Vremennyi Tsentral'nyi Komitet Vserossiiskogo soiuza evreev-voinov*) was the governing body of the VSEV; at the Second Conference in May 1918 it was replaced by a permanent Central Committee (TsEKOVSEV).
9. Rossiiskii gosudarstvennyi arkhiv sotsial'no-politicheskoi istorii (Russian State Archive of Socio-Political History) *fond* 273, *opis'* 1, *delo* 8, *listy* 1-5ob, 6-6ob (henceforth: RGASPI 273/1/8/1-5ob, 6-6ob); RGASPI 273/1/19/22, 24.
10. "A brif fun yidishe soldatn tsum komisar far yidishe inyonim" [A Letter from Jewish Soldiers to the Commissar for Jewish Affairs], *Di varhayt* 1 (8 March 1918): 4.
11. RGASPI 273/1/19/1b-1ob, 10-10ob, 18ob; 27-27ob, 27a; RGASPI 273/1/14/14ob; "Moskva: Soiuz evreev-voinov" [Moscow: The Union of Jewish Soldiers], *Evreiskoe slovo* 6–7 (9 [22] March 1918): 6. On the Moscow OPE library, see Jeffrey Veidlinger,

Jewish Public Culture in the Late Russian Empire (Bloomington: Indiana University Press, 2009), pp. 45–47.
12. RGASPI 273/1/19/2, 8ob, 11; "Khronika: U evreev-voinov" [At the Jewish Soldiers], *Evreiskoe slovo* 3 (11 [24] January 1918): 4.
13. RGASPI 273/1/3/6ob-7ob.
14. M[eir] Grosman, "Di yidishe gezelshaft un di yidishe soldatn" [Jewish Society and the Jewish Soldiers], *Petrograder togblat* 126–135 (17 [30] October 1917): 3–4.
15. RGASPI 273/1/3/6ob-7ob.
16. RGASPI 273/1/3/5; on the practice of inviting Jewish soldiers for meals in the czarist era, see Yohanan Petrovsky-Shtern, *Jews in the Russian Army, 1827–1917: Drafted into Modernity* (Cambridge: Cambridge University Press, 2009), pp. 191–96.
17. M. Serebrianyi, "V Petrograde: Soiuz evreev-Voinov" [In Petrograd: The Union of Jewish Soldiers], *Evreiskaia nedelia* 5 (18 February 1918): 14–15. In 1916 there was already an attempt to build cooperation between OPE, OZR, ORT, and EKOPO; Evgeniia Pevzner, "Evreiskii Komitet pomoshchi zhertvam voiny (1914–1921)" [Jewish Committee for the Relief of War Victims (1914–1921)], *Tirosh* 10 (2010): 145.
18. RGASPI 273/1/10/40. The organizations involved were Jewish Committee for the Relief of War Victims (EKOPO), Society for the Protection of the Health of the Jewish Population (OZE), Jewish Colonization Society (EKO), Society for Spreading Enlightenment among Jews (OPE), Society of Skilled Trades (ORT), and Jewish Relief Society for Victims of Pogroms and the War (EVOPO).
19. RGASPI 273/1/13/59-59ob.
20. RGASPI 273/1/2/1, 21, 22.
21. RGASPI 273/1/8/7-8, 9.
22. RGASPI 273/1/1/2; RGASPI 273/1/9/2; the following cities were represented: Vologda, Kineshma, Kazan', Moscow, Nizhnyi Novgorod, Orel, Orsha, Petrograd, Roslavl', Saratov, Smolensk, Tambov, Tula, Tsaritsyn, Iaroslavl' (two representatives arrived from Vitebsk and Ufa, but were not officially delegated); there were also branches in Petropavlovsk, Riazan', Samara, Simbirsk, Syzran', and Cheliabinsk. An additional twelve candidates were also included; RGASPI 273/1/1/4. See also mandates and questionnaires of delegates on RGASPI 273/1/6/1-33ob.
23. RGASPI 273/1/4/1-2ob.
24. RGASPI 273/1/4/2ob-4ob; see also RGASPI 273/1/11/21-27. Around the same time, VSEV advertisements in newspapers began offering help for family members of POWs in establishing contacts with the latter; "Evrei voenno-plennye" [Jewish POWs], *Evreiskoe slovo* 13–14 (6 [19] May 1918): 6.
25. RGASPI 273/1/4/2ob-3ob. The Moscow VSEV, for instance, intended to utilize specialists trained in Germany to set up a workshop making prosthetic limbs; RGASPI 273/1/11/1-2ob. See the resolutions in: RGASPI 273/1/1/55; republished as Hrynevych and Hrynevych, *Natsional'ne*, p. 131.
26. RGASPI 273/1/2/7-9; RGASPI 273/1/1/56; republished as Hrynevych and Hrynevych, *Natsional'ne*, p. 132.
27. RGASPI 273/1/10/16.
28. RGASPI 273/1/10/4-4ob, 35; RGASPI 273/1/9/49.
29. RGASPI 273/1/9/16-17, 39.
30. RGASPI 273/1/10/64, 68.
31. RGASPI 273/1/13/18-18ob.
32. RGASPI 273/1/9/43, 51.

33. RGASPI 273/1/2/22-23; RGASPI 273/1/8/20, 23ob, 28.
34. RGASPI 273/1/2/22-23; RGASPI 273/1/8/20, 23ob, 28.
35. RGASPI 273/1/8/34-35; the expenses mentioned were 5,420, 3,472, and 2,562 rubles, respectively.
36. RGASPI 273/1/9/21, 51; RGASPI 273/1/10/26.
37. RGASPI 273/1/10/3; "V Moskve: Voennoplennye priekhaly" [In Moscow: The POWs Have Arrived], *Evreiskoe slovo* 13–14 (6 [19] May 1918): 6; "Evrei-voennoplennye," *Bor'ba* 1, nos. 4–5 (25 July 1918): 58–59.
38. On Dimanshtein, see Zvi Gitelman, *Jewish Nationality and Soviet Politics: The Jewish Sections of the CPSU, 1917–1930* (Princeton, NJ: Princeton University Press, 1972), pp. 130–33, 135.
39. "Organizatsiia evreiskoi samooborony" [The Organization of Jewish Self-Defense], *Razsvet* 10 (24 March 1918): 25–26; see also "Arba'a shanim le-mavet Yitzchaq ben-David" [The Fourth Anniversary of Yitzhak ben-David's Death], *Davar*, 26 February 1952, 2; on Trumpeldor's detachment, see, e.g., Aleksandr Mikhailovich Gak, *Iosif Trumpel'dor—chelovek-legenda* [Joseph Trumpeldor: Man and Legend] (Tel Aviv: Aleksandr Gak, 2006), pp. 54–58; and the present author's forthcoming article in the 2017 *CEU Jewish Studies Yearbook*.
40. RGASPI 273/1/23/46ob-47.
41. RGASPI 273/1/19/16.
42. RGASPI 273/1/11/14, 54-54ob = 55-55ob; RGASPI 273/1/19/14, 17.
43. RGASPI 273/1/8/2.
44. RGASPI 273/1/19/28.
45. RGASPI 273/1/19/30; RGASPI 273/1/8/15.
46. "Moskva: Evreiskie organizatsii samooboony" [Moscow: Jewish Self-Defense Organizations], *Evreiskoe slovo* 10 (1 [14] April 1918): 4.
47. RGASPI 273/1/21/2-10ob, 12-32ob.
48. DAKO R-3050/1/122/17-18; GARF R-130/2/212/1-3; GARF R-1318/24/7/3ob = 15ob, 27, 33, 39; RGASPI 272/1/71/8; "Khronika: Bor'ba s pogromami" [Chronicle: Fight against Pogroms], *Bor'ba* 1, nos. 2–3 (9 June 1918): 48–49; "Bor'ba s evreiskimi pogromami" [Fight against Jewish Pogroms], *Evreiskaia mysl'* 27 (28 June 1918): 15; "Evreiskaia zhizn': V Rossii: Postanovlenie soveta narodnykh kommissarov Moskovskoi oblasti po voprosu o preduprediteľ'nykh merakh bor'by s everiskimi pogromami" [Jewish Life: In Russia: The Decision of the Moscow Oblast Sovnarkom on the Question of Preventive Measures for Combating Jewish Pogroms], *Evreiskaia mysl'* (Samara) 4 (4 [17] May 1918): 9; L. B. Miliakova and I. A. Ziuzina, eds., *Kniga pogromov: pogromy na Ukraine, v Belorussii i evropeiskoi chasti Rossii v periode Grazhdanskoi voiny, 1918–1922 gg.: sbornik dokumentov* [The Book of Pogroms: Pogroms in the Ukraine, Belarus and the European Part of Russia in the Civil War Period, 1918–1922: A Collection of Documents] (Moscow: ROSSPEN, 2007), pp. 754–56.
49. RGASPI 273/6/5-33ob.
50. RGASPI 273/1/8/24, 26.
51. RGASPI 273/1/5/26ob, 27ob; quote from l. 27ob.
52. RGASPI 273/1/5/30ob.
53. RGASPI 273/1/5/27-28, 30ob.
54. RGASPI 273/1/5/32ob-34.
55. RGASPI 273/1/1/50-50ob; on Fel'dberg, see RGASPI 273/1/6/11.
56. RGASPI 273/1/1/51-51ob.

57. RGASPI 273/1/1/45-46. On Vilenkin, see, e.g., Tynchenko, *Pid zirkoiu Davida*, pp. 41–44.
58. RGASPI 273/1/1/51ob.
59. RGASPI 273/1/1/45-45ob, 47ob; on Shimelovich, see Gitelman, *Jewish Nationality*, p. 138.
60. RGASPI 273/1/1/45ob-46; quote from l. 45ob.
61. RGASPI 273/1/1/46ob.
62. RGASPI 273/1/1/47-47ob.
63. RGASPI 273/1/1/47-48.
64. RGASPI 273/1/1/56-57; Hrynevych and Hrynevych, *Natsional'ne*, pp. 132–34.
65. RGASPI 273/1/9/15, 26. Apparently, Brams also made a follow-up visit: RGASPI 273/1/9/39.
66. RGASPI 273/1/9/30, 35, 44; RGASPI 273/1/10/5; see also: "Samooborona" [Self-Defense], *Razsvet* 19 (2 June 1918): 21.
67. RGASPI 273/1/10/24-25.
68. RGASPI 273/1/25/5ob.
69. On Evkom locations, see Gitelman, *Jewish Nationality*, pp. 138–44; Shmuel Agurski, *Di yidishe komisariatn un di yidishe komunistishe sektsyes: Protokoln, rezolyutsyes un dokumentn (1918-1921)* [The Jewish Commissariats and the Jewish Communist Sections: Protocols, Resolutions, and Documents (1918–1921)] (Minsk: s.n., 1928), p. 70.
70. RGASPI 273/1/14/1a, 2, 3-3ob, 4ob, 5; RGASPI 273/1/9/75.
71. RGASPI 273/1/18/2, 3.
72. RGASPI 273/1/2/27; on Tambov, see also RGASPI 273/1/1/47.
73. Michael Hickey, "Revolution on the Jewish Street: Smolensk, 1917," *Journal of Social History* 31, no. 4 (1998): 840; Michael C. Hickey, "Smolensk's Jews in War, Revolution, and Civil War," in *Russia's Home Front in War and Revolution, 1914–22*, ed. Sarah Badcock, Liudmila G. Novikova, and Aaron B. Retish (Bloomington: Slavica, 2015), pp. 198–99.
74. RGASPI 273/1/9/65, 70, 75.
75. RGASPI 273/1/9/130-131 = 132-132ob; RGASPI 273/1/10/9 = 28 = 29 = 30 = 31 = 32 = 33 = 48-48ob. According to certificates from the Moscow Military Commissariat, twelve hundred bullets per training were issued to VSEV members: RGASPI 273/1/22/94-97. In late July, the VSEV instructed its Petrograd plenipotentiary to convince the Union of Towns to get permission for the self-defense to train at state-owned shooting ranges: RGASPI 273/1/13/32-32ob.
76. RGASPI 273/1/13/53-54; for a list of Moscow self-defense members, see, RGASPI 273/1/22/1-87.
77. RGASPI 273/1/19/66-66ob.
78. See, e.g., Lewis H. Siegelbaum, *Soviet State and Society between Revolutions, 1918–1929* (Cambridge: Cambridge University Press, 1992), p. 13; Mordekhay Altshuler, *Ha-yevseqtziyah bi-Vrit ha-Mo'atzot, 1918-1930: ben le'umiyut we-qomunizm* [The Jewish Sections of the Communist Party in the Soviet Union, 1918–1930: Between Nationalism and Communism] (Tel Aviv: Sifriyat po'alim, 1980), pp. 23–24.
79. RGASPI 273/1/13/24, 26, 27, 28; see also: ll. 50-51 and "V komissariate po evreiskim delam" [In the Commissariat for Jewish Affairs], *Bor'ba* 1, nos. 4–5 (25 July 1918): 62; *Politika sovetskoi vlasti po natsional'nomu voprosu za tri goda* [The Policies of the Soviet Government on the Nationalities Question for Three Years] (Moscow: Gosizdat, 1920), p. 31. On such measures during the takeover of public organizations, see Romanova, "Evreiskii otdel," p. 62.

80. RGASPI 273/1/13/20-21. In Petrograd, too, the VSEV tried to concentrate Jews in a separate hospital so as to be able to comply with kashrut laws more efficiently; RGASPI 273/1/13/32-32ob.
81. RGASPI 273/1/9/35, 62ob, 90ob, 115-117 = 118-119; RGASPI 273/1/10/3ob; RGASPI 273/1/13/31-31ob.
82. RGASPI 273/1/9/94ob-95 = RGASPI 273/1/10/67; RGASPI 273/1/9/95-95ob = RGASPI 273/1/13/30-30ob.
83. RGASPI 273/1/9/109-110 = 111ob-112ob = 114-114ob = RGASPI 273/1/10/55-55ob. It seems that around this time Tsvibak actually tried to close down the VSEV, but the TsEKOVSEV flatly claimed that he had no right to do so; RGASPI 273/1/9/130-131 = 132-132ob.
84. RGASPI 273/1/13/22-22ob.
85. RGASPI 273/1/10/20-21 = 53-54ob.
86. RGASPI 273/1/13/34-34ob.
87. RGASPI 273/1/9/126-126ob.
88. RGASPI 273/1/9/139-140 = 141-142. On the dining hall, see also RGASPI 273/1/9/143, 144, 145 = 146.
89. RGASPI 273/1/19/79; see also RGASPI 273/1/19/143, 144.
90. Shmuel Agurski, *Der yidisher arbeter in der komunistisher bavegung (1917–1921)* [The Jewish Worker in the Communist Movement (1917–1921)] (Minsk: Melukhe-farlag fun Vaysrusland, 1925), p. 49; Avrom Kirzhnits, *Der yidisher arbeter: Khrestomatye tsu der geshikhte fun der yidisher arbeter, revolutsionerer un sotsialistisher bavegung in Rusland*, vol. 4, *Di yorn 1917–1918* [The Jewish Worker: A Chrestomathy for the History of the Jewish Labor, Revolutionary, and Socialist Movement in Russia: The Years 1917–1918] (Moscow: Shul un bukh, 1928), pp. 261–62; Agurski, *Di yidishe komisariatn*, pp. 50, 59–60; quotation from p. 50. See also Gitelman, *Jewish Nationality*, pp. 145–46.
91. RGASPI 445/1/1/4; see also Elias Tcherikower, *Di ukrayner pogromen in yor 1919* [The Ukrainian Pogroms in the Year 1919] (New York: YIVO, 1965), p. 284; "Iz deiatel'nosti evreiskikh kommunistov" [From the Activities of Jewish Communists], *Zhizn' natsional'nostei* 3 (24 November 1918): 8; see also "Iz deiatel'nosti Narodnogo komisariata po delam natsional'nostei: Evreiskii komisariat" [From the Activities of the People's Commissariat for Nationality Affairs: Jewish Commissariat], *Zhizn' natsional'nostei* 5 (8 December 1918): 7.
92. GARF R-1318/1/550/32; "O zakrytii soiuza evreev-voinov," *Zhizn' natsional'nostei* 2 (17 November 1918): 7; also published in *Politika sovetskoi vlasti*, 32.
93. Beizer, *Evrei Leningrada, 1917–1939*, pp. 244–45.
94. On Jews and Jewish units in the Red Army, see Baruch Gurevitz, "An Attempt to Establish Separate Jewish Units in the Red Army during the Civil War," *Michael: On the History of the Jews in the Diaspora* 6 (1980): 86–101; Oleg Budnitskii, *Russian Jews between the Reds and the Whites*, trans. Timothy J. Portice (Philadelphia: University of Pennsylvania Press, 2012), pp. 356–405.
95. RGASPI 273/1/10/41-42 = 56.
96. RGASPI 273/1/2/16, 19.
97. RGASPI 273/1/1/8-10ob; quotation from l. 10.

Selected Bibliography

Primary Sources

Agurski, Shmuel. *Di yidishe komisariatn un di yidishe komunistishe sektsyes: Protokoln, rezolyutsyes un dokumentn (1918–1921)*. Minsk: s.n., 1928.
Agurski, Shmuel. *Der yidisher arbeter in der komunistisher bavegung (1917–1921)*. Minsk: Melukhe-farlag fun Vaysrusland, 1925.
Hrynevych, Vladyslav, and Liudmyla Hrynevych. *Natsional'ne viis'kove pytannia v diial'nosti Soiuzu ievreïv-voïniv KVO: (lypen' 1917-sichen' 1918 rr.)*. Kiev: Natsional'na akademiia nauk Ukraïny, Instytut istoriï Ukraïny NAN Ukraïny, Instytut politychnykh i etnonatsional'nykh doslidzhen', 2001.
Miliakova, L. B., and I. A. Ziuzina, eds. *Kniga pogromov: pogromy na Ukraine, v Belorussii i evropeiskoi chasti Rossii v periode Grazhdanskoi voiny, 1918--922 gg.: sbornik dokumentov*. Moscow: ROSSPEN, 2007.
Politika sovetskoi vlasti po natsional'nomu voprosu za tri goda. Moscow: Gosizdat, 1920.

Secondary Sources

Altshuler, Mordechai. "The Attitude of the Communist Party of Russia to Jewish National Survival, 1918–1930." *YIVO Annual of Jewish Social Science* 14 (1969): 68–86.
Altshuler, Mordekhay. *Ha-Yevseqtzyah bi-Vrit ha-Mo'atzot, 1918–1930: Ben le'umiyut we-qomunizm*. Tel Aviv: Sifriyat po'alim, 1980.
Beizer, Mikhail. *Evrei Leningrada, 1917–1939: Natsional'naia zhizn' i sovetizatsiia*. Moscow and Jerusalem: Mosty kul'tury, 1999.
Buldakov, Vladimir Prokhorovich. "Freedom, Shortages, Violence: The Origins of the 'Revolutionary Anti-Jewish Pogrom' in Russia, 1917–1918." In *Anti-Jewish Violence: Rethinking the Pogrom in East European History*, edited by Israel Bartal, Jonathan L. Dekel-Chen, David Gaunt, and Natan M. Meir, pp. 74–94. Bloomington: Indiana University Press, 2011.
Budnitskii, Oleg. *Russian Jews between the Reds and the Whites*. Translated by Timothy J. Portice. Philadephia: University of Pennsylvania Press, 2012.
Frankel, Jonathan. "The Paradoxical Politics of Marginality: Thoughts on the Jewish Situation during the Years 1914–1921." In *Crisis, Revolution and Russian Jews*, edited by Jonathan Frankel, pp. 131–54. New York: Cambridge University Press, 2009.
Frenkin, Mikhail Samoilovich. *Russkaia armiia i revoliutsiia, 1917–1918*. Munich: Logos, 1978.
Gatrell, Peter. *A Whole Empire Walking: Refugees in Russia during World War I*. Bloomington: Indiana University Press, 1999.
Gitelman, Zvi. *Jewish Nationality and Soviet Politics: The Jewish Sections of the CPSU, 1917–1930*. Princeton, NJ: Princeton University Press, 1972.
Holquist, Peter. *Making War, Forging Revolution: Russia's Continuum of Crisis, 1914–1921*. Cambridge, MA: Harvard University Press, 2002.
Hrynevych, Vladyslav, and Liudmyla Hrynevych. "Deiatel'nost' soiuza evreev-voinov Kievskogo voennogo okruga (iul' 1917–ianvar' 1918 gg.)." *Vestnik Evreiskogo universiteta v Moskve* 6 (24) (2001): 207–48.
Petrovsky-Shtern, Yohanan. *Jews in the Russian Army, 1827–1917: Drafted into Modernity*. Cambridge: Cambridge University Press, 2009.

Rabinovitch, Simon. *Jewish Rights, National Rites: Nationalism and Autonomy in Late Imperial and Revolutionary Russia.* Stanford, CA: Stanford University Press, 2014.

Romanova, Nina Mikhailovna. "Evreiskii otdel Petrogradskogo komissariata po delam natsional'nostei (1918–1923 gg.)" [*The Jewish Department of the Petrograd Commissariat for Nationality Affairs (1918–1923)*]. *Vestnik Evreiskogo universiteta v Moskve* 10 (1995): 56–69.

Tynchenko, Iaroslav. *Pid zirkoiu Davida: Evreis'ki natsional'ni formuvannia v Ukraini v 1917–1920 rokakh.* Kiev: Tempora, 2014.

von Hagen, Mark. "The Great War and the Mobilization of Ethnicity in the Russian Empire." In *Post-Soviet Political Order: Conflict and State Building*, edited by Barnett R. Rubin and Jack Snyder, pp. 34–57. London: Routledge, 1998.

Zavadivker, Polly. "Blood and Ink: Russian and Soviet Jewish Chroniclers of Catastrophe from World War I to World II." Unpublished PhD dissertation, University of California, Santa Cruz, 2013.

Zipperstein, Steven. "The Politics of Relief: The Transformation of Jewish Communal Life during the First World War." In *The Jews and the European Crisis, 1914–1921*, edited by Jonathan Frankel, *Studies in Contemporary Jewry* 4 (1988): 22–40.

CHAPTER 8

Global Conflict, Local Politics
The Jews of Salonica and World War I
Paris Papamichos Chronakis

On the morning of 16 June 1915 in Salonica, members of such respectable Zionist associations as Maccabi, Max Nordau, Nouveau Club, and Bene Sion passed by Jewish shops in the central marketplace and pressed their owners to boycott the Francophile Jewish newspaper *L'Indépendant* (The Independent). Moving in the streets and squares like "bands of Apache Indians," they tore sheets of the paper in public, beat a young vendor, threw flyers calling the "good Jews" to boycott the newspaper, sent threatening letters to its subscribers, and requested its advertisers to stop publicizing—all in a systematic attempt to silence a paper that, in their view, ran a "vile campaign against the Jewish nation."[1] Those militant Zionists presented themselves as "young Jews," claimed to be the "numerous" and "resolute" spokesmen of "Jewish public opinion," and reproached *L'Indépendant,* whose owners, editors, and readers were all Jewish, as comprised of "French journalists," essentially labeling the local newspaper an instrument of foreign and gentile propaganda.[2]

"Like hounds, the entire vile mob, the scum of the earth, threw itself against the editors Joseph Matarasso and Lazare Nefussy, who can now walk in public only with police protection," noted a pro-French Jewish notable.[3] Worried, the Greek police banned all demonstrations and assemblies in the quay, the city's main meeting point.[4] Tensions, however, escalated as the editors of *L'Indépendant* and their supporters did not remain idle. Picking up the gauntlet, Matarasso and Nefussy counterattacked by denouncing the Zionists as an "occult organization" of "violent thugs."

The editors suggested the Zionists were closely associated with the local German and Austrian consuls and represented not Jewish but German interests.[5] They furthermore alleged that the Zionists were tools of Austrian and German spies who encouraged them to enter the Jewish shops of the marketplace in order to "sow discord and hatred" and "throw the germs of crime and scandal" among the "ignorant [Jewish] crowd."[6]

This ferocious episode was not unique. Between the outbreak of hostilities in the summer of 1914 and northern Greece's November 1916 entry on the side of the Entente, the streets, theaters, and newspapers of neutral Salonica often resembled a battle zone where Jews re-enacted the drama of the Great War.[7] In October 1914 there had been violent confrontations among viewers of a film showing German soldiers surrendering, forcing the police to ban all war movies and newsreels.[8] Even charity events turned into rows between pro-French and pro-German supporters, as occurred in September 1915, when during a screening organized on behalf of the Belgian war victims at the cinema Alhambra, the Jewish audience split in two, with one part hissing at the sight of the Russian flag and the picture of the czar and the other shouting, "Down with the Kaiser," when newsreel scenes of a German sentry appeared on screen. Taken up by the press, the "Alhambra incident" continued to reverberate, deeply dividing the Jewish public.[9] Physical violence was recurrent, and in street demonstrations opponents were lynched. This, indeed, was the case in August 1916 during a pro-Entente rally against Germany's ally Bulgaria, when an angry Francophile Jewish crowd chased and nearly beat to death three coreligionists for shouting pro-German slogans.[10]

Clashes also took a more ritualized form with Franchophile and Germanophile Jews confronting each other in duels to defend their insulted honor. In February 1915 a journalist of the resolutely pro-Entente Jewish newspaper *L'Opinion* challenged to a duel Mentech Bessandji, the Zionist editor in chief of the Jewish, French-language newspaper *Le Nouveau Siècle* (The New Century) and an allegedly "Salonican champion of German views." When the latter declined the challenge, the former immediately reminded Bessandji sarcastically that the duel was mandatory in Germany, a country that had effectively "robbed" him of his "conscience" and "dignity," if not his honor and manhood.[11] The journalist insinuated that support for Germany entailed effeminacy as well as the loss of one's Jewishness.

How are we to account for such acute intra-Jewish tension, a conflict physically and symbolically so violent that it resembled a veritable Jewish civil war, with opponents openly negating each other's ethnic and even gendered identities? Why would the Jews of Salonica clash over a war fought by gentiles far away from their still peaceful lands? Despite Greece's neutrality until June 1917, Salonican Jewry's engagement with the Great

War was deep and multifaceted from the start. In their various capacities as export and import traders, smugglers and profiteers, foreign citizens and Westernized Sephardim, fighters and philanthropists, producers and consumers, Salonican Jews were enmeshed within interweaving business, familial, imperial, and cultural webs that crossed national boundaries and brought the war into their lives. These webs have often passed unnoticed within a historiography largely operating within a national framework, which treats Jewish involvement in World War I through the restrictive interpretative lenses of ethnic solidarity and/or national patriotism and exclusion. Attending to wartime Jewries from the more dynamic perspective of Jewish Diaspora networks rather than the static viewpoint of state-minority relations complicates the historical narrative and helps create a third conceptual space in between neutrality and active engagement.

If, however, the Great War had not just a formative but also a divisive impact on Salonican Jewry, it was because it took distinctly local forms. As I will argue, the war dramatically transformed social and political relations within the community. It turned existing (and long-simmering) ideological, class, and party differences into unbridgeable cleavages, generating a mishmash of competing allegiances to France and Germany, Greece and Salonica, Zionism and assimilation. These overlapping allegiances were felt locally in the city of Salonica, but they were equally the outcome of a complex interaction among local, national, and global actors, Jewish as well as gentile.

First, opposing communal factions, rival ideologies, and competing social classes closed ranks by identifying either with the Franco-British Entente or with the Austro-German Central Powers. In Salonica, the global war followed a local script. Second, Greek Christian politicians, European consuls and ministers, international Jewish organizations, and Salonican Jewish emigrants abroad often read local divisions as direct reflections of the European conflict, attributing to Salonican Jewry a "French" or "German" national identity. In short, the war proved to be a metaphor, a "key symbol," so rich and powerful precisely because local decision-making now operated within a much broader, indeed global, field.[12]

Maelstrom: Transnational Connections and the Experience of the Great War

Historiography on the Jews and modern European wars has occasionally mentioned in passing clashes between Jews in neutral countries to highlight how competing national identifications undermined the sense of a shared Jewish identity and the bonds of religious solidarity. Derek Penslar reminds us of an event that occurred in 1871 in Los Angeles, where German and French Jewish immigrants, all members of the local Alliance Israélite Universelle chapter, brawled over the ongoing Franco-Prussian War.[13] Similarly, new scholarship on the cultural aspects of the war experience in Eastern Europe has begun to note the tensions in multiethnic cities like Warsaw, where the conflicting loyalties of its Russian, German, and Polish gentile (and Jewish?) inhabitants turned the cafés, the city's most emblematic places of tolerant conviviality, into arenas of brutal clashes.[14]

While the Jews of Los Angeles and the gentiles of Warsaw could at least claim some tangible connection or sense of origin to a German, French, or Russian social milieu, the Salonican Jews, by contrast, do not neatly fit this interpretative pattern of divisive nationalism tearing apart a religious community in a multiethnic city. They were Sephardic Jews who had no social but only imagined and affective ties with the opposing parties they supported. Ironically, Salonican Jewry had been for centuries a culturally homogeneous ethno-religious community of about eighty thousand Spanish-speaking Sephardim, who until these events erupted had possessed a strong sense of a distinct cultural identity. Ever since their arrival from Spain to the Ottoman Empire in the late fifteenth century, their distinct language, religion, customs, and demographic superiority in a multiethnic city with much smaller Greek Orthodox and Muslim Turkish populations had gradually coalesced into a coherent identity despite their diverse origins, social divisions, urban distribution, and citizenship status.[15]

Beginning in the mid-1870s these old allegiances began to change as Salonican Jews enthusiastically embraced European modernity, reforming the community's educational system and introducing Western-type schooling. This happened mainly through the efforts of the Alliance Israélite Universelle, a Franco-Jewish educational association committed to civilizing the Jews of the Orient by immersing them in French culture and the doctrine of Jewish emancipation through instruction, not in Judeo-Spanish or Ottoman but rather in French.[16]

From that point on the Jewish community underwent a radical transformation. It diversified socially and culturally as an expanding middle and upper class steeped in French language and culture set the tone of public life and debate within the community and the city at large. French became part and parcel of Jewishness, constituting the second pillar of a distinctive modern Jewish identity, next to Judeo-Spanish.[17] It became the chief medium of public no less than private communication, the language of the press, of associations and public gatherings, of intimate letters, business correspondence, even petitions. It informed a modern sense of Jewishness and as such tied Salonican Jewry as a whole to France. By the early twentieth century, middle-class Salonican Jews, loyal Ottoman citizens nonetheless, celebrated France as their intellectual and spiritual motherland, a beaming light of Western civilization, Jewish emancipation, and local prosperity and progress.[18] Thus, when World War I erupted in the summer of 1914, Salonican Jewry was still a culturally homogeneous group, one that largely sympathized with everything French. Moreover, after centuries of Ottoman rule, they were now full citizens of neutral Greece, the state that had annexed Salonica just two years earlier after defeating the Ottoman armies during the First Balkan War of 1912–13.[19]

Yet, for those French-speaking Jews, residents of a still neutral state on the European periphery, World War I was anything but a faraway echo. Similarly to other diasporic communities in neutral countries, the local Jewish public contemplated its impact on the Jewish condition and the benefits and dangers it could potentially bring.[20] However, in Salonica, the war was not only an intellectual exercise but an all-embracing experience. It was felt on all socioeconomic levels with such intensity and in so many different ways that it blurs conceptual boundaries between neutrality and engagement.

On the economic side, the outbreak of hostilities, in particular Austria-Hungary's attack on Serbia and the Ottoman Empire's entrance to the war on the side of the Central Powers, severed the tight business links connecting Salonica to Central Europe and the Eastern Mediterranean and further disrupted the conduct of commerce that had already been hit hard by the Balkan Wars and the loss of Salonica's vast hinterland. However, the war also brought new business opportunities. The Ottomans' closing of the Dardanelles turned Salonica's port overnight into a gateway to Russia, whereas the imposition of a Franco-British blockade against the Central Powers also made trade with Austria-Hungary an appealing and highly lucrative business.[21] Jewish merchants exploited their transnational business networks and their near monopoly in the import-export trade to successfully adjust to the new circumstances and retain their position in the local economy. Within the city, however, these economic disruptions widened the social divide. Food shortages, rationing, and inflation hit the populous Jewish lower and lower-middle class strata hard, particularly the salaried employees and white-collar workers. As elsewhere, access to food became a new social marker, and consequently, provisioning turned into a key arena of political action shaping new social and political identities. Public discourse on the "cost of life" now pitted a desperate and helpless "people" against a new social enemy, the "profiteer" and "speculator" identified with the "insatiable baker, the greedy butcher, and the avaricious grocer."[22]

Such "class" cleavages within the Jewish community were counterbalanced by the spread of a new sense of Jewish solidarity. Numerous charity drives, public subscription lists, and relief work for the war victims in Europe and the Middle East made the war "real" on the sociocultural side as well. The conflict infused a broad, middle-class sociability, intensively engaging both men and women and mobilizing a new social category, the Jewish youth. Among the Zionists in particular, club lectures on "Judaism and the World War" as well as frequent philanthropic gatherings, bazaars, and public ceremonies supplemented regular fund-raising efforts for the relief of "our brothers in Palestine," the publication of special newspaper editions and their widespread distribution by "Jewish young ladies and gentlemen," and eventually the establishment of a dedicated society, the Lema'an Zion (For Zion's Sake), to coordinate public action.[23] More than sustaining established forms of middle-class philanthropy, the war actually radicalized relief efforts. It recast them (in the minds of the local agents) into a "movement" with local as well as international references.[24] Filling the pages of the newspapers and informing social action, these sustained, focused, and coordinated initiatives reinvigorated local public life and further strengthened the transnational philanthropic networks of Salonican Jews. As was the case with other European and especially American Jewries during the times of war, they, too, could now legitimately claim a place in the global, emotional community of Jewish collectivity brought together as witnesses to the spectacle of unprecedented Jewish suffering and displaying a solidarity that was both "national" and "human."[25]

For some Jews the war even became a harsh reality. Those holding French or Italian citizenship were drafted, hastily leaving Salonica in the late summer of 1914 to fight for a country they had never seen before.[26] Others, although Greek citizens, were nevertheless so animated by a true French patriotism and a youthful idealism (similar to that which had swept the entire continent that summer) that they volunteered to serve in the French army, joining the French Legion.[27] Finally, Salonican Jews who had immigrated to France also joined the ranks of those serving as naturalized French citizens.[28] The gallantry, patriotism, and sacrificial death of some of these Jews was to be subsequently memorialized in obituaries published in the local Jewish newspapers, the fallen "co-citizens" ironically praised for "making a spontaneous holocaust [*sic*] of their life for the grandeur of the fatherland."[29] These newspapers tried hard to bring the war home. Irrespective of their political stance and ideological affiliation, they closely followed the involvement of European Jewry and enthusiastically embraced their coreligionists' active participation, viewing it, like all other Jewries in the belligerent countries, as the ultimate proof of Jewish loyalty to their respective nation-states, as well as a source of Jewish pride, incontestable virility, and renewed self-assertion.[30]

The commercial outlook of Salonican Jewry, its trans-Mediterranean and pan-European trade networks, the multiple citizenships of its members, its strong cultural attachments to France, and the existence of numerous emigrants in the belligerent countries turned the war into a tangible experience. Distant conflicts can have unique reverberations in diasporic and highly mobile communities as the transnational aspects of individual life courses create complex spatialities and shrink real and imaginary distances as much in war as in peace. If, however, the experience of war proved so decisive and immediate, it was not only because the networks of Salonican Jews brought it home. Rather, it was primarily due to the particular local meanings with which it was invested. The lived experience of the war was culturally mediated and symbolically constructed in situ.[31]

The Jewish Schism: The Local Politics of a Global War

In Salonica, the outbreak of the Great War reignited existing political and ideological divisions. By 1914 two opposing political camps vied for communal control while also promoting radically different understandings of Jewishness. On the one side, there were "the Alliancists," a quasi-political faction organized around a network of clubs, the local committee of the Alliance Israélite Universelle, and its male and female alumni associations. Backed by French- and Ladino-language newspapers, this group had grown out of the modern educational system introduced in the city in the mid-1870s by the Alliance. It had spearheaded the reorganization of communal establishments and the curtailment of rabbinic power and had been credited with the spectacular renewal of the community in the later part of the nineteenth century. In control of the communal council and the leading educational and welfare institutions, the Alliancists had long dominated communal affairs, constituting the local political elite. An enlightened aristocracy of sorts, ideologically they echoed the emancipationist discourse of French republican Jewry and espoused a modern understanding of Jewishness as principally a religious demarcation.[32]

On the other side were the rising and assertive Zionists. A late arrival in communal politics, they had experienced a meteoric rise since the Young Turk Revolution of 1908, strengthening their positions during the tumultuous years of political upheaval, war, and border changes that followed. The Zionists managed to broaden, mobilize and radicalize the local public by appealing to all its constituent parts through the establishment of a network of closely associated sports and youth societies, social clubs, and philanthropic associations, as well as an affordable press. Zionism was a loose category of identification. Often called "nationalists," its adherents advocated a form of diasporic cultural nationalism, demanding the physical, moral, and intellectual regeneration of an enfeebled Judaism as well as the renovation of the community, and fostering a more clearly delineated and publicly visible Jewish *ethnic* identity based on the use of Hebrew, body culture, knowledge of Jewish history, and preparation for return to the Land of Israel.[33]

By 1914, the two groups were already at loggerheads, and the war further pitted the one against the other.[34] The numerically weaker Alliancists identified with France by articulating a discourse based on the tropes of cultural indigeneity, kinship, and gratitude. France was their "intellectual homeland," and the Jews of Salonica were its "children" in heart and mind.[35] Like other Eastern European Jews, the Alliancists' Francophile discourse was both generic and specific, fusing human and Jewish dignity.[36] It broadly praised France's "tolerance," "liberalism," and "civilization," as well as more explicitly its pioneering role in "demolishing [that] Jewish Bastille," the "infamous ghetto where our ancestors were parked."[37] In juxtaposition, it condemned France's Jewish opponents as "ungrateful."[38] This discourse informed a wide array of pro-French, Jewish-led activities in Salonica. The Alliancist newspapers *L'Indépendant* and *L'Opinion* hailed French victories and incessantly propagated the Entente cause. The (predominantly Jewish) alumni association of the Mission Laïque Française prided itself in becoming a "center of French propaganda" and flew the tricolor on the occasion of every French victory.[39] Similarly, the alumni of the local Alliance schools, Jews but "French at heart," contributed to the French war effort by organizing fund-raising campaigns for the wounded soldiers and offering them gifts on New Year's Day.[40] These actions were further normalized by being inserted into a longer historical narrative of cordial relations between Salonica and France and presented as a reflection of the close bonds binding together a Jewish city and the French nation.[41] Salonica was imagined as an outpost of French culture.

For their part, the wives of prominent Jewish notables who supported the Alliance Israélite Universelle performed their patriotic duty by running the local chapter of the Union des Femmes de France (French Women's Union), one of the three most important women's associations in France and overseas.[42] Furthermore, pro-French newspapers closely followed the participation of "our co-citizens abroad" in the French war effort, praising those naturalized Salonican Jews, like Dr. Arama, who rose from private soldiers to officers, making "Salonica proud."[43] Such celebratory accounts of individual feats were largely bereft of references to masculine pride or Jewish patriotism. In fact, they were less an expression of Jewish social status, patriotism, and normative virility than they might appear—or than might have been the case elsewhere in Europe.[44] Rather, these jubilant texts were intentionally partisan. They made explicit reference to "co-citizens" so as to directly link the local Alliancist group with local pride, and they praised a "principled" and "generous" France in order to associate the group with France's supposedly widely shared ideals and values.[45] Involvement in the "just" French war effort elevated the local Alliancist Jews into exemplary "Salonicans" at home and abroad. Most crucially, the universally accepted principles that a republican France embodied vindicated their understanding of Jewishness as a non-ethnic but exclusively religious identity marker. By 1914, the Jews of Salonica, former Ottoman subjects and Greek citizens in the making, were hard-pressed to reconsider their erstwhile secure place in a city bound to lose its multiethnic character and in a country eager to assimilate them. By acting the way they did, the Alliancists essentially attempted to convince and mobilize a Jewish public deeply divided over its own post-imperial identity. They resorted to a certain idea of "liberal" and "emancipationist" France to promote a particular, local understanding of an assimilated Jewishness.

The Zionists, on the other hand, looked to the "great and beautiful Italy" and the historical precedent of the Risorgimento as an example of what a people's will for a "free and independent life" could achieve, and in early 1915 they publicly declared their formal neutrality in keeping with the position of the international Zionist movement.[46] At the same time, however, they sympathized with the Central Powers, Germany and Austria-Hungary.[47] Local and international concerns informed their stance. Since 1908, German Jewish involvement in the delicate sphere of Jewish education in Salonica had increased. The more overtly German nationalist Hilfsverein der deutschen Juden (Relief Organization of German Jews) made its presence felt by establishing a superb local school and attracting the support of several local notables (and, no less, the ire of the Alliancists). In 1910 a project was even put forward to transfer the protection of the Jewish schools from the Alliance Israélite Universelle to the German government and replace French with German as the language of instruction in return for sizable German subventions, personnel, and material. This bold plan was eventually rejected by the communal council, but the fact that it was seriously considered suggests the local appeal of a German-backed Zionism as a counterforce to the Alliance.[48]

Antipathy to Russia was a much more important factor, however, in empowering Zionism. The Zionists tapped into a widespread Russophobia—a local reflection of a broader trend within the European and American Jewish publics shaped by recurrent pogroms and intolerant czarist politics.[49] In Salonica the memory of a thousand destitute Jewish refugees (victims of the pogrom in Kishinev, Ukraine) arriving in the city in 1903 was still vivid and often mentioned.[50] Realizing the extent of anti-Russian feelings, the pro-Zionist chief rabbi was forced to claim that support for France was impossible as long as the latter remained allied with the czar.[51] Russia was in fact so unpopular that once the Great War erupted, Jews trampled over Russian flags in plain view, while the raising of the czarist emblem at pro-Entente events was enough to enrage an otherwise sympathetic public.[52] The Zionists systematically exploited this deep-seated anti-Russian sentiment, thereby frustrating the dismayed Alliancists.[53] In their view, a Jew's support for Russia was an inconceivable "crime of treason to his own people." "Whoever dared express Russophile sentiments would be booed by his own brothers," they warned.[54] The Zionists, therefore, connected Jewishness to a resolute anti-Russian stance, countering the Alliancists' similar tying of Jewishness to support for France. Once complementary, Francophilia and Russophobia had now become oppositional. In Salonica, the war intensified the battle between the two political factions by turning the conflict between the Entente and the Central Powers into a struggle of two globally competing constructions of Jewish identity.

Next to Russophobia, a unique local concern further animated the Zionists' pro-German stance, making it particularly popular among the public: a widespread, almost messianic belief that the victory of the Central Powers would lead to a redrawing of borders in the Balkans. For decades, strong ties linked Jewish commerce to Central Europe, and Austro-Hungarian merchandise dominated the local market.[55] Once the war erupted, the initial German military advances fueled a public enthusiasm that a quick German victory would terminate the recently established Greek rule in the city, insert Salonica anew to the Central European economic sphere (as Austria's gateway to the Balkans), and secure the communal prosperity that was so suddenly jeopardized by the unexpected, extraordinary border changes of the Balkan Wars.[56] "A German victory," it was claimed, "would be a dreamed-of, unexpected, and inexhaustible fortune for Salonica."[57] But more than an economic fantasy, Austro-German success was also seen as apparently the only way to avert the "Greek tutelage," the hellenization (read: demise) of Jewish Salonica.[58] The war infused new life into the recent Zionist project of turning the city into a local Zion, an autonomous, internationally administered free port, a "little Jewish republic," as the Zionists termed it.[59] A far-fetched prospect, this idea nevertheless captivated the local popular imagination and tipped the balance of public sympathy in favor of the Central Powers. "This colony," remarked the French consul, "is not Gallophobe. It holds no bad sentiments against us. If only it could be reassured that its secret desire to see Salonica transformed into a free city would materialize under the protection of France and Britain, then it would side with us."[60]

Different visions of Salonica thus determined the choice of side. If for the Alliancists local pride and historical cultural connections spoke in favor of Salonicans' sacrifice for France, for the Zionists local attachment informed instead a daring political stance, the internationalization of Salonica, and made legitimate an enthusiastic support for the Central Powers.

Communal factionalism, the international Jewish movements of Zionism and assimilation, rival imaginings of Jewishness, and competing visions of Salonica informed opposing attitudes to the war. Class divisions added a further layer of differentiation. Salonica's Jewish community was among Europe's most socially stratified, encompassing all elements from the numerous porters and peddlers to a closed-knit group of prominent business magnates.[61] Although the exact social composition of the Alliancist and the Zionist camps is hard to determine, contemporary commentators, Alliancists and Zionists alike, systematically associated the Alliancists with the "aristocracy," the communal elite of notables and entrepreneurs, and the Zionists with the "medianeros," that is, the educated but disenfranchised upcoming middle class of white-collar workers, merchants, and businessmen.[62]

The fierce public debate over the war drew frequently on this local vocabulary of class. Predictably, by drawing from the prevalent understandings of existing social divisions, it also intensified them. The Alliancists in particular prided themselves on being the "social and intellectual aristocracy," the "elite," "those who count."[63] By contrast, they deplored the Zionists as the "small" and "poor" people.[64] References to cultural rather than solely economic capital informed such imaginings of social cleavages. While the upper classes were singled out for their spiritual and moral qualities, for their "ability to think," their sincerity, and the "integrity of their actions," the lower classes were conversely termed an "uncultivated mass" of "fanatics."[65] External understandings neatly corresponded with these self-perceptions of Jewish social hierarchies, generating cross-ethnic allegiances. The Greek Christian press praised the Francophilia of the "Israelite and our own [i.e., gentile] aristocracy," and in April 1915 prominent members of the local Christian and Jewish upper class jointly launched a Greco-French Association to promote the establishment of a French chamber of commerce and commercial museum in the city.[66] Class identity and ethnic cooperation were tied to support for the Entente.

For the Zionists, in contrast, vocabularies of class informed a nationalist rhetoric. The Zionists denounced prominent Alliancists as un-Jewish, their stance determined by their vested economic interests in major Jewish Salonican companies.[67] They further conjured the negative image of Herzl's infamous "Mauschel" to denigrate those respectable upper-class entrepreneurs as seekers of "vulgar profit," as show-offs and "inferior human beings."[68] In political discourse, newspapers and competing factions debated the war (and made it meaningful) through recourse to a familiar language of local class cleavages. Ironically, these polarized political representations of class did not reflect social realities. In everyday life, economic hardship, unemployment and shortages, profiteering and smuggling, were dividing the Jews anew between an impoverished mass of blue- and chiefly white-collar workers (spanning up to and including respectable families) and a new class of capacious nouveaux riches.[69] However, although the war was redrawing social boundaries on the ground, a polemical and politicized class discourse linked Francophilia and Germanophilia with increasingly differentiated class identities.

Beyond the Jewish milieu, national divisions, tearing the Greek Christian polity apart, further exacerbated these communal, ideological, and class cleavages. By mid-1915, the disagreement over Greece's participation in the war between the pro-Ententist Liberal prime minister Eleftherios Venizelos and the neutralist, pro-German King Constantine reached unprecedented heights of political polarization, generating intense political instability and splitting the country in two.[70] The "National Schism," as the conflict between the "Venizelists" and the "Royalists" was termed, involved two different visions of irredentism, of establishing a Greater and Christian Greece.[71] However, it did not leave Salonica's Jewish community untouched either.

In the national elections of June 1915 (essentially a referendum on Greece's entry into the war), the pro-Entente, Alliancist communal elite sided with Venizelos, while the pro-German, middle-class Zionists supported the Royalist parties and their candidate Demetrios Gounaris.[72] Both sides were deeply involved, mobilizing all their forces. Zionist societies carried out all the necessary paperwork, making sure the numerous Jewish masses were registered to vote, while their newspapers urged all Jews to go to the polls "for the triumph of peace and the king."[73] The Alliancists in turn utilized their larger financial resources to support theirs and the gentile Venizelists' electoral campaigns.[74] In the course of a heated debate the two groups fought ferociously against each other. New designations appeared, the "Venizelist Jews" and the "Gounarist Jews," which although sometimes condemned as an "arbitrary" and "monstrous" breakup of a unified collective, nevertheless clearly reflected the emergence of new forms of self-identification that supplemented older ones.[75]

These developing political allegiances were legitimized as well as challenged in the name of national loyalty. The "Gounarist Jews" systematically attacked *L'Indépendant* as traitorous for opening its columns to pro-French articles penned by French, not Greek (Jewish) journalists.[76] In turn, the "Venizelist Jews" retaliated by vehemently labeling the Zionists as anti-patriots—an accusation no other anti-Zionist Jew dared use anywhere else in wartime Europe.[77] Pro-Venizelist Jewish publications mockingly called the Zionist newspaper *Courrier de Salonique* "Kourrier von Salonik" and chastised it for abandoning the defense of Greek and Jewish interests in favor of foreign ones.[78] Similarly, they comprehensively denounced the Zionists as "tepid Greeks," people who treated "Fatherland" as a "dead letter," sided with the Ottoman Turks (Germany's allies and Greece's historic enemy), compromised the dignity and honor of the Jewish community, and created an abyss between Greeks and Jews.[79]

Conversely, the Alliancists fashioned themselves as ardent Greek Jewish patriots.[80] Venizelist Jewish candidates argued that being an anti-Venizelist and a Jew was a contradiction in terms, since only Venizelism was fully compatible with Jewishness.[81] The Alliancist press equally pointed out that support for Venizelos certified particular Jewish qualities: the Jews' love for liberty, progress, and civilization, and no less their devotion to "Hellenism," that particular Western marker of cultural nobility and intellectual supremacy.[82] Even Greek irredentism, the "Great Idea" of integrating all "Greek" populations under a national state by expanding the Greek homeland across the Aegean to Ottoman Asia Minor and northward up to the Black Sea, a dream whose most ardent supporter was the Liberal Venizelos, was domesticated and "Judaicized" by being rebranded a "union of races," a revival of the Alexandrine period of Hellenism.[83]

True Jewishness was therefore associated not only with reverence for France and Salonica but also with support for the Greek Liberal prime minister Venizelos. In the fluid post-Ottoman period of war and transition from empire to nation-state, Jewish allegiance became an increasingly complex issue, with love for Greece and brotherhood with France seen as fully harmonious commitments. The local supporters of an international organization, the Alliance Israélite Universelle, sought to reinvent themselves as both transnational *and* national subjects, demonstrating just how politicized the production of Jewish identities had become and how muddled a process the acquisition of a Greek national identity was. Importantly, though, the sharp allegations of the Alliancists against their Zionist opponents consciously replicated the anti-Zionist rhetoric of the Greek Christian Venizelist press, which termed Zionists and by extension all Jews as inimical, indeed hostile, to Greece.[84] Ironically, by demonstrating their Greekness, the Alliancists ended up legitimizing a negative perception of the Jews as an alien element in the Greek body politic that the Venizelist press had advocated. Pushing for inclusion, they unconsciously promoted exclusion.

The alignment of existing Jewish communal cleavages with broader Greek national divides intensified the intra-Jewish conflicts and made the impact of the war more visceral. Breaking the barriers between communal and national politics, this alignment heightened tensions, transforming the struggle over communal hegemony into a question of national loyalty pitting Jewish "patriots" and "non-patriots" against one another. The case of Salonica Jewry thus adds another dimension to the complex interplay between nationalism and Jewish politics in wartime Europe. Whereas in Britain the anti-Zionists refrained from attacking their opponents as anti-British, and in Germany intra-communal rivalry between Liberals and Zionists blunted a sharper response by the Liberal Jewish establishment to gentile antisemitism, in Greece Salonican Alliancist Jews did not hesitate to instrumentally employ the language of Greek patriotism to shore up support for their own particularistic ends.[85]

Making Jews "French" and "German": Global Readings of Local Allegiances

Turning from the local and national frameworks to the transnational, we see that global influences complemented national and communal politics. Greece's ambivalent neutrality, its precarious gravitation between the Entente and the Central Powers, together with the geostrategic importance of Salonica, its uncertain future, and the still fragile Greek authority over this very recently annexed territory, compelled the Entente and the Central Powers to win over the public opinion of the city's most important group, the local Jewish population. Spies operated and foreign secret services recruited locals Jews.[86] The British, French, Italian, and particularly the German propaganda offices collaborated with local Jewish clubs and employed mass publicity techniques, distributing brochures, bribing journalists, supporting associations, financing existing newspapers, and founding new ones.[87] Great Power war aims and imperialist interests were brought to bear on local strife to such an extent that outsiders came to view Jewish political groups as spokespersons of foreign interests.[88] The French treated local Zionist clubs as branches of Berlin-based societies, whereas Greek officials in the city, worried about where Jewish loyalties lay, warned that the Alliancist Jewish press "had turned into the mouthpiece of French headquarters."[89] If Salonican Jews saw a global war through a local lens, the concerned European nation-states in turn read local clashes as reflections of their global struggle.

Consequently, not only were the stakes of the local debate raised, but Jewish communal politics and local decision-making assumed a global outlook reverberating in Berlin, Paris, and London. Notably, civil society actors, and not just state agencies, proved instrumental in this global turn. In the race to win the hearts and minds of Salonican Jewry, national and international Jewish organizations and prominent personalities collaborated with their respective state authorities. Close collaboration between the German-Israelite Communal Federation and the German foreign ministry probably facilitated German propaganda among Salonican Jews.[90] Similarly, the Franco-Jewish Alliance Israélite Universelle coordinated action with the local branch of the Mission Laïque Française and instructed its local personnel to serve French war interests.[91] It also advised Salonican voters seeking guidance from Paris to vote for Venizelos, the darling of Franco-British liberal circles and a staunch advocate of Greece's entry into the war on the side of the Entente.[92] Salonican pro-Alliance Jews abroad also acted as spokesmen of French interests. In Switzerland, they defended the Francophile Salonican Jewish press against accusations by Swiss scholars and debunked the *Tribune de Lausanne* for attributing to the Jews the electoral defeat of Venizelos in the June 1915 elections.[93]

Finally, in March 1916, Salonican Jews in Paris publicly addressed their fellow brethren back home, refuting German accusations of French mistreatment of them, affirming French hospitality, and asserting their own loyalty to their adopted motherland.[94]

All these debates and appeals, and many more, were reported back to Salonica itself and taken over by the pro- and anti-Ententist press.[95] At a time of border closure and state expansion, such forms of diasporic politics as the pan-European circulation of news and opinions between newspapers in Salonica and elsewhere testify to the durability and malleability of Jewish transnational bonds. What emerged was a fragmentary yet tangible transnational public sphere with a direct impact on local developments. The intervention of international Jewish organizations and émigré communities connected local politics to war propagandas. In doing so, it turned global events into generators of local identities, producing a normative sense of locality, of being a Salonican Jew, linked to Frenchness and, paradoxically, Greekness.

Conclusions: Rethinking Jewish Identities in Times of War

Beginning in the fall of 1915 Salonica and Greece were gradually drawn into the Great War. From October to December 1915 several hundred thousand Entente troops, most of them evacuated from the Dardanelles following the failure of the Gallipoli Campaign, began their disembarkation to push for Greece's entry into the war, support the fledgling Serbian Army, and counter rapid German-Bulgarian advances in Greek Eastern Macedonia. Salonica was now informally administered by the Allied command, and by 3 June 1916 it was formally put under martial law. Three months later, on 30 August 1916, an Allied-backed military coup of pro-Venizelist officers led to the establishment of the Provisional Government of National Defense in the city under the presidency of Venizelos himself. Greece was now territorially torn between a Royalist "Greece of Athens" and a Venizelist "Greece of Salonica." Venizelos fully committed the latter to the Ententist cause, and once he returned to the premiership of a reunited Greece in mid-June 1917, he formally declared war against the Central Powers and their allies.[96]

The Ententist presence, Venizelist rule, and Greece's entry into the war changed the rules of the game between the Alliancists and the Zionists, albeit in unexpected ways. Allied censorship curtailed pro-German views in Zionist publications, while the presence of an ever-increasing army offered unprecedented opportunities for legal business as well as illegal profiteering. The Ententist feelings of Salonica's Jews were consequently strengthened, and by mid-1916 even the Zionists were won over, their publications now castigating German antisemitism and tying the establishment of a Jewish nation-state to Allied victory.[97] On the surface, these developments appeared to vindicate the pro-Entente and pro-Venizelist camp, but in fact they did little to strengthen its grip over the community. In 1917, Wilson's Fourteen Points and eventually the Balfour Declaration made possible the rapprochement of Zionism with the Entente cause as well as Venizelism and increased the Zionists' local acceptance and international status. Even its opponents now took part in the various Zionist celebrations, demonstrations, and congresses to demonstrate Jewish gratitude to the Entente and Jewish prominence in Salonica itself.[98]

By easing tensions, these developments calmed a torn community. With Greece at war, the community finally achieved (a fragile) peace. For if neutrality proved so explosive, it was precisely because it allowed for contrasting readings of the World War in accordance with local cultural codes. A global conflict proved such a divisive local issue precisely because it echoed an entire set of ideological, class, and national cleavages pitting the Francophile and Germanophile Jews against each other as at once "Alliancists" and "Zionists," "upper" and "lower" classes, "Venizelists" and "Royalists," "Greek patriots" and "anti-Greek traitors." The war functioned as a central metaphor conveying a multiplicity of contrasting meanings and constructing bipolar oppositions. To be pro-French or pro-German was much more than an individual's opinion; it was a politicized global identity that was appropriated locally. The war thus solidified a lasting "Jewish Schism," one that intersected with but was not identical to either Greece's "National Schism" or Europe's division in two rival camps, a schism that would largely determine Greek-Jewish politics throughout the postwar period.[99]

These local politics were produced transnationally. Foreign diplomats, the European Jewish press, migrant communities, and international Jewish organizations strove to win over the Jews of Salonica by actively intervening in the local public sphere. It was their presumed "Frenchness" or their ties with Germany that informed Great Power perceptions, attitudes, and actions and eventually deepened communal divides. Paradoxically, the multiple cultural affinities, business networks, and strong diasporic links of Salonican Jewry actually made this fixing of identities possible in the first place. This was a notable development. For elsewhere in Europe, once the patriotic enthusiasm of the first months receded, the war fed an exclusionary nationalism that questioned Jewish loyalty to the gentile nation-in-arms and undermined multipartite imperial identities.[100] But in the fluid, post-Ottoman environment of Jewish Salonica, at the aftermath of the Balkan Wars and with the city's future still undetermined, in a period of transition from empire to nation-state, plural identities proved to be a catalyst for the forging of multiple allegiances as much as the formation of increasingly hardened political stances.

Analyzed from this double, local/transnational perspective, Jewish Salonica adds another dimension to the study of Jewish political (and politicized) identities in wartime Europe. Many historians have approached the question of citizenship, nationality, and the Jews in times of war as a question of inclusion and exclusion. A Jew either was (or aspired to be) part of a national or imperial polity in arms or was denied membership in it as more singular imaginings of the fighting nation gradually predominated in the later years of the war. Moreover, scholars have by and large explored these questions by confining themselves to the national or imperial framework. Attention to transnational processes is rarer and mostly limited to studies of refugee relief, international humanitarian aid, and their social and political implications for givers and receivers. A global conflict is still very much seen through national lenses.[101]

Opening up the field of inquiry, a thick description of the Salonican Jewish community's wartime politics shows that local repercussions of national and global politics were not unidirectional as in many other European countries. These repercussions cannot be adequately analyzed by employing a framework of (global) power and (local) resistance, nor through the selective use of nationalism and patriotism. In Salonica, political identification was a much more complex process since in 1914 the Jews were still trying to navigate a difficult transition from empire to nation-state. In the course of this transition, the eruption of a global conflict acquired uniquely local meanings. Paradoxically, the involvement of rival Great Powers and international Jewry made the war instrumental in producing the local Jewish identity itself, an identity redefined by its relation to Greek, French, German, and Jewish nationalism. The case of Jewish Salonica thus demonstrates how simultaneously global and local (that is, "glocal") the making of post-imperial war subjectivities was, extending beyond the spatial and conceptual framework of the nation.[102]

The story of Salonica's Jewry is nevertheless not just a history of a local exception to a pan-European rule. Quite the contrary: the Great War was a global battle in which numerous Jewish communities struggled with their own identities by appropriating national and global front lines to fight in a very local minefield. The war as a "Jewish war" has therefore to be read from such a double perspective as we begin to acknowledge the importance of transnational movements of peoples and ideas and move beyond the framework of patriotism. And it has to consider not only the Jews of the belligerent nations, but also those residing in the neutral countries. Salonica's neutrality was everything but neutral. Rather, for its Jews, there was a war to fight. And they did fight it with a determination, persuasion, and intensity echoing that of their brethren elsewhere in war-torn Europe.

Paris Papamichos Chronakis is Lecturer in Modern Greek History at the University of Illinois at Chicago. His research explores the transition of the Eastern Mediterranean port-cities from empire to nation-state bringing together the interrelated histories of Sephardi Jewish, Greek Orthodox, and Muslim entrepreneurial elites. With Giorgos Antoniou, he has also been developing digital tools to map social networks during the Holocaust. He was a member of the scientific committee creating the "Database of Greek Jewish Holocaust Survivors' Testimonies" and has published on Greek antisemitism, Greco-Jewish relations, Zionism in Greece, Digital Holocaust Studies, and the Holocaust of Greek Jewry.

Notes

1. "Ces petits messieurs en mal de célébrité," *L'Indépendant*, 16 June 1915, p. 1.
2. "Un peu de pudeur!," *L'Indépendant*, 11 June 1915, p. 1.
3. Joseph Nehama (Salonica) to Jacques Bigart (Paris) (18 June 1915), Archives of the Alliance Israélite Universelle (hereafter Archives AIU), Grèce II C 53.
4. "Communique de la police," *L'Indépendant*, 16 June 1915, p. 3.
5. French Consul (Salonica) to French Ambassador (Athens) (23 July 1915), Ministère des Affaires Etrangères, Centre des Archives Diplomatiques de Nantes (hereafter MAE CADN), Consulat général de France à Salonique, Salonique, Série B, Carton 22.
6. "Comment M. Goudas a organisé les élections en Macédoine," *L'Indépendant*, 17 June 1915, p. 1.
7. Participation in the war deeply divided the Greek political scene, pitting the neutralist and Germanophile King Constantine against the interventionist and Ententophile Liberal prime minister Eleftherios Venizelos. In November 1916 Venizelos, prompted by a group of loyal army officers, established a provisional government of "National Defense" in Salonica and declared the lands of northern Greece and the Aegean archipelago the provisional government controlled at war with the Central Powers. See George Th. Mavrogordatos, *O Ethnikos Dichasmos* [The National Schism] (Athens: Patakis, 2015).
8. "Ēho tēs poleōs" [City Echo], *To Fōs*, 18 October 1915, p. 3.
9. "À propos de l'incident de l'Alhambra," *L'Echo de Salonique*, 12 September 1915, p. 1; "À propos de l'incident de l'Alhambra," *L'Echo de Salonique*, 14 September 1915, p. 2; "Pour les victimes belges," *L'Indépendant*, 12 September 1915, p. 2.
10. "To prochthesinon syllalētērion" [The day before yesterday rally], *To Fōs*, 12 August 1916, p. 1.
11. "Le champion de l'Allemagne," *L'Opinion*, 7 February 1915, p. 2; "Monomachia dēmosiografōn" [Duel between journalists], *To Fōs*, 24 January 1915, p. 3.
12. On the anthropological concept of "key symbol," see the seminal work of Victor Turner, *From Ritual to Theatre: The Human Seriousness of Play* (New York: Performing Arts Journal Publications, 1982).
13. Derek Penslar, *Jews and the Military* (Princeton, NJ: Princeton University Press, 2013), p. 134.
14. Belinda Davis, "Experience, Identity, and Memory: The Legacy of World War I," *Journal of Modern History* 75 (2003): 119–20.
15. Anthony Molho, "The Jewish Community of Salonika: The End of a Long History," *Diaspora* 1 (1991): 100–22; Mark Mazower, *Salonica, City of Ghosts* (New York: Al-

fred A. Knopf, 2005). Population statistics from the Ottoman period are notoriously inaccurate, but all censuses certify to the demographic superiority of the Jews. Rena Molho, *Oi Evraioi tēs Thessalonikēs, 1856–1919: Mia idiaiterē koinotēta* [The Jews of Thessaloniki, 1856-1919: An Exceptional Community] (Athens: Themelio, 2001).
16. Aron Rodrigue, *French Jews, Turkish Jews: The Alliance Israélite Universelle and the Politics of Jewish Schooling in Turkey, 1860–1925* (Bloomington: Indiana University Press, 1990).
17. Ibid., pp. 168, 178; Rodrigue, "From Millet to Minority: Turkish Jewry," in *Paths of Emancipation: Jews, States, and Citizenship*, ed. Pierre Birnbaum and Ira Katznelson (Princeton, NJ: Princeton University Press, 1995), pp. 238–61; Sarah Abrevaya Stein, "The Permeable Boundaries of Ottoman Jewry," in *Boundaries and Belonging: States and Societies in the Struggle to Shape Identities and Local Practices*, ed. Joel S. Migdal (Cambridge: Cambridge University Press, 2004), pp. 49–70.
18. Leon Sciaky, *Farewell to Salonica: City at the Crossroads* (Philadelphia: Paul Dry Books, 2003), pp. 19, 157–59; Association des Anciens élèves de l'Alliance Israélite Universelle, Salonique, *Bulletin Annuel, 1908* (12ème année), pp. 18–21. On the development of an Ottomanist Sephardic sensibility, see Julia Phillips Cohen, *Becoming Ottomans: Sephardi Jews and Imperial Citizenship in the Modern Era* (Oxford: Oxford University Press, 2014).
19. Molho, *Oi Evraioi tēs Thessalonikēs*. On Salonican Jewry during the Balkan Wars, see Mark Levene, "'Ni grec, ni bulgare, ni turk': Salonika Jewry and the Balkan Wars, 1912–1913," *Jahrbuch des Simon-Dubnow-Instituts* 2 (2003): 65–97.
20. "La guerre et les Juifs: Vers l'amélioration de leur sort," *L'Indépendant*, 22 January 1915, p. 5.
21. See the blacklists of merchants trading with the enemy compiled by British and French authorities, including *Trading with the Enemy: Consolidating Statutory List of Persons and Firms in Countries, Other than Enemy Countries, with Whom Persons and Firms in the United Kingdom Are Prohibited from Trading. Complete to 27.04.1917* (London, 1917).
22. "Questions économiques. La cherté de la vie," *L'Indépendant*, 18 July 1915, p. 4. On the importance of consumer politics during World War I, see Maureen Healy, *Vienna and the Fall of the Habsburg Empire: Total War and Everyday Life in World War I* (Cambridge: Cambridge University Press, 2004), chapter 1. On food provisioning and the cultural representations of the "profiteer" in wartime Europe, see Jean-Louis Robert, "The Image of the Profiteer," in *Capital Cities at War: Paris, London, Berlin 1914–1919*, ed. Jay Winter and Jean-Louis Robert, vol. 1 (Cambridge: Cambridge University Press, 1997), pp. 104–131; and Thierry Bonzon and Belinda Davis, "Feeding the Cities," in ibid., pp. 305–41.
23. "Causerie," *Courrier de Salonique*, 22 October 1915, p. 4; "Jewish National Movement: Relief from Salonika for Palestine Jews," *Jewish Chronicle*, 10 September 1915, p. 20; "La cérémonie d' hier," *L'Écho de Salonique*, 4 July 1915, p. 2.
24. "Jewish National Movement: Relief from Salonika for Palestine Jews," *Jewish Chronicle*, 10 September 1915, p. 20.
25. Penslar, *Jews and the Military*, p. 156; "Un Bazar de Charité," *L'Indépendant*, 5 August 1917, p. 2.
26. "La mort d'un héros," *L'Indépendant*, 5 August 1917, p. 1. Later, some would volunteer to fight in Palestine for a country to be. Surprisingly, they would be identified by the British authorities as Jews coming not from a sovereign state or historical region (such as "Poland," "Russia," "America," "England," or "Yemen"), but from a city, "Salonika"—a testimony to the resilience of locality in the configuration of a certain version of

Jewishness. "Jewish National Movement: Conference of Jews in Palestine; Important Address by Major Ormsby-Gore, MP," *Jewish Chronicle*, 16 August 1918, p. 12.

27. See the death certificates of Vitalis Cohen and Leon Allalouf: http://www.memoiredeshommes.sga.defense.gouv.fr/fr/arkotheque/client/mdh/base_morts_pour_la_france_premiere_guerre/detail_fiche.php?ref=11170&debut=0 (accessed 1 November 2015).
28. "Nos concitoyens à l'étranger," *L'Indépendant*, 28 January 1915, p. 1.
29. "Jacques Yahiel," *L'Indépendant*, 5 November 1916, p. 1; "La mort d'un héros," *L'Indépendant*, 5 August 1917, p. 1.
30. Todd Samuel Presner, "Muscle Jews and Airplanes: Modernist Mythologies, the Great War, and the Politics of Regeneration," *Modernism/Modernity* 13, no. 4 (2006): 701–28; Anne Patricia Lloyd, "Jews under Fire: the Jewish Community and Military Service in World War I Britain" (unpublished PhD dissertation, University of Southampton, 2009).
31. On "lived experience" as a discursive construct, see the incisive thoughts of Joan Scott, "The Evidence of Experience," *Critical Inquiry* 17, no. 4 (1991): 773–97.
32. Minna Rozen, *The Last Ottoman Century and Beyond: The Jews in Turkey and the Balkans, 1808–1945* (Ramat-Aviv: Tel Aviv University, Goldstein-Goren Diaspora Research Center, Chair for the History and Culture of the Jews of Salonika and Greece, 2005); Esther Benbassa, *Un grand rabbin sépharade en politique, 1892–1923* (Paris: Presses du CNRS, 1990).
33. On the rise of Zionism in Salonica, see "Nuestra manseves. Dyez anyos antes e agora. Kontribusyones ala istorya del dispertamyento nasyonal en Saloniko," *El Makabeo* 5677 (1916): 13–23; Nehama (Salonica) to AIU (Paris) (19 May 1916), Archives of the AIU, Grèce I G 3. On Zionism in the Ottoman Empire, see Esther Benbassa, "Le Sionisme dans l'Empire Ottoman à l'aube du 20e siècle," *Vingtième Siècle* 24 (1989): 69–80.
34. On previous clashes, see Cohen, *Becoming Ottomans*, chapter 4; Paris Papamichos Chronakis, "The Jewish, Greek, Muslim and Dönme Merchants of Salonica, 1882–1919: Ethnic and Class Transformations in the Course of Hellenization" (unpublished PhD dissertation, University of Crete, 2011); Rena Molho, "The Zionist Movement in Thessaloniki, 1899–1919," in *The Jewish Communities of Southeastern Europe*, ed. I. K. Hassiotis (Thessaloniki: Institute for Balkan Studies, 1997), pp. 327–50; Benbassa, *Un grand rabbin sépharade en politique*.
35. Nehama (Salonica) to AIU (Paris) (11 September 1914), Archives of the AIU, Grèce XVII E 202b; "L'A.I.U. chez le général Franchet d'Espèrey," *L'Indépendant*, 17 July 1918, p. 1; "À la A.A.E. de la M.L.F.," *L'Opinion*, 28 January 1915, p. 3.
36. On Francophile discourses elsewhere in wartime Europe, see Penslar, *Jews and the Military*, pp. 170, 178.
37. "Nos concitoyens à l'étranger," *L'Indépendant*, 28 January 1915, p.1; "À la A.A.E. de la M.L.F.," *L'Indépendant*, 27 January 1915, p. 3; "Le 56ème anniversaire de l'AIU. L'imposante cérémonie d'hier matin," *L'Opinion*, 28 May 1916, p. 3; "Un centre de propagande française," *L'Indépendant*, 7 January 1916, p. 3; "L'A.I.U. chez le général Franchet d'Espèrey," *L'Indépendant*, 7 July 1918, p. 1.
38. "Le boycottage de l'Indépendant," *L'Indépendant*, 18 June 1915, p. 2.
39. "Un centre de propagande française," *L'Indépendant*, 7 January 1916, p. 3.
40. "Une belle manifestation française à l'AAE de la MLF," *L'Indépendant*, 27 January 1915, p. 3; "À la A.A.E. de la M.L.F.," *L'Opinion*, 28 January 1915, p. 3; "Les étrennes des blessés français," *L'Indépendant*, 2 January 1916, p. 2.
41. Ibid.

42. Union des Femmes de France. Procès-verbaux des séances, MAE CADN, Consulat général de France à Salonique, Salonique, Série B, Carton 95. Operating under the auspices of the French Ministry of War, the Union des Femmes de France was a highly prestigious institution offering its services to the war wounded.
43. "Nos concitoyens à l'étranger," *L'Indépendant,* 28 January 1915, p. 1.
44. Penslar, *Jews and the Military*; Margaret H. Darrow, "French Volunteer Nursing and the Myth of War Experience in World War I," *American Historical Review* 101, no. 1 (1996): 80–106.
45. Derek Penslar has noted that such reports functioned as declarations of social acceptance and active citizenship. Penslar, *Jews and the Military,* p. 178.
46. General Maurice Sarrail (Salonica) to C.A.A. (2e Bureau) (Paris) (8 February 1917), Archives de la Défense, 20 N 153; "Communiqué," *L'Indépendant,* 17 February 1915, p. 3.
47. Nehama (Salonica) to AIU (Paris) (19 May 1916), Archives AIU Grèce, I G 3.
48. Lieutenant La Mache (Salonica) to Capitaine Picard (Paris) (16 November 1918), MAE CADN, Consulat général de France à Salonique, Salonique, Série B, Carton 23.
49. Nehama (Salonica) to AIU (Paris) (11 September 1914), Archives AIU Grèce, XVII E 202b.
50. Rena Molho, "Jewish Working Class Neighborhoods Established in Salonica following the 1890 and 1917 Fires," in *Salonica and Istanbul: Social, Political and Cultural Aspects of Jewish Life* (Istanbul: Isis Press, 2002), pp. 173–94; Josephe Saias, *La Grèce et les Israélites de Salonique* (Paris: Imprimerie de la Conférence de la paix, 1919), pp. 38–40.
51. "Salonika Jews Alleged to Be Pro-German," *Jewish Chronicle,* 31 March 1916, p. 10 (quoting Berlin's *Jüdische Presse*); Saias, *La Grèce et les Israélites de Salonique,* p. 40.
52. "À propos de l'incident de l'Alhambra," *L'Echo de Salonique,* 12 September 1915, p. 1; "A German Lie Refuted," *Jewish Chronicle,* 9 April 1915, p. 8.
53. Nehama (Salonica) to AIU (Paris) (11 September 1914), Archives AIU Grèce, XVII E 202b.
54. "À propos de l'incident de l'Alhambra," *L'Echo de Salonique,* 12 September 1915, p. 1.
55. Commandement en chef des Armées Alliées. Etat-Major de l'Armée, 2e bureau (Paris) to (unknown) (14 February 1917), Archives de la Défense, 7 N 723.
56. Sam Yoel (Salonica) to AIU (Paris) (19 August 1919), Archives AIU Grèce, I G 3; Nehama (Salonica) to AIU (Paris) (17 April 1917), Archives AIU Grèce, I G 3; Nehama (Salonica) to AIU (Paris) (8 August 1916), Archives AIU Grèce, II C 53; Nehama (Salonica) to AIU (Paris) (19 May 1916), Archives AIU Grèce, I G 3; Albert Charles Wratislaw, *A Consul in the East* (Edinburgh: W. Blackwood and Sons, 1924).
57. Saias, *La Grèce et les Israélites de Salonique,* p. 40.
58. Nehama (Salonica) to AIU (Paris) (8 August 1916), Archives AIU Grèce, II C 53.
59. Once their earlier plans to internationalize Salonica or turn it into a free city had failed. See N. M. Gelber, "An Attempt to Internationalize Salonica," *Jewish Social Studies* 17, no. 2 (1955): 105–20; Katherine E. Fleming, *Greece, A Jewish History* (Princeton, NJ: Princeton University Press, 2007). The term "little Jewish republic" was used by the French ambassador (London) to Foreign Ministry (Paris) (4 March 1913), MAE CADN, Ambassade de France à Athènes, Fonds A, Carton 288.
60. French Consul (Salonica) to Foreign Minister (Paris) (7 December 1915), MAE CADN Ambassade de France à Athènes, Fonds A, Carton 357.
61. Paul Dumont, "The Social Structure of the Jewish Community of Salonica at the End of the Nineteenth Century," *Southeastern Europe* 5, no. 2 (1979): 33–72.

62. Nehama (Salonica) to Bigart (Paris) (18 June 1915), Archives AIU Grèce II C 53; "Ai eklogai kai oi Evraioi" [The Elections and the Jews], *Israēlitikē Epitheōrēsis*, Year 4, nr. 2, 3, 4, April–June 1915, p. 17.
63. *L'Indépendant* quoted in "Oi Israēlitai kai ai eklogai" [The Israelites and the Elections], *Nea Alētheia*, 3 June 1915, p. 1; Nehama (Salonica) to AIU (Paris) (7 June 1915 and 18 June 1915), Archives AIU Grèce, II C 53; "Le boycottage de l'Indépendant," *L'Opinion*, 18 June 1915, p. 1; "Le crime d'hier," *L'Indépendant*, 14 June 1915, p. 1.
64. "Le bon combat," *L'Opinion*, 19 June 1915, p. 1; Nehama (Salonica) to Bigart (Paris) (18 June 1915), Archives AIU Grèce II C 53; *L'Indépendant* quoted in "Oi Israēlitai kai ai eklogai" [The Israelites and the Elections], *Nea Alētheia*, 3 June 1915, p. 1.
65. "Le crime d'hier," *L'Indépendant*, 14 June 1915, p. 1.
66. "Gallia kai panta Gallia" [France for Ever], *To Fōs*, 19 January 1915, p. 2; "Idrysis ellēnogallikou syndesmou" [Establishment of a Greco-French Association], *To Fōs*, 6 April 1915, p. 3.
67. *El Avenir*, quoted in "Tribune libre. Leur patriotisme," *L'Opinion*, 27 June 1915, p. 1.
68. Theodor Herzl, "Mauschel," *Die Welt* 1, no. 20, 15 October 1897, pp. 1–2.
69. Papamichos Chronakis, "The Jewish, Greek, Muslim and Dönme Merchants of Salonica," chapter 9.
70. On Greece and World War I, see George B. Leontaritis, *Greece and the First World War* (Boulder, CO: East European Monographs, 1990).
71. Michael Llewellyn Smith, *Ionian Vision: Greece in Asia Minor 1919–1922* (Ann Arbor: University of Michigan Press, 1999), chapter 1.
72. The results were devastating for the Alliancists: five out of six Jewish MPs for Salonica were pro-Royalist Zionists. Dimosthenis Dodos, *Oi Evraioi tēs Thessalonikēs stis ekloges tou ellēnikou kratous, 1915–1936* [The Jews of Thessaloniki in the Elections of the Greek State, 1915–1936] (Athens: Savvalas, 2005).
73. "Tous aux urnes pour le triomphe de la politique du Roi et de la paix," *Le Courier de Salonique*, 19 December 1915, p. 1.
74. Nehama (Salonica) to AIU (Paris) (7 June 1915), Archive AIU Grèce II C 53.
75. "Une mise au point nécessaire," *Echo de Salonique*, 4 July 1915, p. 3.
76. "Un peu de pudeur!," *L'Indépendant*, 11 June 1915, p. 1.
77. "Tribune libre. Leur patriotisme," *L'Indépendant*, 27 June 1915. To my knowledge, nowhere in Europe were the Zionists associated with anti-patriotism, as had happened in Salonica. See Stuart A. Cohen, "Ideological Components in Anglo-Jewish Opposition to Zionism before and during the First World War: A Restatement," *Jewish Historical Studies* 30 (1987): 149–62; David Engel, "Patriotism as a Shield: The Liberal Jewish Defense against Antisemitism in Germany during the First World War," *Leo Baeck Institute Year Book* 31 (1986): 147–71; Stefan Vogt, "The First World War: German Nationalism, and the Transformation of German Zionism," *Leo Baeck Institute Year Book* 57 (2012): 267–91; Andrew Koss, "World War I and the Remaking of Jewish Vilna, 1914–1918" (unpublished PhD dissertation, Stanford University, 2010), chapter 1; Ilaria Pavan, "'The Lord of Hosts Is with Us': Italian Rabbis Respond to the Great War," *Jewish History* 29 (2015):137–62; Mario Toscano, "Gli ebrei italiani e la prima guerra mondiale (1915–1918), tra crisi religiosa e fremiti patriottici," in *Ebraismo e antisemitismo in Italia dal 1848 alla Guerra dei sei giorni* (Milan, 2003); Christopher M. Sterba, *Good Americans: Italian and Jewish Immigrants during the First World War* (New York: Oxford University Press, 2003), chapter 1; Steven J. Zipperstein, "The Politics of Relief: The Transformation of Russian Jewish Communal Life during the First World War," in *The Jews and the European Crisis, 1914–1921*, ed. Jonathan Frankel, *Stu-*

dies in Contemporary Jewry 4 (1988): 22–40; Philippe Landau, *Les Juifs de France et la Grande Guerre: Un patriotisme républicain, 1914–1921* (Paris: CNRS Editions, 1999).
78. "Les clients du Kourrier," *L'Indépendant,* 12 April 1916, p. 2; "Les écuries d'Augias. Une campagne se prépare," *L'Indépendant,* 8 February 1916, p. 2; "Le patriotisme scandaleux du Courier de Salonique," *L'Opinion,* 22 January 1916, p. 2.
79. "Tribune libre. À propos des élections," *L'Opinion,* 24 June 1915, p. 2; "Les élections de dimanche," *L'Opinion,* 15 June 1915, p. 1; "Le boycottage de l'Indépendant," *L'Opinion,* 16 June 1915, p. 1; Nehama (Salonica) to Bigart (Paris) (18 June 1915), Archives AIU Grèce, II C 53; "Le bon combat," *L'Opinion,* 19 June 1915, p. 1.
80. Ibid.; "Le boycottage de l'Indépendant," *L'Opinion,* 16 June 1915, p. 1.
81. "Être Israélite et anti-venizeliste sont deux qualités incompatibles," *L'Opinion,* 2 June 1915, p. 1.
82. Ibid.; "Le vrai patriotisme," *L'Opinion,* 10 July 1915; "Le triomphe du Libéralisme," *L'Indépendant,* 11 June 1915, p. 1. On Hellenism in European civilizational and nationalist discourses, see Richard Jenkyns, *The Victorians and Ancient Greece* (Cambridge, MA: Harvard University Press, 1980); Athena S. Leoussi, "Nationalism and Racial Hellenism in Nineteenth-Century England and France," *Ethnic and Racial Studies* 20, no. 1 (1997): 42–68.
83. "Le triomphe du Libéralisme," *L'Indépendant,* 11 June 1915, p. 1. On Venizelos's irredentist views and their popular appeal, see Mark Mazower, "The Messiah and the Bourgeoisie: Venizelos and Politics in Greece, 1909–1912," *The Historical Journal* 35, no. 4 (1992): 885–904.
84. As a moderate participant in the debate hastened to note. "Tribune libre," *L'Opinion,* 23 June 1915 and 26 June 1915, p. 2; *Écho de Salonique,* quoted in "À propos d'assimilation," *L'Opinion,* 27 June 1915, p. 2.
85. Cohen, "Ideological Components in Anglo-Jewish Opposition to Zionism"; Engel, "Patriotism as a Shield."
86. "Ē kataskopeia" [Espionage], *Makedonia,* 21 July 1915), p. 1; General Governor of Macedonia (Salonica) to Foreign Minister (Athens) (10 September 1918), Historical Archives of Macedonia, Archives of the General Government of Macedonia, File 103.
87. "Les israélites de Salonique et la France," *L'Opinion,* 1 February 1915; French Consul (Salonica) to French Ambassador (Athens) (16 June 1915 and 14 June 1915), MAE CADN, Ambassade de France à Athènes, Fonds A, Carton 277; French consul (Salonica) to Foreign Minister (Paris) (15 December 1914), MAE CADN, Consulat général de France à Salonique, Salonique, Série B, Carton 97; Wratislaw (Salonica) to Elliot (Athens) (14 April 1915), NA FO 371/2561; Commandement en chef des Armées Alliées. Etat-Major de l'Armée, 2e bureau (Paris) to (unknown) (14 February 1917), Archives de la Défense, 7 N 723. On the successes of German propaganda among English Jews of German origin, see C. C. Aronsfeld, "Jewish Enemy Aliens in England during the First World War, *Jewish Social Studies* 18, no. 4 (1956): 278. On the techniques the Germans applied, see M. L. Sanders, "Wellington House and British Propaganda during the First World War," *The Historical Journal* 18, no. 1 (1975): 119–46. On the collaboration between the German-Israelite Communal Federation and the German Central Office for Foreign Service, see Penslar, *Jews and the Military,* p. 177. Compared to studies of the home front, Entente and Central Powers propaganda in neutral countries has received much less scholarly attention than it deserves. In his comprehensive study, David Welch leaves out that crucial aspect of German propaganda; David Welch, *Germany, Propaganda and Total War, 1914–1918* (New Brunswick, NJ: Rutgers University Press, 2000).

88. "Na patachthoun" [They must be suppressed], *Makedonia,* 15 September 1915; "German or Jewish, it is the same thing," a young newspaper seller was shouting in the streets of Salonica in 1916. V. Lebedev, *Souvenirs d'un volontaire russe dans l'armée française, 1914–1918* (Paris: Perrin et Cie, 1917), p. 128.
89. French consul (Salonica) to French ambassador (Athens) (23 July 1915), MAE CADN Consulat général de France à Salonique, Salonique, Série B, Carton 22; Thessaloniki Press Bureau (Salonica) to Foreign Ministry (Athens) (11 May 1918), Historical Archive of the Greek Foreign Ministry, New Archive of the History of Jews in Greece.
90. Penslar, *Jews and the Military,* p. 177.
91. AIU (Paris) to Nehama (Salonica) (15 November 1915), Archives AIU Grèce, II C 53; Nehama (Salonica) to AIU (Paris) (7 June 1915), Archives AIU Grèce, II C 53.
92. Alliance (Paris) to Nehama (Salonica) (28 May 1915 and 15 November 1915), Archives AIU Grèce, II C 53.
93. "Le sphinx de Stockholm," *La Tribune de Lausanne,* 24 July 1915, p. 3; "Les Juifs," *L'Indépendant,* 26 July 1915, p. 4.
94. "Une belle lettre. Les Israélites Saloniciens établis en France, à leurs coreligionnaires de Salonique," *L'Opinion,* 11 March 1916, p. 3.
95. "Les Saloniciens se défendent et nous défendent," *Le Courrier de Salonique,* 18 November 1915, pp. 1–2; "Réponse à M. Reiss," *Le Courrier de Salonique,* 19 November 1915, p. 1.
96. Mazower, *Salonica, City of Ghosts,* pp. 286–97.
97. Nehama (Salonica) to AIU (Paris) (19 May 1916), Archives AIU Grèce, I G 3.
98. Yoel (Salonica) to AIU (Paris) (19 August 1919), Archives AIU Grèce, I G 3.
99. Maria Vassilikou, "Politics of the Jewish Community of Salonika in the Inter-war Years: Party Ideologies and Party Competition" (unpublished PhD dissertation, University College London, 1999).
100. Marsha L. Rozenblit, *Reconstructing a National Identity: The Jews of Habsburg Austria during World War I* (New York: Oxford University Press, 2001).
101. Ibid., introduction; David Cesarani, "An Embattled Minority: The Jews in Britain During the First World War," *Immigrants and Minorities* 8, nos. 1–2 (1989): 60–81; Robert Nemes, "Refugees and Antisemitism in Hungary during the First World War," in *Sites of European Antisemitism in the Age of Mass Politics 1880–1918,* ed. Robert Nemes and Daniel Unowsky (Hanover, NH: University Press of New England, 2014), pp. 236–54; David Rechter, *The Jews of Vienna and the First World War* (Oxford: Oxford University Press, 2000); Peter Gatrell, *A Whole Empire Walking: Refugees in Russia during World War I* (Bloomington: Indiana University Press, 1999), chapter 7. My own thinking on citizenship in times of war has been greatly influenced by Sarah Stein's incisive attempt to re-examine citizenship as a spectrum rather than a binary. See Sarah Abrevaya Stein, *Extraterritorial Dreams: European Citizenship, Sephardi Jews, and the Ottoman Twentieth Century* (Chicago: University of Chicago Press, 2016).
102. On the dynamic relationship between global processes and local appropriations, see George Ritzer, *The Globalization of Nothing 2* (Thousand Oaks: Pine Forge Press, 2007).

Selected Bibliography

Primary Sources

Archives of the Alliance Israélite Universelle, Grèce I G 3, II C 53, XVII E 202b
Ministère des Affaires Etrangères, Centre des Archives Diplomatiques de Nantes, Consulat général de France à Salonique, Salonique, Série B, Cartons 22, 23, 95, 97
Ministère des Affaires Etrangères, Centre des Archives Diplomatiques de Nantes, Ambassade de France à Athènes, Fonds A, Cartons 277, 288, 357
Courrier de Salonique (1915)
L'Echo de Salonique (1915–18)
L'Indépendant (1915)
L'Opinion (1915–16)
Le Courier de Salonique (1915)
Makedonia (1915)
Nea Alētheia (1915)
Tò Fōs (1915)

Secondary Sources

Benbassa, Esther. "Le Sionisme dans l'Empire Ottoman à l'aube du 20e siècle." *Vingtième Siècle* 24 (1989): 69–80.
Cesarani, David. "An Embattled Minority: The Jews in Britain during the First World War." *Immigrants and Minorities* 8, nos. 1–2 (1989): 60–81.
Cohen, Stuart A. "Ideological Components in Anglo-Jewish Opposition to Zionism before and during the First World War: A Restatement." *Jewish Historical Studies* 30 (1987): 149–62.
Dodos, Dimosthenis. *Oi Evraioi tēs Thessalonikēs stis ekloges tou ellēnikou kratous, 1915–1936* [The Jews of Thessaloniki in the Elections of the Greek State, 1915–1936]. Athens: Savvalas, 2005.
Dumont, Paul. "The Social Structure of the Jewish Community of Salonica at the End of the Nineteenth Century." *Southeastern Europe* 5, no. 2 (1979): 33–72.
Fleming, Katherine E. *Greece, A Jewish History*. Princeton, NJ: Princeton University Press, 2007.
Koss, Andrew. "World War I and the Remaking of Jewish Vilna, 1914–1918." Unpublished PhD dissertation, Stanford University, 2010.
Landau, Philippe. *Les Juifs de France et la Grande Guerre: Un patriotisme républicain, 1914–1921*. Paris: CNRS Editions, 1999.
Leontaritis, George B. *Greece and the First World War*. Boulder: East European Monographs, 1990.
Levene, Mark. "'Ni grec, ni bulgare, ni turk'—Salonika Jewry and the Balkan Wars, 1912–1913." *Jahrbuch des Simon-Dubnow-Instituts* 2 (2003): 65–97.
Mazower, Mark. *Salonica, City of Ghosts*. New York: Alfred A. Knopf, 2005.
Molho, Rena. *Salonica and Istanbul: Social, Political and Cultural Aspects of Jewish Life*. Istanbul: Isis Press, 2002.
Papamichos Chronakis, Paris. "The Jewish, Greek, Muslim and Dönme Merchants of Salonica, 1882–1919: Ethnic and Class Transformations in the Course of Hellenization." Unpublished PhD dissertation, University of Crete, 2011.

Penslar, Derek. *Jews and the Military.* Princeton, NJ: Princeton University Press, 2013.
Rechter, David. *The Jews of Vienna and the First World War.* Oxford: Oxford University Press, 2000.
Rodrigue, Aron. *French Jews, Turkish Jews: The Alliance Israélite Universelle and the Politics of Jewish Schooling in Turkey, 1860–1925.* Bloomington: Indiana University Press, 1990.
Rozen, Minna. *The Last Ottoman Century and Beyond: The Jews in Turkey and the Balkans, 1808–1945.* Ramat-Aviv: Tel Aviv University, Goldstein-Goren Diaspora Research Center, Chair for the History and Culture of the Jews of Salonika and Greece, 2005.
Rozenblit, Marsha. *Reconstructing a National Identity: The Jews of Habsburg Austria during World War I.* New York: Oxford University Press, 2001.
Sanders, M. L. "Wellington House and British Propaganda during the First World War." *The Historical Journal* 18, no. 1 (1975): 119–46.
Stein, Sarah Abrevaya. *Extraterritorial Dreams. European Citizenship, Sephardi Jews, and the Ottoman Twentieth Century.* Chicago: University of Chicago Press, 2016.
———. "The Permeable Boundaries of Ottoman Jewry." In *Boundaries and Belonging: States and Societies in the Struggle to Shape Identities and Local Practices,* edited by Joel S. Migdal, pp. 49–70. Cambridge: Cambridge University Press, 2004.
Sterba, Christopher M. *Good Americans: Italian and Jewish Immigrants during the First World War.* New York: Oxford University Press, 2003.
Vogt, Stefan. "The First World War: German Nationalism and the Transformation of German Zionism." *Leo Baeck Institute Year Book* 57 (2012): 267–91.
Welch, David. *Germany, Propaganda and Total War, 1914–1918.* New Brunswick, NJ: Rutgers University Press, 2000.
Winter, Jay, and Jean-Louis Robert, eds. *Capital Cities at War: Paris, London, Berlin 1914–1919.* Vol. 1. Cambridge: Cambridge University Press, 1997.

CHAPTER 9

Recounting the Past, Shaping the Future
Ladino Literary Representations of World War I

Devi Mays

The Armistice of Mudros, signed between representatives of the Allied forces and the Ottoman Empire on 30 October 1918, marked the end of Ottoman involvement in World War I. Two weeks later, Allied warships arrived in the Ottoman capital of Constantinople, heralding the beginning of the occupation of the city by British, French, and Italian forces, who would remain in some capacity until 23 September 1923. Constantinople's occupation threw the Ottoman capital into disarray. Greek Orthodox and Armenian residents of the city enthusiastically welcomed Allied forces, waving Greek flags from balconies that lined the Grand Rue de Pera leading from Taksim Square. A Muslim student at the prestigious state Galatasaray Lycée on the Grand Rue described with pain the British, French, Italian, and Greek flags that seemed to dangle from every window after the first day of armistice; a neighboring Greek Orthodox tailor even went so far as to hang a blue and white robe from his window to emulate Greek colors.[1] Thousands of Greek Orthodox Ottomans crowded along terraces, high walls, and the Galata Bridge to cheer the arrival of the Greek warship *Averof*, whose sailors called to those assembled on land, "Awaken, poor subject, awaken and see liberty."[2]

The upending of power dynamics between the city's Muslim and non-Muslim populations was further emphasized several months after the initial occupation, when French general Franchet d'Espèrey rode from the quay below Galata Bridge to the city's French embassy on a white horse given to him by a Greek Orthodox man.[3] The significance of this act was not lost on Constantinople's population, including the city's ninety thousand Jewish residents. All likely knew that Sultan Mehmet the Conqueror had ridden a white horse into Constantinople after capturing the city for the Ottomans from the Byzantines in 1453. The Allied forces saw themselves not only as victors but also as liberators of the city's Christian population, showing a marked preference for the latter when filling jobs ranging from typists to auxiliary police.[4] As French and English supplanted German on signs and in cafés throughout the city, as Interallied forces cobbled together new legal regimes to govern the city, and as international legislators and lobbyists debated the city's ultimate fate, the city's Greek Orthodox and Armenian residents viewed the Allied occupation as an opportunity to publicly express their aspirations for national self-determination.[5] Their public visibility during the occupation would stand in marked contrast to the later enforced silencing of minorities in the early years of the Turkish Republic.[6]

In contrast to the Greek Orthodox and Armenian examples, historians have often presumed the reactions of Constantinople's Jews to the occupying forces in Constantinople and to the surrender of the Ottoman Empire to have been negative or ambivalent, in large part because these historians buy into Ottoman Jewish leaders' successful attempts to mark Ottoman Jews as the faithful, loyal, and uncritical "model minority" of the Ottoman state.[7] The opposition of some Ottoman Jews to broader Ottoman projects and programs, including those of World War I and the military service and home front sacrifices it entailed, have been largely overlooked. Rather, the little work that has been done on Ottoman Jewry during World War I has by and large accepted and repeated tropes of Jewish loyalty, patriotism, and enthusiasm to serve in the army and support the Ottoman war effort—tropes that, while attested to in the (censored) Ladino press of the period and the utterances of communal elites, did not always match realities on the ground.[8] While recent studies have shown that Ottoman Jews in the Balkan Wars of 1912–13 often, but not consistently, publicly supported the Ottoman war effort, issued patriotic calls to arms, and endorsed the first mass mobilization of Ottoman non-Muslims, it should not automatically be assumed that these same attitudes extended to World War I.[9] Several factors were key to a shift in Ottoman Jewish stances on the two conflicts—the earlier Balkan Wars and World War I: in the former case Jews were encouraged to serve as active combatants, while in the latter, they were relegated for the most part to service in demeaning labor battalions; simultaneously, the severe privations of the Ottoman home front further discouraged support for the latter conflict.

Several Ladino novellas and haggadic parodies published in Constantinople in the years of Allied occupation shed light on Constantinopolitan Jews' discontent with World War I, whether experienced by those in the

Ottoman military or on the home front. These works highlight the difficulties that the war created for Constantinopolitan Jews as well as their diverse responses to a future made uncertain by the outcome of the Great War. These texts—reflecting the effects of the war on Ottoman Jewish women, children, and men alike—offer counter-narratives to the familiar characterizations of unquestioning Jewish loyalty to the Ottoman cause. Instead, they shed light on challenges that Ottoman Jewish soldiers faced on the battlefield, as in the Balkan Wars, or, more commonly, in the labor battalions into which Ottoman non-Muslims were conscripted en masse during the Great War. They also reveal strategies of resistance to military service and the hardships of life on the Constantinopolitan home front. As such, these texts add a crucial piece to an Ottoman historiography that has just begun to explore processes and experiences of mobilization, as well as life on the home front, albeit from perspectives that focus primarily on Ottoman Muslims.[10]

I argue that these texts, through the ways in which their respective authors sought to place themselves and the Jewish community, highlight the many possible paths forward that Ottoman Jews could envision as their city was under occupation. Thus, while the scholar of Ladino literature Eliezer Papo has understood Ladino satirical Haggadot as attempts to produce collective memories, shape collective identity, or address collective trauma, I posit that these texts should also be understood as attempts to proffer and shape different collective futures in a period characterized by uncertainty.[11] These texts thereby highlight what literary critic Gary Saul Morson has defined as "sideshadowing." They conjure the "ghostly presence" of the "hypothetical histories [that] shadow actual ones," reminding us as historians that "the temporal world consists not just of actualities and impossibilities but also of real though unactualized possibilities."[12] The period of occupation and uncertainty that immediately followed World War I provided ample fodder for the articulation in Ladino literature of unrealized possible futures for Constantinople's Jewish residents, and often in a manner that drew upon their experiences of World War I.

Four Ladino texts published in Constantinople during the period of occupation form the basis of the analysis that follows. Ladino belles lettres in general combine instruction and entertainment, with a moralizing undertone often buried within the narrative.[13] This instructional purpose is made explicit in the texts examined here, where the aim is to remind the reader of precisely why and how World War I should be remembered and how that relates to the trajectory of the future. Two of the texts—*Techiyat haMetim o El Ofisier Judio* (Resurrecting the Dead, or the Jewish Officer; 5681) and *Los Dos Ermanikos* (The Two Little Siblings; 5681) take the form of novellas—while the second two—*Haggadah dela Gerra por Dia de*

Pesach (Haggadah of the War for the Day of Passover; 1919) and *Haggadah dela Gerra General* (Haggadah of the General War; 1920)—take the form of haggadic parodies.

During World War I itself, the publishing of periodicals and belles lettres in the Ottoman Empire languished, due to both the strictures of wartime censorship and the prohibitive cost of paper.[14] The Allied occupation did not fully lift wartime censorship—Ladino newspapers regularly bore blank columns with a simple note that the censor had excised an article. Nonetheless, it put an end to the hiatus in publishing Ladino novels that spanned 1914 to 1920.[15] Further, the weakened grasp of the Ottoman state during the period of Interallied occupation facilitated open criticisms of Ottoman governmental leaders of a kind that had been censored (or self-censored) under Ottoman rule and criminalized later during the early years of the Turkish Republic.[16] At the same time, the specter of Interallied censorship may have encouraged expressions of approval for the Entente.

Three of the texts in question—the two novellas and the *Haggadah dela Gerra General*—were authored by Eliya Karmona (Constantinople, 1869–1931), the most prolific author of Ladino novellas and the editor of *El Jugeton*, a satirical and humoristic periodical published from the Young Turk Revolution of 1908/9 until Karmona's death in 1931. Most of the over fifty novels that Karmona wrote and published in his lifetime deal with popular themes like death, robbery, and romance in settings beyond Ottoman borders, which both passed Ottoman censorship and appealed to Karmona's audience.[17] As such, the three works examined here are exceptional in that they are all set in and shed light on the quotidian experience of Constantinopolitan Jews during World War I. The fourth work, *Haggadah de la Gerra por Dia de Pesach*, was composed by Nissim Shem-Tov 'Eli, an otherwise-unknown author. In what follows I will analyze these works, showing how they illuminate Ottoman Jewish attitudes toward World War I.

The mass mobilization of Ottoman men into military service—or, in the case of many Ottoman Christians and Jews during World War I, into labor battalions—has captured the interest of historians seeking to understand the effects of war on the Ottoman Empire, due in part to the discovery of a number of diaries of Ottoman soldiers in an empire marked by high rates of illiteracy.[18] Ottoman historian Yiğit Akın, meanwhile, has recently argued that Ottoman women bore most of the brunt of the war on the home front, as the Ottoman state extracted millions of men from society and the economy through mobilization while simultaneously increasingly intervening in the everyday lives of the Ottoman population.[19] Some of these imbricated effects of mobilization on both male soldiers

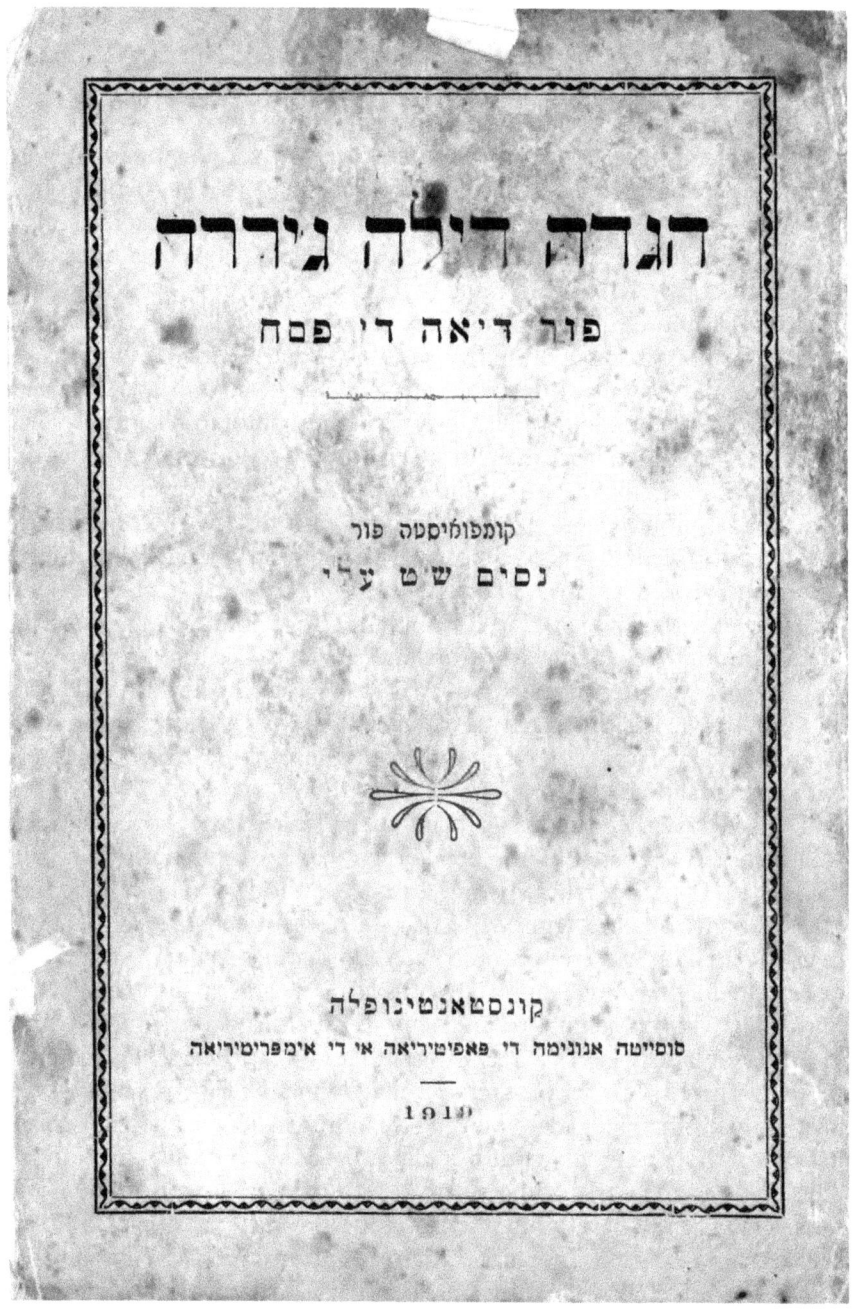

Figure 9.1. *Cover page of Nissim Shem-Tov 'Eli's* Haggadah dela Gerra por Dia de Pesach *(Constantinople: Sosieta Anonima de Papeteria i de Impremeria, 1919).*

and the women who remained behind are explored in Karmona's *Techiyat haMetim* (Resurrecting the Dead), published in 5681 (1920–21) under the subheading of "a true passage from the General War."[20]

As was the case for many of Karmona's stories actually set in Constantinople, Karmona opens *Techiyat haMetim* with an identifiably Jewish date and setting, the morning of 13 Tishrei 5650 (8 October 1889) at the Kahal Kadosh Ahrida in Balat. This was the imperial capital's most recognizably Jewish district and oldest synagogue, as well as the site of the funeral of Sr. Moshe B., a man who "although employed in a great commercial house, was very good and very pious."[21] In the story's nine pages, Karmona focuses on Sr. Moshe B.'s widow, Miriam, as she raises her only child, Abraham. He is a precocious child who matriculates first from the Balat school of the French-Jewish philanthropic Alliance Israélite Universelle and then from the Ottoman *Idadiye* (secondary) school, where he conducts his studies in the Turkish language.[22] However, war is declared three months before Abraham is to earn his law diploma, which would have "secured the livelihood of the mother and son."[23] Instead, Abraham is called up as an *ihtiyat zabıtı* (in Turkish: a "reserve officer") and sent to the Ottoman Harbiye military school in the Pangaltı district of Constantinople. As always, Abraham proves successful, is promoted to the rank of lieutenant (Ladino: *melaazim*, from the Turkish *mülazım*) and is appointed as the instructor of *talum* (Turkish *talım*, "drills") at the barracks in Haydarpaşa on Constantinople's Asian shore before being sent with his battalion to Aleppo.

The narrative then switches to focus on Miriam's anxiety over her son's well-being, exacerbated by the breakdown in the weekly transmission of his letters. The story takes a (for Karmona) typically melodramatic turn once Miriam visits the Ministry of War for news of her son, only to learn that his battalion was entirely destroyed and that her son was either killed or captured by the English. For months she is unable to drink her morning coffee without spilling tears, her head perpetually downturned "in a sad and downcast state." It seems to Miriam a cruel joke when she finds herself gathered with her brother's family around the Passover table as her brother reads the Haggadah to his two children in *lashon* (short for *lashon kodesh*, or "holy tongue") and in Ladino "in order to create affection for religion." He then asks to her to read the passage "Joyous mother and sons, praise *HaShem*."[24] Only then does her brother reveal a card he received from Abraham, in which Abraham informs him that he is alive in Bombay, a British prisoner of war. Miriam waits impatiently for the armistice that will allow her son's return, and on the morning of 13 Adar 5680 (3 March 1920), coinciding with Purim, she greets Abraham on Constantinople's quay, exclaiming as she embraces her son, "Blessed are You, Holy God! In the most miserable and darkest hour, it is You who takes pity on us!"²⁵ As the story's title suggests, the Jewish officer has been resurrected from the death to which his mother was sure he had succumbed.

Within the Jewish time and space into which Karmona weaves World War I and disparate Ottoman military sites in Constantinople, *Techiyat haMetim* refrains from overt political, social, or economic commentary. Unlike the two haggadic parodies discussed below, *Techiyat haMetim* focuses on the rare Ottoman Jew serving in an armed military capacity during a point in Ottoman history in which, as mentioned above, non-Muslims, though draftable since 1909, were primarily mobilized into unarmed labor battalions. The character of Abraham, in contrast to those described as suffering in labor battalions or attempting to dodge the draft, seems to point to the success of Ottoman reforms (Tanzimat) in their efforts to integrate Jews into Ottoman society. Abraham attends not only the Alliance Israélite Universelle school system through which thousands of Ottoman Jewish children passed, but he graduates from a Turkish-language Ottoman secondary school before earning his position as an officer in the Ottoman army. In fact, at no point in the narrative does Abraham's Jewishness serve as a hindrance to his studies or to his military service.

It is Miriam's pain at the ostensible loss of her son that overwhelms the simple narrative of *Techiyat haMetim,* hearkening back to the hardships that Ottoman women faced on the home front. Karmona used the much longer and more complex *Los Dos Ermanikos* (discussed below) to delve into the social and economic effects of World War I on the Ottoman capital city. Here he simply hints at the layered anxieties that war provoked for women left behind as male relatives were mobilized, emigrated to avoid military service, or went into hiding. Abraham's mobilization into the Ottoman military and his eventual disappearance not only provoke the emotional collapse of a widow who finds herself losing her only child. They also produce a circumstance of material insecurity; Abraham was to be his widowed mother's main economic as well as emotional support, and with his assumed loss she risks losing the basis of her future security.

While the character of Abraham points to the potential of Ottoman Jews to integrate into the Ottoman military world as officers, Karmona also includes several details formulated perhaps to appease Allied censors or to reconcile his audience to the British presence in Constantinople. Not only did the armistice allow for Ottoman prisoners of war like Abraham to be returned to their anxious families, but the British also cared well for captured Ottoman troops. In the letter that Abraham sends to Miriam to inform her that he is alive, he makes sure to note that "los Inglizes" viewed him positively. As a British prisoner of war, he "ate extensively, lived like a gentleman [*sinyor*], and received a large monthly allowance for his other expenses."²⁶ This implicitly stood in contrast to the material privation that Ottoman soldiers and those on the home front faced during World War I;

soldiers frequently found their pay in arrears, and they lacked sufficient clothing and supplies, while those on the home front were subject to strict rationing amid a growing scarcity of food, gas, and clothing.[27] Though perhaps not explicitly so, Karmona implies that the British were a benevolent force, not one whose presence in the Ottoman capital should be opposed.

In the much longer *Los Dos Ermanikos,* likewise published in 1921, Karmona addresses the many ways in which the Jewish community of the Ottoman capital experienced the disease, rations, privation, and disruptions of communal beneficence networks that attended World War I. Comprising some sixty-seven pages and published in five volumes, *Los Dos Ermanikos* bears an endnote attesting that "this story is true."[28] Rather than focusing on a mother-son relationship, *Los Dos Ermanikos* tells the story of two young Jewish children, Estreyika and Moshoniko Behar. They live with their parents in Kasımpaşa, a lower-middle class neighborhood with a mixed ethnic and religious residential profile that lay to the north of the Golden Horn on Constantinople's European shore. When their drunkard father dies while wandering home one night, leaving behind their pregnant mother, the Benevolent Society of Women of the Jewish community of Galata-Pera-Şişli provides a monthly allowance to help support the Behar family. The Benevolent Society ensures that Estreyika is placed with a Jewish foster family, while Moshoniko remains with his mother. The narrative thus emphasizes the responsibility that the prewar female benevolent society assumed in caring for Jewish widows and orphans.

However, once war breaks out, the lives of the Behar siblings—illustrative of the Constantinopolitan Jewish community as a whole—are thrown into disarray. Estreyika's adoptive mother dies of the Spanish influenza that accompanied the war, and her adoptive father perishes as a result of the strenuous conditions of the forced labor battalion (*amele taburu*). Forced into the street because the war has effectively halted Jewish philanthropic activity in the city, Estreyika is taken into the home of the non-Jewish wife of a German officer.[29] After his mother dies from exanthematous fever, Moshoniko is meanwhile kidnapped by Aspasia, the married but childless Greek Orthodox neighbor who was his mother's friend. Aspasia had learned Ladino out of her affection for her Jewish friend and had tried to adopt Moshoniko upon his mother's passing, only to be rebuffed by Jewish communal representatives with the words that "a Jewish child should always be Jewish, and a Christian child should always be Christian."[30] Aspasia hides Moshoniko in her mother's house in the predominantly Greek Orthodox neighborhood of Tatavla, from which Moshoniko flees, tired of enduring verbal and physical abuse from Aspasia's mother in Aspasia's absence. He lives in an enclave with other orphaned children under the Galata Bridge, earning barely enough for food by begging in front of the Greek Orthodox church in Taksim Square. A chance encounter with Estreyika, who now lives in a nearby district of the city, provides Moshoniko with a slightly greater degree of material comfort. Estreyika, though fearful that the family's servants and her foster parents will discover the existence of her brother, sneaks portions of her bread rations to him. Strict rationing prevents her from supplying him with more food. The two siblings are reunited only once the war has ceased and a Jewish orphanage that served both male and female children is founded.

While *Techiyat haMetim* focused predominately on the anguish that a mother felt at the possibility of the loss of her only son during the war, *Los Dos Ermanikos* broadens the perspective to include not only the effects of the war on the remnants of the Behar family, but general societal effects as well. World War I, with its large-scale mobilization of men of working age, disrupted social and economic patterns in the city, led to a proliferation of indigent Jewish women and children needing succor from soup kitchens, forced the closing of the city's Jewish orphanage for girls, and threw Ottoman Jewish benevolent societies into a prolonged hiatus.[31] Prior to the outbreak of hostilities, Constantinople contained one Jewish orphanage, located in the district of Şişli to the north of Pera, which housed only orphaned girls. As *Los Dos Ermanikos* suggests, most Ottoman Jewish orphans, including those who still had a living mother but whose father was deceased, would either receive a monthly stipend from local Jewish benevolent societies, be placed with a relative, or be put into foster care in Jewish homes that needed a small additional source of income. The war forced an end to subsidies from the benevolent societies, which no longer had sufficient funds to support a burgeoning number of indigent Jewish women and orphans. By the end of the war, Jewish orphans in the Ottoman capital numbered some twenty-eight hundred, and widows over two thousand.[32] Thousands of Ottoman children, like Moshoniko, were thrown onto the streets, at times banding together for support across ethno-religious lines as they begged and stole in order to survive. It was only in August of 1919 after the declaration of the armistice, Karmona adds, that Madame Naar, the former directress of the Jewish orphanage, was able to work together with English and Turkish police to help address the question of orphans. This prompted the opening of an orphanage in February 1921 that would house Jewish boys and girls alike.[33] It is there that Estreyika and Moshoniko were united.

Indeed, the backdrop for *Los Dos Ermanikos* is the general privation that the war caused in the Ottoman capital. Karmona describes how Estreyika has sufficient food only because of her foster family's position in the German military, "while the most wealthy descended into the plaza in order to attain bread with a lot of money."[34] Indeed, police permits were required to buy more than one loaf of bread a day in the city, and even such provisions were often rank or cut with chaff.³⁵ But if the wealthiest residents of the city faced obstacles in acquiring bread, the problem was far more acute for the majority of the populace. "Our readers will certainly remember," Karmona writes, the great number of male and female Jewish beggars (*sedakarios i sedakarias*) that filled the city's plazas and streets during the war, going from shop to shop, house to house, pleading for assistance and cursing at those who did not aid them.³⁶ As diseases wracked the home front, widows, orphans and beggars proliferated on the streets of the Ottoman capital, a challenge that would take the Ottoman Jewish community and European and American aid organizations years to address.

While *Techiyat haMetim* and *Los Dos Ermanikos* take the form of novellas in recounting the effects of the war on Constantinople's Jewish population, the last two texts we will discuss follow the structure of the Haggadah, the ritualized retelling of the Israelites' exodus from Egypt recounted yearly at Passover. Beginning in the late nineteenth century, Ottoman Jews published Ladino parodies of the Haggadah. These commented on social and political topics ranging from deliberately humorous accounts to critiques of the Jewish nouveaux riches and Zionism to the Balkan Wars, World War I, and (later to) the Israeli War of Independence. Some of these satirical Haggadot were published in the Ladino press, a practice that Ottoman Jewish émigrés carried with them to New York. Others, including these two works, were published as stand-alone chapbooks. As with Ladino publications in general, the extent of readership and the reception of these texts are unknown.³⁷ As noted above, one of the Haggadot on World War I was authored by Eliya Karmona, who had earlier written a haggadic parody recounting the effects of the Balkan Wars. The second was authored by an otherwise unknown author, Nissim Shem-Tov 'Eli.³⁸ While both of these Ladino Haggadot reiterate the importance of remembering the individual and collective trauma of World War I for Ottoman Jews and others—a point emphasized by using the Haggadah as the model for their texts—they also illuminate the divergent ways in which members of the Ottoman Jewish community envisioned their future and the place of Ottoman Jews within it.

Just as the traditional Haggadah recounts the biblical plagues in Egypt, the two Constantinopolitan Haggadot of World War I recount the plagues that "the residents of Turkey"³⁹ and "the people of Constantinople"⁴⁰ suffered during the war years. The ten plagues each author lists focused in particular on the experiences of individuals on the home front without distinction made to religion, and they offer insight into the challenges that war caused in a city where, over the span of six years, the cost of living skyrocketed 1,350 percent.⁴¹ Both texts emphasize general civilian hardship from the requisition of foodstuffs and animals, the "bread of *vesika* [ration-card]" cut with chaff standing in for the "bread of affliction" that the Israelites ate on their exodus from Egypt.[42] In 'Eli's text, these plagues range from lice and mange to hailstorms of bombs and darkness due to lack of gas.[43] Karmona adds the proliferation of orphans, skyrocketing costs of goods, exanthematous fever, and the Spanish influenza, topics that the latter also addresses in *Los Dos Ermanikos*.[44]

The boundaries between suffering on the home front and suffering on the battlefront are blurred in both texts, in what become bitter critiques of the policies of the Young Turk Triumvirate and their German allies. 'Eli's text concludes with a rewritten version of "Chad Gadya" ("One Little Goat"), the classic Passover song that traditionally concludes the seder, a feature lacking in Karmona's less nuanced text. This "Chad Ravia" (or, "What Rage") ends:

> And the conqueror came and he drove away Enver Pasha, who was pleased by the courier who pleased the lieutenant [*yuzbashi*], who approved the clerk [*kyatib*], who reunited with the assistant [*muavin*], who shared with the secret police [*hafiye*], who snatched from the policeman, who stripped the youth, whose father had raised him with much suffering.[45]

This text, in which the Allied forces are equated to God and the Ottoman commander-in-chief Enver Pasha to Pharaoh, blames the father's suffering on all levels of the Ottoman bureaucracy, the actions of all stages of Ottoman authority having dire results for those, like the poor father, on the home front. Similarly, Karmona's rewriting of the classic Passover song "Dayenu" ("It would have been enough for us") begins with "if they had not taken our sons as soldiers [*askyer*], it would have been enough for us," continues with "if they had tormented [*eziyet*] us regularly with the gas and regularly given salaries to the wives of soldiers, it would have been enough for us," and ends with "if they had lengthened the war so much and had behaved as a *ben adam* [human] toward the people [*puevlo*], it would have been enough for us."[46] "Their" lack of accountability to the people manifests itself both in their mobilization of "our sons" and in the unwillingness or inability to pay soldiers' salaries to the wives and widows on the home front, drawing a sharp distinction between Ottoman officials and the Ottoman populace they exploited. Other sources from the period attest that this failure to provide salaries was a problem particularly acute for the spouses of non-Muslim soldiers, the vast majority of whom were mobilized into labor battalions, thus exacerbating difficulties for non-Muslim Ottoman families in the Ottoman capital.[47] In *Techiyat haMetim*, Karmona had presented the possibility of an Ottoman Jewish officer integrated into the Ottoman military structure and presiding over presumably Muslim troops. But in his Haggadah, the Ottoman authorities appear at odds with both those on the home front and those serving in the armed forces.

Indeed, while the Ottoman Ladino press of World War I (in the irregular issues produced), sought to portray Ottoman Jews as eagerly embracing military service for the defense of their Ottoman *patria*, a view commonly accepted by historians, these two texts reveal the suffering endured by Ottoman Jewish soldiers as well as the strategies they used to resist mobilization efforts. The Young Turk Revolution had instated mandatory military service for all Ottoman subjects, although this policy was unevenly implemented well into World War I and contained a number of loopholes.[48] Prior to that period, military service had been generally reserved for Muslim subjects, with non-Muslims paying an exemption tax. Jews were widely conscripted onto the fronts for the Balkan Wars of 1912–13. However, by World War I, Ottoman authorities disarmed most non-Muslim conscripts and sent them into labor battalions away from the fronts, often under conditions so treacherous that one author of Ottoman Sephardic provenance writing for the *American Israelite* equated them to "hard prison labor."[49]

Both Haggadot highlight the cold, hunger, and backbreaking work that those mobilized into labor battalions suffered. ʿEli lays ultimate blame at the feet of the Germans, whose commands Enver followed, "putting over us corporals and sergeants ... they made us lay cobblestones for the old streets of Edirne and Silivri."[50] Karmona elaborates more on the experiences of Jewish soldiers—indeed, in his text, the four children of the Haggadah are portrayed as the "armed soldier," the "unarmed soldier," the man in the labor battalion, and the man hiding in the attic to avoid conscription. All complain of their respective experiences, the first comparing his survival with no food and maltreatment to the resurrection of the dead; the second alludes to those at the home front arranging for a doctor to release him from the barracks; the third—he in the labor battalion—tells of being put to work like a donkey. Finally, Karmona cautions the fourth, the draft dodger, not to emerge from his corner lest he be imprisoned.[51] These strategies of resistance, whether hiding in the attic or having relatives seek a "known" doctor who could grant a "change of environment" and thus a temporary reprieve, linked the battlefront and home front. They suggest the existence of widespread Jewish resistance to the hardships imposed by the Ottoman war effort in both arenas.[52]

I will now turn briefly to the ways in which these texts sought not only to recount and memorialize the past, but to shape the future in a period marked by uncertainty. Indeed, in the years in which these two texts were published, not only was Constantinople occupied, but much of Anatolia had been divided among the Entente victors, Greek forces had landed in Smyrna and were pushing east, and Ottoman soldiers gathered under the leadership of Mustafa Kemal [Atatürk] were challenging both Greek forces and Ottoman continuity. This instability provided the Haggadot authors with the opportunity to forge and disseminate visions of the future. While these designs for the future never materialized, in 1919 and 1920 they were entirely possible outcomes of the war.

The authors' divergent views on what the postwar future would hold become apparent in their treatment of the war and their views on who, beyond God, was ultimately responsible for salvation from the war's hardship. Both excoriate Enver Pasha and Germany and adopt some of the optimistic vision for the future that Erez Manela has characterized as "the Wilsonian moment."[53] While Karmona explicitly mentions US president Wilson's words in favor of world peace, 'Eli's text favors Wilsonian plans for national self-determination. In 'Eli's text, the Allied forces serve as the traditional haggadic parallel to God leading the Israelites out of Egypt. For him, the four children of the Haggadah are the Jew, the Greek, the Armenian, and others "who suffer from the power of Turkey," who are rescued by Allied forces under the guise of divine will, making for them homelands over which they will have dominion.[54] Indeed, in 'Eli's text, the rewriting of the Passover song "Dayenu" ends with a reference to the establishment of a Jewish governing body in Palestine—"if the [victor] made us patrons of Eretz Israel and had not permitted us to form a [governing] chamber, it would have been enough for us."[55]

'Eli's urgent advocacy of Wilsonian national self-determination for Ottoman religious minorities, and for the Jews in particular, casts a different light on narratives that paint Ottoman Jews as simply waiting to see what the outcome of the war would be. This alternative narrative in which Ottoman Jews, like Ottoman Greeks and Armenians, openly displayed support of their own national projects on the streets of occupied Constantinople is further attested to in the memoir of an Ottoman Jew, Nissim Benezra. Benezra has written that the occupation by the Allies revolutionized the lives and behavior of ethnic minorities, including Jews, whose young Zionists came to behave "a bit like Constantinople was a conquered country," marching on parades in full view.[56] Even earlier, the "Dayenu" of another satirical Haggadah published in a Ladino periodical in 1911 had bemoaned the "Zionist foreigners" who caused Ottoman Jews to appear to be disloyal in the eyes of the Ottoman state and "were the cause of the complete ruin of all the Jewish communities" in encouraging public displays of support for the Zionist project.[57] Clearly, the Allied occupation indeed altered Jewish life by making support for Zionism more visible and overt.

But whereas in 'Eli's text, the Ottoman Empire is clearly defunct and the Jewish future lies in Palestine (facilitated by the benevolent intervention of the Entente), Karmona's text offers a future in which the Ottoman Empire persists. Though he casts Ottoman actions in World War I as the result of the Ottoman Triumvirate's desire to "destroy the people," his

Haggadah ends with praise of Sultan Mehmed VI Vahidettin, "who desired peace and brought it," together with the Allies. With no distinction between the various religious and ethnic components of Ottoman society, Karmona leaves open the possibility of an Ottoman future in which there would be "equality among the people."[58] Though he refers favorably to a potential Jewish home in formerly Ottoman Palestine, the future he envisioned in his recounting of the war was one in which the Ottoman Empire persists—albeit with altered borders—where Ottoman Jews, like all others, have a place.

These four texts, produced in the immediate postwar period as Constantinople writhed in uncertainty, cast light on the challenges of life on the home front and negative Jewish perceptions of World War I and Ottoman leadership. They further reveal the authors' divergent forecasts for their community in the face of an uncertain future. The Haggadot emphasize the transformative nature of the experience of World War I for Ottoman Jews, which required that it be remembered and recounted to further generations just as in the case of the traditional Haggadah. For 'Eli, with his enthusiastic adoption of Wilsonian principles of self-determination, "this war, the bread of the ration card, and the military service" must be remembered, because it was this war that "saved our people from captivity"; the grandfather should recount to his children that "he took us forth from there, to bring us to and to give us the land that he promised our fathers."[59] In contrast, Karmona asserts that it is simply the suffering of military service that must be recounted and remembered, closing with a message of Ottoman-Allied unity: "Blessed be He who created Sultan Vahidettin with the Allies who saved the whole world."[60] Meanwhile, while the novellas do not command ritualized remembering of the war, they all highlight the transformations war wrought on levels ranging from individuals and families to Jewish communal organizations and institutions.

The instability of the immediate postwar period began with the occupying presence of Interallied forces in what was once and could still remain the capital city of an Ottoman Empire that might (so far as anyone knew) persist. This ambiguous situation offered the Ottoman Jewish authors of these texts an opportunity to recount their experiences of the war in an environment in which criticism of the Young Turk Triumvirate would no longer be perceived of as disloyal. Julia Phillips Cohen has cogently argued that many Ottoman Jews, particularly among the intellectual and communal elite, attempted to adapt themselves to the changing political landscape of the post-Tanzimat period and insert themselves into both civic and Islamic discourses of Ottomanism by asserting a special affinity with their "Muslim brothers."[61] This narrative, she posits, offered Jews "a special symbolic place at the side of their Muslim compatriots," and was propounded in the Ottoman Jewish press through "selective representations of reality."[62] Further, with the establishment of the Republic of Turkey in 1923 and its subsequent Turkification policies, Turkish Jews too had a vested interest in both de-emphasizing occasions of dissent against the state and in casting themselves as "model citizens," often explicitly in contrast to other ethno-religious minorities.[63] Within both of these frameworks, representations in the Ladino press and elsewhere stressed Ottoman Jewish loyalty during World War I in a variety of ways, such as through the ardent performance of patriotic duty, through fund-raising efforts, and through military service. Nevertheless, this approach tends to skew the historical narrative away from examining moments of Ottoman Jewish dissent against Ottoman policies. This is not to deny that many Ottoman Jews fervently supported the war effort or embraced the opportunity to serve in the Ottoman military, at least initially.[64] However, these four Ladino works offer insight into certain forms of Ottoman Jewish dissatisfaction with or subversion of Ottoman policies and the Ottoman leadership, views that could only be expressed in a period of profound uncertainty and absence of a clear governing structure.

Together, these texts offer insight into the ways in which World War I rocked the Constantinopolitan home front, whether through disease, death, lack of gas, rationed bread, or the proliferation of orphans. So, too, they offer a counter-narrative to that of Ottoman Jews enthusiastically—or even willingly—embracing the call to serve in the Ottoman military. Instead, they offer narratives in which mobilized Jewish Ottomans suffered to an extent that demanded annual commemoration, while hinting at strategies of resistance ranging from bribing doctors to receive leave following mobilization to hiding in attics to avoid mobilization altogether. While such practices do not necessarily reflect a lack of patriotism on the part of Ottoman Jews, they suggest that claims of Jews' complete alignment with the demands of the Ottoman state have been exaggerated. Finally, these texts hint at a period in which the significance of the Great War, though recognized, was not and could not yet be fully understood. Indeed, they suggest that part of the significance of the Great War was that it offered individuals throughout the world the opportunity to envision new frameworks for the future. Together, these texts hint at the multiple possible futures that existed in a single moment for Constantinopolitan Ottoman Jews in the immediate aftermath of Mudros and how the authors attempted to position themselves and their communities in light of what they imagined those futures might hold.

Devi Mays is assistant professor of Judaic studies at the University of Michigan. She was a post-doctoral fellow in modern Jewish studies at the Jewish Theological Seminary. She received an award for her research from the Latin American Jewish Studies Association, and she is currently working on a manuscript, tentatively titled *Forging Ties, Forging Passports: Migration and the Modern Sephardi Diaspora.*

Notes

1. Suat Aray, *Les souvenirs d'une élève de Galatasaray* (Izmir, 1959), pp. 116–17, quoted in Stéphane Yerasimos, "Jeunes et Vieux Turcs dans la tourmente," in *Istanbul, 1914–1923: Capitale d'un monde illusoire ou l'agonie des vieux empires*, ed. Stéphane Yerasimos (Paris: Éditions Autrement, 1992); Henri Mylès, *La fin de Stamboul* (Paris: Éditions E. Sansot, 1921), pp. 162–66.
2. Catherine Laskaridhis, *Quinze mille jours à Constantinople ma patrie* (Athens, 1987), pp. 93–96, quoted in Hélène and Stéphane Yerasimos, "Rêves et cauchemars d'une ville perdue," in Yerasimos, *Istanbul, 1914–1923.*
3. Charles King, *Midnight at the Pera Palace: The Birth of Modern Istanbul* (New York: Norton, 2014), p. 42.
4. Ibid., pp. 41, 64.
5. A. Louise McIlroy, *From a Balcony on the Bosphorus* (London: Country Life, 1924), p. 93; Nissim M. Benezra, *Une enfance juive à Istanbul (1911–1929)* (Istanbul: Isis Press, 1996), p. 83.
6. See Lerna Ekmekçioğlu, *Recovering Armenia: The Limits of Belonging in Post-Genocide Turkey* (Stanford, CA: Stanford University Press, 2016); Rıfat Bali, "The Alternative Way to Come to Terms with the Past: Those Who Try to Forget; Turkey's Jewish Minority," paper presented at "From 'Milieu de Mémoire' to 'Lieu de Mémoire': Istanbul, Izmir, and Athens as Strongholds of Transcultural Societies in the 20th Century" conference at Karl Franzens University, Graz, Austria, June 2005.
7. On Ottoman-Jewish reactions to Allied occupation and Ottoman surrender, see Nur Bilge Criss, *Istanbul under Allied Occupation, 1918–1923* (Leiden: Brill, 1999), p. 48; Nora Seni, "Combien de raisins dans votre thé?," in Yerasimos, *Istanbul, 1914–1923*, p. 171. For more on the process by which Ottoman-Jewish leaders cast themselves as a model minority, see Julia Phillips Cohen, *Becoming Ottoman: Sephardi Jews and Imperial Citizenship in the Modern Era* (Oxford: Oxford University Press, 2014).
8. Stanford Shaw, *The Jews of the Ottoman Empire and the Turkish Republic* (London: Macmillan, 1991); Shaw, "Ottoman Jewry during World War I," *Türk Tarih Kongresi* (1994): 2035–46; Walter F. Weiker, *Ottomans, Turks and the Jewish Polity: A History of the Jews of Turkey* (Lanham: University of America Press, 1992), pp. 234, 241; and Naim Güleryüz, *Türk Yahudileri Tarihi* (Istanbul: Gözlem Gazetecilik Basın ve Yayın, 1993).
9. For Ottoman-Jewish reactions to mobilization during the Balkan Wars, see Eyal Ginio, "'Yehudim 'Othmanim! Hoshu lehatzil et moldatenu!' Yehudim 'Othmanim be-Milhamot ha-Balkan," *Pe'amim* 105–6 (Fall–Winter 2005): 5–28; David Ashkenazi, "Gius Yehudim be-Istanbul le-tseva ha-'othmani be-shanim 1909–1910 be-ra'i ha-'iton 'El Tiempo,'" *Pe'amim* 105–6 (Fall–Winter 2005): 181–218.
10. For mobilization, see Mehmet Beşikçi, *The Ottoman Mobilization of Manpower in the First World War: Between Voluntarism and Resistance* (Leiden: Brill, 2012); for the home front, see Yiğit Akın, "The Ottoman Home Front during World War I: Everyday Politics, Society, and Culture" (unpublished PhD dissertation, Ohio State University, 2011).

11. Eliezer Papo, *Ve-hitalta le-vinkha ba-yom ha-hu: Paradyot Sefaradiyot-Yehudiyot 'al ha-Hagadah shel Pesach* (Jerusalem: Mekhon Ben-Tzvi, 2012); Eliezer Papo, "Hagadat ha-partizanim: tsihok karnevali kaderekh hitmodedut 'im traumot hardifa ve-ha-lohma ve-kaemtsa'i lehavnayat ha-zikaron ha-kvutzati," in *Lashonot Yehudei Sefarad veha-Mizrah ve-sifriuteihem*, ed. David M. Bunis (Jerusalem: Misgav Yerushalayim u-Mosad Bialik, 2009), pp. 142–216; Eliezer Papo, "Reescribir un texto para redefinir una identidad: La Agada de la Guerra para el día de Pesach de Nissim Shem-Tov 'Eli y la autopercepción de los sefaradíes de Turquía después de la Primera Guerra Mundial," in *Ayer y hoy de la prensa en judeoespañol*, ed. Pablo Martín Asuero and Karen Gerson Şarhon (Istanbul: Isis Press, 2007), pp. 113–28; Eliezer Papo, "Konstruksion de la memoria i rekonstruksion de la identidad: Agadot de gerra- un jenero neglejado de la literatura sefaradi," in *Los Sefardíes ante los retos del mundo contemporáneo: identidad y mentalidades*, ed. Paloma Díaz-Mas and María Sánchez Pérez (Madrid: Consejo Superior de Investigaciones Científicas, 2010), pp. 204–24.
12. Gary Saul Morson, *Narrative and Freedom: The Shadows of Time* (New Haven, CT: Yale University Press, 2007), pp. 118–19.
13. Olga Borovaya, *Modern Ladino Culture: Press, Belles Lettres, and Theater in the Late Ottoman Empire* (Bloomington: Indiana University Press, 2012), p. 9.
14. On the effect that rising paper costs had on Ladino publication during World War I, see Alexandre Ben Ghiat, *Livro-Jurnal de la Gerra General* (Izmir: El Meseret, 1919), p. 4.
15. Elena Romero, *La creación literaria en lengua sefardí* (Madrid: Editorial Mapfre, 1992), p. 224.
16. For further discussion of the criminalization of insulting Turkishness (*Türklük*) and the government in the Turkish Republic, see Cemil Koçak, "Ayın Karanlık Yüzü: Tek-Parti Döneminde Gayri Müslim Azınlıklar Aleyhinde Açılan Türklüğu Tahkir Davaları," *Tarih ve Toplum Yeni Yaklaşımlar* 1 (March 2005): 147–208; Rıfat N. Bali, *Bir Türkleştirme Serüveni: Cumhuriyet Yıllarında Türkiye Yahudileri, 1923–1945* (Istanbul: Iletişim, 1999).
17. Romero, *La creación literaria*, pp. 241–43.
18. Mustafa Aksakal notes that "the literate segment of the Ottoman population remained in the single percentage points throughout the war." See Mustafa Aksakal, "The Ottoman Empire," in *The Cambridge History of the First World War*, vol. 1, *Global War*, ed. Jay Winter (Cambridge: Cambridge University Press, 2014), p. 460. Literacy would have been higher among the Ottoman-Jewish population. Soldiers' diaries include, among others, Salim Tamari, *Year of the Locust: A Soldier's Diary and the Erasure of Palestine's Ottoman Past* (Berkeley: University of California Press, 2011); İsmet Görgülü and İzeddin Çalışlar, eds., *On Yıllık Savaşın Günlüğü: Orgeneral İzzettin Çalışların Günlüğü* (Istanbul: Yapı Kredi Yayınları, 1997); Ali Rıza Eti, *Bir Onbaşının Doğu Cephesi Günlüğü*, ed. Gönül Eti (Istanbul: Türkiye İş Bankası Kültür Yayınları, 2009); two diaries of Jewish soldiers mobilized from Ottoman Palestine are published in Glenda Abramson, *Soldiers' Tales: Two Palestinian Jewish Soldiers in the Ottoman Army during the First World War* (Middlesex: Vallentine Mitchell, 2013).
19. Yiğit Akın, "War, Women, and the State: The Politics of Sacrifice in the Ottoman Empire during the First World War," *Journal of Women's History* 26, no. 3 (2014): 12–35.
20. Eliya Karmona, *Techiyat haMetim o El Ofisier Judio: Un Pasaje Verdadero dela Gerra General* (Constantinople: El Jugeton, 1921). Ladino stories often claimed to be recounting true events, but such claims did not mean that stories were indeed true.

21. Karmona, *Techiyat haMetim*, p. 3. On Balat, see Marie-Christine Bornes-Varol, "The Balat Quarter and Its Image: A Study of a Jewish Neighborhood in Istanbul," in *The Jews of the Ottoman Empire*, ed. Avigdor Levy (Princeton, NJ: Darwin Press, 1994), pp. 633–46.
22. On Jewish education in the Ottoman Empire, and particularly the activities of the Alliance Israélite Universelle, see Aron Rodrigue, *French Jews, Turkish Jews: The Alliance Israélite Universelle and the Politics of Jewish Schooling in Turkey, 1860–1925* (Bloomington: Indiana University Press, 1990).
23. Karmona, *Techiyat HaMetim*, p. 5.
24. Ibid., pp. 9–10.
25. Ibid., p. 12.
26. Ibid., p. 11.
27. Melanie Schulze-Tanielian, "Food and Nutrition in the Ottoman Empire," in *1914-1918-online—International Encyclopedia of the First World War*, ed. Ute Daniel et al. (Berlin: Freie Universität Berlin, 2014).
28. Eliya Karmona, *Los Dos Ermanikos* (Constantinople: Impremeria del Jugeton, 1921), p. 67. As with other claims of veracity, this should not be taken at face value. Nonetheless, *Los Dos Ermanikos* indeed engages with a number of themes that were certainly true for the period in question.
29. This, perhaps, alludes to a case that raised attention in 1921 in which a Jewish orphan was fostered and then adopted by a non-Jewish American aid worker. See H. C. Jaquith to Isaac Taranto, 8/3/1921, ID: 352172, Child Care, 1921–1928, Turkey, New York Collection 1921–1932, Joint Distribution Committee Archives (hereafter JDC).
30. Karmona, *Los Dos Ermanikos*, p. 15.
31. Extracts from Letter from Ambassador Elkus, Constantinople, 3/3/1917, ID: 10734, Turkey, General, 1917–1918, 1914–1918 New York Collection, JDC; Benezra, *Une enfance juive à Istanbul*, passim.
32. Statistiques des veuves, orphelins et orphelines de la capitale, 11/4/1920, Constantinople, ID: 238699, Folder: Turkey, Child Care, 1920–1921, 1919–1921, New York Collection, JDC.
33. Karmona, *Los Dos Ermanikos*, p. 64. It is unclear in Karmona's text whether the orphanage to which he refers is that founded in Ortaköy in 1920, the result of a combined effort of the Constantinopolitan Jewish community and the Joint Distribution Committee.
34. Karmona, *Los Dos Ermanikos*, p. 59.
35. King, *Midnight at the Pera Palace*, p. 39.
36. Karmona, *Los Dos Ermanikos*, p. 62.
37. Borovaya, *Modern Ladino Culture*; Sarah Abrevaya Stein, *Making Jews Modern: The Yiddish and Ladino Press in the Russian and Ottoman Empires* (Bloomington: Indiana University Press, 2004).
38. Nissim Shem-Tov 'Eli, *Haggadah dela Gerra por Dia de Pesach* (Constantinople: Sosieta Anonima de Papeteria i de Impremeria, 1919), hereafter *Dia de Pesach*; Eliya Karmona, *Haggadah dela Gerra General* (Constantinople: Impremeria del Jugeton, 1920), hereafter *Gerra General*. For Karmona's earlier haggadic parody, written under the nom-de-plume Rabbi Yotpata, see *Haggadah Echa i Apropiada por la Aniada de la Gerra 5673* (Constantinople, 1913).
39. 'Eli, *Dia de Pesach*, p. 15.
40. Karmona, *Gerra General*, p. 4.

41. François Georgeon, "Au bord du rire et des larmes," p. 88, in Yerasimos, *Istanbul, 1914–1923*.
42. 'Eli, *Dia de Pesach*, p. 3; Karmona, *Gerra General*, p. 5. Indeed, as the war raged on and wheat became increasingly difficult and expensive to acquire in both Constantinople and elsewhere in the empire, bread became cut with other things, ranging from barley and other grains to chaff. For repeated discussions of the composition of bread ingredients in Izmir during the war, see Ben Ghiat, *Livro-Jurnal de la Gerra General*. For more on food provisioning during what became known in Ottoman Syria and Lebanon as the "War of Famine," see Melanie Schulze-Tanielian, "Food and Nutrition in the Ottoman Empire during World War I," in *International Encyclopedia of the First World War*.
43. 'Eli, *Dia de Gerra*, p. 15.
44. Karmona, *Gerra General*, p. 4. For more on disease in the late Ottoman Empire, see Oya Dağlar, *War, Epidemics and Medicine in the Late Ottoman Empire (1912–1918)* (Haarlem: Sota, 2008).
45. 'Eli, *Dia de Pesach*, p. 24.
46. Karmona, *Gerra General*, pp. 5–6.
47. Benezra, *Une enfance juive à Istanbul*, pp. 44–45.
48. Akın, "The Ottoman Home Front," pp. 11–75.
49. Jose M. Estrugo, "More Facts about the Jews in Turkey: Horrors of Turkish Civic and Religious Oppression—Non-Mohammedans Hounded to Death or Emigration," *American Israelite*, 18 June 1925, p. 1; for more on the experiences of Ottoman Jews during World War I with a particular focus on questions of military service and emigration, see Devi Mays, "Transplanting Cosmopolitans: The Migrations of Sephardic Jews to Mexico, 1900–1934" (unpublished PhD dissertation, Indiana University, 2013), pp. 108–33.
50. 'Eli, *Dia de Pesach*, p. 10. The assertion that Germany was ultimately responsible for Ottoman involvement in World War I and behind much of the Ottoman military actions and policies has often been repeated by historians, though recently challenged by Mustafa Aksakal's minute examination of German and Ottoman archival sources. See Mustafa Aksakal, *The Ottoman Road to War in 1914: The Ottoman Empire and the First World War* (Cambridge: Cambridge University Press, 2008).
51. Karmona, *Gerra General*, p. 3.
52. Alexandre Ben Ghiat's diary offers insight into yet another form by which Ottoman Jews evaded military service. Individuals he called *chobeleros* (from the word *chobe*, which signified the robe Ottoman-Jewish religious figures wore) took on the role of religious leaders in order to be exempted from military service. These *chobeleros*, Ben Ghiat explained, were distinct from the *chobelis*, in that the latter were authentic religious figures and had been prior to the war. See Ben Ghiat, *Livro-Jurnal de la Gerra General*, p. 73.
53. Erez Manela, *The Wilsonian Moment: Self-Determination and the International Origins of Anticolonial Nationalism* (Oxford: Oxford University Press, 2007).
54. 'Eli, *Dia de Pesach*, pp. 6–7.
55. 'Eli, *Dia de Pesach*, pp. 17–18.
56. Benezra, *Une enfance juive à Istanbul*, pp. 83–84.
57. *La Haggadah Eskaldada*, in *El Korreo*, 14 Nisan 1911.
58. Karmona, *Gerra General*, pp. 3, 7.
59. 'Eli, *Dia de Pesach*, p. 20.
60. Karmona, *Gerra General*, p. 7.

61. Julia Phillips Cohen, "Between Civic and Islamic Ottomanism: Jewish Imperial Citizenship in the Hamidian Era," *International Journal of Middle East Studies* 44 (2012): 239, 243–44.
62. Ibid., pp. 245–46.
63. Rıfat Bali, *Cumhuriyet Yıllarında Türkiye Yahudileri, Devlet'in Örnek Yurttaşları (1950–2003)* (Istanbul: Kitabevi, 2009); Rıfat Bali, *Musa'nin Evlatları, Cumhuriyet'in Yurttaşları* (Istanbul: İletişim Yayınları, 2001); Marcy Brink-Danan, *Jewish Life in Twenty-First-Century Turkey: The Other Side of Tolerance* (Bloomington: Indiana University Press, 2011).
64. See, for example, the work of Oscar Aguirre-Mandujano on translating the Balkan War diary of Yehuda Leon Behar, which included Ottoman poems "sung by an officer who takes personal pride for the victories of his nation, which is, clearly enough, the Ottoman nation." See "A Soldier's Ladino Poems of Ottoman-Jewish Pride," http://jewishstudies.washington.edu/sephardic-studies/soldier-ladino-poems-ottoman-jewish-pride/.

Selected Bibliography
Primary Sources

Benezra, Nissim M. *Une enfance juive à Istanbul (1911–1929)*. Istanbul: Isis Press, 1996.
Ben Ghiat, Alexandre. *Livro-Jurnal de la Gerra General*. Izmir: El Meseret, 1919.
'Eli, Nissim Shem-Tov. *Haggadah dela Gerra por Dia de Pesach*. Constantinople: Sosieta Anonima de Papeteria i de Impremeria, 1919.
Karmona, Eliya. *Haggadah dela Gerra General*. Constantinople: Impremeria del Jugeton, 1920.
———. *Los Dos Ermanikos*. Constantinople: Impremeria del Jugeton, 1921.
———. *Techiyat haMetim o El Ofisier Judio: Un Pasaje Verdadero dela Gerra General*. Constantinople: El Jugeton, 1921.

Secondary Sources

Ashkenazi, David. "Gius Yehudim be-Istanbul le-tseva ha-'othmani be-shanim 1909–1910 be-ra'i ha-'iton 'El Tiempo,'" *Pe'amim* 105–6 (Fall–Winter 2005): 181–218.
Beşikçi, Mehmet. *The Ottoman Mobilization of Manpower in the First World War: Between Voluntarism and Resistance*. Leiden: Brill, 2012.
Borovaya, Olga. *Modern Ladino Culture: Press, Belles Lettres, and Theater in the Late Ottoman Empire*. Bloomington: Indiana University Press, 2012.
Cohen, Julia Phillips. *Becoming Ottoman: Sephardi Jews and Imperial Citizenship in the Modern Era*. Oxford: Oxford University Press, 2014.
Criss, Nur Bilge. *Istanbul under Allied Occupation, 1918–1923*. Leiden: Brill, 1999.
Ekmekçioğlu, Lerna. *Recovering Armenia: The Limits of Belonging in Post-Genocide Turkey*. Stanford, CA: Stanford University Press, 2016.
Ginio, Eyal. "'Yehudim 'Othmanim! Hoshu lehatzil et moldatenu!' Yehudim 'Othmanim be-Milhamot ha-Balkan," *Pe'amim* 105–6 (Fall–Winter 2005): 5–28.
King, Charles. *Midnight at the Pera Palace: The Birth of Modern Istanbul*. New York: Norton, 2014.

Papo, Eliezer. "Konstruksion de la memoria i rekonstruksion de la identidad: Agadot de gerra- un jenero neglejado de la literatura sefaradi." In *Los Sefardíes ante los retos del mundo contemporáneo: identidad y mentalidades,* edited by Paloma Díaz-Mas and María Sánchez Pérez, pp. 2014–224. Madrid: Consejo Superior de Investigaciones Científicas, 2010.

———. "Reescribir un texto para redefinir una identidad: La Agada de la Guerra para el día de Pesach de Nissim Shem-Tov 'Eli y la autopercepción de los sefaradíes de Turquía después de la Primera Guerra Mundial." In *Ayer y hoy de la prensa en judeoespañol,* edited by Pablo Martín Asuero and Karen Gerson Şarhon, pp. 113–128. Istanbul: Isis Press, 2007.

———. *Ve-hitalta le-vinkha ba-yom ha-hu: Paradyot Sefaradiyot-Yehudiyot 'al ha-Hagadah shel Pesach.* Jerusalem: Mekhon Ben-Tzvi, 2012.

Shaw, Stanford. *The Jews of the Ottoman Empire and the Turkish Republic.* London: Macmillan, 1991.

———. "Ottoman Jewry during World War I." *Türk Tarih Kongresi* (1994): 2035–46.

Yerasimos, Stéphane, ed. *Istanbul, 1914–1923: Capitale d'un monde illusoire ou l'agonie des vieux empires.* Paris: Éditions Autrement, 1992.

CHAPTER 10

Women and the War
The Social and Economic Impact of World War I on Jewish Women in the Traditional Holy Cities of Palestine

Michal Ben Ya'akov

The Jews in Ottoman Palestine were caught up in the conflict of World War I, beginning with its outbreak in the summer of 1914 until well after its cessation in November 1918, and they suffered greatly, as did Jews worldwide, albeit with differences specific to their location and the distinct characteristics of communal demographics and organization.[1] Furthermore, the Great War in late Ottoman Palestine highlights the intersection of natural disasters and man-made upheaval wrought by war and the blurred division between "home front" and "battlefield," as this war involved civilians in general, and Jews in particular, in ways that had not previously occurred.[2] The traditional Holy Cities of Jerusalem, Tiberias, and Safed may be defined as the "home front," as little or no direct fighting occurred within these cities, with Jerusalem and Tiberias serving as rear bases for the Ottoman and German armies. Nevertheless urban civilians experienced the war intimately, and they battled it in many ways. Zionist circles tried many creative solutions to deal with the rising crises, and their efforts to meet wartime problems have been well studied. The more religious Jews in the traditional communities of the Holy Cities, however, have been virtually ignored in studies of wartime Palestine. The diverse and divided religious communities relied on their existing social and economic frameworks to cope, and individuals struggled with various personal strategies, but unfortunately these were inadequate to address the increasing exigencies during the war years.

Those on the economic and social fringes of civilian society, especially the women, bore the brunt of daily survival in Palestine as in Europe, fighting battles on many fronts: poverty, starvation, disease and epidemics, locust plagues, exile, and expulsion. In addition, a combination of international and local conditions converged and accentuated the loneliness and isolation of the Jewish population, as will be described below. From organizational reports and personal diaries, much has been revealed regarding these battles on the home front, but little on how women coped during the war. Based on fragmentary documentation and work on women's strategies for coping with poverty, loneliness, and the exigencies of life in Palestine before the war,[3] this chapter will examine the implications of World War I for Jewish women in the traditional urban communities, with special emphasis on North African and Sephardic Jews, to the extent that sources allow. Norms based on gender distinctions dictated that these women, for the most part, did not have the economic or social resources available to the more affluent Sephardic elite or the Ashkenazic Zionist leadership in the various cities, towns, and newly established agricultural settlements, nor did they participate in the deliberations regarding communal decisions on the allocation of funds. Furthermore, most of those women were living alone: widowed, divorced, or those whose husbands had been drafted into the Ottoman army, or exiled from the country as foreign citizens, or separated from their families by circumstance, abroad when the war broke out and travel became impossible. Some had children to care for; only a few had extended family in Palestine. They did, however, constitute a considerable proportion of the Jewish population in urban centers, and it is these women who battled on the home front for their daily survival and for that of their children.

Home-Front Battles

The most severe problem for the population at large was food—or the lack of it. With the British and French naval blockade of the coast, all supply lines were cut, and the Turkish army and government requisitioned nearly all available foodstuffs. Supplies were soon depleted, particularly in the cities and towns. Already in late August 1914 the newspaper *HaPo'el HaTza'ir* reported, "In Jerusalem, where much of the population is unproductive and sunk in poverty in normal times, the distress is felt most, and the number of those hungry for bread is increasing from day to day."[4] The price of flour began to climb. In November 1915, over a year into the war, Dr. Otis Glazebrook, the American consul in Jerusalem, reported to the State Department that during the previous year the price of rice had increased nearly 600 percent, the price of sugar over 850 percent, and the price of potatoes nearly 430 percent.[5]

Finally the government was forced into action. In Jerusalem, as well as in other provinces in Greater Syria, the Ottoman authorities formed a grain syndicate, which was supposed to purchase grain in Karak, East Jordan, deliver it to the cities, sell the grain at fixed prices, and distribute it among the population,[6] based on vouchers distributed by the various communities.[7] The price of grain that ultimately made it to the market, however, continued to soar, and a black market developed, not to mention the fact that many officials and agents along the way took a share for themselves.[8]

Not only man created havoc in Palestine during the war. At the end of March 1915 and throughout the summer and fall, the situation became even more desperate as swarms of locusts invaded the entire country and devastated what was left of the crops, trees, and greenery, intensifying the shortages already caused by the war.[9] The locusts demolished fields, orchards, and gardens, leaving neither blade nor leaf. A. M. Luntz, in his yearly almanac *Luah Eretz Yisrael* for 1915–16, reported, "The Rabbinical Courts decreed ... that there should be a *Ta'anit Tzibbur*, a public fast day, and the whole day should be one of prayer and petition. After a few days the locusts left. ... However the locusts soon replenished themselves with new larvae."[10] Finally, army orders, government regulations, and citywide communal efforts united under the Central Commission to Fight the Locusts. Every male residing in the cities aged fifteen to sixty was required to collect twenty kilos of locusts and their larvae or pay a fee. Within three days ninety thousand kilo of locusts were collected in Jerusalem alone.[11] Gradually the plague subsided, but barely a home was spared from death by starvation.

Poverty, famine, and abysmal living conditions left the population open to disease. Epidemics of cholera, epidemic typhus or spotted fever, typhoid, dysentery, malaria, and fevers followed in the wake of the locusts and recognized no distinctions between Jews, Muslims, and Christians. The few existing health facilities had no medical supplies, and most of the professional medical staff were alien subjects who had been exiled. Tens were dying by the day, hundreds by the month. A cholera epidemic came in the wake of the Ottoman army, beginning in the north of the country, and continuing south to Jerusalem.[12]

Although wartime shortages, natural disasters, severe poverty, and suffering cut across religious and ethnic divisions, the Jews in Palestine, most of whom lived in the urban centers, suffered in additional ways due to the distinctive characteristics of their communities and personal circumstances.[13] The Jews of Palestine were strongly linked to their brethren abroad, by familial and communal ties as well as by economic dependence.[14] With the outbreak of hostilities in Europe, direct contact with the outside world ceased almost immediately, with the breakdown in international post and civilian sea transportation.[15] In October 1914 the Austrian, German, French, and British post offices in Palestinian cities stopped functioning altogether, and only the Ottoman postal service continued operating. The sense of isolation from the world was intensified during the first year of the war with the closure of most Palestinian newspapers, both in Hebrew and in Arabic. Hebrew newspapers, such as *Ha'Ahdut* and *HaPo'el HaTza'ir*, were shut down, accused of publishing Zionist propaganda and anti-Ottoman articles. Only the *Herut* newspaper, affiliated with the Sephardic community in Jerusalem, continued to function until 1917, and it was the only source of information that the Jewish community had about the outside world. However, the newspaper was strictly censored by the government, which necessitated a very patriotic and loyal Ottoman tone in its reporting.[16] With no mail and no newspapers, there was a feeling of almost complete isolation from the outside world, which was further amplified by the subsequent cessation of foreign shipping into Palestinian harbors.

Perhaps half of the Jews of Palestine in 1914 were foreign subjects.[17] On 1 October 1914, a month before officially joining the war on the side of Germany and Austria-Hungary, the Ottoman government announced a unilateral cancellation of the capitulations, the treaties signed with Western powers that granted privileges to foreign (i.e., non-Ottoman) citizens, protégés, and subjects in the Ottoman Empire. Not only were special rights and privileges abrogated, but foreign post offices and most consular offices were closed, as were foreign banks, resulting in the termination of credit.[18] In April 1915 the *New York Times* reported that "money has ceased to circulate."[19] The combined effects of the uncertain local financial market and the rapid economic deterioration in Europe created an economic crisis. The Zionist Anglo-Palestine Bank, founded in 1902,[20] was closed. Due to the diplomatic intervention of the American ambassador in Turkey, Henry Morgenthau, however, it reopened in various locations and continued to operate on an irregular basis. Thus the distress of the Jewish communities was minimally relieved by paper money and credit.[21]

One of the most drastic results of the first two factors—the break in communications and the abrogation of capitulatory status—was the cessation of monies received from abroad. This devastated the already fragile economic situation existing in the *Yishuv* (the Jewish community of Palestine) and affected both Jews in the religious communities in the Holy Land, for the most part living on the traditional *halukah*, funds collected in the Jewish communities abroad and sent to the Holy Land to maintain them, as well as the Zionist enterprise and the funds contributed from abroad for the building of a new society. Furthermore, as many of the Jews in Palestine were citizens, subjects, or protégés of countries at war with Germany, Austria-Hungary, and their Ottoman ally, they were expelled under suspicion of espionage and treason, usually with little notice. Hemda Ben Yehuda reported in 1918 that "ten thousand Jews left Jerusalem in one week.... In Jaffa 700 Jews were commanded to leave the country in two hours."[22] Others chose to leave before being expelled. While entire families left, it was the male head of the household who was officially expelled, and many times the rest of the family remained in the country. Ashkenazic Jews, most of whom had European protection, were affected more than Sephardim, who were usually Ottoman subjects, but Sephardim also suffered expulsion, since many North African Jews had French or English protection, and Bukharans and others were Russian subjects. Sephardic leaders, including the Chelouche family in Jaffa, Haim Ben-Atar, editor of the Hebrew daily *Herut,* and Avraham Elmaliach in Jerusalem and others were similarly expelled from the cities or elsewhere on charges of Zionist activities or other suspicious actions.

The lack of funds acerbated the famine. Both Arabs and Jews were affected by the hardships, albeit differently.[23] The Jews were hit the hardest, as most were urban residents and thus totally dependent on crops and supplies brought to the city from the surrounding countryside. Arab peasants, while also suffering from shortages due to government regulations and the requisitioning of crops for the Ottoman army, as well as from depleted manpower due to the draft, were usually in a better position to obtain food and exploit the growing black market than the urban Jews. Rural areas were farther from law enforcement agencies, and those living there were often able to escape the draft, enforced labor, and other regulations. On the other hand, however, the civilian population in the urban centers benefited from aid committees and other forms of assistance generally available only in the cities, and the Jews more than others often had access to limited aid and assistance from family and Jewish organizations abroad.

The Immediate Impact of the War on the Jewish Family

Famine, disease, military draft, and deportations had a drastic effect on the demographic composition of the population in general, the Jewish population in particular, and the status of Jewish women.[24] After a meticulous analysis of existing statistics, demographer Uziel O. Schmelz concluded that prior to the war there were approximately 85,000 Jews (with the emphasis on approximately), but at the end of the war only about 50,000 remained alive in Ottoman Palesine,[25] an astounding 59 percent of the original population. For the same period, Schmelz estimated that the overall population of Palestine declined from 800,000 to 700,000.[26]

During the war years a census was undertaken in each of the Jewish communities by the Palestine Office of the Zionist Organization, primarily to coordinate the allocation of aid from American Jews.[27] These statistical records, together with a detailed report by Eliezer Siegfried Hoofien, a Dutch-born banker in Jerusalem who served as representative for the Joint Distribution Committee in Palestine during the later part of the war,[28] and various memoirs, all point to the overall conclusion that not only did the Jewish communities suffer much more than the general population of Palestine, but the mortality rates of the Sephardic population were higher than for other Jews. In his comprehensive report, Hoofien included detailed mortality statistics for Sephardic Jews in Jerusalem during the war years, collected from the communal burial societies (*hevrot kadisha*).[29]

The state of Sephardic communal organizations was especially grave, not only due to limited financial resources but also because they lacked the flexibility needed to deal effectively with the ongoing crisis and because of the large number of splits and divisions within each group and between the different groups. Although the varying definitions and categories in the sources render it difficult to consistently differentiate between subgroups of Sephardic and Oriental (Mizrachi) Jews,[30] the Yemenite and Moroccan Jews seem to have suffered the most. In spite of enormous efforts to unify the community to deal with the situation in a most efficient manner, tensions continued between groups.

The situation in Safed was particularly devastating, with recurrent typhus and cholera epidemics, as well as large numbers of Jews who had left the country. The Palestine Office noted that at the onset of the war 7,000 Jews resided in the city; at its conclusion barely 2,688 Jews remained,[31] a loss of more than 60 percent. This enumeration, conducted in Safed in the month of Adar (February–March) 1919, after the war had officially ended, reveals the full extent of its demographic impact: some 248 women were widows (25.8 percent of the households, which, together with their de-

Table 10.1. *Number of Deaths in Jerusalem among the Sephardic and Mizrachi Communities*

Year	Approx. population	Number of deaths	Mortality rate (per 1000)
1913/1914	16,000	442	27.6
1914/1915	14,600	450	30.9
1915/1916	13,700	1,319	96.3
1916/1917	13,000	936	72.0

Source: Hoofien, *Report to the Joint Distribution Committee*, p. 34.

pendent children and other family members, comprised 558 individuals), 113 women were cut off from their husbands abroad or in the army (11.8 percent of the households, comprising 339 individuals), 91 men were widowers (9.5 percent of the households, comprising 226 individuals), 80 were orphans with neither parent, and only a third of the households included married couples (326 couples, comprising 1,359 individuals, or 50 percent of the community).[32] At the end of the war the situation in Tiberias was less drastic, but nonetheless tragic: 22.6 percent of the households were headed by widows (234 women, of whom 149 were Sephardic and Mizrachi, totaling 556 individuals, including dependent family members), and 5.1 percent by widowers (53 men, 119 individuals). There were 51 orphans, and only 51.5 percent of the households included married couples (534 of the 1,036 households, comprising 2,090 individuals).[33]

High mortality rates for adults and especially for infants and young children due to famine, disease, and appalling living conditions, as well as the draft and the deportation of males, left an enormous number of orphans, of one or both parents. "Everywhere little Jewish children laid down and died in the streets, little families of two, three and four huddled together under the parental guidance of some ten-year-old older brother or sister," Hoofien reported.[34] In April 1918 in Jerusalem alone, there were some 3,000 Jewish orphans, of whom only 420 were in four orphanages.[35] Another demographic distortion affecting women was the small size of the nuclear family—averaging three persons or less, with few young children.[36] This finding reinforces data on high rates of infant mortality and low fertility rates due to famine and poor health and the absence of many men from the country.[37]

Under the dire circumstances created by the effects of the war, how did the Jews of Palestine in general, and in particular, the women living alone, cope with the extreme deprivations, terrible living conditions, and natural calamities, including drought and a locust plague, during the war years?

Coping with the War

In early 1919, only months after the official end of the war and the beginning of British military rule in Palestine, Zvi Hirschfeld, a member of the citywide Jerusalem Food Committee for the Jews, wrote a most heart-rending description of the city:

> During the war the situation of Jerusalem's Jewish residents was most grim, as was the work of those aiding them. ... The elderly, women and babies, their bodies bloated by starvation, lay on the sides of the roads day and night, wailing their cries of hunger. ... Jerusalem residents sold all their valuables to the Circassians for a pittance in order to quiet their hunger. Ritual objects were also passed on to the

hands of outsiders, and Talmudic pages and other holy books were sold to Arab shopkeepers who used them to wrap halva and salted fish.... Whole families were wiped out.... One woman who lived with her three children, told [me], "For two months we have lived on charity—and now even that no longer exists; there is nothing to buy, everything has been used up." When I passed by her house a week later, not one of them was alive—all had died.[38]

At the beginning of the war, the Jewish community in Jerusalem organized independently and tried to support itself. Normally each of the Jewish communities in Jerusalem organized welfare assistance, but in this time of dire need they began to work together. Both religious Jews in the traditional Ashkenazic Old *Yishuv* and the Zionist New *Yishuv* cooperated (more or less) in trying to relieve the suffering. They established or enlarged soup and bread kitchens. Over nine hundred Jews in Jerusalem alone were fed from funds collected in the city in the so-called Bread and Tea Houses (*Batei HaLehem veHaTea*). Those institutions, in which people could receive tea and bread free of charge on a daily basis, grew rapidly and eventually started serving hot meals. It was reported that around three to four hundred people used the services of these houses each day.[39] Mem-

Figure 10.1. *Food Distribution at the Central Soup Kitchen, Jerusalem, World War I. Courtesy of the Central Zionist Archives, Jerusalem, Zadok Basan Collection, photo GNZB 401450.*

bers of the new Zionist organizations and younger members of the elite Sephardic leadership established a Sustenance Committee, which collected food and money for the Bread and Tea Houses.[40] Various communal and individual initiatives also helped alleviate some of the suffering, including the work of Swiss-born Sarah Thérèse Dreyfuss, who established three large soup kitchens in Jerusalem during the war years, feeding some three thousand Jerusalem children daily.[41]

With the deteriorating economic situation, many Jews looked for work of any kind, but little was to be found. Shopkeepers and itinerant peddlers had little or nothing to sell, and as money was scarce or nonexistent, there were no customers. With no money circulating, those who offered their services—craftsmen and artisans, and women who cleaned, prepared food, or sewed—had no one to serve. The Jerusalem Merchants Association (*Agudat HaSoharim*), established in August 1914, was the first institution that purported to unite all Jews living in Jerusalem. The association, composed of the elite of the Sephardic community and Zionist circles in Jerusalem, tried to create as many jobs as possible and to develop a more productive atmosphere among the Jews. The Merchants Association, however, fell apart after a short time.[42] At the onset of the war the Ottoman authorities began drafting men into government labor battalions, and at first many Jews perceived these as an opportunity for paid employment, but the degradation and discrimination they encountered in the battalions quickly dashed their hopes.

Numerous aid and assistance committees (*Va'ad Ha'Siyua*) were organized in the various cities and communities, all attempting to find solutions to the myriad problems.[43] A subcommittee for public works made plans to employ workers, as no one could pay them any longer for their labor. Zvi Leibowitz, a member of the Jerusalem Committee for Public Works, reported that after much discussion, the group forged guidelines, outlining the amount to be paid and the number of days of labor permitted, with the work rotated among the unemployed.[44] Most of the work, however, seemed to have been distributed to men, placing women at a disadvantage, in spite of their numbers in the community. In Hoofien's report to the Joint Distribution Committee on food distribution to schools for August 1917, he noted two workshops for women ("Beth Melacha" and "Schoschannah"), offering them work.[45]

Jerusalem's American Colony[46] initiated efforts to provide employment specifically and exclusively for women whose husbands and fathers were in the army or labor battalions. Their assistance was offered to Jews, Muslims, and Christians alike. In the fall of 1915 Bertha Spafford Vester, leader of the American Colony during the war years, began her Industrial Relief Work project and opened workshops with the assistance of her husband, Fredrick. They made "native" embroidery and lace, which "we felt could be improved and made attractive to Western purchasers,"[47] but they were unable to export the goods. At its height the American Colony employed more than three hundred Muslim, Christian, and Jewish women. Nevertheless, eventually Bertha Vester had to report, "The industry was kept up ... until they [the women] got too hungry and emaciated to work,"[48] and then the workshops ceased to operate. Vester and the American Colony extended additional relief to all residents of the city, regardless of religion, including a soup kitchen, opened with contributions collected in the United States and funneled via the State Department to the American consul, Dr. Glazebrook.[49] By 1917 the kitchen served over a thousand people daily. "It would be impossible to carry on an industrial relief work now. The people are not in a condition to work. It is now simply keeping soul and body together. In some cases our assistance helps; in other cases it is too late,"[50] wrote Vester to her American contributors. In one letter she wrote specifically of the Jews and their deteriorating situation:

> The Gadite or Yemenite Jews and the Morocco and Aleppo Jews are the worst cared for among that class....
>
> It shows the increase in poverty, when last year the Jews would not take our cooked soup, but asked for the uncooked cereals, while this year [1917] they are eager and grateful to get it.[51]

As the fighting got nearer, however, the German officers in the city closed the American Colony soup kitchen, and the death rate soared.

Prostitution, an ever-present source of earnings for young girls and women especially during wartime, became prominent among Jews as others, as many women sold themselves to German and Turkish troops just to ensure food for themselves and their families.[52] Some prostitutes seemingly worked as agents collecting information from government officials and army officers,[53] enabling them and their families to survive. However hushed, the problem came to the forefront after the British conquest in late 1917, and individual women and women's organizations sought to offer alternative vocational opportunities for those women to earn a living and regain their dignity.[54]

Jews in Palestine desperately needed outside assistance. As reports arrived in the neutral United States, American Jews began collecting contributions, organized by the newly established Jewish Joint Distribution Committee of America Funds for Jewish War Sufferers. After much organizational wrangling, negotiations, international diplomacy, and bureaucracy, the Joint managed to send money and food supplies to Palestine through the intervention of Henry Morgenthau in Istanbul and Dr. Glazebrook in Jerusalem. Food and supplies finally arrived in Palestine in the spring of 1915 and its allocation began at Passover. The JDC remained active in Palestine, engaging in lifesaving activities during and after the war.[55]

The committees organizing the distribution of the American aid consisted of men, who prepared the guidelines for work, made the decisions, wrote the reports, and signed the correspondence. Nevertheless, it seems that it was mostly women who carried out the actual work.[56] It was women who went into the homes, huddles, and cellars to distribute the food and aid to those who did not have the strength or will to come themselves. Rachel Atia, for example, granddaughter of the esteemed Rabbi David Ben Shimon, the founding leader of the North African Jewish community, visited homes on behalf of the American Joint Distribution Committee, not only distributing food, but also collecting information on the needs of the poor.[57] Pinchas Ben-Zvi Grayevsky, in his fascinating and unique sketches of women, mostly from the religious communities of Jerusalem, published in some ten booklets in the late 1920s and 1930s, *Bnot Zion veYerushalayim* (Daughters of Zion and Jerusalem), noted some twenty women who assisted in the distribution of aid, privately or under the auspices of one organization or another.[58] These women would otherwise have remained nameless or gone unknown, including Mathilde Cohen, who distributed Sabbath meals to the famished on Friday afternoons and found it painful to see the starving recipients eat as soon as she brought the food, not waiting for the Sabbath.[59]

Long lists of widows and orphans in need of assistance in the various communities and cities testify to the sad story and memorialize their names and existence. According to the wartime census of the Palestine Office of the Zionist Organization in Jaffa, women constituted approximately 55 percent of the urban population in the traditional Jewish centers of Jerusalem, Safed, Tiberias, and Hebron, and 35.8 percent of the adult population were widows (36.9 percent in Jerusalem).[60] This disproportion had been a feature of the traditional urban Jewish communities in Palestine in the nineteenth and early twentieth centuries, with over a third of the urban households headed by widows.[61] The war had introduced a new social and statistical category—those whose husbands were out of the country due to the war—either exiled or abroad prior to August 1914 as traditional emissaries or for work and prevented from returning or even sending monies.[62] In the North African *Ma'aravi* community of Jerusalem, which numbered just under 2,000 Jews in the spring of 1916, an undated report listed over 375 poor widows in need of sustenance, some with dependent children, and many living in communal housing (*batei mehase*).[63] As the situation in the country worsened, Jewish widows and women without husbands in the city were especially hard hit and their situations deteriorated considerably.[64]

Traditional assistance offered by individual women and by the wartime efforts of women's organizations like Ezer Yoldot and Agudat Nashim all worked to reinforce the traditional family unit and thus contribute to the stability and rehabilitation of the community. Simultaneously, through social networking and individual initiatives, many women developed unique strategies for coping with the dire physical circumstances and emotional stress of the continued crisis. Lists for distributing aid show that poor widows often shared living quarters, either in communal almshouses or in private accommodations. Many "adopted" families and assisted them,[65] at the same time receiving moral support and sociability. Others lived with various family members or friends and tried to use their homemaking skills to earn money. Describing the Sephardic neighborhood of Ohel Moshe in Jerusalem, Ya'akov Yehoshua noted the warm relationship between such women.[66] As Helena Znaniecka Lopata has shown in her work on mid-twentieth-century widows in the United States, these women learned to take advantage of a variety of resources, as well as create them, in order to cope with their emotional and physical needs. Personal and social resources, both formal and especially informal, provided the main support outside a normative family.[67] Since many Jewish widows had no family residing in the Holy Cities able to give them support or housing, they created an alternative subculture among themselves. These forms of mutual assistance are much more difficult to document than those of formal organizations or committees, but they are no less "real" and no less important in helping people cope.[68]

Volunteerism and philanthropy have traditionally been spheres of activity for women, associated with their customary home-oriented activities of caring for and nursing the needy. As shown in recent research, as well as in this case study, men generally performed in a more public manner, as a civic duty, organizing aid, while women functioned in a more private, individual manner, assisting the poor and sick.[69] Women in the traditional Jewish communities in Palestine were already deeply involved in the evolving women's organizations prior to the war,[70] and the war gave them greater urgency and afforded them a route into the public sphere, which continued after the war in the traditional communities, as well as in Zionist circles.

Religious women in the Sephardic communities chose these routes as well, simultaneously continuing their traditional way of life and deep compassion for fellow Jews and the Jewish community, while developing new strategies that were neither "modern" nor "traditional," neither "Eastern" nor "Western." They developed new forms of independent resilience, and after the war they were thrust into the public sphere in ways unique to their experiences and their status in the Holy Land. Of course their opportunities for self-expression were always limited by financial resources, exacerbated during the difficult war years, but they combined "modernity" and tradition to suit their particular needs and circumstances. Some acted independently, privately, others in women's organizations. Often it was women who molded the actions decided upon by the men directing communal affairs—as noted by the portraits of women Grayevsky published—and women who ventured out to receive assistance, as testified to by photos of long lines of women at the soup kitchens. Women's resilience can be seen in Hirschfeld's graphic accounts. Women worked to keep their families alive or at least attempted to do so by not submitting to circumstances. The female experience of the devastation may add to our understanding of the war—and responses to it—at a most individual and personal level.

Michal Ben Ya'akov is an associate professor of history at the Efrata School of Education in Jerusalem and director of its graduate program. Her research focuses on nineteenth- and twentieth-century Eretz Israel, with emphasis on North African and Sephardic Jewry, especially women. She has edited three volumes and authored numerous publications, including "Space and Place: North African Women in 19th Century Jerusalem," *HAWWA* (2012); "Hélène Cazès Ben-Attar et ses activés en faveur des réfugiés juifs au Maroc, 1940–1943," in *Les Juifs d'Afrique du Nord face à l'Allemagne nazie*, ed. Dan Michman and Haim Sa'adoun (2018); and "Little Meknes: the Jews of Meknes in 19th century Tiberias," in *Research on the Magreb*, ed. Moshe Bar-Asher, Elimelch Weintreich and Shimon Sharvit, Bar Ilan University [forthcoming, 2018].

Notes

1. Much scholarly research has been published on the Jews of Palestine during World War I. See, for example, Mordechai Eliav, ed., *Siege and Distress, Eretz Israel during the First World War* [Hebrew] (Jerusalem: Yad Izhak Ben-Zvi, 1991); Nathan Efrati, *The Jewish Community in Eretz Israel during World War I* [Hebrew] (Jerusalem: Yad Izhak Ben-Zvi, 1991); Abigail Jacobson, *From Empire to Empire: Jerusalem between Ottoman and British Rule* (Syracuse, NY: Syracuse University Press, 2011); and a series of booklets published almost annually by the Society for the Heritage of World War I in Israel (Jerusalem: Ariel Publishing, 2004–15). For the centennial of World War I, many academic conferences have been held and articles published. Special issues of journals have focused on the Jewish experience during World War I and its aftermath in Palestine/Eretz Israel, including *Zmanim* 126 (2014), *The Jerusalem Quarterly* 56–57 (2014), and *Cathedra* (forthcoming).
2. On this aspect of the European experience of World War I, see, for example, Susan Grayzel, *Women's Identities at War: Gender, Motherhood and Politics in Britain and France during the First World War* (Chapel Hill: University of North Carolina Press, 1999), pp. 11–49, 245. See also Billie Melman, ed., *Borderlines, Genders, and Identities in War and Peace, 1870–1930* (New York and London: Routledge, 1998); on the Jews in Palestine specifically: Billie Melman, "Re-Generation: Nation and the Construction of Gender in Peace and War—Palestine Jews, 1900–1918," pp. 130–37. For the home front in general, see Jay Winter and Antoine Prost, *The Great War in History: Debates*

and *Controversies, 1914 to the Present* (Cambridge: Cambridge University Press, 2005), pp. 152–72.
3. Michal Ben Ya'akov, "Space and Place: North African Women in 19th Century Jerusalem," *HAWWA: Journal of Women of the Middle East and the Islamic World* 10 (2012): 37–58; Ben Ya'akov, "Triple Marginalization: Widow, Immigrant and North African Women: On the Fringes of Jewish Society in 19th Century Eretz-Israel," in *Immigrant Women in Israel* [Hebrew], ed. Pnina Morag Talmon and Yael Atzmon (Jerusalem: Bialik Institute, 2012), pp. 9–42.
4. "Within the Country" [Hebrew], *HaPo'el HaTza'ir* 7, no. 42 (27 August 1914): 10. All translations from the Hebrew are my own.
5. Otis Glazebrook to the State Department, "Increase in Cost of Living Caused by War," 3 November 1915, Consular correspondence, American Consulate in Jerusalem, Record Group 84, Vol. 72, National Archives and Records Administration, College Park, MD, as cited in Abigail Jacobson, "American 'Welfare Politics': American Involvement in Jerusalem during World War I," *Israel Studies* 18, no. 1 (2013): 63, 73n28.
6. *Herut*, 26 October 1916, p. 4, reported that twenty-five thousand kilo of grain was brought to Jerusalem every day from Karak and Salt across the Jordan and distributed to the residents of Jerusalem by the municipality. See also *Herut*, 3 December 1916.
7. Shimon Rubenstein and Zvi Shiloni, *Activities of the General Wheat Committee of Jerusalem during World War I* [Hebrew] (Jerusalem: typewritten in ten copies, 2007), pp. 3a, 4a, 40a.
8. Ronald Storrs, *Orientations* (London: Ivor Nicholson and Watson, 1937), p. 297; Sami Hadawi, "Sodomy, Locust and Cholera: A Jerusalem Witness," *Jerusalem Quarterly* 53 (2013): 24; Bertha Spafford Vester, *Our Jerusalem: An American Family in the Holy City, 1881–1949* (Jerusalem: American Colony and Ariel Publishing, 1988, orig. 1950), pp. 201–2; Linda Schatkowski Schilcher, "The Famine of 1915–1918 in Greater Syria," in *Problems of the Modern Middle East in Historical Perspective: Essays in Honour of Albert Hourani*, ed. John P. Spagnolo (Reading: Ithaca Press, 1992), pp. 229–58.
9. Much documentation exists on the locust plague. See, for example, "Remarkable Details from American Consul on Palestine Locust Plague," *New York Times*, 21 November 1915; Avraham Elmaliach, *Eretz Yisrael Ve'Suriyah Biymey Milhemet Ha-Olam* [Eretz Israel and Syria during the World War] (Jerusalem: Ha'Solel, 1928), vol. 2, pp. 139–44; Salim Tamari, *Year of the Locust: A Soldier's Diary and the Erasure of Palestine's Ottoman Past* (Berkeley: University of California Press, 2011), pp. 107–8 for 23 April 1915. Lars Larson, an American Colony photographer, together with John Whiting, took photographs of the devastation, and these hand-tinted images are archived in the Library of Congress and available on its website, https://www.loc.gov/collections/american-colony-in-jerusalem/articles-and-essays/the-locust-plague-of-1915-photograph-album. Recent scholarship has also examined the locust invasion and its consequences: Jacobson, *From Empire to Empire*, pp. 35–38; Stefanie Wichhart, "The 1915 Locust Plague in Palestine," *Jerusalem Quarterly* 56–57 (2013–14): 29–39; Zachary J. Foster, "The 1915 Locust Attack in Syria and Palestine and Its Role in the Famine during the First World War," *Middle Eastern Studies* 51, no. 3 (2015): 370–94.
10. Abraham Moshe Luntz, *Luah Eretz Yisrael* [Eretz Israel Almanac] 21 (1915–16): 247–48.
11. Elmaliach, *Eretz Yisrael ve-Suriyah*, vol. 2, pp. 139–44. The sources noted here and in note 9 above all cite the rampant corruption of city officials in carrying out the regulations.

12. Dan Barel, *An Ill Wind: Cholera Epidemics and Medical Development in Palestine in the Late Ottoman Period* [Hebrew] (Jerusalem: Bialik, 2011), pp. 187–268. On the 1916 cholera epidemic, see Barel, "Disease in Times of War: Cholera Epidemics in Palestine during WWI," *Korot* 21 (2011–12): 55–74; Dan Barel and Zalman Greenberg, "Illness and Cholera in Tiberias during the First World War," [Hebrew] *Cathedra* 120 (2016): 161–82; Zvi Shilony, "Health Services in Jerusalem," in Eliav, *Siege and Distress* [Hebrew], pp. 61–83; Eran Dolev, "Medical Assistance in World War I," *Ariel* 167, *Eretz-Israel during World War I: The Campaign in the Negev and Sinai* [Hebrew], ed. Ezra Pimental and Eli Schiller (2004): 52–57.
13. For an alternative perspective, see Samir Seikaly, "Unequal Fortunes: the Arabs of Palestine and the Jews during World War I," in *Studia Arabica et Islamica,* ed. Wadad al-Qadi (Beirut: American University of Beirut, 1981), pp. 399–405. He notes, "In fact, and rather paradoxically, the condition of the Jewish minority during the war appears, in retrospect, to have been both less perilous and less difficult than that of the Palestinian Arab majority. For, unprotected by the solicitous care of neutral powers, the Arabs stoically tolerated the harshness of Ottoman rule and the miseries of war. By contrast the Jewish population, neither for the first nor the last time, was sustained by foreign support that went a long way to preserve, very much intact, the existence of a miniscule minority in an empire not over-anxious for the well-being of its minorities" (p. 403). Seikaly also notes that "many Jews refused the offer of Ottoman citizenship. Suffering by choice" (p. 403). Not only do the population statistics noted above refute this claim, but the discussion below addresses this stance.
14. For examples of wartime contacts between the Jews of Palestine and Austria-Hungary, see Mordecai Eliav, *Under Imperial Austrian Protection: Selected Documents from the Archives of the Austrian Consulate in Jerusalem, 1849–1917* [Hebrew] (Jerusalem: Yad Izhak Ben-Zvi, 1985), pp. 415–68; and I. Klausner, "The Assistance Committee in Vienna for the Yishuv in Eretz Israel during World War I" [Hebrew], *Shalem* 1 (Jerusalem: Yad Izhak Ben-Zvi, 1974), pp. 501–523. On the activities of American Jews, see below.
15. "Within the Country" [Hebrew], *HaPo'el HaTza'ir* 7, no. 42, 27 August 1914, p. 10.
16. On Haim Ben-'Attar and the *Herut* newspaper, see Yitzhak Betzalel, "On the Journal 'Ha'Herut' (1909–1917) and on Haim Ben-Atar as Its Editor" [Hebrew], *Pe'amim* 40 (1989): 121–47; on the closure of the newspaper, p. 145; Jacobson, *From Empire to Empire,* pp. 24–25, 87–89. Some short-term Hebrew publications appeared, including *Bayn Hametzarim* in 1915, but these publications appeared very irregularly and did not serve as a replacement for a daily newspaper. See also Mordecai Ben Hillel Ha-Cohen, *Milhemet ha'Amim* [War of the Nations] (Jerusalem: HaSefer Printers, 1929–30), p. 243; Zvi Shiloni, "The Crisis of World War I and Its Effects on the Urban Environment in Jerusalem and Its Jewish Community" [Hebrew] (master's thesis, Hebrew University of Jerusalem, 1981), pp. 119–21.
17. The exact numbers of Jewish foreign citizens and subjects are not known. Approximation based on Uziel O. Schmelz, "The Decline in the Population of Palestine during World War I," in Eliav, *Siege and Distress* [Hebrew], pp. 17–47, esp. p. 22.
18. "Within the Country" [Hebrew], *HaPo'el HaTza'ir* 7, no. 42, 27 August 1914, p. 10; Elmaliach, *Eretz Yisrael Ve'Suriyah,* vol. 1, pp. 118–19; Vester, *Our Jerusalem,* p. 247.
19. " Distress in Jerusalem," *New York Times,* 23 April 1915.
20. The bank was the main financial institution of the Zionist movement in Palestine and functioned under the protection of England. On the history of the Anglo-Palestine Company, see *A Story of a Bank: 75th Anniversary to Bank Leumi Le-Israel, 1902–1977* (Tel Aviv: Bank Leumi, 1977).

21. Yosef Eliahu Chelouche, *Parashat Hai* [Reminiscences of My Life] (Tel Aviv: Strod and Brothers, 1931), p. 261; Jacobson, *From Empire to Empire*, pp. 44–45.
22. Hemda Ben Yehuda, "Jerusalem," in *Jerusalem: Its Redemption and Future, The Great Drama of Deliverance Described by Eyewitnesses*, ed. Hemda Ben Yehuda, Kemper Fullerton, and Edgar J. Banks (New York: Christian Herald, 1918), pp. 30–31.
23. Seikaly, "Unequal Fortunes," pp. 399–405; Vester, *Our Jerusalem*, pp. 257–58, 263–64; Schatkowski Schilcher, "The Famine," pp. 229–58.
24. The issue of the overall demographic effect on the Jewish population has been dealt with in depth elsewhere and is beyond the scope of this article. See Schmelz, "The Decline in the Population," pp. 17–47; Zvi Shiloni, "HaDildul ba'Uchlusiya ha'Yehudit bi'Yerushalayim biTkufat Milhemet ha'Olam ha'Rishona" [The Decline of the Jewish Population in Jerusalem during World War I], in *Mehkarim Bi'Geografiyah Historit-Yishuvit shel Eretz-Israel*, ed. Yehoshua Ben Arieh, Yossi Ben Arzi and Haim Goren (Jerusalem: Yad Izhak Ben-Zvi, 1988), pp. 128–51.
25. Schmelz, "The Decline in the Population," pp. 30–39.
26. Ibid., pp. 26, 30.
27. Palestine Office of the Zionist Organization, *Sfirat Yehudei Eretz Yisrael* [A Count of the Jews of Palestine], 2 vols. (Jaffa: Zionist Organization, 1918–19).
28. Eliezer Siegfried Hoofien, *Report of Mr. S. Hoofien to the Joint Distribution Committee of the American Funds for Jewish War Sufferers, New York, concerning Relief Work in Palestine from August 1st, 1917 to May 31st, 1918* (New York, 1918; reprint, New York: Arno Press, 1977).
29. Ibid., pp. 34–35; using these statistics, see Shiloni, "HaDildul ba'Uchlusiya," pp. 128–51; and a comprehensive discussion in Schmelz, "The Decline of the Population," pp. 43–46, esp. table 7, p. 44.
30. Nitza Druyan and Michal Ben Ya'akov, "Jews from Islamic Countries in Jerusalem at the End of the Ottoman Era," in *The History of the Jewish Community in Eretz Israel since 1882: The Ottoman Period* [Hebrew], ed. Israel Kolatt (Jerusalem: Bialik, 2002), part 2, pp. 211–78, esp. p. 272; Uziel O. Schmelz, "Bayaiot Musagiot b'Mehkar al Edot Yisrael" [Problems in Terminology in Research on Jewish Communities], *Pe'amim* 56 (1993): 125–39.
31. Palestine Office, *Sfirat Yehudei Eretz Yisrael*, vol. 2, p. 20.
32. Ibid., p. 21.
33. Ibid., p. 13.
34. Hoofien, *Report*, p. 35. On the orphans in Jerusalem and the women "visitors" organized to try and deal with the situation, see Ela Ayalon, "'Visitors of Orphans' in Jerusalem" [Hebrew] *Zmanim* 126 (2014): 72-83; Ayalon, "Orphans in the Jewish Community in Jerusalem at the End of the First World War and After: The Story of the 'Palestine Orphan Committee'" [Hebrew], *Historia* 33 (2014): 95–116.
35. Hoofien, *Report*, orphans, pp. 35, 50; Schmelz, "The Decline in the Population," pp. 44–45.
36. Palestine Office, *Sfirat Yehudei Eretz Yisrael*, vols. 1–2, tables for each of the individual cities and communities; vol. 1, p. 7, for Jerusalem; vol. 2, p. 13, for Tiberias; vol. 2, p. 21, for Safed.
37. For a comprehensive analysis, see Schmelz, "The Decline in Population," pp. 39–43.
38. Zvi Hirshfeld, "Jerusalem," *Ha'Aretz Veha'Avoda* [The Land and the Work], Shvat 1919, pp. 80–81.
39. *Herut*, 6 September 1914.

40. Elmaliach, *Eretz Yisrael veSuriyah,* vol. 1, pp. 123–24; Zvi Leibowitz, "The Bread and Tea House: Reminiscences from the Days of the First World War" [Hebrew], in *B'Aliya u'Bivniya: Zichronot u'Masot* (Jerusalem: Rubin Mass, 1953), pp. 114–16; Efrati, *The Jewish Community,* p. 54.
41. Margalit Shilo, "The First World War: An Arena for the Empowerment of Women in the Jewish Community in Palestine," *Journal of Modern Jewish Studies* 1, no. 7 (2008): 3, 10–11. Elmaliach notes some thirty-five institutions that received assistance from the Joint Distribution Committee in 1915 in order to enable some twenty-three thousand to continue their work (Elmaliach, *Eretz Yisrael Ve'Suriyah,* pp. 194–95).
42. *Herut,* 18 January 1916; Efrati, *The Jewish Community,* pp. 54–55, 59–60.
43. Elimaliah, *Eretz Yisrael Ve'Suriyah,* pp. 110–13; Efrati, *The Jewish Community,* pp. 44–51; Zvi Shiloni, "Changes in the Jewish Leadership of Jerusalem during World War I" [Hebrew], *Cathedra* 35 (1985): 64–90; Jacobson, *From Empire to Empire,* pp. 43–44.
44. Zvi Leibowitz, "Jerusalem in the First World War, the Committee for Public Works" [Hebrew], in *B'Aliya u'Bivniya: Zichronot u'Masot* (Jerusalem: Rubin Mass, 1953), pp. 116–18.
45. Hoofien, *Report,* p. 31.
46. The "American Colony" in Jerusalem was established in 1881 by a group of evangelical, utopian Christians from Chicago, led by Anna and Horatio Spafford, and later joined by others from Sweden as well as the United States. They came to help the residents in the Holy Land, regardless of religion. During World War I they were particularly active with philanthropic work, supported by donations from their supporters in the United States. See Vester, *Our Jerusalem*; Helga Dudman and Ruth Kark, *The American Colony: Scenes from a Jerusalem Saga* (Jerusalem: Carta, 1998).
47. Vester, *Our Jerusalem,* p. 252. For a photograph of such a lace embroiderer, see Nirit Shalev-Khalifa and Migdal David, *Jerusalem: A Medical Diagnosis; The History of Jerusalem Reflected in Medicine and Beliefs* [Hebrew and English] (Jerusalem: Tower of David and Yad Izhak Ben-Zvi, 2014), p. 167.
48. Vester, *Our Jerusalem,* p. 252; see also p. 256.
49. On Glazebrook's efforts, see Jacobson, "American Welfare Politics," pp. 56–76.
50. Vester, *Our Jerusalem,* pp. 257.
51. Ibid., pp. 257–58.
52. Vester, *Our Jerusalem,* deals with the severe situation in one sentence only, p. 264. On the presence of prostitutes at parties and their contacts with government and army officials, see Jacobson, *From Empire to Empire,* pp. 71–73; Salim Tamari, "The Short Life of Private Ihsan, Jerusalem 1915," *Jerusalem Quarterly* 30 (Spring 2007): 48. After the British conquest of Jerusalem in December 1917, the situation grew to epidemic proportions; see Margalit Shilo, "The Blight of Prostitution in the Holy City, 1917–1919: Male and Female Perspectives" [Hebrew], *Jerusalem and Eretz Israel* 1 (2003): 173–97; Shilo, "The First World War," pp. 5–8; Shilo, "Women as Victims of War: The British Conquest (1917) and the Blight of Prostitution in the Holy City," *Nashim* 6 (2003): 72–83. On prostitutes in Jerusalem during the prewar period, see Margalit Shilo, *Princess or Prisoner: Jewish Women in Jerusalem, 1840–1914* (Hanover, NH: University Press of New England / Brandeis University Press, 2005), pp. 197–201; Gur Alroey, "Prostitution and Trafficking in Women in Eretz Israel at the Beginning of the 20th Century" [Hebrew], in *Blood Money, Prostitution, Trafficking in Women and Pornography in Israel,* ed. Esther Hertzog and Erella Shadmi (Haifa: Pardes, 2013), pp. 73–88. On prostitution as an expression of the marginality of women in the modern city, see Deborah Bernstein, *Women on the Margins: Gender and Nationalism in Man-*

date Tel Aviv [Hebrew] (Jerusalem: Yad Izhak Ben-Zvi, 2008), pp. 17–19 and numerous references there. On prostitution as a component of the immigrant experience, see Gur Alroey, "Journey to Early Twentieth-Century Palestine as a Jewish Immigrant Experience," *Jewish Social Studies*, n.s. 9, no. 2 (2003): 28–64; on Jaffa, pp. 55–59.
53. A striking example is Alther Levine, who seemingly paid Jewish prostitutes who, in return, provided him with information that they gathered from Turkish, German, and Austrian clients; see Jacobson, *From Empire to Empire*, pp. 72–73.
54. Not only was the subject of prostitution hushed at the time, but also in subsequent research on the effect of the war on the civilian population. This lacuna is now being filled. See, for example, Shilo, "The Blight of Prostitution"; Shilo, "The First World War," pp. 5–8.
55. On American Jewish relief in Palestine, see Elmaliach, *Eretz Yisrael Ve'Suriyah*, pp. 185–96; Alexandra Lee Levin, *Dare to Be Different: A Biography of Louis H. Levin of Baltimore, a Pioneer in Jewish Social Service* (New York: Bloch, 1972), pp. 145–94; Efrati, *The Jewish Community*; Jacobson, "American 'Welfare Politics,'" pp. 56–76; Jaclyn Granick, "Waging Relief: The Politics and Logistics of American Jewish War Relief in Europe and the Near East (1914–1918)," *First World War Studies* 5, no. 1 (2014): 55–68.
56. See, for example, Shilo, "The First World War: An Arena for the Empowerment of Women," pp. 1–15; Ayalon, "'Visitors of Orphans' in Jerusalem"; pp. 72–77; Ayalon, "Orphans in the Jewish Community", pp. 95–116; as well as works on Jewish women in the United States, including Mary McCune, *"The Whole Wide World, without Limits": International Relief, Gender Politics, and American Jewish Women, 1893–1930* (Detroit: Wayne State University Press, 2005), esp. pp. 43–78.
57. David Tidhar, *Encylopedia le'Halutse Ha'Yishuv u'Vonav* [Encyclopedia of the Founders and Builders of Israel] (Tel Aviv: self-published, 1958), vol. 13, p. 4232.
58. Pinhas Ben Zvi Grayevksy, *Bnot Zion veYerushalayim* [Daughters of Zion and Jerusalem], 10 vols. (Jerusalem: Zuckerman Printers, 1929–33; reprint, Jerusalem: Yad Izhak Ben-Zvi, 2000, with all ten issues in one volume with index).
59. Ibid., vol. 6, p. 176.
60. According to Schmelz's computations of the Zionist Organization census (Schmelz, "The Decline in the Population," p. 41, table 6).
61. According to the nineteenth-century census of the Jews initiated by Sir Moses Montefiore, for example, women constituted over 65 percent of the population. Factors of differential ages of marriage and mortality rates between Jewish men and women, particularly among Sephardim, and the rather common phenomenon of widows immigrating to the Holy Land created a situation in which there were large numbers of widows. For a detailed discussion, see Michal Ben Ya'akov, "*Aliyah* in the Lives of North African Jewish Widows: The Realization of a Dream or a Solution to a Problem?," *Nashim* 8 (2004): 5–24.
62. The problem of "abandoned" or "deserted" women, however, was not a new problem and had grown in proportion prior to the war, during the mass waves of migration in the late nineteenth century. However during the war the numbers grew. See Gur Alroey, "Deserted Women in Palestine at the End of the Ottoman Period and the Beginning of the Mandate Period" [Hebrew], *Israel* 15 (2009): 93–116; Shilo, *Princess or Prisoner*, pp. 190–97.
63. Widows in the North African Jewish community, Jerusalem Historical Archives (JHA), Old Yishuv collection, *Edat HaMaaravim*, 274/60. The lists are divided by categories, according to the types of assistance received.

64. Tragically, the arrival of the British did *not* immediately ameliorate the situation, but that, too, is beyond the scope of this study.
65. Ya'akov Yehoshua, *The Story of the Sephardi House in the Jewish Quarter of the Old City of Jerusalem* [Hebrew] (Jerusalem: Reuven Mass, 1976), pp. 149–50.
66. Ya'akov Yehoshua, *Childhood in Old Jerusalem*, part 4, *Neighborhoods in Old Jerusalem* [Hebrew] (Jerusalem: Reuven Mass, 1971), pp. 92–95.
67. Helena Znaniecka Lopata, *Current Widowhood: Myths and Realities* (Thousand Oaks: Sage, 1996), pp. 166–69; Lopata, "Widowhood: World Perspectives on Support Systems," in *Widows*, vol. 1, *The Middle East, Asia and the Pacific* (Durham: Duke University Press, 1987), pp. 1–9; Lopata, *Women as Widows: Support Systems* (New York: Elsevier, 1979), pp. 3–7, 17–18, 255-269.
68. For a discussion of living arrangements for poor widows in nineteenth-century Jerusalem, see Ben Ya'akov, "Space and Place," pp. 42–44. Shilo, "The First World War," p. 11, also mentions such arrangements within the context of Zionist circles.
69. M. Liborakina, "Women's Voluntarism and Philanthropy in Pre-Revolutionary Russia: Building Civil Society," *Voluntas* 7, no. 4 (1996): 367–411; Liborakina, "Women and Philanthropy in Nineteenth-Century Ireland," *Voluntas* 7, no. 4 (1996): 350–64, as cited in Lilach Rosenberg-Freidman, *Revolutionaries Despite Themselves* [Hebrew] (Jerusalem: Yad Izhak Ben-Zvi, 2005), p. 85.
70. On Jewish women in nineteenth-century Jerusalem, see Grayevksy, *Bnot Zion ve Yerushalayim*; Shilo, *Princess or Prisoner*, pp. 122–42; on the war years, see Shilo, "The First World War," pp. 1–15; Ayalon, "'Visitors of Orphans' in Jerusalem," pp. 72–77.

Selected Bibliograpy

Primary Sources

HaPo'el HaTza'ir, 1914

Herut, 1914–1916

Hoofien, Eliezer Siegfried. *Report of Mr. S. Hoofien to the Joint Distribution Committee of the American Funds for Jewish War Sufferers, New York, concerning Relief Work in Palestine from August 1st, 1917 to May 31st, 1918*. New York, 1918. Reprint, New York: Arno Press, 1977.

Palestine Office of the Zionist Organization. *Sfirat Yehudei Eretz Yisrael*. 2 vols. Jaffa: Zionist Organization, 1918–19.

Secondary Sources

Alroey, Gur. "Nashim Azuvot ba-Shalhei ha-Tkufa ha-'Otmanit u-Rashit ha-Mandat." *Israel* 15 (2009): 93–116.

Ben Ya'akov, Michal. "Space and Place: North African Women in 19th Century Jerusalem." *HAWWA: Journal of Women of the Middle East and the Islamic World* 10 (2012): 37–58.

Efrati, Nathan. *Mi-Mashber le-Tikvah: Ha-Yishuv ha-Yehudi be-Erets-Yisrael be-Milḥemet-ha-'Olam ha-Rishonah*. Jerusalem: Yad Izhak Ben-Zvi, 1991.

Elmaliach, Avraham. *Eretz Israel ve-Suriyah bi-Yemey Milḥemet Ha-'Olam*. Jerusalem: Ha'Solel, 1928.

Grayevksy, Pinhas Ben Zvi. *Bnot Zion ve-Yerushalayim*. 10 vols. Jerusalem: Zuckerman Printers, 1929–33; reprint, Jerusalem: Yad Izhak Ben-Zvi, 2000.

Jacobson, Abigail. *From Empire to Empire: Jerusalem between Ottoman and British Rule.* Syracuse, NY: Syracuse University Press, 2011.

Schilcher, Linda Schatkowski. "The Famine of 1915–1918 in Greater Syria." In *Problems of the Modern Middle East in Historical Perspective: Essays in Honour of Albert Hourani*, edited by John P. Spagnolo, pp. 229–58. Reading: Ithaca Press, 1992.

Schmelz, Uziel O. "Hitma'atut Uchlusiat Eretz-Israel bi-Milhemet ha-'Olam ha-Rishona." In *Ba-Matzor u-Ba-Matzok: Eretz-Israel bi-Milhemet ha-'Olam ha-Rishona,* edited by Mordecai Eliav, pp. 17–47. Jerusalem: Yad Izhak Ben-Zvi, 1991.

Seikaly, Samir. "Unequal Fortunes: The Arabs of Palestine and the Jews during World War I." In *Studia Arabica et Islamica,* edited by Wadad al-Qadi, pp. 399–406. Beirut: American University of Beirut, 1981.

Shilo, Margalit. "Women as Victims of War: The British Conquest (1917) and the Blight of Prostitution in the Holy City." *Nashim* 6 (2003): 72–83.

Shiloni, Zvi. "HaDildul ba'Uchlusiya ha'Yehudit bi'Yerushalayim biTkufat Milhemet ha-'Olam ha'Rishona." In *Mehkarim Bi'Geografiyah Historit-Yishuvit shel Eretz Yisrael,* edited by Yehoshua Ben Arieh, Yossi Ben Arzi, and Haim Goren, pp. 128–51. Jerusalem: Yad Izhak Ben-Zvi, 1988.

Vester, Bertha Spafford. *Our Jerusalem: An American Family in the Holy City, 1881–1949.* Beirut: Middle East Export Press, 1950; reprint, Jerusalem: American Colony and Ariel Publishing, 1988.

CHAPTER 11

Baghdadi Jews in the Ottoman Military during World War I

Reeva Spector Simon

On 5 November 1914, Britain declared war on the Ottoman Empire, which had entered World War I on the side of Germany. Far from Istanbul at the provincial headquarters in Baghdad, the announcement was greeted with the beating of drums as the Turks prepared for the military buildup that was required to meet the British army advancing from India to southern Iraq, to counter hostilities in Syria/Palestine, and to thwart the Russian threat against Turkey in the Caucasus. Baghdadi Jews, like other citizens of the Ottoman Empire, were conscripted into the army and sent to the front. But instead of combat units, most Jews were assigned to labor battalions, where large numbers suffered and died. The military experience of Baghdadi Jews during World War I exemplified the end of a period of anticipation for inclusion in Ottoman society that had begun with the process of modernization and the promise of ultimate equality initiated in the nineteenth century, stalled at the beginning of the twentieth, and momentarily revived with the euphoria accompanying the secular Young Turk coup of 1908. For the Jews of Baghdad, whether on the battlefield or at home, the war years were not only catastrophic; they marked a turning point in Iraqi-Jewish history.[1]

The Jewish Community

In 1914 the Jewish community of Baghdad, where most Iraqi Jews lived, numbered some fifty thousand people and played a key role in the commercial life of the city. Under various regimes, a number of Jews were financial advisors, dealers in foreign currency, and bankers to the rulers. They also participated in the burgeoning international trade, networking with coreligionists from India to Hong Kong and Manchester to supply British manufactured goods to the region, and began to corner foreign commerce. By the turn of the twentieth century, Jews had already begun the process of modernization when schools established by the Alliance Israélite Universelle were opened in Baghdad. Jews learned European languages and received secular education in the Alliance schools and in the Ottoman government secondary schools that were established later. These skills would prepare them to become the translators and physicians that the Turks would find so useful during World War I. The wealthy commercial elites and professionals, however, represented only 5 percent of the Baghdad Jewish population. Thirty percent of the male population was made up of clerks, petty traders, retail shop owners, and employees. The rest were poor and included immigrants from Mosul and Kirkuk. The community supported schools, a hospital, and help for the indigent funded through charitable contributions and a community tax on kosher meat.[2]

By 1914, it seemed that the reforms and modernization programs known as the Tanzimat undertaken by Istanbul during the nineteenth century were taking hold. Until then, Jewish political participation within an Islamic polity as well as military participation were proscribed, because as non-Muslims, Jews could never be part of the ruling elite. Classed as *dhimmi* (*ahl al-dhimma*), Jews were a protected minority that had religious autonomy but were subject to a special tax, the *jizya,* in addition to demeaning restrictions on Jewish life that were embodied in what came to be known as the Pact of Omar. This dominant-subordinate relationship between Muslims and Jews that had existed since the advent of Islam legally ended with the Tanzimat. In 1908, Jews, other minorities, and Westernized Muslim elites supported the more secular regime instituted by the Young Turks.[3] They foresaw a future of inclusion in the official life of the Ottoman Empire as citizens; they had seats in the newly constituted parliament and were subject to military conscription.

Ottoman Military Reform from 1908 to 1914

Before we turn to the events of World War I, however, it is important to understand how reform of the Ottoman military affected the Jews and the local reaction to Jews serving in the army. On the official level, leaders of the Jewish community, including Haham Hayim Nahum, chief rabbi of the Ottoman Empire, supported Jewish military service and applauded the fact that Jews were now truly citizens of the empire, a sentiment echoed by Djavid Bey, the minister of finance, who expressed "great satisfaction" at Jewish support and devotion for the new regime.[4] The chief rabbi intervened with the government to increase the number of Jews eligible for officer candidacy and to ease conditions overall for Jews who were conscripted into the army. Five Jewish students who, in 1906, had attended the Ottoman military preparatory school (*rushdiye*) in Baghdad were already studying at the Military College in Istanbul, from which four graduated, were commissioned as lieutenants, and served in World War I. Until the war, the number of Jews attending the government military preparatory school gradually increased, and seven Baghdadi Jews had even formed a committee in 1910 to consider establishing a similar Jewish school.[5] When, however, the government instituted a quota on the number of non-Muslims who could attend the Military College, Haham Nahum interceded with the government to allow more Baghdadi Jews to pursue careers as military officers, arguing that the 4 percent quota allotted to Ottoman Jewry did not take into account the fact that the proportion of Jews in Baghdad was considerably higher than in the empire overall.[6] Due to his efforts, by 1913, authorities in Baghdad were instructed to admit Jews into the military and government schools without restrictions,[7] but the rest of the students coming up through the Baghdad school system did not graduate as officers because of the outbreak of World War I. Jews attended classes, even those on Qur'an, but were excused for two hours on Saturday morning so that they could attend synagogue.[8]

The chief rabbi also sought to temper the impact of military service on ordinary conscripts. Most faced three years of active duty, or two if stationed in cholera-prone Baghdad or other unhealthy climes. This was in addition to service in the reserves, which could amount to twenty years of military service from approximately the age of twenty to forty.[9] The rabbi appealed for military exemptions for hardship cases as well as for rabbis and yeshiva students, requested the appointment of Jewish chaplains in units where there were also imams and priests officiating, and asked that Jewish holidays (Yom Kippur, Rosh Hashanah, and Passover) be designated as official leave time.[10] At one point, contemporary newspaper reports in the West concluded that the question of kosher food was waived for Ottoman soldiers because service to the fatherland took precedence,[11] but other reports demonstrate that the issue of kosher food led to different responses depending on circumstance. Some soldiers were released to eat at the homes of coreligionists; at times, the Ministry of War determined that all soldiers had to eat together, since it was forbidden to differentiate between Muslims and non-Muslims; and at one point, military doctors decided that soldiers could bring their own cooking utensils with them rather than eat from the "collective pot."[12] The government rejected the creation of separate Jewish units, but there were Jewish representatives on the committees that made decisions about hardship cases.[13]

Enthusiasm on the official level, however, belied the fact that generally most Jews tried to avoid military service if they could. Until World War I, it was relatively easy for minorities to pay a military exemption fee (*bedel askari*)—in essence, a replacement for the *jizya*. Levied by the government on a communal basis, the tax was an important source of local revenue, especially at a time when the government could not absorb all of the men called up under universal military conscription.[14] It was assessed by community leaders and, in the case of the Jewish community, remitted to the government treasurer by the chief rabbi of Baghdad, who represented his constituents. The assessment became a source of communal conflict if it was administered inequitably or if the government extorted the money. It was not uncommon for those who refused to pay to be arrested and thrown in jail on the eve of Jewish holidays and released only when relatives or friends agreed to pay, a method the Turks would also employ.[15]

In Baghdad, the period of the Young Turk regime brought a new governor as well as a local opposition to his administration. Arabs opposed Governor Nazim Pasha's enforcement of the use of Turkish as the official language and the fact that he surrounded himself with Turkish subordinates. He replaced Arab military retirees with Turkish officers and even had Jewish advisors.[16] Devout Muslims were not pleased with the changes in the traditional roles that now placed non-Muslims equal to Muslims, nor were they happy with the new social life in Baghdad—music and floor shows in the cafés along the river and the riverboats plying the Tigris. They criticized the young Turkish officers for smoking on Ramadan and for their general lack of religious observance.[17] Clerics viewed the Young Turk proclamations of liberty, equality, and justice as manifestations of their secular apostasy and suspected Jewish influence.[18] Soon after the Young Turk accession to power, Jews were attacked in Baghdad and Mosul as part of a Muslim backlash against Jewish support for Young Turk policies.[19]

The Ottomans also had to deal with the reality that most Muslims strongly opposed non-Muslims serving in the military, bearing arms, or holding any commission of significance. Some firmly believed that Jews could not function in a combat situation because of a verse in the Qur'an that talked about paralyzing Jewish hands. Iraqi popular culture presented negative depictions of Jews in the military, including, for example, the image of a Jewish recruit holding a gun and hiding behind a hedge in terror, with the caption asking "whether or not the shot went through," or verses in a popular song that spoke of the "pitiful plight of Jewish recruits" ("Under the slogan of liberty, oh our sovereign, your army is Jewish").[20] Despite the reports that Christians and Jews recruited for military service were "giving good satisfaction" in the campaign to pacify the Iraqi southern area of Muntafiq,[21] Muslims soon expressed their feelings about the use of Jewish recruits from Baghdad in tribal areas when Shiites of the region attacked the local Jews. The chief rabbi interceded, and the minister of war ordered the commandant of the troops at Baghdad to arrest or punish the troublemakers, but he also instructed him not to send any more Jewish soldiers to the district.[22]

In 1910 Nazim Pasha, who was appointed as both governor of Baghdad (which had authority over Mosul and Basra) and commander of the Sixth Army Corps, improved living conditions in the city by having streets widened and cleaned, public gardens opened, and shops painted.[23] The city was policed, and vagabonds, vagrants, and petty thieves were put to work building army barracks.[24] As the military headquarters for the province, Baghdad became a major induction center for a reorganized Turkish army. There were now permanent barracks on the Persian side of the Tigris that quartered some four thousand men. German military advisors supervised training, and there were daily drills and maneuvers throughout the summer. The American representative in Baghdad noted the efficiency of the troops and the marked improvement in uniforms and equipment. The German consul general took credit for the reorganization of the Ottoman military: "If you want to see the German army," he noted, "here it is in front of you."[25] The army was also better fed, clothed, and housed than the majority of the people. Food supply was supervised. Contractors delivered meat, vegetables, and fruit, and bread was freshly baked.[26]

In 1912–13 (at the time of the Balkan Wars) the newly constituted Ottoman military failed its first major challenge. The government galvanized all of the institutions of a modern state—press and propaganda, bureaucracy, and the reorganized military. The Turks began the war in an atmosphere of patriotic rather than religious enthusiasm in an attempt to garner the support of all citizens, Muslims and non-Muslims alike, in the national struggle to maintain the integrity of the Ottoman Empire.[27] Very quickly, the benefits of inducting non-Muslims into the army were seriously questioned because of the opposition of Muslim soldiers to the idea of non-Muslims bearing arms and even more so to Muslims serving under non-Muslims. Although few soldiers from Iraq were sent to the Balkans because they were needed to keep local order at home,[28] most of the Christian and Jewish recruits who served in the Balkan Wars were disarmed and served in labor battalions used in road construction and transport behind the lines.[29] The government allowed men to purchase exemption from service, and after the news spread that most of the Baghdad Jews sent to the Balkans died of cold and hunger, many even married for a dowry in order to have the money to pay the military tax.[30] It should also be noted that the *bedel askari* was the second most important revenue stream for the government.³¹ The two-year protracted period of conflict demonstrated the failure of the conscription program and the new methods of logistics and supply. The war ended in military defeat, with heavy casualties.

World War I Mobilization

Despite their attempts to repair a reserve system that had completely broken down during the Balkan Wars and to overhaul the Turkish military, the Ottomans were not prepared when World War I broke out in 1914. The military triumvirate of Enver, Talat, and Cemal (Jamal) had taken control of the government, and Enver with his German advisors was in the process of reorganizing the armed forces. But the army was operating at reduced strength because of heavy casualties incurred during the Balkan Wars and inexperience due to Enver's policy of removing older, seasoned, non-commissioned military officers. Added to the manpower shortage was a lack of reserve artillery or technical formations. The only combat-hardened unit was sent to Gallipoli. The Third Army (Caucasus) and the Second Army (Syria), to which many Jewish conscripts were sent, were both in the process of being reconstituted. Eventually, they would deploy Baghdadi Jews to the Caucasus or to Syria en route to Egypt and the campaign to take the Suez Canal.³²

With the beginning of hostilities in Europe, on 2 August 1914, the Ottoman government ordered a general mobilization. The penalty for desertion was death. Although the Ottoman Empire was not yet officially at war, martial law was imposed on Baghdad due partly to local opposition to conscription.³³ The protocol that was developed for military conscription called for orderly induction by year, so that during the summer of 1914, the classes of 1893 and 1894 (each cohort had about 90,000 men) were to be inducted, with the goal of eventually reaching a million men.³⁴ Baghdad province was scheduled to furnish 15,000 men immediately, sending 10,000 to Mosul and 5,000 to Basra. Younger classes of reservists, recruits aged twenty-three to thirty, were drafted into active units, while men aged thirty to thirty-eight were sent to depot formations where they received a few weeks of rudimentary training and were then sent home with instructions to be ready to join units within twenty-four hours' notice. But in mid-August, with the very warm weather in Baghdad and the threat of outbreaks of cholera because of contaminated drinking water, men called to the colors were sent home to eat and sleep and report back the next day, because local authorities were unable to feed, clothe, and transport them. Many who were on their way to Mosul returned to Baghdad too ill to fight, and a number died en route.³⁵

By 29 October, when the Ottoman Empire entered the war on the side of Germany, the call-up was more haphazard, and popular reaction was less than exuberant. The 5 November British declaration of war on the Ottoman Empire was marked in Baghdad by the beating of drums that signaled general military conscription. "I was eight at the time," writes Abraham Twena, "and I saw an unforgettable scene. Moslem women went out beating their breasts, shouting mournful songs. Jewish women looked out tearfully from their doors and windows. Jewish young men began to escape into hiding-places, waiting for the storm to pass." Muslims and Jews cursed the authorities.[36] Thousands of Jews who were of military age were signed up; but by November, despite the elaborate plans on paper, there were no induction offices, draft notices, or lists of specific names in age groups.[37] Placards were posted on walls calling up reservists up to age forty-five. The British doubted that the Ottomans could reach their induction goal even if they succeeded in provoking a rising of Muslims in Egypt, India, and the Caucasus against the British and the Russians.[38]

In 1916, men between ages fifteen and fifty-five were being called up, and according to British reports, the following year 12 percent of the inductees were between the ages of sixteen and nineteen.[39] In Baghdad, patrol groups of military inspectors and citizen clerks working for the military bureaucracy took to the streets and went from house to house looking for and seizing able-bodied young men who seemed eligible even if they were not of draft age. One of them, the father of Yitzhak Bar Moshe, was taken at random, and the documents presented proving his age were destroyed. Bar Moshe's grandfather was certain that his own fasting, chain-smoking, and praying for seventeen days saved his son, who deserted and managed to escape.[40] Yehuda Barshan's father decided to flee Baghdad when he found himself inside the military barracks. He crept outside and joined those already in line for uniforms and then ran toward the Tigris, hiding in a tower overlooking the river. He realized that he could not return home, because not only would the gendarmes be looking for him, but they would also be on the lookout for anyone else they could conscript. In his case, bribery and assistance from a Muslim friend facilitated his escape from military service.[41] Some men managed to remain in Baghdad, hiding in specially prepared rooms where men were even able to gather and pray in a proper quorum (minyan).[42] Others were dragged away.

Once inducted, conscripts were taken to military barracks where they answered roll call and were issued one-size-fits-all "moldy," often ragged uniforms, which had to last them for more than a year.[43] Journalists reported that when fighting the British in Mesopotamia (Iraq), Ottoman soldiers stripped British corpses of their uniforms and especially shoes, because it was not unusual for the soldiers to march and fight barefoot or with their feet covered in rags. Shoes were unavailable on the Palestine front, and men were issued yellow Bedouin slippers that were bound to their feet with rope, while men on garrison duty wore shoes made of straw with wooden soles.[44] In Syria the war is still known as "the barefoot war";[45] the situation on the Caucasus front was even worse.

The army also lacked equipment. The military was short some two hundred thousand rifles along with the requisite ammunition. In November 1914, of the nine thousand Ottoman reservists stationed at Baghdad, four thousand were without rifles. If guns were issued, often they were rusty.[46] The situation was somewhat better in Palestine, where Alexander Aaronsohn, a Jewish volunteer in the Ottoman army, underwent training despite a shortage of ammunition. Men were divided into groups of fifty, put under the charge of a young non-commissioned officer who had recently graduated from the Ottoman Military Academy, or drilled by an Arab soldier who had been in the service for several years. But there was little target shooting, and once the Ottoman Empire entered the war, the army stopped training minorities.[47] "The final blow," Aaronsohn wrote,

> came one morning when all the Jewish and Christian soldiers of our regiment were called out and told that henceforth they were to serve in the *taboor amlieh*, or working corps. The object of this action, plainly enough, was to conciliate and flatter the Mohammedan population, and at the same time to put the Jews and Christians, who for the most part favored the cause of the Allies, in a position where they would be least dangerous. We were disarmed; our uniforms were taken away, and we became hard-driven "gangsters." I shall never forget the humiliation of that day when we, who, after all, were the best-disciplined troops of the lot, were first herded to our work pushing wheelbarrows and handling spades, by grinning Arabs, rifle on shoulder.[48]

Sensitive to Muslim reaction, the Ottomans adopted a different approach to World War I than they did in the preceding Balkan conflict.

Unlike the Balkan Wars where the Young Turks did not want to appear anti-Christian, World War I was promoted as a Muslim war and the call to jihad was used as a deliberate tactic to mobilize Muslims against the British Empire. In an attempt to secure the loyalty of its Ottoman subjects as well as of Muslims generally, the Turkish leadership acceded to the advice of German Orientalists and had the Sheikh al-Islam (the chief Muslim cleric) and the Sultan (in residence, but not in power) sign a declaration of jihad, or holy war, against the European powers. "Following in the footsteps of the Prophet of the whole Moslem world," Muslims were told, "we must put apart all our personal concerns at a time like this, and must be ready against the enemies of our religion who are towards Moslems in every instance devoid of any sign of pity. We must also bear in mind that we are categorically obliged to sacrifice, when required, our souls for that purpose."[49] With the general mobilization of Ottoman forces, the declaration made it incumbent upon all Muslims to take up the struggle and sacrifice themselves against those who would destroy Islam. It was a call to unity of all Muslims from North Africa to India to rise up against the Russian, French, and British imperial powers.[50] For the Ottoman Turks, it was particularly important to ensure the loyalty of the Arabs in the empire, with whom there was a mutual antipathy at a time when nascent Arab nationalist sentiments threatened to impede Turkish efforts in the war against the British in Egypt. There had already been rumblings during the Balkan Wars of an Arab uprising in southern Iraq.[51] By 1916, facing an Arab revolt against the Turks in Syria and Palestine in addition to the general opposition to non-Muslims in the military, the Turks disarmed minorities and sent Christian and Jewish conscripts to work in labor battalions.[52]

Military Service and Deployment

On 6 November 1914, the day after they declared war, the British, who had anticipated the possibility of an Ottoman-German alliance, sent troops from India to invade southern Iraq and take Fao. The Ottomans, on the other hand, planning for offensives against the British at the Suez Canal and in the Caucasus against Russia, whom they thought would be bogged down in hostilities against Germany and Austria-Hungary, were totally unprepared for the British invasion. They sent troops to defend Basra, but on 17 November, after losing Kut al-Zayn, a village south of the city, the Ottomans decided to evacuate Basra and withdrew to Qurna. On 22 November, the British entered Basra without resistance and drove the Turks from Qurna and advanced north until the Ottoman army stopped them at Kut al-'Amara and held it until 1917. Basra, under British civil administration, was hardly affected by the rest of the war and provided sanctuary behind British lines for Iraqi deserters.

Jews were sent south to Basra, but once the city was in British hands, they were deployed to other fronts. Some were sent to Palestine on the way to the Suez Canal; most of the Iraqi troops, however, were sent to the Caucasus. Mosul was a major embarkation center for Iraqi draftees on their way to the front. The Iraqi Twelfth Corps, stationed in Mosul, was deployed to Syria with troops stationed in Aleppo, Homs, Damascus, and along the coastline of Palestine.[53] As men from Irbil and Kirkuk arrived, manpower shortages in these units were filled with conscripts already in Mosul, many of whom were Jews. At one point there were more than fifteen hundred Jewish soldiers in Mosul, leading the chief rabbi of Mosul, Rabbi Eliahu Barzani, to request that Jews have the day off on Yom Kippur, and in the spring the Jewish community helped the forty Jewish soldiers who had arrived from Basra a few days before Passover celebrate the holiday with local families.[54] Some young men who were not so fortunate were sent off without training or uniforms to units on their way to Suez. Marching through Palestine in a series of night marches in order to avoid detection by British reconnaissance seaplanes, Jews called this group from Mosul the "Match Battalion" because they were sent out at night and used matches to light their way.[55]

The Turkish attacks on the Suez Canal in February 1915 and again in August 1916 were unsuccessful but required troops to guard the Hejaz railway, not only because of the British threat but also because of Arab attacks, especially after the beginning of the Arab Revolt. It is interesting to note that there were Jews involved in the Arab Revolt who, like many Iraqi soldiers in the Ottoman army, joined Faisal's army after they were taken prisoner by the British. Some one hundred Iraqi Jews headed by two Jewish officers "came from the prisoner camps to fight under the banners of King Hussain," Prime Minister Nuri Sa`id told members of the Baghdad Staff College in 1947. "The British and French commands tried to separate these volunteers from their other brethren and employ them in the Palestine front, but they did not succeed, as they insisted to serve under the Arab flag in the Hejaz."[56]

For the most part, however, Jewish conscripts were assigned to labor battalions to build roads or engage in other non-military duties. There were 70 to 120 labor battalions active at any given time, whose overall strength varied from twenty-five to fifty thousand men. Some performed office, factory, or agricultural work, but most recruits worked on road repair and transport. The work was onerous. Aaronsohn provides a description of road building between Safed and Tiberias, a link in the military highway from Damascus to the coast:

> From six in the morning till seven at night we were hard at it, except for one hour's rest at noon. While we had money, it was possible to get some slight relief by bribing our taskmasters; but this soon came to an end, and we had to endure their brutality as best we could. The wheelbarrows we used were the property of a French company which, before the war, was undertaking a highway to Beirut. No grease was provided for the wheels, so that there was a maddening squeaking and squealing in addition to the difficulty of pushing the barrows. One day I suggested to an inspection officer that if the wheels were not greased the axles would be burned out. He agreed with me and issued an order that the men were to provide their own oil to lubricate the wheels![57]

The soldiers were underfed and suffered from malnutrition and disease. Men dreaded being sent to labor camps and deserted when they could. The narrator in the story "The Soldier and the Ass" ("Hahayal vehapirda") by Israeli author Yehuda Burla, who served in the Ottoman army, captures the despair of soldiers in describing the dreaded Labor Camp Six near Beersheba, which, over the winter due to flood and disease, was reduced from one thousand to four hundred men:

> Ten by ten the labourers pass by. They walk with faltering steps, there is no sound of life in this camp. Soldiers, in a manner of speaking, covered in rags, without the merest sign of a uniform; their heads are bent, their faces thin—fragments of human beings with the marks of misery and humiliation on their faces ... these are the comrades of those drowned in the floods, suffering from typhus ... and here—this is the place of horror and evil that people talk about in the cities in fear and trembling—"the Amaliyah Centre," as this sixth centre is known, barren, black of fortune. ... And this is where the train goes, the rails laid by the human casualties, victims of hunger, disease.[58]

It was not unusual for half the men in units to desert on the way to the front.

Conditions were especially harsh on the Russian front, where many Iraqi Jews were sent in 1915 as a result of Enver's ill-fated offensive against the Russians in the Caucasus (December 1914–January 1915). As an ally of the Central Powers, the Ottoman Empire's role was to draw British and Russian troops away from the European front; but rather than take a defensive position against the Russians, as some of his German advisors recommended, in December 1914 Enver Pasha decided to unleash a winter offensive in the Caucasus designed to hold off a Russian advance into eastern Turkey and to destroy the Kars-Sarikamish and Tiflis railways. His plan required reinforcements for the Turkish Third Army, critically short of men, uniforms, equipment, ammunition, and horses, which now faced the Russian forces near Erzerum.[59] The men would come from the Thirteenth Corps from Mesopotamia, which was now deployed northward, stripping Iraq of regular troops. The division sent from Baghdad included many Jewish conscripts who, sent without adequate winter clothing, extra fuel, or food rations, would never return.[60]

Deployment to the Caucasus was difficult and complicated. The British estimated that it took between four and six weeks to get from Istanbul to the Palestinian front by rail and seven weeks to reach Mesopotamia. The route taken by the Thirteenth Corps from Mesopotamia on their way to the Caucasus and the Twelfth Corps in Syria conflicted as troops intersected with each other and crossed lines, delaying deployment northward.[61] In addition, the Ottoman Empire's fifty-seven hundred miles of single-track railroad had major gaps. This was due to the fact that the vaunted Berlin to Baghdad railway had never been completed, so that, for example, only the first twenty-five miles of rail north of Baghdad was operable.[62] The reinforcements sent from Baghdad had to travel by barge up the Tigris and Euphrates Rivers and then foot-march first into the Anatolian heartland and then through the eight-thousand-foot mountains, snowbound passes, and mountain ridges deep in snow in temperatures of –50°C. The railway connections between the fronts in the Caucasus and Europe were interrupted where they crossed the Taurus and Amanos mountain ranges, making it necessary to load and unload the trains four times. Everything—shells, including artillery shells, and sacks of fodder for the animals—had to be carried long distances over roads that were already in a state of disrepair when the war began and were steadily deteriorating under the heavy military traffic. Pack animals, especially camels, were in short supply, as Arabs were unwilling to sell them to the Turkish army unless paid in gold, so that a large portion of the supplies were carried on the backs of the men of the labor battalions who were also required to repair the roads and the railway lines. By February–March, the Thirty-Sixth Infantry Division arrived from Iraq; the Thirty-Seventh Infantry Division (part of the Thirteenth Corps) never arrived. [63]

Feeding and supplying the army was also a problem, although in theory the Arab provinces produced enough grain to support the local population and the armies on the Mesopotamian and Palestinian fronts. Even Syria had a grain surplus until the disastrous locust plague of 1915. But throughout the war, the Ottoman Empire exported grain to the Central Powers in exchange for arms despite its own manpower shortage, a situation that led to a reduction in crop harvest and a decline of 40 percent in the production of foodstuffs. Food supply also varied from location to location depending on transportation and proximity to grain-producing areas and the purchase of grain by the local commissariat. Troops in eastern Syria (Hawran), for example, had more food than troops in Nablus and Jaffa, while troops in eastern Anatolia on the Caucasus front suffered food shortages because of the Armenian genocide and deportations, which resulted not only in a lack of manpower but in the creation of an agricultural wasteland. Often when the men baked bread, they mixed the wheat with ground beans and barley. Troops were supposed to receive two hot meals per day of bulgur soup and meat stew (ox, sheep, or camel meat) depending on availability of animals, which were becoming scarce because of the lack of grazing for tens of thousands of animals and wood for fuel needed for cooking. The men supplemented their food rations with local fruits and vegetables—dates, figs, raisins, olives—but these, too, were not available to most, creating a serious problem of scurvy, which seems to have affected approximately 20 percent of the army. Generally, troops on the front lines fared better than those in garrison stations or communication duty or the civilian urban population.[64]

For soldiers in the Ottoman army, the lack of adequate food—complicated by the famine in Syria and inadequate clothing—made troops particularly susceptible to the diseases that killed 50 percent of those affected.

Malaria, typhus, typhoid, syphilis, cholera, and dysentery were rampant. Sanitation was minimal, a situation made worse by the lack not only of firewood, which hampered heating water, but also of basic medical supplies, which, like field hospitals and even physicians, were unavailable because of the British blockade that cut off all trade with the Ottoman Empire. As a result of the combined effects of cold, starvation, and typhus, of the ninety thousand troops of the Third Army who took part in the Caucasus campaign, only twelve thousand survived into spring.[65] It was estimated that fifty thousand men deserted in 1916 from the retreating Ottoman forces during a second Russian offensive and that seven times as many men died of illness as died of wounds during the war.[66] By December 1917 most units were operating at half strength due to casualties and desertion.

As word trickled back to Baghdad about the horrific conditions at the front, especially in the Caucasus, more and more Jews took advantage of opportunities to avoid being sent away. By 1916, as Ottomans needed more bureaucrats and extended military exemptions to top civil servants, judges, and lower civil servants, such as policemen and railway clerks, more men were needed to fill those positions.[67] These exemptions also applied to rabbis, cantors, judges, and religious officials. Others, if they could, found civilian jobs in the military or worked for the railroad, in hospitals or in supply.[68]

Knowledge of European languages became especially useful for service behind the front lines. Jewish reserve officers who were not deployed to the front and, even if they had in some cases been given commands[69] tended to be young men like Salman Shina, who had some secular education. Finishing the course of study at the Alliance school, Shina went on to the Turkish government school in 1913–14 as the only Jew in his class. With the outbreak of the war, he remained in Baghdad, where the Turks desperately needed translators in order to communicate with their German advisors, using French as the common language. Later, they would need men to read captured British documents or to interrogate British captives in the prisoner-of-war camps and hospitals who did not speak Arabic or Turkish.[70] Like Shina, these translators were often Jews who, having studied in the Alliance schools, knew French and English. In Mosul, the site of a Turkish prisoner-of-war camp for Allied detainees,[71] Salim Da'ud Semakh, who had studied in an Alliance school and was drafted as a "special soldier," went to work in Mosul first as a clerk and then for the military commander of Mosul, who had him translate for Allied prisoners at the POW camp. He received a letter of commendation for his work from Enver Pasha.[72]

Payment for exemption from military service was still possible, but it was becoming more challenging. The buyout, which had to be paid in gold, was an important revenue stream for the Ottoman government, so that as the price rose, the government forced civilians to use Turkish-issued paper money, which was steadily losing value, and removed gold from the local market.[73] At the beginning of the war, the cost was thirty Turkish pounds, a sum that many Baghdadi Jews could not afford and had to borrow;[74] in April 1915, it was fifty Turkish pounds at a time when the government tried to reduce the number of exempted males and even made Muslim foreign residents eligible for the draft, citing the Sultan's call for jihad. But even then men could pay as much as forty-five pounds.[75] It was estimated that some three thousand men in Baghdad had purchased exemption by paying forty-three gold pounds ($189.20 US gold in 1914) each, for a total of about $567,600 in gold.[76]

As a consequence of the terrible conditions, despite the heavy penalties, men deserted. In Mosul, men who hid in basements were typically discovered despite the fact that according to the law, officials had to be escorted by a member of the community, who could sound a warning in time for men to change their hiding places and go to surrounding villages. One, Salah ben-Yona, spent four years in different cellars. While in hiding, he learned shoemaking and sent shoes to government officials. The authorities learned of this graft by chance and assessed him the equivalent of sixty-five lira in paper money, because of inflation of the Turkish pound.[77]

Most deserters fled en route to the front, especially when passing close to home or village, roaming the countryside and living off the land. Some joined robber bands, causing problems for the army, which had to send troops to pacify them. By 1916, in Palestine and Syria, Bedouin were offered a reward of five Ottoman pounds for every deserter they brought in.[78] Desertion was even more dangerous because of likely attack by Arabs, Turks, or Persians, who thought that soldiers hid gold in their bellies.[79]

Jews fled to Persia, and many who were sent to Basra at the beginning of the war stayed there after the British occupation.[80] Others, like Salman Shina, who remained in Iraq during the initial hostilities translating for German air officers, one of whom flew strapped to the wing of his plane and dropped bombs on British positions in southern Iraq, headed south once the British moved north to Baghdad and the Turks began to retreat. Traveling downriver by boat, Shina surrendered to the British; but as a loyal Ottoman subject, he tells us that he did not translate for them.[81] Basra, which remained a destination for Iraqis seeking to evade service in the Ottoman army, grew to a Jewish wartime population of four to five thousand people.[82]

Impact of Mobilization on the Home Front

Baghdad was under martial law, and with the Ottoman Empire at war with Britain, a major Iraqi trading partner, commerce came to a standstill.[83] Merchants and those working in the commercial sector were hit hardest. For Jews, many of whom fell into this category either as large-scale importers or *bazaaris* on a smaller scale, the war had disastrous effects on individuals and the community as a whole. With trade routes closed, the prices of commodities soared, accompanied by inflation as the Turks forced the use of "valueless promissory notes" to compensate for goods and warehouses that were "requisitioned."[84] Jews, accused of hoarding goods and gold, were arrested, tortured, and executed when they tried to conserve the gold needed for payment in lieu of military service.[85]

Women and children left behind by the men who were either drafted, had fled, or were executed had to be supported by the community, which now suffered from double taxation: Jews contributed heavily to the Ottoman war effort in men and materiel and now had to support some six thousand destitute dependents, including three hundred orphans.[86] The food shortages and floods from the overflowing Tigris that compounded the hardship affecting Baghdad were followed by an epidemic of cholera that left sixty-two hundred Jews homeless.[87] The chief rabbi informed the American ambassador in Constantinople that out of a population of fifty thousand, ten thousand people needed aid and the Jewish community was unable to cope with the situation. The ambassador passed on the request to an American Jewish relief organization, the American Joint Distribution Committee, which began to provide assistance in 1918.[88]

As the Turks retreated in 1917, taking anything of value with them, the city of Baghdad was a pale reflection of its prewar bustle: "The streets of the inner town, through which it was hard to move in 1912," an eyewitness noted, "gaped emptily, the shops were mostly closed, the coffee houses only half filled. ... Groups of soldiers appeared occasionally here and there. ... There was no longer any life in the town, one of the busiest in the Orient."[89] Economic life was dead and public services ceased to exist.[90]

Throughout the war years, whether at the front or at home, the Jews of Baghdad suffered the deprivations of war, famine, and disease.[91] The Ottoman patriotism exhibited by young Westernized Jews that was generated by the Tanzimat and the secular Young Turk Revolution died with the war. Treated not as equal citizens of the empire, but once again as *dhimmi* minorities, Jews now placed their fate and faith in the West. Is it any wonder then that they eagerly awaited the British advance north from Basra and that when the British occupied Baghdad in March 1917, the Jewish community declared a *yom ha-nes,* a "holiday of deliverance"?[92] Only a decade or so later, as a result of the postwar dissolution of the Ottoman Empire and the creation of the British mandate of Iraq, the Baghdadi Jewish community reconstituted itself and was revitalized to become

Iraq's middle class and one of the most important Jewish communities in the Middle East.

Reeva S. Simon served as associate director of the Middle East Institute at Columbia University and was professor of history at Yeshiva University. Among her publications are *Iraq Between the Two World Wars: The Militarist Origins of Tyranny* and *Spies and Holy Wars: The Middle East in Twentieth Century Crime Fiction*. She also coauthored *Conflict, Conquest, and Conversion: Two Thousand Years of Christian Missions in the Middle East* and coedited *The Jews of the Middle East and North Africa in Modern Times*.

Notes

1. This study is based on British, German, and Turkish accounts of the war; British and US diplomatic archives; archives and histories of the Iraqi Jewish communities; interview transcripts; Iraqi memoirs; comparative studies of Jewish communal experience in Palestine, Turkey, and the Balkans; and literature.
2. Elie Kedourie, "The Jews of Baghdad in 1910," in *Arabic Political Memoirs and Other Studies* (London: Frank Cass, 1974), pp. 267–71.
3. On Jewish support for the Young Turks, see M. Sükrü Hanioglu, "Jews in the Young Turk Movement in the 1908 Revolution," in *The Jews of the Ottoman Empire*, ed. Avigdor Levy (Princeton, NJ: Darwin Press, 1994), pp. 519–26.
4. *Jewish Chronicle*, 16 July 1909.
5. Kedourie, "The Jews of Baghdad in 1910," p. 269.
6. Population figures for the Ottoman Empire as a whole were 75 percent Muslim, 21 percent Christian, and 4 percent Jewish (*Jewish Chronicle*, 28 June 1912). Kazzaz considers that the policy to reduce the number of Jews in the military academy was part of the Turkish conservative reaction in 1912 to the liberal Young Turk regime; Nissim Kazzaz, *The Jews in Iraq in the Twentieth Century* [Hebrew] (Jerusalem: Ben Zvi Institute, 1991), p. 87.
7. *Jewish Chronicle*, 28 June 1912; *American Jewish Yearbook* (1912–13), p. 184; (1913–14), p. 345. Gertrude Bell in *Amurath to Amurath* cites the number of Baghdad Jews interested as one hundred (Gertrude Lowthian Bell, *Amurath to Amurath: A Journey Along the Banks of the Euphrates* [London: Macmillan, 1924], p. 187), but Yosef Meir thinks that her number is too high; to his knowledge twenty Jews were admitted to the military high school in the first group (Yosef Meir, *Across the Desert* [Hebrew] [Tel-Aviv: Ma`arakhot, 1973], p. 14).
8. Records of the Oral History Collection, Institute for Contemporary Jewry, Hebrew University. Hayyim Shalom, one of the first Jews in military school, later an officer in the Iraqi police, did not finish because of health reasons.
9. Erik Jan Zürcher, "The Ottoman Conscription System, 1844–1914," *International Review of Social History* 43 (1998): 442. On the impact of cholera on Baghdad, see Paul Dumont, "Jews, Muslims, and Cholera: Intercommunal Relations in Baghdad at the

End of the Nineteenth Century," in *The Jews of the Ottoman Empire*, ed. Avigdor Levy (Princeton, NJ: Darwin Press, 1994), pp. 353–72.
10. David Ashkenazi, "Conscription of Jews in Istanbul in the Ottoman Army 1909–1910 as Seen through the Newspaper *el-Tiempo*" [Hebrew], *Pe'amim* 105–6 (2005): 202–3. Muslim religious functionaries and seminary students were also exempt from military service. It was reported that young Muslims went on pilgrimage to Mecca when threatened with military recruitment (Zürcher, "The Ottoman Conscription System," p. 444).
11. *Jewish Chronicle*, 16 July 1909; also published in the Istanbul Ladino newspaper *el-Tiempo* (Ashkenazi, "Conscription of Jews," pp. 203–4).
12. Michelle U. Campos, *Ottoman Brothers: Muslims, Christians, and Jews in Early Twentieth-Century Palestine* (Stanford, CA: Stanford University Press, 2011), p. 285, f. 77, citing the Hebrew newspaper *Ha-Herut* (23 November 1910; 14 December 1910). "On a few occasions the Moslem and Christian soldiers have messed together, which, the Chief of Staff says, is a great step forward"; quoted in Muhammad Gholi Majd, *Iraq in World War I: From Ottoman Rule to British Conquest* (Lanham, MD: University Press of America, 2006), p. 14. Majd's account of World War I is drawn primarily from US diplomatic dispatches and British studies of the Mesopotamian campaign.
13. *Jewish Chronicle*, 16 July 1909.
14. Zürcher, "The Ottoman Conscription System," p. 446.
15. Heskail Elkabir, "Memoirs" (Or Yehuda: Babylonian Jewry Heritage Center Archives), pp. 7, 21.
16. Notably Abraham El-Kabir. See Daphne Tsimchoni, "The Beginnings of Modernization among the Jews of Iraq in the Nineteenth Century until 1914" [Hebrew], *Pe'amim* 36 (1988): 7–34.
17. Great Britain, FO 371/560, Ramsay to Government, Baghdad, 19 October 1908. Nazim Pasha's opponents circulated a pamphlet detailing their opposition; see FO 424/224, Gerard Lowther to Sir Edward Grey, Constantinople, 21 September 1910.
18. See correspondence from A. Franco, AIU teacher, from Baghdad to Paris, 28 May 1909, on his advice to Jews not to be outspokenly in favor of the Young Turk regime, because of a backlash by Muslims against Jews and Christians; Archives of the AIU, Irak I.C.4, quoted in Aron Rodrigue, *Images of Sephardi and Eastern Jewries in Transition: The Teachers of the Alliance Israélite Universelle, 1860–1939* (Seattle: University of Washington Press, 1993), pp. 263–65.
19. FO 371/560, Ramsay to Government of India, forwarded to Sir Edward Grey, Baghdad, 19 October 1908.
20. A. S. Elkabir, "My Communal Life or Death of a Community" (Or Yehuda: Babylonian Jewry Heritage Center Archives), pp. 15–16.
21. Majd, *Iraq in World War I*, p. 14.
22. *Jewish Chronicle*, 15 April 1910.
23. Elkabir, "My Communal Life or Death of a Community," p. 15: "The Jews had to perform another national duty on a communal basis. The maintenance and consolidation of the lands surrounding Baghdad were undertaken by the local population. A certain part of the land ran along the Jewish quarters and it was the duty of the Chief Rabbi to provide the labour, materials, transport and other necessities when the district was threatened by flood from the overflowing Tigris. I have once seen the Chief Rabbi presiding over the operations from a tent planted in the neighbourhood and exhorting young men and children in their hard, sometimes dangerous work, often with no remuneration at all."

24. FO 371/1008, translation of Firman of appointment of Nazim Pasha, Civil and Military Governor of Baghdad, 30 November 1909.
25. Quoted in Majd, *Iraq in World War I*, p. 14. Beginning in 1882, German officers advised the Ottoman military; General Colmar von der Goltz restructured the Turkey army and standardized the organization; and German advisors remained through World War I. See Reeva Spector Simon, *Iraq Between the Two World Wars: The Militarist Origins of Tyranny* (New York: Columbia University Press, 2004), pp. 7–40.
26. Elkabir, "Memoirs," p. 75.
27. Eyal Ginio, "Mobilizing the Ottoman Nation during the Balkan Wars (1912–1913): Awakening from the Ottoman Dream," *War in History* 12 (2005): 161, 164.
28. Majd, *Iraq in World War I*, pp. 21–22.
29. Leyla Neyzi, "Trauma, Narrative and Silence: The Military Journal of a Jewish 'Soldier' in Turkey during the Greco-Turkish War," *Turcica* 35 (2003): 297.
30. Abraham Hayim Twena, *Jewry of Iraq: Dispersion and Liberation*, part 7 (Ramla: Geula Synagogue, 1979), p. 18.
31. Zürcher, "The Ottoman Conscription System," pp. 446–49.
32. Edward J. Erickson, *Ordered to Die: A History of the Ottoman Army in the First World War* (Westport, CT: Greenwood Press, 2001), pp. 7–11.
33. Ibid., p. 50.
34. Ibid., p. 7; Erik Jan Zürcher, "Between Death and Desertion: The Experience of the Ottoman Soldier in World War I," *Turcica* 28 (1996): 241. The goal of one million men was never reached. After deducting the number of men who could pay exemption tax, it was estimated that only three-quarters of the number of men called up for military service joined; the rest were rejected for reasons of health.
35. Majd, *Iraq in World War I*, pp. 52–53.
36. Twena, *Jewry of Iraq*, p. 18.
37. The Ottomans had a better idea of the number of non-Muslims eligible for conscription in Palestine than they did in Baghdad or Mosul. See Byron D. Cannon, "Local Demographic Patterns and Ottoman Military Conscription: A Preliminary Survey of the Hebron District in Palestine, 1914–17," in *The Middle East and North Africa: Essays in Honor of J. C. Hurewitz*, ed. Reeva S. Simon (New York: Columbia University Middle East Institute, 1990), pp. 43–70.
38. FO 371/2143, Telegram 11 August 1914.
39. Zürcher, "Between Death and Desertion," p. 242.
40. Isaac Bar-Moshe, *A House in Baghdad* [Hebrew] (Jerusalem: Sephardi Council of Jerusalem, 1982), pp. 6–7.
41. Yehuda (Gurg'i) Barshan, *A Jew under the Shadow of Islam: Reminiscences from Baghdad* [Hebrew] (Ramat Gan: Y. Barshan, 1997), pp. 14–27.
42. Twena, *Jewry of Iraq*, p. 19.
43. Barshan, *A Jew under the Shadow of Islam*, pp. 16–17; Alexander Aaronsohn, a Jew from Zichron Yaakov who signed up voluntarily, noted that although the Turkish uniforms were of conventional European cut with good boots, conscripts were given "old, discarded, and dirty" uniforms, the "clothes of some unknown Arab legionary, who, perhaps, had died of cholera at Mecca or Yemen." He and his Jewish colleagues bribed Turkish officers and purchased new uniforms. Bribing officers was also useful in changing sleeping arrangements from dilapidated mosques to hotel rooms. See Alexander Aaronsohn, *With the Turks in Palestine* (Boston: Houghton Mifflin, 1916), pp. 12, 17.

44. Zürcher, "Between Death and Desertion," pp. 247–48. See also A. J. Barker, *The First Iraq War 1914–1918: Britain's Mesopotamian Campaign* (New York: Enigma, 2009), p. 227.
45. Ibid., p. 247.
46. F. J. Moberly, *The Campaign in Mesopotamia, 1914–1918* (London: Imperial War Museum, 1997), p. 31; Barshan, *A Jew under the Shadow of Islam*, pp. 16–17.
47. Aaronsohn, *With the Turks in Palestine*, pp. 12–13.
48. Ibid., pp. 23–24.
49. Quoted in Majd, *Iraq in World War I*, p. 51.
50. Mustafa Aksakal, "'Holy War Made in Germany'? Ottoman Origins of the 1914 Jihad," *War in History* 18 (2011): 184–99.
51. Majd, *Iraq in World War I*, p. 21.
52. This was the British-supported rebellion led by Faisal, the son of Sherif Hussein of Mecca, and T. E. Lawrence.
53. Erickson, *Ordered to Die*, p. 69.
54. Yaron Harel, "The Importance of the Archive of the Hakham Bashi in Istanbul for the History of Ottoman Jewry," in *Frontiers of Ottoman Studies: State, Province, and the West*, ed. Colin Imber and Keiko Kiyotaki (London: I. B. Tauris, 2005), p. 262; Ezra Laniado, *The Jews of Mosul* [Hebrew] (Tirat Karmel: Be-hotsa'at ha-Makhon le-heker Yahadut Motsl, 1981), pp. 93, 95.
55. Erickson, *Ordered to Die*, p. 70; Laniado, *The Jews of Mosul*, p. 92.
56. Submitted by Meer Basri to *The Scribe* 72 (September 1999), http://www.dangoor.com/72frame.htm 11/19/10 //. See also Eliezer Tauber, *The Arab Movements in World War I* (London: Frank Cass, 1993), pp. 118–19; Ghassan R. Atiyyah, *Iraq 1908–1921: A Political Study* (Beirut: Arab Institute for Research and Publishing, 1973), p. 105.
57. Aaronsohn, *With the Turks in Palestine*, pp. 24–25.
58. Yehuda Burla, "The Soldier and the Ass" ("Hahayal vehapirda"), translation in Glenda Abramson, *Hebrew Writing of the First World War* (London: Vallentine Mitchell, 2008), p. 338.
59. Erickson, *Ordered to Die*, pp. 40–41.
60. Nir Shohat, *Story of Exile* [Hebrew] (Jerusalem: Ha-Agudah le-kidum ha-mehkar veha-yetsirah me-yesodam shel yots'e 'Irak be Yisra'el, 1981), p. 121; Mehmet Arif Olcen, *Vetluga Memoir: A Turkish Prisoner of War in Russia, 1916–1918* (Gainesville: University Press of Florida, 1995), pp. 14–19.
61. Erickson, *Ordered to Die*, pp. 43–47.
62. Majd, *Iraq in World War I*, p. 52.
63. Zürcher, "Between Death and Desertion," p. 251; Erik Jan Zürcher, "Ottoman Labour Battalion in World War I" (Leiden Project Working Papers Archive, 2002), no pagination.
64. In 1916 troops at the Dardanelles were issued nine hundred grams of bread daily, whereas in Mesopotamia in 1918, they were given three hundred grams (Zürcher, "Between Death and Desertion," pp. 248–51); L. Schatkowski Schilcher, "The Famine of 1915–1918 in Greater Syria," in *Problems of the Modern Middle East in Historical Perspective: Essays in Honour of Albert Hourani* (Reading: Ithaca Press, 1992). Aaronsohn notes that they had to purchase food, and if the troops were not paid, their rations were affected. When the government provided food, he ate boiled rice (Aaronsohn, *With the Turks in Palestine*, p. 11).
65. Erickson, *Ordered to Die*, pp. 52–60, 105–8. According to Olcen, nearly one-half (c. 45,000) of the men froze to death; Olcen, *Vetluga Memoir*, 26.

66. There are no exact figures for Turkish World War I casualties. According to British sources, 325,000 Ottoman soldiers were killed in action, and between 400,000 and 700,000 men were wounded. Of the wounded, approximately 60,000 died of their wounds. More than 400,000, or one-seventh of the armed forces, died of disease. Approximately 250,000 were missing or captive, and some 500,000 men deserted (Zürcher, "Between Death and Desertion," pp. 244–45, 254–57).
67. Zürcher, "The Ottoman Conscription System," p. 444.
68. Laniado, *The Jews of Mosul*, p. 93; Elkabir, "My Communal Life or Death of a Community," p. 16; Salman Shina, *From Babylonia to Zion* [Hebrew] (Tel Aviv: s.n., 1955), p. 18.
69. Shohat, *Story of Exile*, p. 123.
70. Shina, *From Babylonia to Zion*, pp. 12–13.
71. Majd, *Iraq in World War I*, p. 54.
72. Laniado, *The Jews of Mosul*, p. 96.
73. Ibid., p. 92.
74. Elkabir, "Memoirs," p. 7.
75. Zürcher, "Between Death and Desertion," p. 242.
76. Majd, *Iraq in World War I*, p. 376.
77. Laniado, *The Jews of Mosul*, pp. 93–94. Hiding rooms were a part of house construction in Baghdad. Some men found work in their hideouts and even prayed in a proper minyan; Twena, *Jewry of Iraq*, p. 19.
78. Zürcher, "Between Death and Desertion," pp. 245–46.
79. Barshan, *A Jew under the Shadow of Islam*, p. 28
80. Laniado, *The Jews of Mosul*, p. 93; Elkabir, "My Communal Life or Death of a Community," pp. 16, 88.
81. Shina, *From Babylonia to Zion*, pp. 12–24.
82. Hayyim J. Cohen, *The Jews of the Middle East 1860–1972* (Jerusalem: Israel Universities Press, 1973), p. 73.
83. FO 371/2143, 10 August 1914.
84. Elkabir, "My Communal Life," p. 88; Abraham Ben-Jacob, *A History of the Jews of Iraq* [Hebrew] (Jerusalem: Kiryat Sefer, 1965), p. 149.
85. Edmund Candler, *The Long Road to Baghdad* (London: Cassell, 1919), pp. 120–21. There were instances of Muslims paying the bail for Jews who were arrested; Twena, *Jewry of Iraq*, p. 19.
86. Records of the American Jewish Joint Distribution Committee (JDC) of the Years 1914–1918, Folder Mesopotamia, Baghdad, 1917–1919, Doc ID #7827, Letter from Ambassador Elkus, 4 April 1917.
87. Majd, *Iraq in World War I*, pp. 400–403.
88. JDC, Doc ID#7828. Copy of document sent to Washington. Oscar S. Neizer to Secretary of State, "Aid for Jews at Baghdad Sought," Baghdad, 4 April 1917; #7877, Letter from I. Bassam, 10 February 1918.
89. Quoted in Atiyyah, *Iraq 1908–1921*, pp. 95–96.
90. Stephen Hemsley Longrigg, *Iraq 1900 to 1950* (London: Oxford University Press, 1953), pp. 93–94.
91. After 1917, Mosul, cut off from Baghdad, underwent similar economic hardship. It was estimated that famine killed some eight thousand people. FO 371/4149 Mosul Division Report for November 1918.
92. Elkabir, "Memoirs," p. 132.

Selected Bibliography

Primary Sources

Aaronsohn, Alexander. *With the Turks in Palestine.* Boston: Houghton Mifflin, 1916.
Bar-Moshe, Isaac. *A House in Baghdad* [Hebrew]. Jerusalem: Sephardi Council of Jerusalem 1982.
Barshan, Yehuda. *A Jew under the Shadow of Islam: Reminiscences from Baghdad* [Hebrew]. Ramat Gan: Y. Barshan, 1997.
Elkabir, A. S. "My Communal Life or Death of a Community." Or Yehuda: Babylonian Jewry Heritage Center Archives.
Elkabir, Heskail. "Memoirs." Or Yehuda: Babylonian Jewry Heritage Center Archives.
Meir, Yosef. *Across the Desert* [Hebrew]. Tel Aviv: Ma'arakhot, 1973.
Shina, Salman. *From Babylonia to Zion* [Hebrew]. Tel Aviv, 1955.
Shohat, Nir. *Story of Exile* [Hebrew]. Jerusalem: Ha-Agudah le-kidum ha-mehkar vehayetsirah me-yesodam shel yots'e 'Irak be Yisra'el, 1981.

Secondary Sources

Erickson, Edward J. *Ordered to Die: A History of the Ottoman Army in the First World War.* Westport, CT: Greenwood Press, 2001.
Kedourie, Elie. "The Jews of Baghdad in 1910." In *Arabic Political Memoirs and Other Studies,* pp. 267–71. London: Frank Cass, 1974.
Laniado, Ezra. *The Jews of Mosul* [Hebrew]. Tirat Karmel: Be-hotsa'at ha-Makhon le-heker Yahadut Motsl, 1981.
Majd, Muhammad Gholi Majd. *Iraq in World War I: From Ottoman Rule to British Conquest.* Lanham, MD: University Press of America, 2006.
Moberly, F. J. *The Campaign in Mesopotamia, 1914–1918.* London: Imperial War Museum, 1997.
Twena, Abraham Hayim. *Jewry of Iraq: Dispersion and Liberation.* Part 7. Ramla: Geula Synagogue, 1979.
Zürcher, Erik Jan. "Between Death and Desertion: The Experience of the Ottoman Soldier in World War I." *Turcica* 28 (1996): 235–58.
———. "The Ottoman Conscription System, 1844–1914." *International Review of Social History* 43 (1998): 437–49.

CHAPTER 12

Unintentional Pluralists
Military Policy, Jewish Servicemen, and the Development of Tri-Faith America during World War I

Jessica Cooperman

In March 1918 Chester Teller, executive secretary of the National Jewish Welfare Board, spoke at the annual meeting of the Jewish Publication Society. It had been almost a year since the United States had entered World War I, the war effort was in full swing, and Teller spoke as the representative of the only Jewish agency in the country authorized by the War Department to provide for the spiritual, emotional, and moral welfare of the troops. Teller's message to his audience was filled with optimism, not just the war, but about the state of American democracy and the position of Jews in American society. He told his audience:

> We do the work of the larger American community when we remind them that America permits them to be Jews—nay, as we, want[s] them to be Jews for what they *as Jews* [italics in original] may contribute to the permanent culture-values of America in the making.... Thank God we understand now better than ever before what America means.... The democracy for which we are fighting now is not a democracy that merely tolerates distinctive culture values—it insists upon them. ... It challenges every man to be himself and to look to his neighbor likewise to be himself.[1]

Teller may have been overly optimistic in his assessment of the character of American democracy in the early twentieth century. The years following the war certainly did not see universal acceptance of the diversity he described. In fact, the interwar period was characterized, in many ways, by expressions of intolerance for "distinctive culture values" and hostility toward the people who brought them to American shores. In the 1920s immigration was restricted and restructured in an attempt to keep the country looking and behaving as it did in the 1890s, membership in racist and nativist organizations like the Ku Klux Klan grew, and political radicals were targeted by those who, in the wake of Communist revolutions and uprisings, grew increasingly scared of "Reds."[2] Jews were certainly not the only targets of racial, ethnic, and religious hostility in the years that followed World War I, but there is real evidence that Teller overestimated American society's willingness to see Jews as positive contributors to the culture and strength of the country.

It is certainly because of this well-documented evidence of interwar racism, nativism, and antisemitism that historians have at times turned to the experiences of World War II to explain how the United States eventually made the transition from a country that demanded "100 percent Americanism" of its citizens, to a country that embraced religious pluralism as a value inherent within American democracy. In recent years, scholars have looked at the lived experiences of men who served in the World War II American military and compellingly described the many ways that both the intensity of combat and the long boring hours of life on military bases helped them to build relationships that challenged, and eventually broke down, the prejudices they brought with them into the military. Civilian and military leaders did their parts as well, using educational programs and wartime propaganda to applaud cultural and religious—although not racial—diversity and to advocate for a sense of shared Americanism that unified men of different backgrounds.[3]

The impact of government and military policies enacted during World War I on this process of transformation is, however, often underestimated. Thomas Bruscino, in his study *A Nation Forged in War: How World War II Taught Americans to Get Along*, for example, notes the widespread presence of attitudes similar to Teller's among World War I American doughboys and military officials. Faced with evidence of the "wave of antiradical, anti-immigrant, anti-Semitic, and anti-Catholic feelings" that characterized the interwar period, however, Bruscino concludes that the American military experience of World War I was simply too small and too short to effectively root out deeply entrenched prejudices.[4]

In many ways, this is of course correct. Cultural and religious pluralism did not loom large in public discourse or popular culture in the interwar period, certainly not in comparison to the much more public campaigns for religious pluralism that emerged following World War II.[5] But as a result of World War I, new ideas about religious pluralism, and in particular about the place of Judaism in American society, became embedded within structures of the American military and within the expectations of at least some of the men who fought that war. These changes, while perhaps not big enough to hold back the wave of anti-immigrant, anti-Jewish sentiment that followed the armistice, made an impact nonetheless and became a crucial step toward America's transformation into what sociologist Will Herberg, writing in the 1950s, famously called a country of "Protestant, Catholic, and Jew."[6]

When the United States entered World War I, such a transformation was not obviously in the works. There is little indication that the US War Department intended to use the war as an opportunity to usher in a new age of religious pluralism. It did, however, intend to find a way to build a conscription military that could both fight and win the war and serve as a kind of laboratory in which the ideals of progressive era social engineering could be tried and measured. Perhaps the most well-known example of these wartime experiments was the IQ testing of nearly two million soldiers conducted under the auspices of the American Psychological Association; but there were many other ways that the military became a site for trying out new ideas about how best to assess, and hopefully improve, the behavior of American citizens.[7]

The secretary of war, Newton Baker, was particularly concerned with using the powers of the military to safeguard the morality of the men. Baker had risen to national prominence as an anti-vice crusader in Cleveland, Ohio, where he served as mayor. In Cleveland, Baker had used city government to offer alternatives to less "wholesome" forms of entertainment. He created well-lit, well-supervised, municipally owned dance halls to draw people away from private dance halls, which he believed overcharged and exposed young women to exploitation. He founded the Cleveland Symphony Orchestra to offer a family-friendly antidote to the lure of the saloon.[8] In his role as secretary of war, Baker intended to build structures and services within the military that would offer servicemen similarly wholesome options intended to keep them away from the temptations of alcohol and prostitution. As in Cleveland, Baker's program focused on both moralistic and pragmatic policies. He wished to promote what he saw as a morally upright atmosphere in American military camps, but he also knew that both venereal disease and alcohol poisoning had taken a heavy toll on Allied troops. Government reports noted that the French army had recorded a million cases of syphilis and gonorrhea since the start of the war.[9] In an era before the discovery of antibiotics, these infections proved devastating to military strength and to the morale and health of both the troops and their families on the home front. Baker wanted to assure Americans that their sons, brothers, and husbands would not meet a similar fate. In one of his more famous speeches, Secretary Baker proclaimed that he wanted to send American men into war armed to face more than just the Hun:

> I want them armed.... I want them to have an invisible armor to take with them. I want them to have an armor made up of a set of social habits and a state of social mind born in the training camps, a new soldier state of mind, so that when they get overseas and are removed from the reach of our comforting and restraining and helpful hand, they will have gotten such a set of habits as will constitute a moral and intellectual armor for their protection overseas.[10]

To forge this armor, Baker oversaw the creation of the Commission on Training Camp Activities (CTCA), which he charged with providing the sort of wholesome recreational programs for soldiers and sailors that he had sought to implement in Cleveland and that he believed would stave off the sort of "immoral" behaviors that threatened them overseas. As Baker insisted in his 1917 annual report to Congress, "The significant thing about a true civilization is its spontaneous upward tendency and the young American instinctively prefers sound and healthy occupations and recreations, if the opportunity to enjoy them be but offered."[11] The CTCA would, therefore, be placed in charge of offering young American men the sort of healthy recreations that Baker believed they longed for and deserved.

Running these programs was, however, a different matter. Neither the War Department nor the military had a staff ready to implement the sorts of soldiers' welfare services that Baker envisioned, and both had other concerns to attend to as the country geared up for war. The CTCA thus decided to turn to a civilian agency for help in crafting the invisible moral armor that American soldiers and sailors would carry with them to battle. With the blessings of President Wilson, who described its work as bearing "such a direct relation to efficiency, ... happiness, content, and morale of the personnel" that he was granting it official recognition "as a valuable adjunct and asset to the service,"[12] the CTCA handed the day-to-day job of caring for the moral well-being of American men to the civilian agency they felt was most suited to this type of work—the YMCA, or Young Men's Christian Association.

The choice of the YMCA reveals just how little concerned Baker and his colleagues were with religious pluralism. While the YMCA had experience working with American soldiers dating back to the Civil War, it was an avowedly Protestant organization that expressly prohibited the participation of Catholics on its War Council and described "the final test of ... [the Y secretary's] efficiency" as "how largely he is able to lead men, one by one, through his personal influence, through Bible classes and meetings as well as through the participation of the individual in service for others, to accept and follow Jesus Christ."[13]

Instead of a gesture toward greater pluralism, the selection of the YMCA demonstrates the extent to which Baker and others at the CTCA were blind to their own denominational biases. Raymond Fosdick, another Progressive reformer (and brother of Protestant theologian Harry Emerson Fosdick), who Baker appointed as chairman of the CTCA, insisted in his memoirs that "Baker and I had assumed—and I think that most of my associates on the Commission shared the assumption—that the approach of the YMCA to its work in the camps would be nonsectarian. We thought that it would represent an American contribution without relation to creed or any other divisive factor."[14] Fosdick's recollections sound sincere, but the idea that the YMCA, an evangelizing organization headed by general secretary John Mott, who is remembered among his many other accomplishments for his book entitled *The Evangelization of the World in this Generation,* would conduct a nonsectarian program "without relation to creed" seems far-fetched.[15] The YMCA had long used social, recreational, and particularly athletic programs as tools to help lead men to Christ.[16] The chance to minister to the more than four million young American men who served in the World War I American Expeditionary Forces represented an unparalleled opportunity to extend the association's mission. The YMCA was eager to seize such an opportunity and unequivocal in stating its objectives in the army and navy as "1. To lead men in Christ. 2. To keep professing Christians loyal to their Lord. 3. To relate all who come under the Association's influence to the principles and aims of the Kingdom of God."[17] By selecting the YMCA, Baker, Fosdick, and the CTCA made explicit what we might call the "invisible sectarianism" of their approach to caring for the moral and spiritual welfare of American servicemen. For while they insisted that soldiers' welfare programs were, in theory, to be entirely American in character, it proved difficult for them, in practice, to disentangle Americanism from Protestantism. They made it clear, moreover, that they understood the encouragement of sobriety and sexual restraint among American men not merely in terms of providing wholesome alternatives to the dance hall and the saloon, but also of religious guidance, instruction, and practice.

General John Pershing wholeheartedly agreed with this understanding of the needs of servicemen. Upon assuming command of the American Expeditionary Forces, Pershing demanded that the Chaplains Corps be reorganized and vastly expanded. In his memoirs he reflected:

> In recommending an increase in the number of chaplains, my reason was that I regarded the value of religious influence among our troops during the war as of special importance. Many temptations confronted our soldiers abroad and it seemed to me that the presence, the example, and the counsel of chaplains of the right sort would exert an excellent moral effect, especially among men without experience away from home.[18]

Pershing was no more interested in pluralism than his colleagues at the War Department. However once both military and civilian leaders explicitly tied the welfare of soldiers to the provision of religious counsel and access to religious services, they opened the door to arguments that *all* soldiers and sailors needed religion in order to serve their country and therefore that the religions of all of the men had something crucial to contribute to the American war effort. As Fosdick continued in his memoir:

> It was with real dismay, therefore, that I learned that the YMCA had no real Catholic representation on its newly formed War Work Council. My reaction was that it was an inadvertence, but I was told that the omission was "a necessity." ... Under the circumstances we seemed to have no choice, and we decided that the Knights of Columbus, a Catholic organization, whose application for admission to the camps was pending before our Commission, should be included in the program.[19]

In a conflict in which Catholic men were expected to comprise one-third of all American servicemen, it was not possible to leave them without the spiritual care that the War Department and General Pershing argued that they required and that Catholic organizations, like the Knights of Columbus, demanded that they have. Jews certainly composed a far smaller percentage of the US fighting forces, but with nearly 250,000 Jewish men serving in the US military, Fosdick's claim that the War Department had no choice but to provide for the moral and spiritual care of soldiers not represented under the YMCA came to have significant implications for the development of a more religiously pluralist military policy.[20]

The very existence of the Jewish Welfare Board, the organization that Chester Teller represented while delivering his rousing speech on the importance of diversity in American democracy, is itself evidence of how claims about the need for religion among the troops came to reshape policy. For while Baker had assumed that the YMCA would be the only civilian agency needed in order to build the invisible armor he wished to provide for the troops, Jewish and Catholic organizations rejected this assumption and seized the opportunity to assert that it was necessary to "help the morale of the army by preserving among our own men ethical and religious values and the finer aspects of personality."[21] Leaders of the Knights of Columbus called on their secretaries to make sure that "the Catholic identity and activity is not submerged" in the provision of welfare services, and stressed that "if the YMCA is conducting an Evangelical institute, it is very essential that we conduct a Catholic program."[22] Cyrus Adler, one of the founders of the Jewish Welfare Board, argued that in order to implement a new program of services designed to protect the moral welfare of the troops, it was necessary "to make adequate provision especially for the needs of soldiers and sailors of the Jewish faith, whose particular requirements could be fulfilled only by an understanding Jewish organization."²³ As it became clear that Jewish and Catholic men, or at least their self-appointed representatives, would not accept the guidance and counsel of the YMCA, provision had to be made for the appointment of Jewish and Catholic agencies to help forge the moral armor Baker desired. It was in this way that the Jewish Welfare Board and the Knights of Columbus came to stand alongside the YMCA as part of a triumvirate of government-sanctioned soldiers' welfare organizations—one Protestant, one Catholic, one Jewish.

The expanded military chaplaincy requested by General Pershing offers an even better example of how the perceived need to provide religious support to all servicemen created an unexpected path to pluralism. The American Jewish military chaplaincy had existed in theory since the Civil War, but because the selection of chaplains was dependent upon the religion of the majority of men in a regiment, and Jews never represented the majority, it remained impossible, in practice, to appoint a Jewish chaplain.²⁴ During World War I, however, with an unprecedented number of Jews in American military service, the Jewish Welfare Board pushed for legislation to create a mechanism for the appointment of chaplains at large, with a rank of lieutenant, who would serve minority religious groups not previously represented within the Chaplains Corps. The number of rabbis who served in an official capacity as chaplains during the war was not large in comparison to the number of chaplains overall. By the end of the war twenty-five rabbis had received commissions, and they served in a Chaplains Corps that had swelled from its prewar size of 146 to more than 2,000 men.²⁵ The percentage of Jewish chaplains was thus small—smaller than the percentage of Jewish soldiers, who composed around 5 percent of the military—but the policy changes that permitted rabbis to serve as chaplains and the impact this had on shaping both Jewish and non-Jewish expectations for American democracy were far from insignificant.

As part of their commission as chaplains-at-large, Jewish military chaplains counseled and preached to all American servicemen, not merely the Jewish ones. The ideas and values they expressed in their role as chaplain thus had a wide and potentially diverse audience of soldiers and sailors. At this time when the government and the military both agreed they were most in need of guidance, these young men might have been offered lessons like the one given by Chaplain Morris Lazaron, who urged the men to remember:

> You have worked, trained, served, suffered, sacrificed together! … You've eaten and lived with Mohammedan, Confucian, Buddhist, Catholic, Protestant and Jew. Haven't you found some good in all? … Think, each of you, of some pal you had who was Catholic, Jew or Protestant. It's the man that counts! … Break down the artificial barriers of ecclesiastical denomination! Demand that in the world you've saved for democracy, democracy be practiced!²⁶

The Jewish Welfare Board also sent Jewish chaplains suggestions for Shabbat sermons that emphasized the American nature of Judaism by connecting the stories of the Hebrew Bible with American history and American values. One memo, for example, suggested a quotation from Abraham Lincoln to help clarify the Torah portion *Chayye Sarah* ("The Life of Sarah"; Genesis 23:1–25:18) on the themes of duty and national idealism.[27] Another paralleled Abraham's migration from the land of his fathers to the story of Roger Williams and compared the sacrifice of Isaac, dubbed "Abraham's Quest of Pure Worship," to both the "implicit obedience" of the soldier and efforts to abolish child labor.[28] A sermon outline provided for the Torah portion *Toledoth* ("Generations"; Genesis 25:19–28:9) interpreted the conflict between Jacob and Esau as a useful device for explaining the global conflict in which the country fought, while reinforcing the Jew's commitment to American democratic ideals. The outline explained:

> Esau represents the element that craves for worldly power and domination, wielding the sword to attain it ... the very thing that the Teuton has typified with all the menace that that constitutes for the world, human liberty and civilization. Jacob on the other hand, stands for the ideals that the Allied nations have made their own, the love of truth and justice, the securing of peace for all the world, the extending of the blessings of freedom to all nations. These are the very ideals to which the Jew has always been committed.... The Kaiser-ridden Prussian hordes have not availed against the idealism, the love of freedom, reverence for moral standards, respect for the rights and liberties of mankind, which animate altruistic humanitarian, noble America and her Allies.[29]

In each of these suggestions, the Jewish Welfare Board sought to shape the type of Judaism presented in American military camps and the image of Jews reflected in the religious services and programs held in the military. The connection between Judaism, patriotism, and American democracy was central to this effort. In addition to sermon suggestions that linked Judaism to America and American history, the Jewish Welfare Board distributed pamphlets for the soldiers that reinforced this connection and even suggested that Judaism provided the model for American democracy. The pamphlet entitled *Golden Rule Hillel* paralleled the life of the Jewish sage Rabbi Hillel with that of Abraham Lincoln and drew a connection between Hillel's legal rulings and the development of American law and democracy:

> Poor and proud, Hillel supported himself by manual labor while he was securing his education. Like Abraham Lincoln, he was a woodchopper.... Hillel's career is a shining example of the democratic principle which has always prevailed in Jewish life, of the opportunity open to all men of talents, however humble their origin, to achieve position in the republic of Jewish learning.... Some of his innovations

anticipate in a striking way the developments under similar circumstances of the common law of England and the United States many centuries later.³⁰

Through sermons, pamphlets, and the simple presence of rabbis on military bases, in military hospitals, and with the army on the Western front, the presence of both Jews and Judaism within the structure of the American military was normalized, and an opportunity was created for instructing non-Jewish Americans about the values they shared with their Jewish compatriots. Jewish chaplains, as officially recognized representatives of Judaism in the military, were able to project an image of Jews serving side by side with their Protestant and Catholic countrymen and of Judaism as a crucial component of the United States' religious heritage and spiritual strength.

Stories about Jewish chaplains also reached beyond the front and the military base. Newspapers at home carried stories about rabbis in the service, thus extending the reach of their message of shared values and cooperation between American Protestants, Catholics, and Jews. Chaplain Elkan Voorsanger, the "fighting rabbi of the New York Seventy-Seventh Division," was interviewed for an article in the *New York Times* entitled "A Fighting Rabbi: Captain Voorsanger Went to France as a Buck Private and Found Religion Drew No Lines." In the article, Voorsanger described Yom Kippur services in France: "In France there were no distinctions.... A Chaplain was a Chaplain, not a Jewish Chaplain, a Catholic Chaplain, or a Protestant Chaplain. Each Chaplain was responsible for the religion of every man, and it didn't matter to us how a man prayed, but that he prayed. A Catholic Chaplain organized Yom Kippur services for the Jewish men," Voorsanger explained. Voorsanger had been delayed in his arrival for holiday services. When he arrived at the abandoned cathedral where the men were gathered, the Catholic chaplain came out to meet him. "I was afraid you wouldn't get here," the Catholic chaplain said, "I got your men together and started them off with a prayer. We had arranged to conduct services ourselves in case you didn't come." Voorsanger continued, "I took up the services where he had left off, and after the traditional prayers were over and we had given them a brief soldierly talk, the men filed out of the cathedral and went on with the business of fighting."³¹

The words of chaplains like Voorsanger and others were clearly didactic. They were intended to educate audiences of Jews and non-Jews, soldiers and citizens, in the lesson of pluralism and the shared values of Jews and Christians. They urged all Americans to show their patriotism and honor the sacrifices made by servicemen by setting aside prejudice and embracing a more democratic future, in which Protestants, Catholics, and Jews worked together as friends and equals. Not all readers and listeners were inspired by these sentiments. Both Secretary Baker and Raymond

Fosdick at the CTCA remained skeptical about the benefits of allowing Catholic and Jewish participation in the country's soldiers' welfare programs. In much of his communication with the Jewish Welfare Board, Fosdick stood by the position that the YMCA offered "an American contribution without relation to creed or any other divisive factor,"[32] but that the presence of Catholic and Jewish soldiers' welfare agencies provided only "sectarian representation,"[33] which could be detrimental to the unity among the troops. By the end of the war, both Fosdick and Baker argued in internal documents and memoranda that the presence not only of the Knights of Columbus and the Jewish Welfare Board, but even of the YMCA had hindered the development of a "spirit of cohesion and unity" among the men by emphasizing the distinct presence of Protestants, Catholics, and Jews in the military. Secretary Baker wrote:

> The Welfare Societies, here under consideration, are all of them admittedly and professedly based upon religious distinctions. Their very presence, therefore; their insignia; their literature; their songs, and the bais [sic] of their representatives lead to a constant emphasis being placed upon religious differences among the soldiers and tend not to bring about a unity of feeling in recreational association but segregation into religious groups. This, I believe, to be an unfortunate influence among the young men in the camps.[34]

Fosdick, in his report to Baker on the activities of the various civilian welfare agencies, put the matter even more bluntly. He wrote, "I have come increasingly to the belief, in two years of intimate association with this work, that the sectarian basis underlying much of it is fundamentally wrong.... Sectarian stratification is the worst possible basis for social work with the Army."[35]

Sectarian stratification may have seemed counterproductive to Baker and Fosdick, but to American Jews and Catholics it offered a powerful response to the "invisible sectarianism" that had guided government policy at the start of the war. Insisting on the distinctive religious needs of Jewish and Catholic soldiers and sailors was far preferable to the unrestricted ministrations of the YMCA or the assumption that Americanism was synonymous with Protestantism. The work of the Knights of Columbus and the Jewish Welfare Board and the service of Jewish and Catholic chaplains may have emphasized the presence of three distinct religious traditions in the army and navy, but to them, this was not an undesirable goal. By taking advantage of the War Department's decision to empower the YMCA to protect the morals of American servicemen, Jews and Catholics managed to assert the necessity of their equal inclusion, alongside Protestants, in the religious life of the US military.

Through this achievement in military policy, even those skeptical about tri-faith collaboration and religious pluralism encountered these ideas again and again via the military chaplaincy, postwar commemorations, and the work of new agencies that emerged in the postwar period. Raymond Fosdick may have lamented the necessity of organizing soldiers' welfare programs around three sectarian organizations in his internal communications, but following the armistice, in public postwar celebrations, he had little choice but to applaud the accomplishments of his commission and its civilian partners. Speaking before the annual meeting of the Jewish Welfare Board just after the war's end, Fosdick stressed the triumph of tri-faith cooperation and touted the Americanness of each of the faiths that had cooperated in the project of providing soldiers' welfare services. He told his audience:

> I know that some of you here have had the privilege of going up in an aeroplane and you know just exactly how the ground recedes as the machine rises and how the details and unimportant things tend to disappear. You know that as you get higher the fundamental things become very plain, but the fences all disappear. I can't help thinking that that has been the result of this work in connection with these three great organizations—the fences have disappeared, the sectarian lines have vanished, and this work that has been carried on has not been carried on as Jewish work or Protestant work or Catholic work; it has been fundamentally an American work carried on for all the troops in the camps without regard to faith.[36]

Fosdick may have simply been putting on a cheerful face in front of a room of men and women who had contributed to his wartime programs, but the message of post–World War I religious pluralism had other supporters as well. Although the years following the war witnessed a rise in both anti-Catholicism and antisemitism, they also saw the establishment of the National Conference of Christians and Jews, an organization founded in 1928 to "promote justice, amity, and cooperation among Protestants, Catholics, and Jews"[37] and organized through collaborative efforts of co-chairmen from each of the different faiths represented, including the by then former secretary of war Newton Baker, who served as the first Protestant co-chair. Rabbi Voorsanger continued to work for the Jewish Welfare Board, serving as overseas director after World War I and as chaplaincy commissioner during World War II.[38] Rabbi Lazaron remained in the Army Officers' Reserve Corps until 1953. He represented American Jews as one of four officiating chaplains at the burial of the Unknown Soldier in Arlington National Cemetery in 1921. He also helped to found the Military Chaplains Association, which focused on interfaith cooperation among chaplains, and like Secretary Baker, he became involved with the work of the National Conference of Christians and Jews, touring the country with a Catholic priest and Protestant minister to promote interfaith dialogue.[39]

Beyond all this, however, the lasting impact of these World War I discussions of pluralism can be seen in the structure of the US military and in programs sanctioned and sponsored by the government for the welfare of American servicemen. When the United States geared up for World War II, there was no need to debate whether Jewish soldiers would require the guidance of what Cyrus Adler has called "an understanding Jewish organization" as part of the country's plans to provide for the spiritual well-being of the troops. Instead, the Jewish Welfare Board, the YMCA, and the National Catholic Community Service together helped to build the United Service Organization (USO) and worked as Protestant, Catholic, and Jew under its umbrella.[40] Nor was there any need to contemplate whether and by what means rabbis could be commissioned as chaplains. The mechanisms for these appointments were already in place, and 311 rabbis received commissions as World War II American military chaplains.[41] Both of these policies had become part of the business of organizing and running a conscription military, and through them religious pluralism became part of the training of soldiers and the patriotic rhetoric of American democracy.

It may be the case that it was only during the United States' more extensive military engagement in World War II that ideas about religious pluralism and the equal partnership of Protestant, Catholic, and Jew became part of public discourse and American popular culture, but it is worth noting that this shift was facilitated in no small part by the meaningful changes to government and military policy made during World War I. This dynamic should remind us to consider the connections not just between these two world wars, but between public sentiment and government policy—and not necessarily policies intended to shift public opinion. The insertion of religion into strategic decisions about how to build a more efficient and morally upright American military reflected a lack of interest in religious pluralism rather than an attempt to instill it among the troops. Nonetheless once these policy changes were made, their implications for American understandings of religion, democracy, and pluralism became very real. The porous nature of the boundary between religion and the policies guiding soldiers' welfare programs during World War I allowed claims about America as a country of three faiths to seep into the structures of the American military and the policies by which it ran. Through this process, the US government gradually, and sometimes reluctantly, relinquished the "invisible sectarianism" that had led men like Baker and Fosdick to see Protestantism as synonymous with Americanism and came to endorse, and even embrace, new notions of American religious pluralism and the tri-faith partnership between Protestant, Catholic, and Jew.

Jessica Cooperman is the director of Jewish studies and assistant professor of religion studies at Muhlenberg College. Her book *Making Judaism Safe for America: World War I and the Origins of Religious Pluralism* is forthcoming with New York University Press. Her other research interests include American-Jewish education in the interwar period and interfaith movements in postwar America.

Notes

1. From *The Jewish Welfare Board*, a published version of an address given by Chester Teller at the Thirty-First Annual Meeting of the Jewish Publication Society of America, 24 March 1918, p. 4.
2. On some of the tensions of the "tribal twenties," see John Higham, *Strangers in the Land: Patterns of American Nativism, 1860–1925* (New Brunswick, NJ: Rutgers University Press, 1994); Nancy McKean, *Behind the Mask of Chivalry: The Making of the Second Ku Klux Klan* (New York: Oxford University Press, 1995); Victoria Saker Woeste, *Henry Ford's War on Jews and the Legal Battle against Hate Speech* (Stanford, CA: Stanford University Press, 2013); and Gary Gerstle, *American Crucible: Race and Nation in the Twentieth Century* (Princeton, NJ: Princeton University Press, 2001), chapter 3.
3. On the experiences of US soldiers, see Thomas Bruscino, *A Nation Forged in War: How World War II Taught Americans to Get Along* (Knoxville: University of Tennessee Press, 2010); Deborah Dash Moore, *GI Jews: How World War II Changed a Generation* (Cambridge, MA: Belknap Press of Harvard University Press, 2004); Deborah Dash Moore, "Jewish GIs and the Creation of the Judeo-Christian Tradition," in *Religion and American Culture: A Journal of Interpretation* 8, no. 1 (Winter 1998): 31–53. On military and civilian programs designed to promote "tri-faith goodwill" during the war, see Kevin Schultz, *Tri-Faith America: How Catholics and Jews Held Postwar America to Its Protestant Promise* (New York: Oxford University Press, 2011), pp. 43–67.
4. Bruscino, *A Nation Forged in War*, pp. 47–55.
5. For some examples of scholarship on this topic, see Schultz, *Tri-Faith America*; Marc Dollinger, *The Quest for Inclusion: Jews and Liberalism in Modern America* (Princeton, NJ: Princeton University Press, 2000); Lila Corwin Berman, *Speaking of Jews: Rabbis, Intellectuals, and the Creation of an American Public Identity* (Berkeley: University of California Press, 2009); Stuart Svonkin, *Jews against Prejudice: American Jews and the Fight for Civil Liberties* (New York: Columbia University Press, 1997); and Matthew Headstrom, *The Rise of Liberal Religion: Book Culture and American Spirituality in the Twentieth Century* (New York: Oxford University Press, 2015).
6. Will Herberg, *Protestant, Catholic, and Jew: An Essay in American Religious Sociology* (Chicago: University of Chicago Press, 1983).
7. On IQ testing, see Stephen Jay Gould, *The Mismeasure of Man* (New York: W. W. Norton, 1981). On other types of social experiments, see, for examples, Jennifer Keene, *Doughboys: The Great War and the Remaking of America* (Baltimore: Johns Hopkins University Press, 2001); Nancy Bristow, *Making Men Moral: Social Engineering during the Great War* (New York: New York University Press, 1996); Nancy Gentile Ford,

Americans All! Foreign-Born Soldiers in World War I (College Station, TX: Texas A&M University Press, 2001); and Christopher Capozzola, *Uncle Sam Wants You: World War I and the Making of the Modern American Citizen* (New York: Oxford University Press, 2010).

8. See Douglas B. Craig, *Progressives at War: William G. McAdoo and Newton D. Baker, 1863–1941* (Baltimore: Johns Hopkins University Press, 2013), pp. 57–58. For more on Baker, see Daniel R. Beaver, *Newton D. Baker and the American War Effort, 1917–1919* (Lincoln: University of Nebraska Press, 1966).

9. Craig, *Progressives at War,* p. 163. For more information on venereal disease in the World War I military and the battle against it, see Donald Smythe, "Venereal Disease: The AEF's Experience," *Prologue* 9, no. 2 (1977): 65–74; Fred Baldwin, "Invisible Armor," *American Quarterly* 16, no. 3 (1964): 432–44; and Alan Brandt, *No Magic Bullet* (New York: Oxford University Press, 1987).

10. From Baker's speech "Invisible Armor," printed in his *Frontiers of Freedom* (New York: George H. Doran, 1918), pp. 94–95.

11. Quoted in Beaver, *Newton D. Baker and the American War Effort,* p. 221.

12. John Mott, "The War Work of the Young Men's Christian Associations of the United States," *Annals of the Academy of Political and Social Science* 79, "War Relief Work" (September 1918): 204.

13. Raymond Fosdick, *Strictly Confidential Report on Non-military Organizations Serving with the AEF* (Washington DC: CTCA, 27 July 1918), p. 25.

14. Raymond Fosdick, *Chronicles of a Generation: An Autobiography* (New York: Harper & Brothers, 1958), p. 149. According to an editorial by B'nai B'rith president George Fox printed in the *Jewish Monitor* of Fort Worth, Texas, both Catholics and Jews were also rejected as YMCA workers. See *Jewish Monitor,* September 1918, in General Correspondence 1917–1920, Records of the War Department General and Special Staffs, RG-165, National Archives and Records Administration, College Park, MD.

15. The book was published by the Student Volunteer Movement for Foreign Missions in 1905. Mott received the Nobel Peace Prize in 1946 for promoting religious brotherhood across national borders (according to the Nobel Prize Foundation). For a biography of Mott, see Howard Hopkins, *John R. Mott 1865–1955: A Biography* (Grand Rapids, MI: Eerdmans, 1979).

16. See Gustav Wrathall, *Take the Young Stranger by the Hand: Same Sex Relationships and the YMCA* (Chicago: University of Chicago Press, 1998); Thomas Winters, *Making Men Making Class: The YMCA and Working Men 1877–1920* (Chicago: University of Chicago Press, 2002). For the definitive history of the YMCA, see Howard Hopkins, *The History of the YMCA in North America* (New York: Association Press, 1951). On the connections between evangelical Christianity and physical fitness, see Tony Ladd, *Muscular Christianity: Evangelical Protestants and the Development of American Sport* (Grand Rapids, MI: Baker Books, 1999); Clifford Putney, *Muscular Christianity: Manhood and Sports in Protestant America, 1880–1920* (Cambridge, MA: Harvard University Press, 2001); Alexandra Lord, "Models of Masculinity: Sex Education, the United States Public Health Service, and the YMCA, 1919–1924," *Journal of the History of Medicine* 58 (April 2003): 123–58.

17. William H. Taft and Frederick Morgan Harris, *Service with Fighting Men: An Account of the Work of the Young Men's Christian Associations in the World War* (New York: Association Press, 1933), pp. 297–98.

18. General John J. Pershing, *My Experiences in the World War,* vol. 1 (New York: Frederick A. Stokes, 1931), p. 284. For histories of the US military chaplaincy during this pe-

riod, see Richard Budd, *Serving Two Masters: The Development of the American Military Chaplaincy, 1860–1920* (Lincoln: University of Nebraska Press, 2002), particularly chapters 5–6, pp. 92–155. See also John Piper, "American Churches in World War I," *Journal of the American Academy of Religion* 38, no. 2 (June 1970): 147–55; and Earl F. Stover, *Up from Handymen: The United States Army Chaplaincy 1865–1920* (Washington DC: Office of the Chief of Chaplains, Department of the Army, 1978). For a more recent discussion of the institution of the military chaplaincy and religious pluralism, see Ronit Stahl, "God, War, and Politics: The American Military Chaplaincy and the Making of a Multi-Religious Nation" (PhD dissertation, University of Michigan, 2014).
19. Fosdick, *Chronicles of a Generation,* p. 149.
20. *The War Report of American Jews: The First Report of Office of War Records,* published by the American Jewish Committee in 1919, estimated that between 150,000 and 200,000 Jewish men served in the US Armed Forces in World War I. These figures were repeated in later reports, including *Jews in the World War: A Study in Jewish Patriotism and Heroism* (New York: Jewish War Veterans, 1941); and J. George Fredman and Louis Falk, *Jews in American Wars* (New York: Jewish War Veterans of the United States of America, 1942). Louis Barish's *Rabbis in Uniform: The Story of the American Military Chaplaincy* (New York: Jonathan David, 1962) claims that there were approximately 250,000 Jewish-American soldiers in the American Expeditionary Forces (p. 10). Albert Isaac Slomovitz, in *The Fighting Rabbis: Jewish Military Chaplains and American History* (New York: New York University Press, 1999), also cites this number (p. 54).
21. *American Jewish Chronicle,* 13 September 1918, article by David de Sola Pool.
22. Christopher Kauffman, *Faith and Fraternalism: The History of the Knights of Columbus, 1882–1982* (New York: Harper & Row, 1982), pp. 209, 211.
23. *Jewish Welfare Board, Final Report of War Emergency Activities* (New York, 1920), p. 13.
24. For a history of the Jewish military chaplaincy, see Slomovitz, *The Fighting Rabbis.*
25. See Richard Budd, *Serving Two Masters: The Development of American Military Chaplaincy, 1860–1920* (Lincoln: University of Nebraska Press, 2002), p. 124.
26. A meditation entitled "What Has It Meant to You?" from Morris Lazaron, *Side Arms: Readings, Prayers and Meditations for Soldiers and Sailors* (Baltimore: Lord Baltimore Press, 1918), pp. 33–34.
27. "Sermon Suggestions for Sabbath *Chayye Sarah,*" 2 November 1918, American Jewish Historical Society, P-58, Box 1, Folder "JWB 1918-1919."
28. "Comments on *Sedra Veyera,*" 26 October 1918, American Jewish Historical Society, P-58, Box 1, Folder "JWB 1918-1919."
29. "Sermon Outline for Shabbat *Toledoth,* 9 November 1918, Esau and Jacob—Character Types," American Jewish Historical Society, P-58, Box 1, Folder "JWB 1918-1919."
30. Rabbi Moses Hyamson, *"Golden Rule" Hillel* (New York: Jewish Welfare Board, 1918), pp. 1–5.
31. *New York Times,* 12 October 1919.
32. Fosdick, *Chronicles of a Generation,* p. 149.
33. Letter from Fosdick to Cutler, 29 September 1917, American Jewish Historical Society, I-180, Box 343, folder "War Department 1917–1920" (no. 1 of 2).
34. Letter from secretary of war Newton Baker, published in the War Department Circular No. 507, 8 November 1919, Seeley Mudd Manuscript Library, Raymond Fosdick Papers, MC-055, Box 24, Folder 7. See also the "Memorandum and American War-Work Agencies and Their Co-Ordination" in the same collection, Box 24, Folder 6.

35. Raymond Fosdick, *Report to the Secretary of War on the Activities of Welfare Organization Serving with the A.E.F.* (n.d.), pp. 10–11.
36. Raymond Fosdick's address to the JWB Annual Meeting, *JWB First Annual Report* (New York, 1919), p. 12.
37. "The Purpose and Program of the National Conference of Christians and Jews," *Journal of Educational Sociology* 16, no. 6, "United We'll Stand" (February 1943): 324–26.
38. See obituaries for Rabbi Voorsanger in the *New York Times* (p. 31) and *Milwaukee Journal* (p. 14) from 3 May 1963.
39. "Biographical Sketch," Morris S. Lazaron Papers, Manuscript Collection No. 71, American Jewish Archives. See also Schultz, *Tri-Faith America*, pp. 35–41.
40. Frank L. Weil, "USO—Its Origin, History and Significance," 31 May 1943, American Jewish Historical Society, I-337, Box 43, Folder "Addresses: 1940-1957."
41. Slomovitz, *The Fighting Rabbis*, p. 75.

Selected Bibliography

Bristow, Nancy. *Making Men Moral: Social Engineering during the Great War.* New York: New York University Press, 1996.

Bruscino, Thomas. *A Nation Forged in War: How World War II Taught Americans to Get Along.* Knoxville: University of Tennessee Press, 2010.

Capozzola, Christopher. *Uncle Sam Wants You: World War I and the Making of the Modern American Citizen.* New York: Oxford University Press, 2010.

Craig, Douglas B. *Progressives at War: William G. McAdoo and Newton D. Baker, 1863–1941.* Baltimore: Johns Hopkins University Press, 2013.

Dawley, Alan. *Changing the World: American Progressives in War and Revolution.* Princeton, NJ: Princeton University Press, 2003.

Ebel, Jonathan. *Faith in the Fight: Religion and the American Soldier in the Great War.* Princeton, NJ: Princeton University Press, 2010.

Gentile Ford, Nancy. *Americans All! Foreign-Born Soldiers in World War I.* College Station, TX: Texas A&M University Press, 2001.

Keene, Jennifer. *Doughboys: The Great War and the Remaking of America.* Baltimore: Johns Hopkins University Press, 2001.

Moore, Deborah Dash. *GI Jews: How World War II Changed a Generation.* Cambridge, MA: Harvard University Press, 2004.

Penslar, Derek J. *Jews and the Military: A History.* Princeton, NJ: Princeton University Press, 2013.

Schultz, Kevin. *Tri-Faith America: How Catholics and Jews Held Postwar America to its Protestant Promise.* New York: Oxford University Press, 2011.

Slomovitz, Albert Isaac. *The Fighting Rabbis: Jewish Military Chaplains and American History.* New York: New York University Press, 1999.

CHAPTER 13

American Yiddish Socialists at the Wartime Crossroads
Patriotism and Nationalism versus Proletarian Internationalism

Gennady Estraikh

The ideology of the New York Yiddish daily *Forverts* (Forward) has a unique place in the spectrum of Jewish socialist beliefs and ideals. In its early period, that is at the turn of the twentieth century, this ideology, or Forvertsism (as it was sometimes called), developed under the strong influence of German and Russian Marxism. Any symptoms of Jewish nationalism were taboo, even shameful in those years. Change began in 1903, when Abraham Cahan, one of the founders of the newspaper, returned to its helm after several hiatuses and remained the editor in chief until his death in 1951. He defined to a significant degree the nature of Forvertsism. A man of huge ambitions, Cahan was determined to transcend the relatively narrow circle of committed socialists and run a newspaper for a mass readership. Among other things (notably choosing a style accessible to the audience composed predominantly of scantily educated speakers of different Yiddish dialects), Cahan's strategy implied the application to the newspaper's content the populist-cum-nationalist criteria "is it good or bad for the Jews?" This was only partially a purely pragmatic turn. To all appearances, Cahan sincerely assumed that an alloy of socialism and mild nationalism was what the Jewish masses needed. As this essay aims to show, wartime developments and debates contributed to make Jewish nationalism—in the form of anti-assimilationism and cross-class ethnic solidarity—more pronounced in the ideology of the *Forverts*.

Figure 13.1. *Abraham Cahan. Courtesy of the* Forverts *Archive.*

The Collapse of the Socialist International

In 1912, when the Jewish (in fact Yiddish-language) Socialist Federation (JSF) was formed at a convention held in Patterson, New Jersey, the Socialist Party of America (SPA) allowed foreign-language federations to act as autonomous subsections whose members simultaneously belonged to the broader socialist community of full-right party card-carriers.[1] This was the time when, following the defeat of the 1905 revolution, hundreds of Jewish socialists, notably Bundists, left Russia and settled in the United States, reinforcing and transforming the Jewish constituent of the American socialist movement. For all that, the JSF, the third largest federation (after the Finish and German ones) in the party, had grouped only a minority of Yiddish speakers of various non-Zionist socialist persuasions. Jacob Benjamin (Yankev) Salutsky, secretary general of the JSF, found it painful to realize that many of his Bundist comrades had chosen not to join the federation. Yet although the JSF had rather modest membership numbers—less than 2,000 in 1913, about 5,000 in 1915, and 6,000 in 1916—Salutsky and his like comforted themselves with the thought that it played a vital role as an incubator, powerhouse, and network for activists.[2]

Belonging to the broad socialist movement was an important element of the JSF members' ideological outlook. They were proud to be part of the Socialist (or Second) International, which, since its establishment in Paris in July 1889, had functioned as an alliance of socialist parties that by 1914 boasted a total membership of over two million people and 811 representatives in European parliaments. The German and French social democrats formed particularly strong parliamentary factions—over one-fourth of seats in the German Reichstag and over one-sixth of seats in the French Chambers of Deputies.[3] However, the final session of the International Socialist Bureau held at Brussels on 29 July 1914 and its strongly worded call to intensify efforts against the war became, in effect, the last sigh of the Socialist International. Moreover, the famous final phrase of Marx and Engels's 1848 *Communist Manifesto,* "Proletarian of all countries, unite!" (which appeared on the front page of every *Forverts* issue: "Arbeter fun ale lender, fareynikt aykh"), turned into an empty slogan on 4 August 1914, when social democratic deputies in Germany and France voted for war credits and by that vote aligned themselves with their bellicose governments. This and similar manifestations of socialists' flag-waving in Belgium, Great Britain, and Austria-Hungary had undermined one more postulate of the manifesto: "The workers have no fatherland."[4] In mid-September 1914, the leadership of the SPA sent a cable to Western European socialist party officials urging them to "exert every influence on their respective governments to have warring countries accept mediation by the United States." It was a cry in the desert.[5]

The belatedness of the entry of United States into the war allowed SPA members to be forthright in supporting a pacifist viewpoint or in expressing partial sympathy without risking censorship from their leadership or the government. Thus, Salutsky rejected unqualifiedly the party leadership's pacifist slogans because he, arguably in unison with the majority of his comrades, believed that the war, despite its attendant horror, would bring revolutionary transformations in such countries as Russia and Germany.[6] As immigrants from Russia, members of the JSF had serious grievances against the Russian regime and could not be neutral in their emotions, even if their party leadership claimed impartiality. The Yiddish socialist press, including its flagship daily *Forverts,* established in 1897, always paid special attention to exposing the anti-Jewish policy of the Russian imperial regime. In the fall of 1913, for example, the *Forverts* editors both stimulated and satisfied their readers' interest by allocating up to half of the newspaper space to coverage of the blood libel trial of the Kiev Jewish resident Mendel Beilis. A reader's wife complained to the editors that every time her husband "finishes reading something in the newspaper about the bloodthirsty trial he gets so upset, so nervous, that he sometimes shows signs of madness."[7] Soon after the beginning of the trial, a *Forverts* editorial suggested that a few dozen military ships sent by the civilized world to the shores of Russia would be the best way to force the czarist government to stop the prosecution against Beilis.[8]

Following the outbreak of the war, on 7 August 1914 the *Forverts* editor Abraham Cahan wrote that "all civilized people [must] sympathize with Germany. Every victory she attains over Russia is a source of joy." On 10 December 1914, Cahan asserted that Russia's defeat would become the catalyst to bring down the Romanov autocracy, whereas Germany's defeat was fraught with danger for social democracy: "If Russia should defeat Germany the labor movement would suffer, and German militarism would only then become a mighty force, because all Germans will support the army to ward off Russian despotism."[9] Ironically, the *Forverts* kept publishing photos of Jewish soldiers who distinguished themselves in action and were decorated with the St. George Cross, Russia's highest military honor, although the editors realized the incongruity of publishing such images next to articles that lamented the plight of Russian and Austria-Hungarian Jews subjected to hostile or even barbaric treatment by the imperial army.[10] Avrom Lessin, editor of the New York–based socialist journal *Tsukunft* (Future), then owned by the Forward Association, publisher of the *Forverts,* did not believe in the patriotism and bravery of Russian-Jewish soldiers. He argued that pacifism had been inherent to Diasporic Jews, who at all times inclined to intellectual and spiritual rather than military bravery, hence:

> Speaking between us (we know that our enemies don't understand Yiddish), we can reveal the truth: all the Jewish battlefield bravery venerated nowadays in newspapers is, in reality, a result of our limitless cowardice. The Jew in the trenches is shaking in his boots, afraid of not being able to do his duty, and therefore he behaves so nervously heroic. And behind the pomp surrounding the glamorous rows of Jewish holders of the St. George Cross we still see the scared eyes of our victimized people—a people that has been scattered over the world for two thousand years.[11]

In its July 1916 issue the *Tsukunft* published Abraham Reisen's story "The Four Heroes" ("Di fir heldn"), which praised the soldiers who had been court-martialed and executed for refusing to fight in the war.[12]

Morris Hillquit, who played a paramount role in the SPA (serving as its international secretary until 1913) and was closely linked with Yiddish-speaking socialists, strove to prevent the party and its voting constituency from being fractured by war-related debates. He advocated a policy of "watchful waiting," hoping that "the shattered International" would resurrect once the war came to an end.[13] Popular at that time was the notion that internationalism was inherent to capitalist society and only consequently to the socialist movement. Following this logic, international links would unquestionably reappear with the restoration of peace, creating a framework for the revival of socialist internationalism.[14] On 1 May 1915, the Chicago-based newspaper *American Socialist* featured an article written by Hillquit entitled "The 'Collapse' of the International." A Yiddish translation of this article came out in the bilingual English-Yiddish monthly the *Ladies' Garment Worker*, published by the International Ladies' Garment Workers' Union (ILGWU), which carried a headline in the form of a question: "Had the International Collapsed?" Hillquit, an old friend of Abraham Cahan and onetime lawyer for the ILGWU, gave his answer to this question: he had no worries about the "soul" of socialism but doubted whether its "form"—the Socialist International—would survive the war.[15]

The *Forverts*, whose ideological roots were nourished by German socialism, paid particular attention to the situation in the German Social Democratic Party (SPD) and supported its pro-war stand. On 23 April 1915, Cahan returned from Europe, where for two months he had traveled under the aegis of the German Kriegspresseamt (Military Press Agency). His reports praised various aspects of Germany's "civilized culture" and pilloried Russia's "barbarism." The success of his journey was indisputable, and his anti-Russian articles resulted in, or at least contributed to, soaring circulation for the *Forverts* from 176,124 in January 1915 to 200,267 in the beginning of April.[16] Cahan's reports appeared also in the *New York Globe*. In 1917, the year of the United States' entrance into the war, he would be accused of acting "for the cause of the Kaiser" as an agent recruited by the co-chairman of the SPD parliamentary group, Philipp Scheidemann, during the latter's 1913 American trip. Significantly, Scheidemann, who was not Jewish, wrote for the *Forverts* as its Berlin correspondent. Cahan rejected the accusations as "an absurd and clumsy fabrication from beginning to end."[17]

On 30 July 1915, the newspaper reported that hundreds of German antiwar socialists, including several members of the Reichstag, published an open letter criticizing the leadership of the party for supporting the militarist policy of government. This letter was an indication that by the end of the first year of the war an increasing number of German socialists realized that territorial conquests were the real purpose of the fighting. Still, judging by the editorial comment, the *Forverts* opposed this dissent in the ranks of the SPD. Readers learned that a much larger number of

SPD members had not signed the letter, knowing that the majority of Belgian, French, and British socialists advocated continuation of the war until full victory over Germany. The editorial comment explained that such a victory would facilitate "a triumph of Russian despotism."[18]

Meanwhile, the *Ladies' Garment Worker* noted that "the only rumors about peace that one can hear nowadays in Europe and America emanate primarily from socialist and [trade-union] organized workers."[19] In an article published in the *Tsukunft*, Benjamin Feigenbaum, a veteran Marxist radical and crusader against all signs of Jewish nationalism, wrote about attempts of European socialists to bridge or disconnect their internationalist ideology with loyalty to their countries, characterizing these attempts as "the birth pangs of a new International."[20] In its Independence Day issue of 1915, the *Forverts* informed its readers that a group of Russian socialists and some of their German peers were making attempts to split up the international socialist movement by creating a new Socialist International, which would unite only those socialists who "had not become nationalistically inclined during the ongoing war."[21] Indeed, on 15 September 1915, a group of socialists representing various European parties, factions, and groupings assembled in Zimmerwald, a little village outside Berne. Among the Russian delegates were the Bolsheviks Vladimir Lenin and Grigory Zinoviev, the Mensheviks Julius Martov and Pavel Akselrod, and Leon Trotsky. Trotsky was at that time leader of a separate group known under the name of its Parisian periodical *Nashe Delo* (Our Course). The conference called for "peace without annexations" and thus opposed the patriotic trend in the socialist parties in the belligerent countries. At the same time, many people perceived the antiwar stance of the Zimmerwald Conference as essentially favoring Germany, which by that time had achieved very significant territorial gains in Europe and could benefit from ending the war at that point.[22]

Reflections on the Zimmerwald Conference

It took the *Forverts* almost a month to publish preliminary information about the Zimmerwald Conference. The newspaper emphasized somewhat mawkishly the "absolute friendship which dominated the debates between participants who represented combatant countries. They trusted each other like friends do."[23] In reality, virtually the day after the conference eight of its participants formed a splinter group, which became known as Zimmerwald Left. Led by Lenin, they united behind the slogan "Transformation of the imperialist war into a civil war," which echoed Carl von Clausewitz's understanding of warfare as "the continuation of politics by other, namely violent means."[24] The Zimmerwald Conference and then, in April 1916, a second conference, or the Second Zimmerwald, in Kienthal, also near Berne, formed what was tagged the "internationalist" strain in the socialist movement, while the Zimmerwald Left became the embryo of the future Third International, or Comintern. In fact, the term "Third International" itself was already broached positively and negatively in the context of the conference, although its initiators had emphasized their loyalty to the existing International.

The tendency to discard the Second International and form a third one was mentioned, for instance, in an article written for the *Tsukunft* by Vladimir Kossovski (Nokhem Mendl Levinson), one of the founders of the Bund in 1897. In 1915 one of the five members of the Bund's Foreign Committee, Kossovski did not go to the conference, feeling that it "could bring nothing good."[25] However, he took part in the Second Zimmerwald. Characteristically, Kossovski had problems mailing his text to New York, because the French military censorship had imposed a ban on all reports about the antiwar socialist gathering.[26] An old adversary of Lenin, Kossovski emphasized that the Bolshevik leader was "a principled divider [*tseshpalter*], inclined to use surgical operations as a universal healing aid for all conflicts in the labor movement," and that he tended to see a traitor in anyone who "disagreed with his Torah." According to Kossovski, Lenin wanted to render irrelevant any opposition and to use adventurous methods of struggle.[27] While the famous socialists of Western Europe supported their countries' military efforts, Lenin, who attacked such socialists as apologists for the bourgeois-imperialist war and betrayers of the proletariat, appeared as a leader whose influence transcended Bolshevik circles. Moreover, Bolshevism, a product of the essentially internal Russian Menshevik-Bolshevik schism contrived by Lenin in 1903, for the first time emerged from the radical margins of the socialist movement as an ideology capable of becoming a force in the international arena, notably among those socialists who longed for return to international solidarity.[28]

In October 1915, American socialists welcomed a guest, Alexandra Kollontai, an offspring of a Russian aristocratic family with a reputation as a prolific writer and lecturer on social and sexual questions from a socialist and feminist point of view. A veteran of the Russian Social Democratic Labor Party (RSDLP), she had recently broken with the Mensheviks and joined Lenin's Bolshevik faction, attracted by its antiwar stand. Ludwig Lore, editor of the *New York Volkszeitung,* and several other members of the German Socialist Federation invited her to come to America as an agitator against the pro-war attitudes among its members. Karl Liebknecht, one of the leaders of the left-wing, antiwar faction of the SPD, had suggested that the American German socialists invite her, an accomplished polyglot. Indeed, she spoke to various-language audiences, giving 123 lectures during her four-month sojourn in the United States.[29]

Abraham Cahan met Kollontai when she gave a talk, presumably in Russian, for a narrow circle of leading socialists, including Morris Hillquit (who, known in his pre-American youth as Moyshe Hillkowitz, studied in Riga at a Russian gymnasium) and the Mensheviks Sergei and Anna Ingerman. Cahan was not impressed by Kollontai's arguments and dismissed the Zimmerwald program as "utopian." The JSF, dominated by adherents of the Bund (from 1912, a federated part of the Menshevik party), also remained initially largely indifferent to "internationalism." However, the mood had changed very quickly. In November 1915, the JSF's Executive Committee supported the political line developed at the Zimmerwald Conference, seeing it as the return to the principles of class struggle and internationalism. The two members of the committee who opposed endorsing the Zimmerwald Conference were representatives of the *Forverts*.[30] One of them, the labor editor of the newspaper, was known in Russia as the Bundist David Lipets, but he appeared in New York in 1913 carrying the name of Max Goldfarb, "with the title of 'Dr.' suddenly and mysteriously affixed before his name."[31] Like Goldfarb, Moissaye Olgin (Novomiski), the second representative of the *Forverts*, was a recent Bundist arrival from Europe.

In terms of the SPA's pecking order, the JSF was a higher-hierarchical body and as such purported to exert control over the *Forverts*. Yet although the *Forverts* considered the JSF as its direct link with the SPA, and its editors and staff writers were JSF's members, it never acted as an organ of the federation. In fact, relations between the JSF and the newspaper were punctuated by ups and downs. Cahan looked down on the leading figures of the JSF and from time to time censured them, feeling empowered by his influence as editor in chief of the world's largest Yiddish—and America's largest socialist—periodical.[32] In comparison, by 1912 the English-language socialist daily *New York Call* had reached its peak circulation of thirty-two thousand.[33] From the perspective of over three decades in America, Cahan believed that the leaders of the JSF were too hotheaded and wrongly understood socialist goals in the United States.

By the time the JSF's National Executive Committee discussed the issue of Zimmerwald, the conference manifesto had already received support not only from the Executive Committee of the Socialist Party, but even from the German Socialist Federation, despite the fact that in Germany itself the SPD opposed it.[34] The American labor reformer William English Walling, whose 1908 book *Russia's Message: The True World Import of the Revolution* contained interviews with Russian revolutionaries and described Lenin as "perhaps the most popular leader in Russia," wrote in the *New York Times*:

The Socialist advocates of an immediate peace on the basis of a German victory have succeeded in reconstructing "the International." In the middle of September they held an international conference at Zimmerwald in Switzerland—and this conference has had an immediate and complete success in the Socialist world.... The Executive Committee of the American Socialist Party has now endorsed the conference and the party press shows—without exception—that sentiment is overwhelmingly in favor of the Zimmerwald program.[35]

Not all socialists supported the Zimmerwald Left, which aimed at an immediate creation of a new International equipped with Lenin's world revolutionary strategy. In fact, the Executive Committee of the JSF stressed in its resolution that it supported the Zimmerwald Manifesto, but it considered the International Socialist Commission established at the Zimmerwald Conference as a temporary body rather than an alternative to the existing International. Thus the JSF also distanced itself from the Socialist Propaganda League, formed by a group of SPA members who called for the collaboration of European and American revolutionary socialists to form a Third International.[36] In general, the majority of American socialists opposed both the current bloodshed and the idea of waging a local or worldwide revolutionary war.[37] Cahan, convinced that his life "was inextricably linked with the destinies of the more than two million Jews who landed in the United States between 1881 and 1924,"[38] tended to reflect the mood of his readership and in principle opposed the war and American participation in it. At the same time, he was reluctant to subscribe to any antiwar strategy that showed signs of being impractical, could harm the unity of the socialist movement, or could lead to Russia's victory.

Significantly, Cahan's disagreement with the decision of the party's National Executive Committee could not be qualified as an act of serious disobedience, because according to Arthur Le Sueur, then a leading figure in the SPA, neither the Zimmerwald Conference nor the SPA's endorsement were "official." He explained:

The best that can be said for the endorsement is that it demonstrated that at least three members of the National Executive Committee stood for principles of Internationalism as against Nationalism, which has apparently destroyed the high idealism of the International movement.... The endorsement was never meant to bind the Party in the United States, but was intended to bring to the fore for discussion, the questions in Militarism, and Nationalism.[39]

Here and in other publications of that time the term "nationalism" usually encompassed both "love of country" and "love of nation." In fact, the synonymous usage of "patriotism" and "nationalism" was rather characteristic of the literature, scholarly and popular, through the entire twentieth century.[40]

On 24 November 1915, a few days before the meeting of the JSF's National Executive Committee, the *Forverts* featured Cahan's article entitled "What Can Socialists Do Now Concerning the Horrible War?" He emphasized that only three of the five members of the highest executive organ of the party voted for endorsing the ideological platform of Zimmerwald. He considered this platform harmful, because it brought dangerous discord, exacerbating the deepening ideological rift between those who advocated the primacy of revolutionary means of struggle for socialism and others who prescribed reformist means. It was not in Cahan's nature, particularly after reaching a mature age, to subscribe to one person's conceptual system. Still, he found Eduard Bernstein's revision of Marxism appealing, especially his assertion that socialism could be achieved through gradual reforms from within a capitalist system. Whereas the Zimmerwald Manifesto was, Cahan believed, futile, pointless talk, he cautioned his readers from ridiculing socialists for talking rather than doing something, because the movement kept growing and its influence became stronger.[41]

While Kossovski's attitude to the Zimmerwald Conference was clearly colored by his dislike for Lenin, Cahan found the Bolshevik leader pleasant to talk to when they had met in Kraków in 1912.[42] As a practical man, however, Cahan considered the conference in Switzerland not only harmful but also pointless, because it could not stop the bloodshed. He compared the effectiveness of the Zimmerwald program to the ability of prayer to stop a fire. Rather, he maintained that nothing meaningful could be done before the end of the hostilities. Only Russia's military defeat in the war could create conditions for the long-awaited overthrow of the Russian monarchy: "In this war, I am on the side of Germany, because Russia is a dark despotic power, while England and France support this bloodthirsty beast. I am sure that German's victory would bring happiness to my people, to Jews, and be a victory for progress in general." He asked: Would it be better, for instance, if German socialists began to sabotage their country's war efforts and, as a result, allow the army of Nicolas II to occupy Germany? And he answered: No, it would be a terrible blow to progress. Whether the socialists like it or not, the war demanded that citizens think first of all about defending their countries. Thus it was unfair to accuse the socialists of France, Germany, Austria, and Belgium of betraying the principles of class struggle.[43]

Cahan believed that the Zimmerwald Conference deviated from Marxism and demonstrated anarchist tendencies, rushing to simplistic conclusions similar to what had happened a quarter of a century earlier, when American anarchists accused socialists of not demanding an immediate revolution. He also disagreed with the Zimmerwald call to preserve prewar borders ("no enforced incorporation either of wholly or partly occupied countries").[44] In particular, he did not see a reason for keeping the Russian borders intact. Thus, he reckoned that Kurland culturally belonged to Germany. Although he certainly could not argue the same about Lite—which encompassed more or less the territory of the historical Grand Duchy of Lithuania—he maintained that the population of these areas had much better prospects under German rule. The idea of detaching Poland and Lithuania from Russia and bringing them under German control had been advocated by Cahan and many other American Jewish socialists at least since December 1914.[45]

The Phantom of Internationalism

In his often cited February 1915 article "Democracy Versus the Melting-Pot," Horace M. Kallen noted that Americanization had liberated rather than suppressed nationality.[46] Cahan's Americanization is a good case in point. In 1890, Cahan wrote, "The only Jewish question we recognize is the question of how to prevent such 'Jewish Questions' from arising" in the United States.[47] Still, in 1891 he tried to raise the Jewish Question during the Second International's congress in Brussels. The congress, however, decided that "the question proposed by the delegation of the groups of American socialists of the Jewish language has no place here, and passes to the order of the day." It also instructed "the workers of the Jewish language" to fight for emancipation by uniting with their countries' workers and socialist parties.[48]

It was easier to formulate such a resolution than to stay immune to Jewish problems. Following the Kishinev pogrom in 1903, dogmatic socialists diagnosed Jewish nationalism in the *Forverts* articles sympathetic toward the victims. Cahan retorted that such hypertrophied internationalism revealed the malaise associated with Jewish life in the Diaspora, which made Jews accustomed to subjection.[49] Around the same time, Shmuel Peskin, an influential socialist activist and journalist, wrote in the *Forverts* that the Kishinev pogrom and, earlier, the Dreyfus case, made irrelevant the slogan, which used to appear as a banner at conventions, "We are Yiddish-speaking socialists rather than Jewish socialists." According to Peskin, Jewish socialists had no reason to be ashamed of preserving the Jewish nation and its language and culture.[50] The Mendel Beilis and Leo Frank cases made the *Forverts* even less "ashamed" of its constituency's primordial ancestry. The Cahan-led *Forverts* developed an idiosyncratic outlook, or Forvertsism, which combined commitment to both socialism and Jewishness and often applied an ethnocentric yardstick ("is it good or bad for Jews?") to American and international events.[51]

To be sure, not all socialists found this outlook supportable. Among the "dissidents" was M. Baranov (Moyshe Gormidor), who in his youth studied at the Saint Petersburg University and was active in the Populist movement. After emigrating, he turned to socialism and became an active contributor to the early Yiddish socialist press in England, although he wrote his articles in Russian. In 1895, he came to America, where he also initially wrote in Russian but eventually developed a fine Yiddish journalistic style. His column "In Passing" was particularly popular with the intellectual segment of *Forverts* readers. On Friday, which was traditionally a dentist's day off in New York (Baranov had a successful dentist practice and did not depend financially on his journalistic honoraria), the Baranov apartment would turn into a salon for Russian-speaking intellectuals, with Cahan and his wife Anna Bronstein among its regulars.[52]

Notwithstanding their friendly relations, Cahan often challenged Baranov's judgments and published his articles with editorial disclaimers, known as *podkoves,* or "horseshoes." In October 1914, the *Forverts* featured several polemical articles by Baranov and Cahan. Baranov, who described himself as "almost the only Jew who did not beseech God to help Germans capture Paris, jump [across the English Channel] into London, and parade through Warsaw," was filled with indignation at ethno-centrists:

> How can our Jewish patriots feel unashamed of manifesting their egotism? Let the whole world end up lying in ruins, as long as [the Russian czar] Nicholas is punished for the Kishinev pogrom; let France be trampled down, England destroyed, Belgium turned into a province of Germany, and Serbia, Montenegro, and Albania become Austrian provinces—let all these things happen for only one purpose: to take revenge on the Russian czar.[53]

Although Cahan belonged to the same generation of Russian Jewish radicals as Baranov, he did not share his unconditional internationalism. He retorted:

> Every nation cares about itself, but only Jews are supposed to care about other people rather than about themselves. All people, apart from Jews, are allowed to be national egotists. We, however, must forget the Kishinev massacre and the Beilis trial and worry only about non-Jews—about Serbia, Montenegro, and Albania.[54]

Some have argued that it was only following his 1925 emotional trip to Palestine that Cahan resolved to respond to the mood of the readers and allow "Jewish nationalist" material to appear in his newspaper, but in fact such material appeared earlier. To be sure, for many socialists, the nation-building project in Palestine was an anathema or at best a waste of proletarian energy.[55] In fact, on 3 July 1915, following the Zionist convention held in Boston, the *Forverts* featured an editorial, entitled "If Jews Would Have Gotten the Land of Israel," that reveals Cahan's view on this issue. In its almost poetic introductory lines the editorial described the war as a period in world history that could be compared with "a summer storm pouring down and hailing on the one side of the street, while golden beams of sun rays become already visible on the other side of the street." In less poetic words, the article admitted that the war might bring the realization of various national dreams, and therefore, the *Forverts* was ready to assume a slightly more conciliatory stance toward the Zionist project. Still, the editors remained skeptical about a Jewish state as a solution for all Jews, the vast majority of whom would continue to live scattered all over the world, because—according to the Yiddish saying—Jews preferred to rest in their graves among Jews, but to make a living among non-Jews (*in keyver zol men lign tsvishn yidn, ober khayune zol men makhn tsvishn goyim*). Thus, Jewish workers could not give up their fight for equality and brotherhood in the countries of their residence.[56]

In 1915 the newspaper only slightly modified its attitude to the Zionist program and continued to criticize it in the coming years, explaining, for instance, in a 1922 editorial that it "believes and preaches international socialism, the brotherhood of all people, believes and hopes that in the future all people will be one happy socialist humanity and all people will live as brothers."[57] During World War I, however, ideologists of the *Forverts* circle revealed an increased interest in various aspects of nationalism, echoing concurrent debates both in the socialist and the general American press. While socialist ideologists were trying to identify the roots of patriotism shown by people in various walks of life, American politicians and journalists debated over ethnic nationalism and identity, linking it to the question of foreign-born Americans' patriotic loyalty in the context of the military preparedness campaign.[58]

No doubt, there were also other reasons why Jewish nationalism had garnered the attention of Cahan and other American socialist ideologues. First of all, many Jewish immigrants, including readers of the *Forverts*, showed clear signs of deep Jewish national feelings. *Der Tog* (Day), launched in New York in November 1914 as a nonpartisan liberal daily favoring Jewish diasporic and territorial nation-building, already had a circulation of seventy-six thousand in 1915.[59] Secondly, the Jewish socialist landscape in America had changed following the arrival of hundreds of nationally conscious Bundists, who had left Russia following the defeat of the 1905 revolution. In addition to creating the Bolshevik-Menshevik divide in the ranks of Russia's social democrats, the results of the 1903 congress of the RSDLP had defined the Bund's attitude to the national question. From this point on, the precedence of primordial Jewish ties over general revolutionary sentiment became constant in the Bund's ideological stand.[60] Also inescapable was the fact that the Labor Zionist movement, whose members belonged to the 1913-established Jewish National Workers' Alliance rather than the JSF, had been growing exponentially since the beginning of the war.[61]

In his article published on 20 July 1915 as part of a series of opinion pieces by *Forverts* authors, Cahan addressed the issues of internationalism and nationalism, lumping together patriotism with ethnic loyalty. He maintained that it was natural for every progressive, civilized man to be both a nationalist and an assimilator. Even if people dressed similarly, listened to the same operas, and read the same scholarly literature, they remained more devoted to their own countries. To be an internationalist did not mean to have exactly the same feelings for every person and nation. He sarcastically reminded his readers that "the Socialist Party does not demand it from us." At the same time, he admitted that some Jewish socialists, especially in the older generation (he certainly meant such veterans as Benjamin Feigenbaum), used to, and sometimes continued to, harbor extreme views, suppressing in themselves any trait of specific sentiments toward Jews.[62] Cahan later recalled that as a newly inducted socialist he, too, "believed literally" that it was his "sacred duty to love all equally."[63]

Apparently reflecting the prevailing Bundist ethos of the time, Kossovski argued that patriotism did not contradict internationalism. He saw it as a logical concomitant of the principle of national self-determination. This view did not stop Kossovski and other members of the Bund's Foreign Committee from endorsing the Zimmerwald antiwar manifesto.[64] The prominent Bundist A. Litvak (party and pen name of Chaim-Yankl Helfand), who became active in the JSF after arriving early in 1915 in New York to handle the affairs of the Bund's Central Committee,[65] welcomed the Zimmerwald Manifesto, believing that it could unite all socialists in the belligerent countries in their fight for peace. At the same time, he realized that one could not expect, for instance, French socialists to join this drive if their German counterparts continued to support their government's military campaign. However, Litvak and others pictured a response to the Zimmerwald Manifesto in the form of a worldwide awakening of class conscience and the antiwar solidarity of socialist parties and groups. He mentioned *inter alia* one more merit of Zimmerwald: it was the best answer to Cahan's refusal to believe that internationalism had a strong foothold among Jewish socialists.[66] Advocates of Zimmerwald emerged also among *Forverts* journalists, notably Benjamin Feigenbaum and Hertz Burgin, a later alumnus of the same Vilna-based Jewish Teachers Training Institute from which Cahan graduated in 1891, a year before his emigration to America.

In three articles published in the last days of 1915, Cahan laid bare his views on internationalism. First of all, he did not see how German and Russian socialists could internationally cooperate as equal partners. In Russia, an agrarian country, socialists' influence was miniscule and they simply were not able to force the government to stop the war, whereas German socialists represented a very strong force and could seriously affect their country's ability to fight with Russia. More significantly, the experience of the war brought him to the conclusion that internationalism was hardly present at all among socialists; it remained more of an ideal, an aspiration. As a result, there was no reason to mourn for something that, in actuality, never existed. Cahan ridiculed such Marxist purists as Feigenbaum, who kept arguing that internationalism had already become an integral part of the socialist outlook, and compared him to those adherents of Hasidism who remained unshakable in their faith in miracle-making rebbes even if their "miracles" never materialized. Feigenbaum and socialists of his kind had replanted their fanaticism from Hasidism to Marxism and religiously revered every word of the great socialist thinker. Although Cahan professed to respect Marx deeply and highly value the great man's economic theories, he saw Marx as a human being who, despite his genius, was fallible. Cahan disagreed with Marx's views on Jews. In general, he was not ready to "put in pawn" his brains to anyone, even to Marx.[67]

Cahan accepted Baranov's argument that internationalism had become part and parcel of contemporary economic, cultural, and academic life, but he stuck to his guns, rejecting the Zimmerwald's postulate of the precedence of internationalism over nationalism in the outlook of contemporary socialists and, generally, workers. Moreover, he did not believe that proletarians would ever in the foreseeable future be able to immunize themselves from national feelings. He also could not forgive the Zimmerwald Conference for mistakenly chastising European socialist leaders as culprits of the war.[68]

The Effect of the Wartime Debates

Jay Winter distinguishes three central effects of World War I on Jewish life: first, the "centripetal movement" of millions of Jews caused by being drafted into or volunteering for the belligerent armies; second, the "centrifugal movement" of other millions of Jews turned by the war into refugees; and third, the transformation of the states in the remapped Europe "into more invasive, centralized and authoritarian entities."[69] The war also engendered far-reaching changes in the international socialist movement, including its Jewish constituents. Abraham Cahan, a towering—and for many people, also sinister—figure in the American-Jewish labor movement, demonstrated his perspicacity by predicting the destructive effect of Zimmerwald on the socialist movement. Conceived to create a new ideological and organizational foundation for socialist unity, the conference had instead opened the door to a schism whose consequences would dominate the political landscape in the coming decades of the twentieth century.[70]

It took some time to consolidate the American supporters of the Zimmerwald Left. Finally, on 17 February 1917, the International Conference of Socialist Organizations and Groups convened in New York. Despite its grand name, it was a rather small gathering, representing almost exclusively Eastern European socialist groups. The conference issued a resolution characterizing the Zimmerwald movement as "the embryo of the Third International." Significantly, neither the JSF nor any other Jewish socialist group sent their representatives to this forum.[71]

The internationalist ideas of Zimmerwald found strong support among the Russian-language (some of them Jewish) socialists who coalesced around their New York daily *Novyi mir* (New World). The *Forverts* praised the *Novyi mir* as "the only Russian daily socialist organ in America, which conducts highly valuable work among Russian workers.... Such an organ is vitally needed for the [socialist] movement in general, but particularly for the Jewish movement, because the Jewish workers have uniquely frequent and close contacts with the Russian workers."[72] In mid-January 1917, Leon Trotsky arrived in New York and joined the editorial board of the newspaper. During his short sojourn (less than three months), he published articles (translated from Russian) in the *Forverts* and the *Tsukunft* and established friendly relations with several *Forverts* writers, including Goldfarb and Olgin. Sholem Asch—a regular *Forverts* and *Tsukunft* contributor, whose Yiddish literary career was on an upward curve—acted as a guarantor of Trotsky's debt and, in the end, had to pay when Trotsky departed from New York without completing the payments on the furniture he had purchased for his Bronx apartment.[73] The collaboration of Trotsky, known as a vociferous advocate of the Zimmerwald-style "internationalism," with the openly pro-German Yiddish newspaper raised the eyebrows of many, who interpreted it as proof of his ties with Russia's enemies.[74]

In domestic politics, the *Forverts* argued that if the American radicals' efforts to fight against a war declaration "were to be of no avail and if war should break out, and if the country were in danger of attack, then the Socialists would take up arms and stand shoulder to shoulder with non-Socialist citizens in the fight against the enemy, as they are now doing in Germany, Austria, and France."[75] The *Forverts* demonstrated a similar stand in March 1917, when the American press discussed the rumors of a treaty between Germany, Mexico, and Japan. The Yiddish daily wrote about its patriotism and appealed to the socialists of the United States to be ready to defend their country. Baruch Charney Vladeck, city editor of the paper at that time (elected that year to the New York Board of Aldermen), wrote—with Cahan's approval, but contrary to the pacifist stand of the SPA's leaders—that if Mexico was really going to attack the country, then every socialist, every citizen, and every resident of the country would fight to protect the American Republic."[76]

Leon Trotsky criticized this patriotic sentiment, insisting that only military industrialists could benefit from America's participation in the war against Germany. As a result, Trotsky announced his break with the *Forverts*. "He rushed into the editorial rooms, straight into Cahan's office. Angry shouts were soon heard, the loud voices of Cahan and Trotsky mingling together. Several minutes later, Trotsky stormed out and left without saying good-bye to anybody."[77] In later years this episode colored Cahan's attitude toward Trotsky. Thus, in 1926 Cahan revealed his satisfaction with Stalin's victory over the "wild, bloodthirsty tactics and rhetoric of [chairman of the Comintern Grigori] Zinoviev and Trotsky."[78] Trotsky, in his turn, characterized the *Forverts* (which he, not knowing Yiddish, could not read) as "a newspaper with the stale odor of sentimentally philistine socialism, almost ready for the most perfidious betrayals."[79]

After the United States entered the war on 6 April 1917, the danger of being closed threatened all periodicals that had revealed pro-German sympathies, especially when the Espionage Act of 15 June 1917 gave the postmaster general the power to suspend or revoke the financially crucial second-class mailing privilege. By mid-September 1917, more than one hundred periodicals were under post office investigation. At the beginning of October 1917, Cahan had to defend his newspaper. He did not (and could not) deny that *Forverts* agitated against America's participation in the war, but—he argued—it only reflected the editors' adherence to the doctrine of defensive wars and did not mean that the newspaper supported Germany or was disloyal to the United States. Indeed, on the eve of the first registration day for the draft on 5 June 1917, Cahan stated, "The paper I represent preaches faithful and loyal citizenship ... every man between the ages of twenty-one and thirty must do his duty tomorrow."[80]

In the end, the newspaper was saved thanks to the intercession of such influential figures as the head of the American Federation of Labor, Samuel Gompers, and the chairman of the American Jewish Committee, Louis Marshall.[81] Nonetheless, until the end of the war (in fact, until 24 November 1918, although an armistice was signed on 11 November), war-related material in each issue of the newspaper had to be translated into English in order to obtain permission of the post office authorities to print. Censorship resulted in additional expenses (a translator, a typist, and a notary public had been added to the staff) and often interrupted the normal rhythm of the newspaper's production and distribution. Cahan expanded the role of proofreaders, ordering them to delete any word or phrase that could be interpreted as non-patriotic. At the same time, all these tribulations had a silver lining, because the image of a state-persecuted newspaper appealed to many socialist-minded readers. By the end of the war, *Forverts* had established itself more firmly in the general Yiddish-speaking community rather than only in socialist circles. According to Cahan's model of a socialist and people's newspaper, Jewish interests could prevail over socialist doctrinaire views of contemporary politics.[82] Yet, Cahan urged socialists to restrain their Jewish nationalism, because he worried that some of them had turned into chauvinists. He failed to define clearly the difference between nationalism and chauvinism but argued that a Jewish chauvinist and a Polish pogromist belonged to essentially the same dangerous category of people.[83]

The alliance formed during the war by "internationalists" of various socialist parties and groupings proved to be a loose one. Not all those socialists who upheld the Zimmerwald Conference's decisions later joined the communist movement.[84] On the other hand, Max Goldfarb and Moyshe Olgin, who denounced the conference, would turn into committed communists. Goldfarb's meteoric career rise in the Soviet party and state machinery would bring him into an influential position in the apparatus of the Third International, or Comintern, established in 1919.[85] In 1915 Olgin ridiculed the Zimmerwald Conference for its practical impotence and psychological harm and lambasted Bolsheviks in his doctorate earned at Columbia University in 1918 (a version of his thesis came out in book form in 1917 entitled *The Soul of the Russian Revolution*), but in 1921 he played a central role among those radicals who steered the JSF toward the Third International, creating a schism that persisted in the American Jewish Left virtually till the end of the twentieth century. In his capacity as the leading political and cultural pundit among Yiddish-speaking American communists, Olgin wrote, "Weak was the voice of Zimmerwald. But it was [the voice of] truth. It showed the right way to peace. It indicated the only consistent direction to the future."[86]

The fault lines that had emerged in the socialist movement developed into battle lines between the Third (Communist) International and the rump Second International. Eduard Bernstein explained to *Forverts* readers that Bolshevism was a peculiar variety of socialist-like thinking rather than a form of socialism. He maintained that leaders of the Comintern sought "to create a centralized dictatorial organization, which would grasp control over socialist parties of all countries."[87] Until the mid-1930s, Comintern ideologists remained devoted to Zimmerwald and did not find anything positive in patriotism or nation-state building.[88] Cahan could not make peace with this kind of "internationalism." His newspaper remained loyal to its social democratic roots, although the socialist movement emerged from the Comintern-caused split "fearfully weakened."[89] In 1925, two years after the establishment of the Labor and Socialist International as the continuation of the Second International, Cahan went to its congress held in Marseilles, where he—together with Morris Hillquit, Victor Berger, the first Socialist elected to the US House of Representatives in 1910, and Jacob Panken, an organizer of the ILGWU and the first Socialist to be elected to New York City's Municipal Court—represented the SPA. By that time, many socialist ideologists had changed their attitude to Zionism, finding appealing the idea of "positive colonial policy" in general and of the Labor Zionists' plan in particular. This plan suggested using trade unions and cooperatives to extend control over the economy of Palestine. Through this prism, Jewish settlers appeared as emissaries of socialism in the backward Orient.[90] Meanwhile, neither Poland nor the Soviet Union seemed to be places for successful application of social democratic ideas among broad masses of Jews.

From Marseilles, Cahan went to Palestine. In 1921, he had written that Palestine never appealed to him "as a land for Jews" and that Zionism "stank through-and-through with dangerous chauvinism."[91] Four years later, "Jerusalem the eternal city, the Western Wall, a relic of the Temple—all these spoke to his heart and inner being. It was as if a dam within him had burst, and all the Jewish content stored deep in his heart gushed out."[92] This trip signified an alteration of the newspaper's course: although Forvertsism, modified during World War I in the direction of embracing some elements of Jewish nationalism, continued to be critical of most basic tenets of the Zionist ideology, it warmed to Labor Zionist projects in Palestine.[93]

Cahan would also disavow Marx's definition of religion as "the opium of the people" and make known his revised understanding of Jewishness: "A Jew remains a Jew even if he is an atheist. Nonetheless, he ceases being Jewish if he converts to any other creed."[94] (It was as if he foresaw that a version of this definition would appear in the later Israeli Law of Return.)[95] Hillel Rogoff, a veteran journalist of the *Forverts* and its editor from 1951 to 1962, stressed that Cahan's and other *Forverts* writers' warming to religion did not reflect a decline in the strength of their freethinking. Rather, it revealed the strengthening of the streak of Jewish nationalism in their ideological makeup.[96]

Gennady Estraikh is a professor at the Skirball Department of Hebrew and Judaic Studies, New York University, where he also directs the Shvidler Project for the History of the Jews of the Soviet Union. An expert in Jewish intellectual history and Yiddish language and literature, he has published *Soviet Yiddish* (1999); *In Harness: Yiddish Writers' Romance with Communism* (2005); *Yiddish in the Cold War* (2008); and *Yiddish Literary Life in Moscow* (in Russian, 2015).

Notes

1. Jacob Sholem Hertz, *Di yidishe sotsyalistishe bavegung in Amerike* (New York: Der Veker, 1954), p. 143; Tony Michels, *A Fire in Their Hearts: Yiddish Socialists in New York* (Cambridge, MA: Harvard University Press, 2005), p. 172.
2. Yankev Salutsky, "Di federatsye un der Bund," *Der yidisher sotsyalist*, 30 January 1914, p. 5; "Boyt di vokhnblat fun der yidisher sotsyalistisher federatsye," *Forverts*, 6 September 1915, p. 4; Max Gordfarb, "Di yidishe sotsyalistishe federatsye: ir plats in der yidisher arbeter-bavegung," *Forverts*, 30 April 1916, p. 5; Charles Leinenweber, "The Class and Ethnic Bases of New York City Socialism, 1904–1915," *Labor History* 22, no. 1 (1981): 51. On Salutsky, see Michels, *A Fire in Their Hearts*, pp. 173–74.
3. Max Goldfarb, "Di trayb-koykhes fun der milkhome," in *Di milkhome, ire urzakhn un oyszikhtn* (New York: Jewish Socialist Federation, 1914), pp. 36–37.
4. On the ambiguous theoretical legacy left by Marx on nationalism-related questions, see, e.g., Shlomo Avineri, "Marxism and Nationalism," *Journal of Contemporary History* 26, nos. 3–4 (1991): 637–57.
5. *American Labor Year Book, 1917–18*, ed. Alexander Trachtenberg (New York: Rand School of Social Science, 1918), p. 11.
6. Yankev Salutsky, "Der internatsyonal in krig," in *Di milkhome, ire urzakhn un oyszikhtn* (New York: Jewish Socialist Federation, 1914), pp. 43–47.
7. Harvey R. Greenberg and Rima R. Greenberg, "'A Bintel Brief': The Editor as Complete Therapist," *Psychiatric Quarterly* 52, no. 3 (1980): 227.
8. "Oyf der stsene un hinter der stsene fun dem Beylis-protses," *Forverts*, 12 October 1913, p. 6.
9. As quoted in Joseph Rappaport, "Jewish Immigrants and World War I: A Study of American Yiddish Press Reactions" (PhD dissertation, Columbia University, 1951), p. 90.
10. "Dos bild un der artikl ibern bild oyf dize peydzsh," *Forverts*, 25 July 1915, p. 4.
11. Avrom Lessin, "Tsum nayem yor!," *Tsukunft* 1 (1916): 1–4.
12. Abraham Reisen, "Di fir heldn," *Tsukunft*, July 1916, pp. 561–62.
13. Brian Lloyd, *Left Out: Pragmatism, Exceptionalism, and the Poverty of American Marxism, 1890–1922* (Baltimore and London: Johns Hopkins University Press, 1992), pp. 325–26.
14. See, e.g., M. Baranov, "Farbaygeyendik," *Forverts*, 25 November 1915, p. 4; Jacob Milch, *Sotsyalizm, milkhome un natsyonalizm* (New York: Max N. Maisel, 1916), pp. 71–75.
15. Morris Hillquit, "The 'Collapse' of the International," *American Socialist*, 1 May 1915, p. 3; Hillquit, "Iz der internatsyonal gefaln?," *Ladies' Garment Worker*, June 1915, pp. 26–28.
16. The 1915 circulation of 196,079 is listed in Mordechai Soltes, "The Yiddish Press: An Americanizing Agency," *American Jewish Yearbook* 26 (1924–25): 335.
17. Gennady Estraikh, "Viewing World War I from across the Ocean: The New York Yiddish Daily *Forverts* on the Plight of East European Jews," *Jews and Slavs* 23 (2013): 380.
18. "An ofener briv fun 700 daytshe sotsyalistn," *Forverts*, 30 July 1915, p. 4.
19. "Sotsyalistishe fridns-klangen," *Ladies' Garment Worker*, August 1915, p. 35.
20. Benjamin Feigenboim, "Di geburts-veyenishn fun a nayem internatsyonal," *Tsukunft* 9 (1915): 793–97.
21. "In der sotsyalistisher velt," *Forverts*, 4 July 1915, p. 3.

22. Olga Hess Gankin and Harold Henry Fisher, *The Bolsheviks and the World War: The Origin of the Third International* (Stanford, CA: Stanford University Press, 1940), pp. 617–18, 621–22.
23. "In der sotsyalistisher velt," *Forverts,* 11 October 1915, p. 2.
24. Sean McMeekin, *The Red Millionaire: A Political Biography of Willi Münzenberg* (New Haven, CT: Yale University Press, 2003), p. 35.
25. *Di geshikhte fun Bund,* ed. Gregor Aronson et al., vol. 3 (New York: Unzer Tsait, 1966), p. 23.
26. See also L. [Julius] Martov, "Di ayzerne frantsoyzishe tsenzur," *Forverts,* 4 April 1916, p. 2.
27. Vladimir Kossovski, "Der tsveyter tsi der driter internatsyonal? Ayndrukn fun der konferents in Tsimervald," *Tsukunft,* 2 (1916): 173–76.
28. See, e.g., Stanley W. Page, "Lenin's Assumption of International Proletarian Leadership," *Journal of Modern History* 26, no. 3 (1954): 233–45.
29. Cathy Porter, *Alexandra Kollontai: The Lonely Struggle of the Woman Who Defied Lenin* (New York: Dial Press, 1980), pp. 225–34.
30. A. Litvak, "Far vos ikh bin far Tsimervald," *Di naye velt,* 10 December 1915, pp. 4–5; Hertz, *Di yidishe sotsyalistishe bavegung in Amerike,* pp. 159–60.
31. David P. Hornstein, *Arthur Ewert: A Life for the Comintern* (Lanham, MD, and London: University Press of America, 1993), p. 67.
32. See, e.g., Hertz, *Di yidishe sotsyalistishe bavegung in Amerike,* pp. 142–44.
33. Ira Kipnis, *The American Socialist Movement 1897–1912* (New York: Monthly Review Press, 1972), p. 252.
34. "Tsimervald un Yapan," *Di naye velt,* 26 November 1915, pp. 1–2.
35. William English Walling, "Socialist Attitude Toward Peace at Any Price," *New York Times,* 14 November 1915 (Sunday Magazine), p. 19.
36. Hertz, *Di yidishe sotsyalistishe bavegung in Amerike,* pp. 159–60; Theodore Draper, *The Roots of American Communism* (New York: Viking Press, 1957), pp. 68–69.
37. Lloyd, *Left Out,* p. 21.
38. Gerald Sorin, "Tradition and Change: American Jewish Socialists as Agents of Acculturation," *American Jewish History* 79, no. 1 (1989): 39.
39. Arthur Le Sueur, "The Zimmerwald Conference and Its Endorsement by the Party N.E.C.," *American Socialist,* 27 November 1915, p. 3.
40. Maurizio Viroli, *For Love of Country: An Essay on Patriotism and Nationalism* (Oxford: Oxford University Press, 1995), p. 1.
41. Abraham Cahan, "Vos kenen sotsyalistn itst ton vegn der shreklekher milkhome?," *Forverts,* 24 November 1915, p. 4.
42. Abraham Cahan, *Bleter fun mayn lebn* 5 (New York: Forward, 1931), pp. 130–32.
43. Abraham Cahan, "Vos kenen sotsyalistn itst ton vegn der shreklekher milkhome?," *Forverts,* 24 November 1915, p. 4.
44. Gankin and Fisher, *The Bolsheviks and the World War,* pp. 332.
45. Egmont Zechlin, *Die deutsche Politik und die Juden im Ersten Weltkrieg* (Gottingen: Vandenhoeck & Ruprecht, 1969), p. 467.
46. Tim Prchal and Tony Trigilio, eds., *Visions and Divisions: American Immigration Literature, 1870–1930* (New Brunswick, NJ: Rutgers University Press, 2008), p. 302.
47. Tony Michels, "Speaking to Moyshe": The Early Socialist Yiddish Press and Its Readers," *Jewish History* 14 (2000): 58.
48. Ezra Mendelsohn, "The Jewish Socialist Movement and the Second International, 1889–1914: The Struggle for Recognition," *Jewish Social Studies* 26, no. 3 (1964): 133–34.

49. Abraham Cahan, "Vos heyst 'nit-internatsyonal,'" *Forverts,* 30 July 1903, p. 4.
50. Shmuel Peskin, "Vi fun yidish-shprekhndike sotsyalistn vern mir yidishe sotsyalistn," *Forverts,* 3 June 1903, p. 4; Peskin, "Muzn mir zayn yidn, oder mir kenen oykh veln blaybn yidn?," *Forverts,* 12 June 1903, p. 4. See also David Shub, *Fun di amolike yorn: bletlekh zikhroynes* (New York: Tsiko, 1970), p. 61.
51. See, e.g., Tsevi Hirsh Margoshes, *Der "forvertsizm"* (New York: s.n., 1922).
52. Shub, *Fun di amolike yorn,* p. 425.
53. Ibid.
54. Ibid.
55. See, e.g., Melech Epstein, *Profiles of Eleven* (Detroit: Wayne University Press, 1965), p. 96.
56. "Ven yidn zoln krign Eretz-yisroyel," *Forverts,* 3 July 1915, p. 3.
57. Shelby Alan Shapiro, "Words to the Wives: The Jewish Press, Immigrant Women, and Identity Construction, 1895–1925" (PhD dissertation, University of Maryland, 2009), p. 63; see also p. 117.
58. R. Craig Nation, *War on War: Lenin, the Zimmerwald Left, and the Origins of the Communist International* (Durham and London: Duke University Press, 1989), pp. 106–12; Leslie J. Vaughan, "Cosmopolitanism, Ethnicity and American Identity: Randolph Bourne's 'Trans-National America,'" *Journal of American Studies* 25, no. 3 (1991): 448.
59. Soltes, "The Yiddish Press: An Americanizing Agency," p. 335.
60. Charles E. Woodhouse and Henry J. Tobias, "Primordial Ties and Political Process in Pre-Revolutionary Russia: The Case of the Jewish Bund," *Comparative Studies in Society and History* 8, no. 3 (1966): 342.
61. See, e.g., Mark A. Raider, *The Emergence of American Zionism* (New York: New York University Press, 1998), p. 41.
62. Abraham Cahan, "Natsyonalizmus," *Forverts,* 20 July 1915, pp. 4–5.
63. Abraham Cahan, *The Education of Abraham Cahan* (Philadelphia: Jewish Publication Society of America, 1969), p. 146.
64. *Di geshikhte fun Bund,* pp. 26, 28.
65. Jonathan Frankel, *Prophecy and Politics: Socialism, Nationalism, and the Russian Jews, 1862–1917* (Cambridge and New York: Cambridge University Press, 1918), p. 512.
66. A. Litvak, "Far vos ikh bin far Tsimervald," *Di naye velt,* 10 December 1915, pp. 4–5; Litvak, "Notitsn," *Di naye velt,* 24 December 1915, p. 4.
67. Abraham Cahan, "Der internatsyonal," *Forverts,* 27 December 1915, p. 5; Cahan, "Far vos ken nokh nit zayn keyn emeser internatsyonal?," *Forverts,* 29 December 1915, p. 5; Cahan, "Iz di gantse milkhome a trik?," *Forverts,* 31 December 1915, p. 5.
68. Abraham Cahan, "Genose Baranovs internatsyonal," *Forverts,* 2 March 1916, p. 4. See also M. Baranov, "Der internatsyonal—far dem krig, yetst un nokh dem krig," *Forverts,* 25 February 1916, p. 5.
69. Jay Winter, "The Great War and Jewish Memory," *European Judaism* 48, no. 1 (2015): 6.
70. Nation, *War on War,* p. 91.
71. Draper, *The Roots of American Communism,* pp. 82–83.
72. "Helft breklen Nikolays aynflus in Amerike," *Forverts,* 9 October 1915, p. 6.
73. Frederic C. Giffin, "Leon Trotsky in New York City," *New York History* 9, no. 4 (1968): 400. Olgin translated into English the book by Leon Trotsky, *Our Revolution: Essays on Working-Class and International Revolution, 1904–1917* (New York: H. Holt, 1918).

74. Shub, *Fun di amolike yorn,* pp. 449–51, 473–74; Richard B. Spence, "Hidden Agendas: Spies, Lies and Intrigue Surrounding Trotsky's American Visit of January–April 1917," *Revolutionary Russia* 21, no.1 (2008): 33–55.
75. As quoted in Rappaport, *Jewish Immigrants and World War I,* p. 193.
76. "Der barikht vegn Daytshlands plan zikh tsu fareynikn mit Yapan un Meksika," *Forverts,* 2 March 1917, p. 1. An emergency SPA convention in April 1917 proclaimed its "unalterable opposition to the war." See Horace B. Davis, *Nationalism and Socialism* (New York: New York University Press, 1967), p. 180.
77. Melech Epstein, *Jewish Labor in U.S.A., 1914–1952: An Industrial, Political and Cultural History of the Jewish Labor Movement* (New York: Ktav, 1969), p. 76. See also Ian D. Thatcher, "Leon Trotsky in New York City," *Historical Research* 69, no. 169 (1996): 175–76.
78. Gennady Estraikh, "The Berlin Bureau of the *Forverts,*" in *Yiddish in Weimar Berlin,* ed. Gennady Estraikh and Mikhail Krutikov (Oxford: Legenda, 2010), p. 152. See also Shub, *Fun di amolike yorn,* p. 475; Thatcher, "Leon Trotsky in New York City," pp. 175–76; Ian D. Thatcher, *Leon Trotsky and World War One: August 1914–February 1917* (Houndmills and London: Macmillan Press, 2000), pp. 203–5.
79. Leon Trotsky, *My Life: An Attempt at an Autobiography* (Mineola, NY: Dover, 2007), pp. 275–76.
80. Christopher M. Sterba, *Good Americans: Italian and Jewish Immigrants during the First World War* (New York: Oxford University Press, 2003), p. 61.
81. "Editor Defends Forward: Abraham Cahan Says His Paper Has Been Loyal to America," *New York Times,* 8 October 1917, p. 18; Shub, *Fun di amolike yorn,* p. 523.
82. *"Forverts" almanakh 1935,* ed. Baruch Vladeck (New York: Forward, 1935), p. 319; S. Rabinovitsh, "A tsimer in 'Forverts' vu m'arbet af misteyks," *Forverts,* 25 April 1937, section 2, p. 12; Lucy S. Dawidowicz, "Louis Marshall and 'The Jewish Daily Forward': An Episode in Wartime Censorship (1917–1918)," in *For Max Weinreich on His Seventieth Birthday—Studies in Jewish Languages, Literature and Society* (The Hague: Mouton, 1964), pp. 31–43.
83. Abraham Cahan, "Natsyonalizm un shovinizm," *Forverts,* 10 July 1920, pp. 8–9.
84. See K. Lemberg, "Vos iz gevorn fun di zimervaldistn?," *Forverts,* 1 May 1922, p. 3; Francis King, "Between Bolshevism and Menshevism: The Social-Democrat Internationalists in the Russian Revolution," *Revolutionary Russia* 9, no. 1 (1996): 1–18.
85. Gennady Estraikh, "Mnogolikii David Lipets: evrei v russkoi revoliutsii," *Arkhiv evreiskoi istorii* 7 (2012): 225–41.
86. Hertz, *Di yidishe sotsyalistishe bavegung in Amerike,* p. 204. See also Moyshe Olgin, "Mir torn nit zayn keyn rikhter ibern arbeter-klas fun Eyrope," *Forverts,* 20 December 1915, p. 5.
87. Eduard Bernstein, "Edvard Bernshteyn iber di shtraytn un shpaltungen in der daytsher sotsyal-demokratye," *Forverts,* 14 November 1920, p. 3.
88. See a detailed analysis in Andrei L. Iurganov, *Russkoe natsional'noe gosudarstvo: zhiznennyi mir istorikov epokhi stalinizma* (Moscow: RGGU, 2011).
89. William M. Feigenbaum, "The Pernicious Influence of the Third International on the Labor Movement," *Forverts,* 6 March 1927, English section, p. 2.
90. Paul Kelemen, "In the Name of Socialism: Zionism and European Social Democracy in the Inter-War Years," *International Review of Social History* 41, no. 3 (1996): 334–39.
91. Abraham Cahan, "Far vos a sotsyalist ken nit zayn keyn tsienist," *Forverts,* 5 May 1921, p. 4.

92. Yaacov N. Goldstein, *Jewish Socialists in the United States: The Cahan Debate 1925-1926* (Brighton: Sussex Academic Press, 1998), p. 25.
93. Ibid., pp. 55–56.
94. Abraham Cahan, *Sholem Ash's nayer veg* (New York: n.p., 1941), p. 4.
95. See, e.g., Izhak Englard, "Law and Religion in Israel," *American Journal of Comparative Law* 35, no. 1 (1987): 195; Nahshon Perez, "Israel's Law of Return: A Qualified Justification," *Modern Judaism* 31, no. 1 (2011): 61.
96. Hillel Rogoff, "Religye oyf der yidisher gas," *Forverts*, 24 November 1956, p. 6.

Selected Bibliography
Primary Sources

Forverts
Di milkhome, ire urzakhn un oyszikhtn. New York: Jewish Socialist Federation, 1914.

Secondary Sources

Estraikh, Gennady. "Viewing World War I from across the Ocean: The New York Yiddish Daily *Forverts* on the Plight of East European Jews." *Jews and Slavs* 23 (2013): 371–84.
Goldstein, Yaacov N. *Jewish Socialists in the United States: The Cahan Debate 1925-1926.* Brighton: Sussex Academic Press, 1998.
Hertz, Jacob Sholem. *Di yidishe sotsyalistishe bavegung in Amerike.* New York: Der Veker, 1954.
King, Francis. "Between Bolshevism and Menshevism: The Social-Democrat Internationalists in the Russian Revolution." *Revolutionary Russia* 9, no. 1 (1996): 1–18.
Mendelsohn, Ezra. "The Jewish Socialist Movement and the Second International, 1889–1914: The Struggle for Recognition." *Jewish Social Studies* 26, no. 3 (1964): 131–45.
Michels, Tony. *A Fire in Their Hearts: Yiddish Socialists in New York.* Cambridge, MA: Harvard University Press, 2005.
———. "Speaking to Moyshe": The Early Socialist Yiddish Press and Its Readers." *Jewish History* 14 (2000): 51–82.
Nation, R. Craig. *War on War: Lenin, the Zimmerwald Left, and the Origins of the Communist International.* Durham and London: Duke University Press, 1989.
Page, Stanley W. "Lenin's Assumption of International Proletarian Leadership." *Journal of Modern History* 26, no. 3 (1954): 233–45.
Porter, Cathy. *Alexandra Kollontai: The Lonely Struggle of the Woman Who Defied Lenin.* New York: Dial Press, 1980.
Rappaport, Joseph. "Jewish Immigrants and World War I: A Study of American Yiddish Press Reactions." Unpublished PhD dissertation, Columbia University, 1951.
Sorin, Gerald. "Tradition and Change: American Jewish Socialists as Agents of Acculturation." *American Jewish History* 79, no. 1 (1989): 37–54.
Sterba, Christopher M. *Good Americans: Italian and Jewish Immigrants during the First World War.* New York: Oxford University Press, 2003.
Woodhouse, Charles E., and Henry J. Tobias. "Primordial Ties and Political Process in Pre-Revolutionary Russia: The Case of the Jewish Bund." *Comparative Studies in Society and History* 8, no. 3 (1966): 331–60.

CHAPTER 14

Louis Marshall during World War I
Change and Continuity in Jewish Culture and Politics

M. M. Silver

Evidence pointing to World War I as a turning point in Jewish affairs in America seems overwhelming. American Jewry's social and demographic character changed fundamentally as a result of the war. Accelerated by wartime fervor, nativist forces in American culture and politics mobilized quickly after the armistice, and by the mid-1920s they had slammed the country's doors to immigrants from Southern and Eastern Europe. This development, coupled with the victory of the Communist revolution in Russia, ended the forty-year era of mass immigration of upward of two million Eastern European Jews to the United States.

As Americanization processes surged forward during the war, any hope for the perpetuation of a semi-autonomous, ethno-national Jewish culture—a culture rooted in Yiddish, New York City neighborhoods, and left-wing politics—effectively vanished. Basing their judgments on relatively objective yardsticks of this culture, such as Yiddish press circulation figures, historians have argued that this Jewish immigrant culture in the United States reached its peak in 1917.[1] In other words, in the war's aftermath the immigrants' American-born descendants increasingly took charge of communal affairs.

Does such broad recapitulation of events overstate the extent to which Jewish matters in the United States were irreparably altered by the Great War and by processes it unleashed? Are we able to trace lines of continuity in Jewish politics in America dating from a decade (or more) before 1914 and lasting through the 1920s, before the upheavals wrought by world depression and the Nazi onslaught? Was American-Jewish political culture singularly transformed during World War I? Are we misled by symbols of Jewish exceptionality and accomplishment into thinking that the process by which masses of Jewish immigrants Americanized during and after the war was distinctive?

This chapter discusses the issue of change and continuity in American-Jewish life during World War I by focusing on the community leadership activities of Louis Marshall (1856–1929). This choice, of course, is not perfectly representative of wartime Jewry in the United States. Many individuals represented important organizational trends and ideological currents in American-Jewish life during the tumultuous war years. Louis Brandeis, who became a Supreme Court justice in 1916, helped catapult Zionism to an unprecedented measure of communal influence during the war; and other major American Jewish figures, such as Stephen Wise, a Reform rabbi connected to an array of left-liberal sociopolitical causes, built bridges between Zionism and new organizational efforts, such as the American Jewish Congress. This pattern of Zionism serving as a platform for cultural or organizational development during the war applies to gender issues, since Hadassah, the Women's Zionist Organization of America (founded in 1912), consolidated impressively during the war; in fact, as the armistice arrived, Hadassah's medical initiatives ranked among the best-organized and best-funded Zionist initiatives in British-controlled Palestine. Marshall operated on the patrician, "uptown" pole of American-Jewish life, generally comprising Jews of Central European origins. On the other socioeconomic pole of Jewish life in New York City, colloquially known as "downtown," a number of remarkable figures (e.g., Abraham Cahan, Joseph Barondess, Morris Hillquit) were connected to vibrant subcultures of Yiddish journalism, labor union activism, and left-wing politics. These figures represented constituencies of Jewish immigrants who were frequently anti-war and who were also defiantly unhappy about the prospect of fighting on the side of the detested Russian czarist regime. While key American Jewish locales, such New York City's immigrant-filled Lower East Side and its elite uptown neighborhoods, are frequently thought of as the home of freethinking radicals or of highly acculturated, modernized Jews, no causal generalizations can be made about the religious or secular dispositions of American Jews who crucially contributed toward communal organizations during the war. For instance, one of the founding constituent groups of the landmark Joint Distribution Committee (the Central Relief Committee) was driven by Orthodox Jews such as Harry Fischel and Leon Kamaiky.

Nevertheless, a combination of events that transpired during and after the Great War positioned Louis Marshall with an unusual degree of leverage and authority to influence community events.[2] In addition to the banker Jacob Schiff's decline and death (in 1920), these include Marshall's energetic ascendance in new organizational structures (e.g., the American Jewish Committee, formed almost a decade before the war, and the Joint Distribution Committee); his willingness to negotiate terms of accommodation between settled American "non-Zionist" Jews and the world Zionist movement; his increasing contacts with communal Jewish leaders in other countries; his deep involvement with key, non-Orthodox, religious institutions in American Jewish life; his network of contacts, as a highly respected attorney, in New York State and the country as a whole; and the experience he garnered in years before the war as a leading advocate of Jewish and non-Jewish immigration rights to America. Arguably, more than the case of any other single individual, Louis Marshall and his activities and orientations during World War I provide a benchmark for examining the ways in which American-Jewish developments differed from or overlapped with the transformations of other American minorities or Diaspora Jewish communities.

Focusing on Marshall's activities, attitudes, and circumstances, this chapter raises questions about the extent to which World War I constituted a transformative experience for American Jewry. By comparing Marshall's situation and endeavors to those of other leaders of ethnic minority groups in the United States and also to those of Jewish leaders in other key Diaspora communities, we gain a richer sense of lines of *continuity* in American-Jewish experience. Frequently, Marshall's perceptions and deeds were not qualitatively different from the outlook and actions of communal stewards from other American ethnic groups, and there is also intriguing overlap between his World War I endeavors and those of Jewish leaders in European lands, including some who imagined themselves to be in ideological opposition to the sort of conservative, pro-capitalist politics Marshall represented. Drawn from comparative analysis, these findings limit the extent to which World War I can be regarded a revolution in American-Jewish life.

On the other hand, such revised understanding of World War I as a period of commonality and continuation in American-Jewish experience, both with regard to the American ethnic arena and also world Jewish politics, should not be taken too far. In several fundamental senses, the war years were distinctive and transformative for American Jews, and these changes and developments are also clearly reflected in this wartime phase of Marshall's career. Since these transformative aspects are detailed at length in extant scholarship on Marshall, there is no need to elaborate upon this point; one organizational example can suffice as a reminder of how the World War I experience could produce near-revolutionary change in American-Jewish life.

During the war, Marshall presided over the institutionalization of an ethos of Jewish solidarity (*Klal Yisrael*) in American Jewish affairs, specifically via the establishment of the Joint Distribution Committee a few months after the war's eruption (25 October 1914), at a meeting held at Temple Emanu-El in New York City. As an instrument devised to provide relief for impoverished or war-stricken Jewish communities overseas, the Joint was a groundbreaking endeavor for American Jews.

In the early months of American neutrality, Marshall shrewdly drew a distinction between American-Jewish political partisanship and intervention, which he considered unduly perilous to European Jews on one or the other side of the conflict, and charitable work for overseas Jews, which he considered imperative.[3] When the invitations went out for the constituent Emanu-El meeting, important sectors of American Jewry, including the B'nai B'rith organization and a section of the Reform rabbinical leadership, disputed this distinction and worried that moves taken by Marshall and the American Jewish Committee (AJC) would mire American Jews in accusations regarding disloyalty or pro-German bias. Bringing disparate groups and individuals together, demanding that skeptics overcome their doubts, Marshall displayed leadership in the period of the Joint's formation and early activities.

Figure 14.1. *Meeting of the Joint Distribution Committee Executive Committee, 1918. Louis Marshall is seated front, far left. Painting by Geza Fischer, 1929. Courtesy of the American Jewish Joint Distribution Committee.*

The Joint's emergence was transformative in terms of the huge levels of practical support provided by the organization and also in terms of reorienting American Jewry's understanding of its place in the world. The cumulative quantitative impact of this event—in the decade that ensued after the Joint's October 1914 establishment, the organization disbursed over $58 million in forty countries—marks a qualitative leap beyond anything American Jews had done in overseas relief before 1914.[4]

However dramatic such an example of sweeping organizational or sociopolitical change in American-Jewish life during World War I might be, it is nonetheless possible to delineate lines of continuity between the communal leadership model Louis Marshall personified, on the one hand, and other ethnic leadership models in the New York City context and broad American setting and also ongoing Jewish political models in other Diaspora settings, on the other hand.

In American-Jewish politics, Marshall functioned as a centrist-integrationist figure, and his work in this capacity preceded and succeeded the World War I crisis. As to why this function had so little staying power in historical memory, Steven Zipperstein's comment regarding the Russian-Jewish political context[5] can, I believe, be extended to America's nonracial ethnic politics in general. As Zipperstein implies, Jewish and other ethnonational leaders who sought moderate, accommodating, or creatively elastic positions on contentious issues tend to be relegated to the sidelines by posterity, whereas groups or individuals who articulated ideologically rigid, resolute, or extreme stances became the retrospective stars of historical study. So the centrist role Marshall played may not have been inscribed indelibly in historical memory, but it was a consistent part of the American ethnic landscape.[6] The tenacious durability of this integrationist function is evidenced by the fact that despite the excruciating loyalty tests and tensions of the various neutrality and mobilization phases of the World War I experience in America, it was possible for the country's ethnic leaders to conduct business more or less as usual.

Marshall's closest counterpart in the other white ethnic group that consolidated in America after a mass immigration and whose loyalties were directly challenged by overseas developments during World War I was William Bourke Cockran (1854–1923), an Irish American attorney who served his New York City constituency during seven terms in the US House of Representatives.[7] Unlike Marshall, the Ireland-born Cockran became a professional politician in the United States. As an anti-Bryan Democrat, he championed the urban working class by fighting for various hard currency and free trade positions toward which Marshall was antagonistic or apathetic. More importantly, Cockran and Marshall represented groups that were structured dissimilarly in urban milieus and that pursued dissimilar advancement strategies. The Irish-dominated political machines in New York and other cities catered to mid-nineteenth-century immigrants and their children and either overlooked or impeded the enfranchisement of later, early twentieth-century immigrant groups from Southern and Eastern Europe. And by distributing patronage spoils and services to Irish Americans in lower-middle-class urban settings, the machines tended to retard their constituencies' advancement in white-collar roles.[8]

Despite such differences of political outlook and of their groups' empowerment orientations, Marshall and Cockran played markedly similar ethnic roles. Cockran spent his political career jousting with machine bosses such as Richard Croker, believing that were Tammany Hall's excesses not trimmed, the integration of Americanizing Irish immigrants would be impaired. Marshall's calculations in his sometimes volatile dealings with the Jewish immigrant ghetto in New York City were similar in that he was constantly worried about the "un-American" implications of organized radicalism or crime networks. Well-connected as a Catholic layman, Cockran periodically took on overseas ethno-religious errands, as in the case of his trip to the Vatican in 1897 at the behest of the archbishop of New York, who was worried about the evolving crisis with Cuba. A famed orator in his day (Winston Churchill, whom Cockran mentored, colorfully alluded to this talent[9]), Cockran was an impassioned advocate of Irish independence. "For more than thirty years," writes one of his biographers, Cockran's "was the most powerful voice raised in America on behalf of Irish Home Rule."[10] In such pro-Irish advocacy, Cockran had a knack for "repackaging" this independence message to "suit [American] audiences typically uninterested or disinterested in the fate of Ireland," one historian of Irish New Yorkers comments.[11] With the substitution of relevant terms, the remark applies to Marshall's advocacy on behalf of Jews in czarist Russia or, at times, Zionism. When Cockran insisted in a 1913 address to the US Senate that Irish independence was not a parochial issue but rather a genuine test of America's democratic values and commitments,[12] he implemented the same rhetorical strategy Marshall had deployed a year earlier, in the American Jewish Committee's famous crusade for the abrogation of America's commercial treaty with Russia.[13]

The pattern of Cockran's responses to events of World War I, along with specific details of his communal leadership activity, have noticeably strong parallels in Marshall's broad orientation and laborious daily activities. Like Marshall, Cockran faced a tricky and taxing dilemma: how could such a centrist-integrationist maintain his overall pro-Americanization orientation in communal affairs when immigrant (or second-generation) masses in his community harbored ongoing contempt for the political regime that controlled the community's overseas coreligionists or compatriots and when that regime belonged to the Entente powers to which America was becoming indelibly aligned? In both cases (England's control over Ireland and Imperial Russia's rule of millions of Jews), events during early and middle phases of the Great War exacerbated the American ethnic group's hatred of the overseas regime and its reservations about America's impending wartime alliance with the regime.[14] Cockran struggled to bridge between his lifelong commitment toward his community's Americanization and his community's (and his own) revulsion at English behavior toward Ireland and reservations about America's inexorable drift toward the Entente. That his tactics and strategy during the war precisely mirror Marshall's suggests one sense in which American-Jewish affairs in this period are not singular and instead belong overall to an American integrationist ethnic rubric.

An advocate of world disarmament before the war, Cockran invested some effort in peace-related work after July 1914. In a letter sent to Wilson in early 1915, he urged the president to intervene with the warring powers and try to negotiate a settlement; later that year, in November, he publicized this faith in Wilson in an acclaimed "Plea for Peace" address in Chicago ("Providence has placed in the hands of the president power not merely to effect restoration of peace but to secure general disarmament," Cockran declared).[15] Complementing such broad expressions of idealistic sentiment in the early phase of the war, Cockran delivered three practical messages to his fellow Irish Americans. First, they must remain neutral ("It is the plain duty of Irish Americans, as of all Americans, to refrain scrupulously from any word or act which may be construed as urging a single man to enlist on either side of this war," he declaimed in November 1914[16]). Second, no matter how strongly he himself or Irish American compatriots might feel about Irish Home Rule, the fate of Irish men and women "who live in England is a matter they must decide for themselves."[17] Third, however distasteful it was for himself and other Irish Americans to contemplate an eventual call to arms in alliance with England, Cockran felt it imperative to prepare his community for this, perhaps inevitable, eventuality.

The third point of this message was the most complicated one to drive home, but Cockran felt committed to it in the period of American neutrality both out of a realistic assessment of the probable outcome of American policy and due to a conviction that the Entente powers were fighting autocracy, in defense of democracy. His private correspondence is filled with attempts to formulate this third point in a fashion that might be persuasive in his community ("In defense of democratic civilization England and her allies are now battling. Irishmen are therefore bound by their own interest to take up arms in defense not of England but of the object for which she and her allies are contending," he wrote in one letter[18]).

Cockran's tripartite approach succinctly summarizes the Jewish communal leader Louis Marshall's program during the first, American neutrality phase of the war. Like Cockran, he insisted that American Jews must remain neutral, largely out of patriotic deference to the country's policy. Since Jews resided in Europe and elsewhere on both sides of the conflict, the Jewish leader's argument in favor of neutrality included considerations absent from Cockan's advocacy ("The Jews, more than any other people, have always been regarded as hostages for each other, and it is therefore incumbent upon the Jews of America to bear that fact in mind, at every instant, lest that, in their zeal, they accomplish the very mischief they are seeking to prevent," Marshall explained[19]). During the war, Marshall translated Cockran's second point into Jewish terms by repeatedly citing Jacob Schiff's dictum that the "Russian Jewish question would be solved in Russia."[20] Like Cockran, Marshall wrestled with the impending circumstance of America's having to ally with a detested regime (Russia, from the standpoint of Jewish Americans) in order to join the global campaign against monarchic despotism and for democracy. Compared to his Irish American counterpart, Marshall seemed a bit less torn by this dilemma, because his loathing of German autocracy was deeply and personally felt (a circumstance that set him apart from Schiff and other prominent members of the "uptown" German-Jewish elite with whom he was associated) and because he believed it probable that the war would bring about regime change in Russia. Hence, Marshall's formulation of this third point was more resolute than that of the Irish America leader's. Just a few days after the war's eruption, Marshall wrote to his AJC colleague and confidante Cyrus Alder, "I am now anxious that England and France, even though it may mean a victory for Russia as well, shall put an end to the militarism and arrogance of Germany."[21]

Cockran's fidelity to this third point was tested poignantly in spring 1916, in the aftermath of the Easter Rebellion, a tragic event whose climax was (as he phrased it) a "barbaric massacre," featuring England's execution of "fifteen Irish patriots and martyrs, fifteen poets of unquestioned genius, writers of unusual brilliancy, scholars of the highest attainments."[22] In mid-May 1916, when he spoke at an Irish American protest rally held at Carnegie Hall, Cockran's blood was boiling, and he stopped just short of rescinding publicly this third point about the utility of allying with England in a global campaign for democracy. Could this tactic really be palatable when England's brutal suppression of the Easter Rising placed it outside of the orbit of civilization? At times in this address, Cockran indulged incendiary anti-English rhetoric reminiscent of the way downtown Jewish radicals spoke with vengeful contempt of czarist Russia at the start of the war ("The bleeding of Russia rejoices my heart," wrote the Yiddish poet Morris Rosenfeld). "I am here to make a confession," Cockran, a speaker identified by Winston Churchill as his oratorical inspiration, told the breathless Carnegie Hall audience:

> For thirty years I was one among many Irishmen who believed that it was the part of wisdom of Irishmen to forget the dreary history of wrongs and oppressions extending over seven centuries in the hope that in the better day which we believed to be dawning these two nations might be able to unite in productive cooperation. But the government of England, from the day it was established in Ireland, was avowedly intended to exterminate the Irish people.... I do not believe that there is a sensible man in the world who would contend for an instant that a political system which acknowledges that it must destroy the best of those subject to it in order that the worst may be raised to power can be tolerated with any regard for the interest of civilization.[23]

The turning point in Cockran's wartime communal leadership activity occurred exactly at this juncture of his Carnegie Hall address, when agitated listeners began to chant, "Down with England!" Reclaiming his role as an integrationist leader, Cockran instinctively switched modes and dropped the insurrectionary, anti-English rhetoric. "No, ladies and gentlemen, not even now do I want to say down with any nation. I am here to say only up with Ireland!"[24]

A shade of difference in the climactic moments of the two communal leaders' wartime advocacy is telling. In early 1916, Marshall, representing the American Jewish Committee, tensely negotiated with the Zionists a compromise agreement for the formation of the American Jewish Congress; weeks later and through the early summer,[25] Cockran barely managed to revive his faith in this third principle of alliance with a detested regime for the higher purpose of fighting for democracy. In other words, the American-Jewish leadership seemed to be a step ahead, because essentially it was arguing about how to organize itself to exploit postwar opportunities that would arise after the inevitability of America's entry in the war and an Entente triumph, whereas the Irish American leadership was trying to resolve itself fully in favor of a fight with the Entente.

Nonetheless, as circumstances evolved in 1917 and America joined the fight, Marshall and Cockran ended up in exactly the same place, zealously advocating an all-out campaign against German autocracy, which they both depicted as the scourge of civilization. In late 1917, Cockran bellicosely told audiences that "the existence of the German empire is absolutely inconsistent with the safety of our civilization."[26] Six months later, writing to his oldest son James, who was in uniform in France, Marshall reiterated this premise, fuming impatiently in favor of a final, decisive offensive: "Why are we waiting? Unless the house of Hohenzollern is defeated, militarism will be rampant and the world bankrupt in every sense of the word."[27]

Overriding their own communities' distaste for particular aspects of the alliance with the Entente, the wartime activities of these two integrationist leaders traced the same arc. The inner logic of adapting genuine, politically contrarian sentiment to the practical needs of accommodating patriotism was identical in the Jewish-American and Irish American cases.

These contrarian, anti-Russian and anti-English impulses were defused not just by communal leadership (or by the outbreak of revolution in Russia in February 1917), but also by dynamics of local politics and society in America's diverse urban settings. A fascinating example of how inclusive realities in New York City militated against the possibility that thirty-five years of Jewish radicalism[28] would produce a World War I outcome of anti-patriotic Jewish exceptionalism is the city's 1917 mayoral race, which featured the candidacy of an antiwar Jewish socialist, Morris Hillquit.

From the standpoint of the communal steward Louis Marshall, the prospect of Hillquit, and his "treasonous" antiwar position,[29] making a strong showing in the race was almost apocalyptic. A few days before the issuance of the Balfour Declaration, Marshall was not thinking about the implications of allied support for a Jewish national home in Palestine.[30] Instead, he declared dramatically that a vote for Hillquit on election day (November 6) would "imperil the condition of Jews throughout the world."[31] Marshall was worried that Hillquit's candidacy could become a spur to antisemitism, and his anxiety had some foundation. Local press coverage, such as a *New York Herald* piece on October 25, lambasted Hillquit for his refusal to take part in the Second Liberty Loan drive, accused him of aspiring to become "the mayor of Berlin," and caricatured him as a bomb-wielding maniac.[32]

Hillquit's antiwar candidacy did not really reflect a special communal situation wrought by masses of Jewish immigrant radicals in the city. From the standpoint of patriotic integrationist leaders like Marshall and Cockran, the city's Irish Americans were comparably vulnerable, since Tammany Hall's candidate, John Francis ("Red Mike") Hylan was also widely excoriated as being anti-patriotic. The incumbent, John Purroy Mitchel, campaigned on the premise that his Tammany rival was pro-German; with former president Theodore Roosevelt standing by his side at campaign rallies, Mitchel declared that a vote for any of his rivals would "give comfort to the enemy," and citing Hylan's association with the German-leaning William Randolph Hearst, Mitchel grimly warned city residents against voting for "Hearst, Hylan and the Hohenzollerns."[33] For his part, and as reported in the *New York Times* a few days before election day, Hylan deflected Mitchel's aspersions about his lack of loyalty and attested to unwavering support of President Wilson's policies;[34] meantime Tammany was dispatching wrecking crews to smash Hillquit's street rallies, and on election day its operatives stuffed ballot boxes for Hylan.[35]

The election results were surprising. Tammany's candidate, Hylan, won handily, taking 293,000 votes, whereas the socialist Hillquit received an eyebrow-raising 21 percent of the vote, and his tally (138,000 votes) came quite close to the vote total (148,000) of the defeated incumbent, Mitchel. Some commentators around the country viewed these mayoral race results as a "defeat of the principles of Americanism" in New York City; they published sententious columns questioning "the city's affinity with the United States."[36]

Despite such journalistic chatter, there was never really any prospect of one of the city's ethnic-immigrant populations, Jewish or Irish, facing a special predicament forged by the antiwar sentiment of many of its members. City officials mobilized rapidly after the election and invested significant resources with the aim of rebranding the city as a solidly pro-American milieu. To dispel speculation about mass anti-draft sentiment in the city and to accentuate its patriotism, the municipality sponsored a two-week pro-America festival, called "Hero Land," at the Grand Central Palace in midtown Manhattan.[37] The newly elected mayor, Red Mike Hylan, solemnly joined this campaign, promising the *New York Times* on November 7 that "I am as good an American as any man." By spring 1918, ethnic groups in the city were outdoing themselves to exhibit pro-war patriotism via purchases of the Third Liberty Loan. In the Jewish community, union activist Joseph Barondess combed the Lower East Side for subscriptions to the loan, and uptown, Temple Emanu-El lavished $500,000 in patriotic bonds.[38]

Scholarly examinations of urban ethnic neighborhoods in this period, including one study of Italian and Jewish immigrants during the Great War, confirm that intriguing episodes such as Hillquit's anti-establishment candidacy do not really reflect lasting, extraordinary sociopolitical circumstances in New York's Jewish community. If anything, Christopher Sterba argues, controversies such as the heated 1917 mayoral race involving Hillquit's antiwar socialism or Hylan's alleged pro-Germanism had the effect of stimulating pro-American responses in ethnic communities and accelerating ongoing assimilatory dynamics in them.[39]

Turning to the sphere of global Jewish politics, the evidence of continuity in Louis Marshall's wartime activities in this sphere is at least as impressive as it is in the domestic American ethnic context. A compelling example of the need to examine Marshall's wartime undertakings closely and to distinguish between their seemingly transformative aspects and their character as a connecting bridge between prewar and postwar trends in world Jewish politics is the American Jewish Congress debate.

In some ways, the American Jewish Congress debate represented an unprecedented American-Jewish exercise in internal self-regulation and self-definition. Indeed, in view of ongoing American-Jewish concerns about double loyalty, the Congress's wartime establishment appears as a highly unusual development. Overcoming fears of creating a "state within a state," American Jews created a democratically representative, autonomous organization to articulate their separate, ethno-national desires or demands at a postwar peace conference.

This certainly had never happened before, and so historians have depicted the establishment of the American Jewish Congress during World War I as an entirely distinctive, positively transformative or curiously different, American-Jewish experience. Since their findings and arguments are familiar, they can be summarized quickly, before we move to an alternative perception of the Congress's emergence as evidence of continuity in global Jewish politics in a period that begins a decade before 1914 and continues well into the interwar years.

The American Jewish Congress's establishment colorfully illustrates the way elites and masses in Jewish America labored to find common ground. Some commentators, most notably Lucy Dawidowicz,[40] have interpreted Marshall's initial reservations and eventual accommodation during the Congress debate as reflecting a social transformation in American Jewish life during the Great War. This was a period of mounting cohesion between the Jewish masses and classes, between the *"Yidden"* and the *"Yehudim,"* they claim.

Indeed, in view of the way the American Jewish Committee elite capitulated during this debate, it is tempting to view the Congress episode as a kind of political coming-out party for Eastern European immigrant Jews in America. Shifting the metaphor somewhat, I think the Congress debate put the paramount issues of communal control and communal participation (vis-à-vis the old Central European Jewish establishment and the more recently arrived Eastern European Jews) at the center of the table, whereas before the war they were hardly felt at the edge of its cloth.

This debate was exhausting in detail and also heavily weighted in individual or institutional ego, and it was predicated upon confusing and transient global political circumstances (particularly the state of the regimes in Russia). Despite such complicating factors, Zionist-oriented historians, most prominently Jonathan Frankel, have identified this debate as a truly exceptional event (Frankel called it the "most remarkable episode" in American Jewish history).[41] This historical school sees the Congress's establishment as proof that conspicuously national Jewish political formations could take root in the United States.

Whether one sees it as a freakish exception, as firm precedent, or as symbolically significant foreshadowing, the fact that 335,000 Jewish Americans cast ballots in June 1917 to elect representatives for action on issues of global Jewish import must mean something. When we think of subsequent central issues of American-Jewish politics that necessitated overseas action and some compromise formula between mass interest and elite command of resources, the American Jewish Committee–American

Jewish Congress clash during World War I has to be regarded as a highly intriguing episode of consequence.

These arguments about the American Jewish Congress's exceptional or revolutionary status are quite persuasive, but I believe that a broad view of global Jewish politics also necessitates an alternative or supplementary perception of World War I as a bridge between antebellum and postbellum trends in Jewish experience.

Louis Marshall's wartime activities regarding the American Jewish Congress unfolded within conceptual frames that had been devised by Zionists and also by Jewish autonomy activists in the Jewish nationalist historian Simon Dubnow's camp,[42] roughly at the time of the 1903 Kishinev pogrom. Of course, Marshall's wartime actions had multiple determinants, but his contestation with these antebellum Jewish nationalist or quasi-nationalist (autonomy) modes represents the one abiding impetus in his work, starting with the American Jewish Congress wartime debates and continuing through his endeavors on behalf of the Joint Distribution Committee (particularly the Agro-Joint project for Jewish colonies in the Soviet Union) and his Jewish Agency discussions in the 1920s. Interestingly, the exact same thing can be said about his close comrades and bitter foes in overseas Diaspora communities who operated before, during, and after the Great War, and so we will conclude this discussion by briefly examining two Eastern European examples of this phenomenon of continuity in Jewish politics.

Maksim Vinaver, a lawyer who founded with Simon Dubnow in 1892 a pioneering Russian historiography project,[43] sometimes went by the moniker "the Louis Marshall of Russia."[44] Vinaver gained prominence after the Kishinev pogrom, when he turned a futile victims' compensation proceeding into a boldly rhetorical courtroom indictment of antisemitism.[45] As a Constitutional Democrat (Kadet) member of the first Duma in 1905–6, Vinaver exploited the parliamentary soapbox—his was, one scholar writes, "the first appearance of a Jewish politician in a Russian political institution demanding in public the abolition of all restrictions [on] Russian Jews."[46] The rhetorical cadences in Vinaver's condemnation of Nicholas II's failure to mention the Jews in his throne speech ("We will support only that government which represents the will of the people"[47]) recall Marshall's most inspired oratory for Jewish rights.

Like Marshall, Vinaver was a moderate integrationist and not a Jewish nationalist. However, his remarkably courageous work as a defender of Jewish rights in this post-Kishinev period (he spent three months in prison after the Duma's collapse) was directly responsive to key developments in Zionist politics.

After Kishinev, the Russian Zionists were forced to think realistically about their movement's short-term and long-term goals at a time when their world movement was considering and rejecting England's proposal for Jewish settlement in East Africa. The Russian Zionists convened in Helsingfors (Helsinki) in November 1906 and endorsed the *Gegenwartsarbeit* strategy of "working in the present."[48] Essentially this Helsingfors "present work" plank provided a warrant for Russian Zionists to become an independent movement in Russian politics. In turn, this development compelled liberals and non-Zionists like Vinaver and Dubnow to form independent Jewish factions of their own,[49] each advocating differing degrees of centralization for the empire's Jewish communities and of inclusion of its Orthodox Jews (Vinaver's faction was called the Evreiskaia Narodinaia Gruppa [ENG]).[50]

Vinaver emerged in this post-Kishinev, first Duma period as a leading Jewish advocate because he was closely attentive to the alarm and grievances felt by Jewish masses and because he shrewdly seized opportunities and exploited his professional expertise to explain Jewish needs to Christian society. That more or less the same thing can be said about Louis Marshall means that primary dynamics of Jewish leadership (though not its results) were similar in radically disparate political circumstances of Jewish life, in czarist Russia and democratic America, and they well preceded the World War I crisis.

This last point bears repeating: though they preceded by a decade the celebrated debate about the formation of an American Jewish Congress, the main contours of the Russian discussions about *Gegenwartsarbeit*, the ENG, and Dubnow's autonomy schemes uncannily resemble the salient features of the American Jewish controversy in which Marshall's decentralized, inclusive preferences were challenged during World War I by secularized Zionist and by non-Zionist Yiddish autonomy plans.

A still more striking illustration of the way global Jewish politics were fashioned by 1903–5 (Kishinev and Uganda era) Jewish nationalist and Jewish autonomy models rather than by the convulsions of the Great War is to be found in postwar Poland. There, in metaphorical and direct senses, Louis Marshall's wartime work was perpetuated by a man—Yitzhak Grunbaum—who virulently opposed one of Marshall's key international Jewish efforts in the 1920s, that is, the expansion of the Jewish Agency, and who conceptualized his defense of the implementation of the minority rights accord in terms of the old Zionist standard of *Gegenwartsarbeit* and who was himself an affiliated Zionist.

As the Second Polish Republic took root, secular Jewish politicians in the new country regarded the minority rights treaty negotiated by Marshall and his Jewish delegation comrades at the Paris Peace Conference as a "great victory." As Ezra Mendelsohn notes, they touted it as a "magna carta, in that it specifically referred to the Jews as a minority with national, not only religious, rights."[51]

The Polish Zionists and other secular Jewish politicians talked about the new country in 1919 as though it were America seventy years later, that is, as though Poland's majority might have a normative inclination to regard the state as a heterogeneous multicultural entity. If anything, Poland in 1919 was more like what America had been half a century before, with the former's Jewish population a beaten-down minority, the juridical equivalent of the latter's emancipated, but largely unwanted blacks. The tale of dissonance between Jewish aspirations and Polish realities is complicated, poignant, and well-known.[52] For our purposes, it suffices to allude to Grunbaum, who in the early 1920s lobbied as vociferously as anyone else in Poland on behalf of this chimeric notion of the minority rights accord as a Jewish "magna carta."

Formally, Grunbaum represented one faction, the General Zionists, within a Jewish national movement in Poland that was splintered by differing regional temperaments (his group, from central or "Congress" Poland, was more ideologically combative than Zionists from Galicia, the southeast region of the state). The Zionists vied with the socialist Bund in an ongoing competition to win new recruits within a Jewish society rent by insuperable ideological differences, including the Orthodox Agudat Israel and also outright assimilationists, who were a numerically significant group, perhaps 10 percent of the country's Jewish population.[53]

If Grunbaum's failure was preordained, his political maneuvering in the Sejm up to Jozef Pilsudski's 1926 coup against the parliament, which opened a new, not necessarily worsened chapter in interwar Polish-Jewish history, was surely as significant as anything else that happened in global Jewish politics in this era. Grunbaum's risky decision in 1922 to combat the state's gerrymandering and enhance Jewish political influence via the establishment of a parliamentary minorities bloc with Germans, Ukrainians, and others, displayed considerable ingenuity and accomplished goals.[54]

Poland was the place in the postwar world where the fulfillment of a Jewish rights agenda would have vindicated the platform forged by the American Jewish Committee and the American Jewish Congress during their torturous wartime debates. In performances that thrilled Eastern European Jews, Grunbaum stared down jeering National Democrat (Endek) delegates in the Sejm and campaigned for that agenda. Starting in 1919, when we review the rhetoric he deployed and the contents of his campaign, his parliamentary appearances verily beg for description as being Louis Marshall-esque.[55] As though he had ripped a page from an AJC handbook, Grunbaum rigorously dissected and criticized archaic laws such as an 1841 statute that required Jewish communities to pay special fees whenever members of their communities were treated in hospitals. In autumn 1920, when anti-Semites in the Polish Sejm characterized Bolshevism as a Jewish conspiracy for world domination, Grunbaum deflated this conspiratorial myth of "Jewish Bolshevism" by pointing out that the new Soviet government was enacting anti-Jewish policies. At this time in America, when Henry Ford had started to disseminate *The Protocols of the Elders of Zion*, Marshall was developing precisely this same contention, holding that Bolshevism could not be a camouflage for Jewish empowerment everywhere, because if it were that, why would the Soviets persecute Jews, as they were then doing?

However, in view of Yitzhak Grunbaum's Jewish political persona, it would be a bad joke to adduce from such comparisons that he was the "Louis Marshall of Poland." In contradistinction to the non-Zionist Marshall, for whom Americanization was one ultimate component of any identity construction, Grunbaum dexterously believed that the obtainment of national rights in Poland was part of the Zionist *Gegenwartsarbeit* program, whose ultimate objective would be the ingathering of the exiles in Eretz Israel and the establishment of the Jewish state.

In fact, Grunbaum was one of three Jewish newspaper editors responsible for this Zionist ideology of "present work" in the Diaspora (the other two were Vladimir Jabotinsky and Avraham Ben-David Edelson). The ideology was first fashioned at a meeting held in Landvorovo, near Vilna, in July 1906, when these editors of Russian-, Polish-, and Yiddish-language newspapers responded to the Kishinev and Uganda controversies by declaring that work to establish communal institutions and promote Jewish rights in Eastern Europe could constitute an important preparatory phase for Zionism. A few months later, at the Russian Zionist Helsingfors conference, the trio brokered the adoption of this idea and various refinements to it.[56]

Imagining himself as part of a Jewish nationalist revolution in the Diaspora that proceeded upward from the bottom, from the rank and file, Grunbaum flamboyantly positioned himself in the 1920s against perceived American-Jewish plutocrats like Marshall or Felix Warburg. During that decade, Marshall worked substantively, albeit slowly and often bitterly, with Chaim Weizmann, for the purpose of including so-called non-Zionists, essentially wealthy American-Jewish philanthropists who recoiled from the vision of a Jewish state, on the Jewish Agency.[57] For years, right up to Marshall's death and the consummation of the Jewish Agency agreement, Grunbaum petulantly berated Weizmann for his unholy alliance with American-Jewish moneybags.[58] Generally the Polish Zionist became associated with the dictum that Jewish settlement in Eretz Israel "could wait" if it depended on the patronage of wealthy bankers like Warburg or the diplomacy of *galut shtadlanim* (lobbyists or intercessors) like Marshall.

Before and after the Great War, political brand labels and ideological nomenclature continued to divide Jews from differing Diaspora settings, even as the same rights and liberties agenda was shared by all of them. In accommodating America, a centrist integrationist like Louis Marshall fought against restrictive Sunday laws or residential covenants; in uninviting Poland after the war, Zionists like Yitzhak Grunbaum fought for the same thing, while proclaiming their disgust for everything that *galut* assimilationists like Marshall stood for.

To some extent, Jewish politics in this pre-Holocaust period can be seen as a case of arrested development. Jews who all shared the same overall vision of democratic empowerment separated among themselves on the basis of old ideological programs, and they ignored changes in basic geopolitical realities, as though the Russian imperial system to which the three newspaper editors had originally applied the concept of *Gegenwartsarbeit* posed the same challenges as the Second Polish Republic. Similarly, as Carole Fink elucidates in detail, naively or disingenuously they related to urgent contemporary distress in timeworn, anachronistic pogrom terminology.[59] Such time-warp phenomena occurred because Jewish political outlooks were locked in place by events (the Kishinev pogrom, the Uganda debates) that transpired a decade before 1914. Remarkably, World War I had not unhinged them.

Though he was a shrewdly discerning and highly experienced participant in communal affairs, Louis Marshall began the postwar era noticeably confused by the issues addressed in this chapter. Were organizational and political initiatives that had taken root during the Great War onetime occurrences, or could the energy and commitments that had animated them be sustained in the new, postwar era?

As confetti in armistice celebrations draped the street outside his office building, Marshall busily planned efforts to assist in the postwar strengthening of Jewish life in Poland,[60] the community whose future was likely to prove whether Wilsonian wartime promises about democratization and American Jewish Congress concerns about minority rights' protections could be effectively translated on the ground. As months passed by, and after he returned to a triumphal reception following his work for Jewish minority rights at the peace conference, Marshall judged that Polish Jewry's future depended on American Jewry continuing with the explosive expansion of overseas funding it had triggered during the war years via the formation and operation of the Joint Distribution Committee. Accordingly, he brought ambitious plans for the economic "reconstruction" of Polish Jewry to prominent Joint donors such as Julius Rosenwald and Felix Warburg; but, frustratingly, he discovered that the philanthropic amplitude American Jews had displayed within the emergency atmosphere of war was receding rapidly with the world at peace. "I have not changed my views on the need for a banking and financing corporation" to assist Eastern European Jews, he wrote to Jacob Billikopf in May 1920. "Our difficulty has been that men who were expected to invest substantial sums have been up to the present time unwilling to assume leadership."[61]

Sometimes Marshall had premonitions that wartime Jewish idealism and pioneering commitments would not be sustained in the 1920s, and this thought left him visibly uncomfortable. Probably the most poignant example of this problem of change and continuity—that is, the issue of whether wartime American Jewish efforts and accomplishments had lasting value—centered on the minority rights accord to whose obtainment Marshall had labored arduously and effectively in Paris. Were Jewish leaders around the world positioned to continue their lobbying work, to ensure that the "Magna Carta of the Jews" would really improve the circumstances of Eastern European Jews? In spring 1920, Eastern European Jews who had worked with Marshall on the Jewish delegation at the peace conference asked him repeatedly to organize follow-up meetings, in order to monitor the implementation of the minority rights accord. Intimidated by the circulation of the antisemitic *Protocols of the Elders of Zion* in America, Marshall demurred; he did not think that the re-formation of an international Jewish delegation was a wise idea, under the new circumstances of rising antisemitism. His rationalizations in this connection hinted strongly at the rapid draining of wartime vigor and idealism in Jewish communal work: "You and my European friends know that I am no coward, and that the interests of Jewry are my greatest concern, but there is a time when the most courageous men must be discreet, and not add fuel to the flames of suspicion," he wrote to one former colleague from the Paris Committee of Jewish Delegations.[62]

To what extent were the Joint, the American Jewish Congress, the Paris Committee, and many other American-Jewish wartime initiatives appropriate passing responses to a onetime occurrence of global distress? Alternatively, to what extent did they entail ongoing responsibility—that is, in a newly globalized Jewish community, were Marshall and his elite American-Jewish associates supposed to take on a global role of Jewish stewardship, running projects for the benefit of indigent and persecuted brethren in the overseas "downtown" of Eastern Europe just as they had been doing for the benefit of downtown Jews in New York for the past couple of decades? Working energetically yet inconclusively on projects such as Jewish colonization in the Soviet Crimea or non-Zionist inclusion on the Jewish Agency, Louis Marshall struggled to frame answers to these questions in the 1920s, just as American Jews and their historians have been debating them ever since.

M. M. Silver is a professor of modern Jewish history at the Max Stern College of Emek Yezreel in Israel. His books in Hebrew and English include *Louis Marshall and the Rise of Jewish Ethnicity in America* (2013) and *In the Service of the West: A New Look at Modern Jewish History* (Hebrew, 2014). He studied modern Jewish history at the Hebrew University of Jerusalem, and he lives in the Galilee

Notes

1. Henry Feingold, *Lest Memory Cease: Finding Meaning in the American Jewish Past* (Syracuse, NY: Syracuse University Press, 1996), pp. 175–76.
2. For an extended discussion, see M. M. Silver, *Louis Marshall and the Rise of Jewish Ethnicity in America: A Biography* (Syracuse, NY: Syracuse University Press, 2013).
3. Ibid., pp. 262–65.
4. Analysis and figures here are based on Zosa Szajkowski, "Concord and Discord in American Jewish Overseas Relief, 1914–1924," *YIVO Annual of Jewish Social Science* 14 (1969): 99–158.
5. Steven Zipperstein, *Imagining Russian Jewry: Memory, History, Identity* (Seattle: University of Washington Press, 1999), p. 38.
6. Research in American ethnic history underscores the impact of elite leaders upon modes of integration and also persistent ethnic separatism among an array of immigrant groups. One such study that follows this influence exerted by what it terms "traditional progressive" leaders is Victor Greene, *American Immigrant Leaders 1800–1910: Marginality and Identity* (Baltimore: Johns Hopkins University Press, 1987).
7. Biographical details from Mary Kelly, *The Shamrock and the Lily: The New York Irish and the Creation of a Transatlantic Identity 1845–1921* (New York: Peter Lang, 2005), pp. 164–67.
8. Steven Erie, *Rainbow's End: Irish Americans and the Dilemmas of Urban Machine Politics, 1840–1985* (Berkeley: University of California Press, 1988), pp. 7–8, 91–95.
9. Michael McMenamin and Curt Zoller, *Becoming Winston Churchill: The Untold Story of Young Winston and His American Mentor* (Westport, CT: Greenwood, 2007).
10. James McGurrin, *Bourke Cockran: A Free Lance in American Politics* (New York: Arno Press, 1948), p. 219.
11. Kelly, *The Shamrock and the Lily,* p. 166.
12. Ibid.
13. Marshall routinely declared in this campaign that revoking the Russian trade treaty, owing to czarist antisemitism, was an American issue, not a Jewish one. Silver, *Louis Marshall,* p. 195.
14. In the Irish case, this dynamic might have been more pointed. The manner in which suppression of the 1916 Easter Rising in Ireland galvanized anti-English feeling among Irish Americans had no single, obvious wartime counterpart among Russian-Jewish immigrants in America, since in this Jewish case the most important symbolic precipitants of anti-Russian feeling occurred in the decade preceding the war, starting with the 1903 Kishinev pogrom.
15. McGurrin, *Bourke Cockran,* pp. 302–3.
16. Cockran letter to William Dillon, 6 November 1914, William Bourke Cockran Papers, New York Public Library, Box 22.
17. Cockran letter to Gertrude Kelly, 6 October 1914, Cockran Papers, Box 22.

18. Cockran letter to Dillon, 6 November 1914.
19. Marshall's address to the New York Kehillah Convention, April 1915, in Silver, *Louis Marshall*, p. 277.
20. Silver, *Louis Marshall*, p. 308.
21. Ibid., p. 253.
22. Transcript of Carnegie Hall address, New York City, 14 May 1916, Cockran Papers, Box 28, Folder 2.
23. Ibid.
24. Ibid.
25. In June 1916, Cockran publicly espoused American intervention in Ireland, citing as a precedent America's late nineteenth-century intervention against Spain, on behalf of Cuban patriots. Speech in Boston, 25 June 1916, Cockran Papers, Box 28, Folder 2.
26. Speech drafts, December 1917, Cockran Papers, Box 28, Folder 2.
27. Silver, *Louis Marshall*, p. 336.
28. For New York Jewish radicalism, see Tony Michels, *A Fire in Their Hearts: Yiddish Socialists in New York* (Cambridge MA: Harvard University Press, 2005).
29. For analysis of this perception of Hillquit as a traitor, see Frederick C. Giffin, "Morris Hillquit and the War Issue in the New York Mayoralty Campaign of 1917," *International Social Science Review* 74 (1999): 115–28.
30. Zosa Szajkowski, "The Jews and New York City's Mayoralty Election of 1917," *Jewish Social Studies* 32, no. 4 (1970): 286–306.
31. Silver, *Louis Marshall*, p. 322.
32. Cited in Ross Wilson, *New York and the First World War* (Dorchester: Routledge, 2014), pp. 177–78.
33. Ibid., p. 179.
34. Ibid.
35. Erie, *Rainbow's End*, pp. 104–5.
36. Wilson, *New York and the First World War*, p. 180.
37. Ibid., p. 181.
38. Ibid., p. 193.
39. Christopher M. Sterba, *Good Americans: Italian and Jewish Immigrants during the First World War* (New York: Oxford University Press, 2003), p. 162, and passim.
40. Lucy Dawidowicz, "Louis Marshall and the *Jewish Daily Forward*: An Episode in Wartime Censorship, 1917–1918," in *For Max Weinreich on His Seventieth Birthday: Studies in Jewish Languages, Literature and Society* (The Hague: Mouton, 1964), pp. 31–43.
41. Jonathan Frankel, "The Jewish Socialists and the American Jewish Congress Movement," *YIVO Annual of Jewish Social Science* 16 (1976): 202–341; Silver, *Louis Marshall*, p. 258.
42. In some examples explored below it is difficult to determine whether ideas of Jewish semi-autonomy in the Diaspora or even of nationalist "work in the present" derive from Zionist sources or from Dubnow's theories of diaspora nationalism. For a recent study that tends to identify Dubnow as a primary influence in early twentieth-century Jewish politics and the Zionists as a secondary influence, see Simon Rabinovitch, *Jewish Rights, National Rites: Nationalism and Autonomy in Late Imperial and Revolutionary Russia* (Stanford, CA: Stanford University Press, 2014). My own sense is that more often than not, Dubnow followed the Zionists' example, and not vice versa (as Rabinovitch implies), but sorting out this line of causality is not germane to the argument pursued below.

43. Christoph Gassenchmidt, *Jewish Liberal Politics in Tsarist Russia 1900–1914* (Houndsmills, Basingstoke, Hampshire: Macmillan in association with St. Anthony's College, Oxford, 1995), p. 7; Maksim Vinaver, "When Lawyers Studied History," in *The Golden Tradition: Jewish Life and Thought in Eastern Europe*, ed. Lucy Dawidowicz (New York: Holt, Rinehart and Winston, 1967), pp. 242–48.
44. Oscar Janowsky, *The Jews and Minority Rights, 1898–1919* (New York: AMS Press, 1966), pp. 91–92.
45. Benjamin Nathans, *Beyond the Pale: The Jewish Encounter with Late Imperial Russia* (Berkeley: University of California Press, 2002), p. 308.
46. Gassenchmidt, *Jewish Liberal Politics*, p. 39. See also Louis Greenberg, *The Jews in Russia: The Struggle for Emancipation* (New Haven, CT: Yale University Press, 1951), vol. 2, p. 117; Sidney Harcave, "The Jewish Question in the First State Duma" *Jewish Social Studies* 6 (1944): 161; B. A. Maklakov, "1905–1906 Godi," in *M.M. Vinaver i russkaia obschchestvennost nachala XX reka* (Paris, 1937), pp. 53–97.
47. Vinaver, "When Lawyers Studied History," pp. 241–42.
48. Janowsky, *The Jews and Minority Rights*, p. 109.
49. Again, Rabinovitch, *Jewish Rights, National Rites*, disputes the way I have formulated this chain of influence. He argues forcefully that Dubnow's autonomy conceptualizations frequently set a standard in Russian-Jewish politics to which the Zionists were essentially responsive. Nonetheless, this section's argument holds true on either interpretation: a decade before the American Jewish Congress debate, Vinaver, a Russian-Jewish non-Zionist, was locked in a stand-off with Zionists in ways uncannily similar to Marshall's subsequent situation.
50. Gassenchmidt, *Jewish Liberal Politics*, pp. 48–55.
51. Ezra Mendelsohn, *The Jews of East Central Europe between the World Wars* (Bloomington: Indiana University Press, 1983), p. 35.
52. See, for instance, Celia Heller, *On the Edge of Destruction: Jews of Poland between the Two World Wars* (New York: Columbia University Press, 1977).
53. For Grunbaum's biography and activities, see Mendelsohn, *The Jews of East Central Europe*, pp. 53–58; Roman Frister, *No Compromise* [Hebrew] (Tel Aviv: Zmora Bitan Press, 1987). For postwar Zionism in Poland, see Ezra Mendelsohn, *Zionism in Poland: The Formative Years, 1915–1926* (New Haven, CT: Yale University Press, 1981).
54. Mendelsohn, *Zionism in Poland*, pp. 213–22.
55. Analysis and examples from Yitzhak Grunbaum, *Speeches in the Polish Sejm* [Hebrew] (Jerusalem: Neumann Books, 1963).
56. Frister, *No Compromise*, pp. 27–29; Yitzhak Grunbaum, *A Generation on Trial* [Hebrew] (Jerusalem: Bialik Institute, 1951), pp. 64–85.
57. Silver, *Louis Marshall*, pp. 490–525.
58. See, for instance, Grunbaum's 1928 open letter to Weizmann, reprinted in Grunbaum, *A Generation on Trial*, pp. 170–74.
59. See, for instance, Fink's analysis of the April 1919 disturbances in Pinsk, in Carole Fink, *Defending the Rights of Others: The Great Powers, the Jews, and International Minority Protection 1878–1938* (Cambridge: Cambridge University Press, 2004), pp. 183–85.
60. Silver, *Louis Marshall*, p. 344.
61. Matthew Silver, "Louis Marshall and the Democratization of Jewish Identity," *American Jewish History* 94 (March–June 2008): 55.
62. Marshall to Dr. Salkind, 20 April 1920, in ibid., p. 57.

Selected Bibliography

Primary Sources

Grunbaum, Yitzhak. *Speeches in the Polish Sejm* [Hebrew]. Jerusalem: Neumann Books, 1963.
Reznikoff, Charles, ed. *Louis Marshall: Champion of Liberty, Selected Papers and Addresses.* Philadelphia: Jewish Publication Society of America, 1957.
William Bourke Cockran Papers, New York Public Library.

Secondary Sources

Dawidowicz, Lucy. "Louis Marshall and the *Jewish Daily Forward*: An Episode in Wartime Censorship, 1917–1918." In *For Max Weinreich on His Seventieth Birthday: Studies in Jewish Languages, Literature and Society*, pp. 31–43. The Hague: Mouton, 1964.
Erie, Steven. *Rainbow's End: Irish Americans and the Dilemmas of Urban Machine Politics, 1840–1985.* Berkeley: University of California Press, 1988.
Feingold, Henry. *Lest Memory Cease: Finding Meaning in the American Jewish Past.* Syracuse, NY: Syracuse University Press, 1996.
Fink, Carole. *Defending the Rights of Others: The Great Powers, the Jews, and International Minority Protection 1878–1938.* Cambridge: Cambridge University Press, 2004.
Frankel, Jonathan. "The Jewish Socialists and the American Jewish Congress Movement." *YIVO Annual of Jewish Social Science* 16 (1976): 202–341.
———. *Prophecy and Politics: Socialism, Nationalism and the Russian Jews 1862–1917.* Cambridge: Cambridge University Press, 1981.
Frister, Roman. *No Compromise* [Hebrew]. Tel Aviv: Zmora Bitan Press, 1987.
Gassenchmidt, Christoph. *Jewish Liberal Politics in Tsarist Russia 1900–1914.* Houndsmills, Basingstoke, Hampshire: Macmillan in association with St. Anthony's College, Oxford, 1995.
Giffin, Frederick C. "Morris Hillquit and the War Issue in the New York Mayoralty Campaign of 1917." *International Social Science Review* 74 (1999): 115–28.
Greene, Victor. *American Immigrant Leaders 1800–1910: Marginality and Identity.* Baltimore: Johns Hopkins University Press, 1987.
Heller, Celia. *On the Edge of Destruction: Jews of Poland between the Two World Wars.* New York: Columbia University Press, 1977.
Janowsky, Oscar. *The Jews and Minority Rights, 1898–1919.* New York: Columbia University Press, 1933; reprint, New York: AMS Press, 1966.
Kelly, Mary. *The Shamrock and the Lily: The New York Irish and the Creation of a Transatlantic Identity 1845–1921.* New York: Peter Lang, 2005.
McGurrin, James. *Bourke Cockran: A Free Lance in American Politics.* New York: Arno Press, 1948.
Mendelsohn, Ezra. *The Jews of East Central Europe between the World Wars.* Bloomington: Indiana University Press, 1983.
Michels, Tony. *A Fire in Their Hearts: Yiddish Socialists in New York.* Cambridge, MA: Harvard University Press, 2005.
Nathans, Benjamin. *Beyond the Pale: The Jewish Encounter with Late Imperial Russia.* Berkeley: University of California Press, 2002.
Rabinovitch, Simon. *Jewish Rights, National Rites: Nationalism and Autonomy in Late Imperial and Revolutionary Russia.* Stanford, CA: Stanford University Press, 2014.

Silver, M. M. *Louis Marshall and the Rise of Jewish Ethnicity in America: A Biography.* Syracuse: Syracuse University Press, 2013.
Sterba, Christopher M. *Good Americans: Italian and Jewish Immigrants During the First World War.* New York: Oxford University Press, 2003.
Szajkowski, Zosa. "Concord and Discord in American Jewish Overseas Relief, 1914–1924." *YIVO Annual of Jewish Social Science* 14 (1969): 99–158.
———. "The Jews and New York City's Mayoralty Election of 1917," *Jewish Social Studies* 32, no. 4 (1970): 286–306.
Vinaver, Maksim. "When Lawyers Studied History." In *The Golden Tradition: Jewish Life and Thought in Eastern Europe,* ed. Lucy Dawidowicz, pp. 242–48. New York: Holt, Rinehart and Winston, 1967.
Wilson, Ross. *New York and the First World War.* Dorchester: Routledge, 2014.
Zipperstein, Steven. *Imagining Russian Jewry: Memory, History, Identity.* Seattle: University of Washington Press, 1999.

Index

Aaronsohn, Alexander, 249, 251, 259n43
Adler, Cyrus, 268, 274
Akselrod, Pavel, 284
Algeria, 6, 22, 87, 88, 90, 91–92
Alliance Israélite Universelle, 24, 28n19, 65, 67, 70, 71, 178, 181–83, 187, 188, 206, 207, 243, 254
"Alliancists" (in Salonica), 181–90
Alsace-Lorraine, 6, 35, 86, 87, 88, 96–102
American Colony, 230, 231, 235n9, 238n46. *See also* Jerusalem
American Israelite, 212. *See also* press
American Jewish Committee, 26, 305–6, 308, 311–14, 317
American Jewish Congress, 9, 24, 70, 313–17, 319–20
American Jewish Historical Society, xii
American Jewish Joint Distribution Committee (AJJDC, JDC), 9, 24, 63–64, 116, 132, 137–9, 144, 227, 230–32, 238n41, 256, 304–7, 315, 319
American Relief Administration (ARA), 132, 136, 139
American Revolution, 21
American Socialist, 283
Anarchism, 288
Anglo-Jewish Association, 24
Anglo-Palestine Bank, 225, 236n20
An-sky, S. (Shloyme Zanvyl Rapoport), 133–4
Antisemitism, 5, 21–22, 34–39, 41, 44–46, 48, 57, 62, 74, 87–88, 91, 93–96, 98, 100, 114, 119, 144, 157–58, 264–65, 273, 317–18
Anti-war sentiment, 60–61, 203, 211–12, 214, 304
Appelbaum, Peter C., 4
Arabs, 224, 226, 229, 230, 231, 236n13
Arct, Stanisław, 26
Armenians, 201–2, 213
Armistice of Mudros, 201, 207, 215
Asch, Sholem, 294
Ashkenazi Jews (in Palestine), 223, 226, 229
Association of Jewish Organizations in Germany for the Protection of the Rights of the Jews of the East, 10, 24
Atatürk, Mustafa Kemal, 212
Auschwitz, 3
Austria (Republic), 17, 43–44
Austria-Hungary, 17, 19, 34, 36, 42, 113, 114, 176, 179, 184, 281, 288, 290, 294
    Jews in, 34, 35–39, 113
    See also Habsburg Empire; Habsburg Monarchy

Baghdad, 7, 242, 245–48
    wartime conditions in, 253–57
Baghdad, Jews in, 242, 257n6
    and Arab Revolt, 251
    and desertion from Ottoman Army, 248, 252, 254–55
    and economic activity, 243
    and education, 243–44
    and labor battalions, 242, 246, 249, 251–52

and military conscription, 244, 245, 248, 250–55
and military service, 244, 245, 257
and Muslim opposition to military service of, 245–46
Baker, Newton, 265–66, 272
Balfour, Arthur James, 68, 70
Balfour Declaration, 2, 4, 27n11, 40–41, 64, 67, 70, 73, 190, 312
Balkan Wars (1912–13), 5, 7, 179, 184, 190, 202–3, 210, 212, 246–47, 249
Ballin, Albert, 58
Bankers (Jewish), 10, 26, 62, 227, 305
Baranov, M. (Gormidor, Moyshe) 289–90, 293
Baron, Salo, 29n23
Barondess, Joseph, 304, 313
Barrès, Maurice, 93
Basch, Victor, 58
Basra, 250, 255
Bavaria, 21–22
Beggars, 208–10
Beilis, Mendel, 282, 289–90
Belgium, 281, 288, 290
Beneš, Eduard, 66
Ben Ya'akov, Michal, 8–9
Bereg County, 112, 119
Berger, Victor, 297
Bergson, Henri, 59
Berlin, 283
Berlin, Congress of, 23, 28n25
Berne, 284–85
Bernstein, Eduard, 288, 296
Bessarabia, 43
Bible, 96, 266, 270
Bigart, Jacques, 70
Black wedding (*shvartze khasene*), 143
Bleichröder, Gerson, 28n25
Bloch, Abraham, 87, 88–96, 100, 102, 103
Bloch, David, 87, 96–102
Bloch, Edmond, 95
Bloch, Joseph Samuel, 121
Bloch, Marc, 1–2
Board of Deputies of British Jews, 24
Bogen, Boris, 139
Bohemia, 38, 41–42, 44–45, 113, 117, 124

Bologna, 22
Bolsheviks, 57, 158
Bolshevism, 284–85, 288, 291, 296
Borderlands, 87–88, 100
Borsod County, 122
Boston, 290
Brams, Iakov, 158–60, 164
Brandeis, Louis, 69
Brătianu, Ian, 66
British Army in Palestine, 231
Brody, 123
Bronstein, Anna, 290
Brusilov Offensive, 37, 124
Buber, Martin, 60
Buczacz, 113, 123
Budapest, 9, 112–13, 115–16, 117–25
  Jewish community in, 112, 115, 117–19, 122–23, 125, 129
Bulgaria, 23, 189
Bukovina, 34, 36, 39, 43, 113, 119, 123
Bund, 40, 46, 158–59, 160–62, 280–81, 285–86, 290–92, 317
Burgin, Hertz, 292
Burla, Yehuda, 251–52

Cahan, Abraham, 279, 280, 282–283, 286–97, 304
  and anti-Russian attitudes, 282–83, 288
  and Palestine, 290–91, 297
  and pro-German attitudes, 282–83, 288–89
Carlebach, Joseph, 61
Caro, Ezekiel, 116
Caucasus, 242, 247, 252–54
Censorship, 202, 204, 207
Center for Jewish History, 6
Central Powers, 177, 179, 188–89
  and Galicia, 113, 123
Chamber of Deputies (France), 281
Chaplains, 267, 269–74; *See also* Jewish Chaplains
Chelouche, 226
Chicago, 283
Cholera, 224–27
Christians, 224, 230–31, 238n46
Chronakis, Paris Papamichos, 8
Churchill, Winston, 308, 310–11

citizenship, 191
    and resource distribution, 115
    Austrian, 113, 116–117
    Hungarian, 117, 119–21
Clausewitz, Carl von, 284
Clemenceau, Georges, 66, 70
Cockran, William Bourke, 307–12
Cohen, Hermann, 60
Colonies, 86–88, 91, 102
Comité des Délégations Juives, 10, 24, 71, 320
Commemoration, 85–86, 88, 93, 95, 98, 101, 102
Commission on Training Camp Activities (CTCA), 266
Committee for the East, 60
Committee on New States, 72
Conjoint Foreign Committee, 24
Constantine, King of Greece, 186, 189
Constantinople, 7
    Jews in, 201–16
    occupation of, 201–4, 207–8, 213
Cooperman, Jessica, 7
Corber, Erin, 6
Cordon sanitaire, 133, 136
Czech nationalists, 44
Czechoslovakia, 17, 42–44, 48, 66, 72

Damascus blood libel, 22
Deák, Ferenc, 114
Deportations, 39–40
Der Tog (Day), 291
Dimanshtein, Simon, 157, 170n38
Disease, 208, 210–11, 215, 224, 227, 247, 251–52, 256; *See also* typhus
Disinfection, 135–38, 141
Dmowski, Roman, 65–66
Dreyfus Affair, 22
Dreyfuss, Sarah Thérèse, 230
Dubnow, Simon, 20
Durkheim, Émile, 59

Eastern European Jews, 39, 47, 48
Eastern Front, 24, 113, 119, 124, 131, 133
Egyenlőség [Equality], 115, 116, 119, 120
Egypt, 247
Einstein, Albert, 61

EKOPO (Evreiskii komitet pomoshchi zhertvam voiny, Jewish Committee for the Relief of War Victims), 134
'Eli, Nissim Shem-Tov, 204–05, 210–14
Elmaniach, Avraham, 226
Engel, David, 10
Engels, Friedrich, 281
England, 288, 290
Enlightenment, 21–22
Entente, 177, 188
Enver Pasha, 211, 213
Espionage Act, 295
Estonia, 17
Estraikh, Gennady, 7, 9
Eötvös, József, 114
Evkom (Jewish Commissariat), 153, 156–58, 160–65, 167
Evsektsiia (Jewish Section of the Communist Party), 165

Fascism, 33. *See also* Nazis
Faisal, Emir, 68
Fareynikte (United Jewish Socialist Workers Party), 158, 162
Feigenbaum, Benjamin, 284, 292–93
Felsőzsolcza, 122
Ferencváros train station, 115
Fink, Carole, 8, 9
Forverts (Forward), 279–84, 286, 288–92, 294–97. *See also* press
Forvertsism, 279, 289, 297
Forward Association, 282
Fosdick, Raymond, 267–68, 272–73
Fourteen Points, 42
France, 8, 22, 68–70, 85–103, 182, 281, 288, 290, 294
    Jews in, 6
    Salonican Jews in, 180, 182, 189
Franco-Prussian War of 1871, 178
Frank, Leo, 289
Franz Joseph (Emperor), 37, 44, 113, 124, 128n63
French Republic, 85–86, 90–91, 94, 98–100, 102
French Revolution, 20, 21
Freud, Sigmund, 59, 63
Frey, Gottfried, 135, 142
Fried, Alfred Hermann, 61
Friedman, Isaiah, 4

Fulda, Ludwig, 59

Galanta, 121
Galicia, 34, 36–37, 39–42, 113–114, 119, 123, 134, 137
    Jews of, 112, 114–18, 120–22, 124–25
Gallipoli Campaign, 189
Gegenwartsarbeit, 316, 318–19
German-Israelite Communal Federation, 188
German-Jewish Committee for the Liberation of Russian Jewry, 9
German Military Press Agency (*Kriegspresseamt*), 283
Germans, 33, 42–44
German Social Democratic Party, 283
German Socialist Federation, 285–86
Germany, 2, 17, 22, 41–42, 63–66, 71–72, 176, 184, 281–284, 286, 288–90, 294–95
    1916 military census (*Judenzählung*) in, 5, 38
    Jews of, 4, 34–37, 41
    policy in Russian-Poland, 40; See also Poland, German occupation of
Gilchrist, Harry, 136
Glazebrook, Otis, 223–24, 231
Goldfarb, Max, 286, 294, 296
Gompers, Samuel, 295
Great Britain, 8, 22, 25, 64, 67–68, 69–70, 281
    Foreign Office, 25
    See also England
Greece, 63–64, 72, 175–76, 184, 186, 188–89
Greek Orthodox, 201–2, 208–9, 213
Grunbaum, Yitzhak, 316–19
Győr, 121–22

Haas, Ludwig, 135, 140–41
Habsburg army, 38–39
Habsburg Empire, 17, 19, 23. See also Austria-Hungary
Habsburg Monarchy, 2, 5, 33–34, 37–38, 41–42, 44, 114
    Jews of, 8, 9, 34, 35–39, 113
    See also Austria-Hungary

Habsburg "umpire", 37, 41
Hadassah, Women's Zionist Organization of America, 304
Haggadot, 203–4, 207, 210, 214
Halicz, 123
Halukah, 8, 225
Hasidim, 38, 45
    and public health, 140–41
Hasidism, 293
Headlam-Morley, James, 72
Hearst, William Randolph, 312
"Hep! Hep" riots, 21
Hero, 85–103
Hertzka, Yella, 61
Herut, 225–26, 236n16
Herzl, Theodor, 185
Hilfsverein der deutschen Juden, 183
Hillquit, Morris, 282–83, 286, 297, 304, 312–13
Holocaust, 2–3, 6, 26
Holy Cities, 222, 233
Home Front, 38, 47–48, 202–4, 207–12, 214–15, 222–24, 226–8, 230, 232, 255–56
Hoofien, Eliezer Siegfried, 227–28, 230
Hoover, Herbert, 136, 139
Horthy, Miklós, 44
House, Edward, 69, 71
Hungarians, 33, 42–44
Hungary, 17, 34, 39, 43–44
    and Jewish refugees in Budapest, 117–119
    and Jewish soldiers in, 120
    and migration of Galician Jews into, 114–15
    and provincial Jewish communities in, 121–23
    and refugee aid in, 116
    and refugee arrival in, 113
    and repatriation policy of, 124–25
Hygiene, 140–41

Immigrants (Jewish), 4, 38, 90–91, 93–96
Ingerman, Anna, 286
Ingerman, Sergei, 286
International Ladies' Garment Workers' Union, 283

Internationalism, 286–87, 289–90, 292–94, 296
Iraq, 17
Israeli Law of Return, 297
Israelitische Allianz zu Wien, 116, 124
Italy, 37, 42, 183

Jacobs, Aletta, 61
Jacobson, Abigail, 4
Janco, Georges, 63
Janco, Marcel, 63
János, Sándor, 115–18, 123–24
Japan, 25, 70, 294
Jerusalem, 8, 222–25, 229–30, 232–33, 236n6
Jewish chaplains, 6, 38, 47, 88–92, 94, 244, 269–71, 274
Jewish Chronicle, 58–59
Jewish ethnicity, 34, 48, 178, 181, 289–90, 303, 314
Jewish loyalty, 114–115, 119–20, 125. See also Patriotism (Jewish)
Jewish National Committees, 46
Jewish national identity, 2, 33, 35, 39, 45, 47, 152, 181, 185, 191, 279, 289–91, 297, 314
Jewish national rights, 40, 46, 47, 213, 318
Jewish National Workers' Alliance, 291
Jewish Party, 45
Jewish pride, 180
Jewish Socialist Federation (JSF), 280–81, 286–87, 294, 296
Jewish soldiers, 6–7
    in Austria-Hungary, 38, 47, 118, 120
    in France, 86–89, 91–92, 98, 102, 117, 125
    in Ottoman Empire, 5, 203, 206–7, 211–12, 223, 243–45, 250, 254–55
    in Russia, 151, 154, 160–61, 166, 282
    in United States, 7, 268–69, 274
Jewish solidarity, 178–80
Jewish Teachers Training Institute (Vilna), 292
Jewish Welfare Board (JWB), 268–70, 272–74

Jewish women, 9, 39, 47–48, 203–4, 206–9
    in Ottoman Palestine, 222–34
Jews
    in Austria-Hungary, 8, 17, 34–37, 39
    in Baghdad, 242–57
    in Constantinople, 201–16
    in Czechoslovakia, 17, 42, 44–46
    in England, 5, 34–37
    in France, 6, 34–35, 37, 85–103
    in Germany, 5, 17, 34, 39, 41, 63
    in Hungary, 17, 34, 44, 112–26
    in Italy, 34
    in Lithuania, 45–47
    in North Africa, 223, 226, 232
    in Ottoman Empire, 17, 201–15, 222–34, 242–57
    in Palestine, 8, 222–34
    in Poland, 9, 17, 33, 42, 45–46, 65, 131–44, 317
    in Romania, 17, 34, 43, 47
    in Russia, 17, 34–37, 39–40, 47, 62, 133–34, 144, 152–3, 166
    in Salonica, 8, 175–91
    in Soviet Union, 17, 35, 46–47, 151–67
    in United States, 5, 7, 8–9, 57, 60, 62–63, 65, 68, 139, 141, 180, 183, 227, 231, 263–75, 279–97, 303–20
Joint Distribution Committee (JDC). See American Jewish Joint Distribution Committee
Judenzählung, 5, 38
Jüdisches Hilfskomitee für Polen und Litauen, 137
Jüdische Zeitung, 123

Kallen, Horace M., 289
Kálmán, Mihály, 10
Karmona, Eliya, 204, 206, 209–14
Keleti [Eastern] train station, 112, 115
Kertész, Antál, 122
Kienthal, 285
King-Crane Commission, 69
Kishinev Pogrom, 289, 290, 315–16, 318–19
Klein-Pejšová, Rebekah, 9

Index 331

Kollontai, Alexandra, 285–86
Kossovski, Vladimir, 285, 288, 292
Kraków, 113, 143, 147–148 n50, 288
Kurima, 119
Kurland, 289

Labor and Socialist International, 296–97
Labor Battalions (*amele taburu*) 202–4, 207–8, 211–12, 230, 242, 246, 249, 251–53
Ladies' Garment Worker, 283–84
Ladino, 202–4, 208, 210, 212–13, 215
Landauer, Gustav, 61
Lansing, Robert, 69
Latvia, 17
Lazaron, Morris, 269
League of Nations, 17, 67, 68–74, 137–38
Lebanon, 17
Lemberg/Lwów/L'viv, 19, 41, 116, 122–23, 136–37
Lenin, Vladimir, 35, 64, 69, 284–88
Lessin, Avrom, 282
Le Sueur, Arthur, 287
Liebknecht, Karl, 285–86
Lipets, David; *See* Goldfarb, Max
Lissauer, Ernst, 60
Lithuania, 17, 35, 40, 289
Litvak, A. (Chaim-Yankl Helfand), 292
Lloyd George, David, 65–66, 68, 70
Locust plague, 223–24, 228, 235n9, 253
Łódź, 133–34
Łomża, 134
Lore, Ludwig, 285
Los Angeles, 177–78
Lublin, 134
Luxemburg, Rosa, 61

Mack, Julian, 69, 71
Magyars; *See* Hungarians
Márkmaros County, 112, 119–20
Mármarossziget, 116
Marne (Battle of the), 88
Marseilles, 297
Marshall, Louis, 7, 26, 65, 71–72, 74, 295, 303–21
Martov, Julius, 284

Marx, Karl, 281, 297, 298n4
Marxism, 279, 284, 288, 293
Masaryk, Tomáš, 44, 46
Mays, Devi, 7
McMahon-Hussein Agreement (1915), 67
Mehmed VI Vahidettin, Sultan, 214
Menshivism, 284–86, 291
Mexico, 294–95
Michaelson, L. B., 26
Migration, 17–19
Military, United States, 133, 136
Military service, 203, 211–12, 214–15
Miller, David Hunter, 71
Minority rights, 2, 4, 57, 316–17, 320
Minority Treaties, 2, 4, 26, 27n11, 70–74
Misař, Olga, 61
Mission Laïque Française, 182
Mobilization, military, 204–7, 209, 212, 215
Modigliani, Giuseppe, 61
Montefiore, Moses, 10
Montenegro, 23, 290
Monuments, 85, 87, 95–100, 101, 103
Moravia, 38, 41–42, 44–45, 112–13, 116–17, 124
Morgenthau, Henry, 72, 225, 231
Mortara Case, 22
Moscow, 152–66
Mosse, Werner, 4
Mosul, 250–51
Múlt és Jövő [Past and Future], 122
Muslims, 201, 211, 214

Nagyvárad/Grosswardein/Oradea, 124
Nahum, Haham Hayim, 243–44
Nationalism, 37, 41, 48, 60, 95, 178, 181, 187, 190, 191, 279, 284, 287, 289–93, 296–97
National minorities, 33
National self-determination, 33, 42, 202, 213–14
Nazis, 20, 26, 41, 90, 103, 141, 304
New York, 9, 279, 282, 285–86, 290–92, 294, 297
New York Call, 286
New York Volkszeitung, 285
Nikolsburg/Mikulov, 116

NILI, 64
non-Muslims (in Ottoman Empire), 201–3, 211–12
Novyi mir (New World), 294
Nyiregyhaza, 119

Ober Ost, 135
Olgin (Novomiski), Moyshe (Moissaye), 286, 294
Ónod, 122
Oppenheim, Max von, 62
Orphans, 208–10, 228, 232, 237n34
Österreichische Wochenschrift, 121, 124
Ostjuden, 144
Ottoman authorities, 222–26, 230, 236n13
Ottoman Empire, 2, 5–6, 8, 17, 23, 25, 41, 57, 62, 64, 67, 178–79, 186, 201–2, 214, 225–26, 242
    and wartime casualties, 254, 261n66
    and Germany, 246, 259n25
    and military conscription, 246, 247–50, 258n10, 259n37
    and military training and equipment, 248–49, 259n43
    and Young Turk Revolution, 181
    Jewish attitudes towards, 211–15, 225, 242, 245, 248–50, 256
    Jewish military service in, 7, 243–48, 250–55
    Jews in, 7, 202, 210–11, 243–44
Ottoman Public Debt, 25, 29n32
OZE (Obshchestvo okhraneniia zdorov'ia evreiskogo naseleniia, Society for the Protection of the Health of the Jewish Population), 133–34

Pacifism, 61, 281–82, 294
Paderewski, Ignacy, 65
Paix et Droit, 24
Pale of Settlement, 2, 39–40, 58, 62
Palestine, 8–9, 17, 24, 62–63, 67–70, 180, 213–14, 222–34, 242, 249, 251–52, 290–91, 297
Panken, Jacob, 297
Panter, Sarah, 4
Paris, 19, 281, 284, 290

Paris Peace Conference, 2, 4, 26, 28n11, 46, 57, 65–74, 316, 319–20
Patriotism (Jewish), 1, 35–37, 114, 202, 212–15, 282, 284, 287, 290–92, 294–96
Patterson, NJ, 280
Paucker, Arnold, 4
Permanent Court of International Justice, 73
Pershing, John, 267–68
Peskin, Shmuel, 289
Pester Lloyd, 116
Petrograd, 152–53, 157–58
Philadelphia, 24
Philanthropy, 208, 209. *See also* Relief work (Jewish)
Pilsudski, Jozef, 317
Pogroms, 22, 41–42, 45–46, 71, 131, 135, 139, 151, 154, 158, 161–63, 165, 183
Poilu, 86–88, 101–2
Poland, 9, 17, 19, 26, 28n11, 33, 35, 37, 42, 44, 61–63, 71–72, 133, 145
    German occupation of, 61–62, 131–33, 135, 137, 141–43, 145
Polish Minority Treaty, 42, 71–74
Polish nationalists, 41, 44
Populist movement (in Russia), 290
Post-imperial identity, 187, 190–91
Pöstyén/Piešt'any, 117, 121
Pozsony/Pressburg (later Bratislava), 121
Press, 59, 61, 63–65, 98, 103, 185, 190, 244, 246, 283, 287, 291, 294, 312
    American Jewish, 60
    antisemitic, 120
    French-Jewish, 89, 90–91, 96
    Habsburg Jewish, 36, 118, 120–21, 123
    Salonican Jewish, 175–76, 178, 180, 186–89
    Ottoman Jewish, 202, 210, 212, 214, 215
    Yiddish, 281, 290, 303
    Zionist, 37, 180, 181, 186, 223, 225
Prisoners-of-War, 206–7
    Jewish, 151–52, 154–67
Propaganda, 188

Prostitution, 231, 238n52, 239nn53–54
Przemyśl, 113

Rathenau, Walter, 58
Rationing, 208–9, 212, 214–15
Red Army, 157–58, 165, 167
Red Cross, 132
Refugee Aid Committee, 123
Refugees (Jewish), 38, 112, 115,
   133–34, 136–37, 152
  aid for, 116–17, 120
  and provincial Jewish communities,
   121–22
  Galician and Bukovinian, 38–39,
   118, 122–25
  Hungarian, 118–21, 125
  in Austria, 116–18, 122
  in Hungary, 38, 112–26
  in Russia, 40, 133–34, 165
  perceptions of, 114–15, 119, 122
  repatriation of, 123–25
Reichstag (Germany), 281, 283
Reinach, Joseph, 60
Reisen, Abraham, 282
Relief work (Jewish), 38–39, 152,
   163–67, 179–180, 229–33
  and Jewish women, 39, 182,
   232–33
Religion, 297
Religious pluralism, 264–65, 268, 271,
   273–74
Republicanism (in France), 86–88, 94,
   100–02
Rogoff, Hillel, 297
Romania, 17, 23, 28n25, 33, 43–44, 57,
   63–66, 72
Rosenfeld, Morris, 310
Rosenthal, Daniel, 9
Rosenthal, Léon, 61
Roth, Jack J., 3
Rothschild family, 23, 25
Rothschild, Lord Nathan (Natty), 25
Rozenblit, Marsha L., 4, 8–9, 19
Ruppin, Arthur, 18–19
Russia/Russian Empire, 2, 10, 17–19,
   22, 25, 33, 35, 37, 39, 41–42, 63–64,
   112, 122–23, 179, 183–84, 280–94
Russian-American Commercial Treaty,
   28n25

Russian army, 113, 119–20, 123,
   126n4, 128n44, 151
Russian Poland, 37, 39–40, 61, 131, 134
Russian Revolution of 1905, 280, 291
Russian Revolutions of 1917, 4, 27n11,
   35, 63–64, 151–52, 158, 303, 312
Russian Social Democratic Labor Party,
   285
Russo-Japanese War, 25, 28n25
Russophobia, 176, 183–84

Sacred Union of Peoples, 87, 92–94,
   102
Safed, 8, 222, 227–28, 232
Sajólád, 122
Salonica, 8
  anti-Russian sentiment in, 176,
   183–84
  as a "Jewish Republic," 184
  clashes in, 175–76
  class divisions in, 179, 184–85, 190
  economic impact of the war in,
   179, 185, 189
  enemy propaganda in, 188, 190
  Entente troops in, 189
  French culture and identity in,
   177–79
  French perceptions of Zionism in,
   188
  Greek-Christian attitudes towards
   Jews in, 185–88
  Jewish attitudes to Greece in, 184,
   186–87, 189–90
  Jewish identity in, 178–84, 187,
   191
  Jewish perceptions of, 182, 184
  Jewish relief work in, 179–80
  Jewish support for Venizelos in,
   186–87, 190
  Jewish women's relief work in, 182
  Jews in French Army from, 180,
   182
  Movement of National Defense in,
   189
  National elections of June 1915 in,
   186, 188
  National Schism in, 189–90
  Pro-Entente support in, 176, 182,
   185–86, 189–90

Pro-French attitudes of Jews in, 176–84, 186–91
Pro-German attitudes of Jews in, 176–77, 183–86, 188, 190–91
Support for Alliance Israélite Universelle in, 178, 181–82, 185–88
Transnational politics in, 188–90
Zionist/anti-Zionist conflict in, 175–76, 181–83, 187, 189–90
Zionists in, 175–76, 180–81, 183–90
Zionist support for the Royalists in, 186
Salutsky, Jacob Benjamin, 281
Sambor, 123
Sáros, 112, 119, 123
Sátoraljaújhely, 116
Schiff, Jacob, 10, 28n25, 62, 305, 310
Schneidemann, Philipp, 283
Scholem, Gershom, 61
Schück, Mayer, 122
"Second Thirty Years War," 3, 6
Sée, Eugène, 67
Self Defense, Jewish, in Russia, 152, 154, 157–63, 165–66
Self-determination; *See* National Self Determination
Sephardic Jews, 223, 225–28, 230, 233, 239n61
    from Salonica abroad, 180
    in France, 180, 182, 189
    in Lausanne, 188
    in Palestine, 222, 225–27, 230
    in Salonica, 175–91
Serbia, 23, 179, 189, 290
Shina, Salman, 254, 255
Shukman, Harold, 4
Silber, Marcos, 4
Silver, M.M., 7, 9
Simon, Reeva Spector, 7–8
Slovakia, 42–45
Śniatyn, 113
Socialism, 280–81, 283–91, 295–97
Socialist Party of America (SPA), 280, 286, 287, 297
Socialist Propaganda League, 287
Socialist (Second) International, 281, 283–85, 287, 289, 297

Soldiers; *See* Jewish soldiers
Somme (Battle of), 3
Soup kitchens, 229
"Southern storms"; *See* pogroms
Soviet Union, 17, 33, 35, 46–47
Stalin, Josef, 35, 295
Stalinism, 47
Stanislau/Stanisławów, 116, 122–23, 148n51
St. George Cross, 282
Stomfa/Stupava, 121
Strasbourg, 96, 99–100
Straus, Isaac, 60
Stryj, 122–23
Suez Canal Company, 25
Sykes-Picot Agreement (1916), 67
Syria, 17, 112, 242, 247
Szatmár County, 116

Taft, William Howard, 29n25
Tammany Hall, 308, 312
Temple Emanu-El, 306, 313
Third International (Comintern), 285, 293, 296
Tiberias, 222, 228, 232
Tisza, István, 121
Torah, 285
TOZ (Towarzystwo Ochrony Zdrowia Ludności Żydowskiej, Society for the Protection of the Health of the Jewish Population), 133
Transylvania, 43
Treaty of Berlin (1878), 57
Treaty of Brest-Litovsk (1918), 64
Trotsky, Leon, 64, 284, 294–95
Tsukunft (Future), 282, 284–85, 294
Turka, 123
Turkey, 17, 204, 215
Typhus, 9, 131–44, 224, 227
Tzara, Tristan, 63

Ujdiósgyőr, 122
Ukraine, 46, 151
Ukrainians, 33, 41–43
Ungarisch Hradisch/ Hradiště Uherské, 117–18, 122, 125
Ung County, 112, 119–20
Union of Jewish Soldiers (VSEV), 10, 151–167

Union patriotique des Français israélites (UPFI), 95, 100
United States, 19, 22, 25–26, 62, 66, 68–69
  Army of, 264–66, 273–74
  entry into World War I, 5
  religious pluralism in, 264–65, 268, 271, 273–74
Universalism, 86–88, 94, 102

Vázsonyi, Vilmos, 120
Venizelos, Eleftherios, 66, 186, 188–89
Verdun (battle of), 3
Versailles Treaty, 28n11, 33, 41, 43
Vester, Bertha Spafford, 230–31
Veterans, 94–96
Veterans' associations, 94–95, 101
Vienna, 38–39, 112–13, 115–16, 118, 121, 124–25
Vilna/Wilno, 136–37
Vinaver, Maksim, 315–16
Vladeck, Baruch Charney, 294
Volunteers, 88–89, 91, 95–96, 98, 101–2
VSEV; *See* Union of Jewish Soldiers

Walling, William English, 286
Warburg family, 25
Warburg, Felix, 139
War finance, 25
Warsaw, 40, 131, 134, 136, 139–40, 142–43, 178, 290
Weimar constitution, 17
Weimar Republic, 41
Weizmann, Chaim, 64, 68–69
Western Wall (Jerusalem), 297
Widows, 207, 209–11
Wilson, Woodrow, 23, 42, 65–66, 68–73, 266, 309, 312, 319
Wise, Stephen, 69
Wolf, Lucien, 58, 62–63, 65, 70–74
Wolff, Theodor, 58
Women; *See* Jewish women
World War I
  and "Thirty Years War of the Twentieth Century," 3
  armistice ending, 9
  as a Muslim war, 249–50
  horrors of, 33, 85
  in general scholarship, 3–4
  local understandings of, 177, 181–87
  neglect of in Jewish historical scholarship, 2–5
  transnational politics during, 188–92
World War II, 3, 5, 264, 274

Yiddish, 7, 34–35, 46–47, 153–54, 279–83, 286, 289–91, 294–95, 303
Young Men's Christian Association (YMCA), 7, 266–68, 272, 274
Young Turk Revolution, 181, 204, 212, 256
Young Turks, 211, 214, 242–43, 245
Yugoslavia, 17, 72

Zaleszczyki, 113
Zangwill, Israel, 56
Zboró, 119, 127n37
Zechlin, Egmont, 4
Zemplén County, 112, 116, 119, 123
Zimmerwald Conference, 284–88, 292, 294–95
Zinoviev, Grigory, 284, 295
Zionism, 40, 48, 57, 59–60, 64, 67, 69, 175–76, 180, 183, 210, 213–14, 290–91, 297
  in Salonica, 175–76, 180–81, 183–85, 190
  in United States, 304
Zionist Anglo-Palestine Bank, 225
Zionists, 20, 37, 40–41, 45–46, 60, 64, 66–67, 69–70, 153, 155, 158–60, 162, 166, 175–76, 180–81, 183, 213, 316–17
  in Palestine, 222, 225, 230, 233
Zweig, Arnold, 60, 63
Zweig, Stefan, 32–33, 48, 59, 63

www.ingramcontent.com/pod-product-compliance
Lightning Source LLC
Chambersburg PA
CBHW072143100526
44589CB00015B/2063